SECOND LIVES

I0309845

SECOND LIVES

Black-Market Melodramas
and the Reinvention
of Television

MICHAEL SZALAY

The University of Chicago Press
Chicago and London

The University of Chicago Press, Chicago 60637
The University of Chicago Press, Ltd., London
© 2023 by The University of Chicago
All rights reserved. No part of this book may be used or reproduced in any manner whatsoever without written permission, except in the case of brief quotations in critical articles and reviews. For more information, contact the University of Chicago Press, 1427 E. 60th St., Chicago, IL 60637.
Published 2023
Printed in the United States of America

32 31 30 29 28 27 26 25 24 23   1 2 3 4 5

ISBN-13: 978-0-226-82048-4 (cloth)
ISBN-13: 978-0-226-82480-2 (paper)
ISBN-13: 978-0-226-82479-6 (e-book)
DOI: https://doi.org/10.7208/chicago/9780226824796.001.0001

Library of Congress Cataloging-in-Publication Data

Names: Szalay, Michael, 1967– author.
Title: Second lives : black-market melodramas and the reinvention of television / Michael Szalay.
Other titles: Black-market melodramas and the reinvention of television
Description: Chicago ; London : The University of Chicago Press, 2023. | Includes bibliographical references and index.
Identifiers: LCCN 2022022553 | ISBN 9780226820484 (cloth) | ISBN 9780226824802 (paperback) | ISBN 9780226824796 (ebook)
Subjects: LCSH: Fiction television programs—United States—History and criticism. | Television series—United States—History and criticism. | Television programs—United States—History—21st century
Classification: LCC PN1992.3.U5 S93 2023 | DDC 791.450973—dc23/eng/20220726
LC record available at https://lccn.loc.gov/2022022553

For my parents

Contents

Introduction: Television's Second Life · 1

1. The Gangster Mourning Play · 45

2. The Informal Abject
Housework and Reproduction in *Weeds* and
Orange Is the New Black · 83

3. AMC's White-Collar Supremacy
Breaking Bad, *Mad Men*, and *Halt and Catch Fire* · 129

4. Managed Hearts
The Americans and News Corporation · 173

5. Waiting for the End
Twin Peaks, *The Wire*, *Queen Sugar*, and *Atlanta* · 213

Conclusion: Streaming and You · 261

Acknowledgments · 285
Notes · 287
Index · 311

INTRODUCTION
Television's Second Life

"So this is it? We just keep going?" June Hoffman asks her husband on *Forever* upon learning their afterlife is all but identical to their life before they died, organized as it was by daily routines and a quiet, dogged boredom. Audiences might have asked themselves similarly despairing questions, when confronting the glut of TV released over the last two decades about characters stuck in some kind of limbo. A large number of supernaturally inclined serials treated purgatory more or less literally, as an indeterminate realm between life and death.[1] Others treated it notionally. On *Peaky Blinders*, a character mused that her cursed Romani family lived "somewhere between life and death, waiting to move on" (4.6). In *Maniac* and *Russian Doll*, purgatory literalized stalled mourning and inescapable grief. Sometimes purgatory described institutions in whose shadow life becomes oppressively invariant. On *Orange Is the New Black*, an inmate wondered whether "we're already dead, and this is limbo" (5.2); on *Queen Sugar*, an activist calls the penal system a "purgatory for all of us" (1.12).

The overarching narratives that often defined these serials did not mitigate so much as heighten their purgatorial feel. It's only when characters remember their past, after all, that they become conscious of what feels stuck about their lives. In *Six Feet Under*, Nate Fisher Sr. appeared to his widow Ruth in a dream. "Stalled again," he said, ostensibly about the family car, but really about the family and ultimately the narrative itself. "Won't go forward, won't go back" (1.9). Characters kept going, and we kept watching, but it wasn't always clear where it was all headed—or why we were stuck in purgatory at all. To what real-life listlessness and claustrophobia did TV purgatories respond? Surely no one thing, though undeniable patterns do emerge. *Game of Thrones* evoked an ambient geopolitical stasis; the dead walked the earth and we stalled for years before an oncoming winter, waiting for the birth of a new political order, while stuck ourselves in a zombie US Empire. It is in fact impossible to disentangle the TV that I'll be discussing from the ongoing, generalized decline of US political and economic power. Nevertheless, on the whole, the serials below discover purgatory where *Forever* does, in a given family's everyday routines. "I'm sick of waiting for my life to begin," says Andy Botwin on *Weeds*. "I'm in perpetual purgatory" (8.9). He was not alone. Tony Soprano and his family struck Geoffrey O'Brien as "zombies"—or "ghosts of people who hadn't quite died."[2] The *Mad Men* opening credits feature Don Draper falling from a skyscraper, but never reaching bottom. Walter White learns he has terminal cancer at *Breaking Bad*'s start, but he stays almost dead for quite some time. In these serials and many others, purgatories derive from a pervasive and destabilizing confusion of family life on the one hand and the labor required to sustain it on the other. Characters might move daily between home and work; but in other ways, they find it hard to know where one begins and the other ends. As a consequence, family life feels neither saving nor damning, but interminable and gray. Ultimately, I will argue, that state of affairs registers the relatively late effects on the white middle class of the deindustrialization that has defined US life for roughly fifty years.

Given their tropism toward tedium and their orientation to viewers at risk of experiencing the same, it is not surprising that TV about family life often invokes narrative traditions in which characters discover some escape from the everyday, less into heaven or hell than simply something more vivifying. On *Undone*, a dead father asks his living daughter "to make a choice . . . you can go back to the life you were living. And just keep living it, and living it, and living it. Or you could try something different. A life that doesn't follow a paint-by-numbers timeline. . . . A life where anything can happen, at any time" (1.2). *Undone* borrows its fantasy landscape from *The Wizard of Oz*. *Lost* borrows from *Alice in Wonderland*. Both echo *The Matrix*, which asks Neo to choose between a blue pill that will return him to his humdrum life and a red pill that will give him, among much else, the power of flight. But none of these sources would prove as influential to TV's evolution as the gangster film—that great "No," as Robert Warshow had it, to the optimism and ordinariness of American life. The same year Warner Bros. released *The Matrix*, another Time Warner property, *The Sopranos*, took viewers down a different rabbit hole into a differently stylized underground, in the name of a more prosaic truth. It inaugurated a new genre—I call it "the black-market melodrama"—in which part or all of a (usually) white, middle-class family leads two lives, one routine and the other typically illegal and dangerous.

The black-market melodrama includes thirty-minute comedy and sixty-minute drama formats, almost always on streaming or cable-supported TV, in which characters live secret second lives. Many serial melodramas about gangsters and black markets have appeared over the last twenty years, from *Gomorrah* and *Narcos* to *Snowfall*, *Godfather of Harlem*, *Mayans M.C.*, and *Gangs of London*. The lawbreaking on offer in these programs requires secrecy, to be sure, but these gangsters typically have only one job. My genre features characters who typically have two, and who have two lives rather than one: an official and legal life and one lived—at the genre's core—in or proximate to black markets for illegal goods or services: *The Sopranos* (loan sharking, drugs, stolen goods), *Weeds* (marijuana), *Hung* (sex work), *Breaking Bad* (meth), *Sons of Anarchy* (guns), *Peaky Blinders* (guns, alcohol), *Ozark* (drugs, money laundering), and so on. These programs have been among the most crucial to television's reinvention, and the pages that follow register the diffusion and transformation of their secret lives across a larger TV field. Broadly rather than narrowly conceived, the black-market melodrama mediates that larger influence, insofar as it includes a diversity of secret second lives.[3] I define the genre in this more expansive sense, as including secret lives defined by murder (*Dexter*, *Bloodline*, season 1 of *Fargo*, *Barry*, *You*), espionage (*Homeland*, *Turn*, *The Americans*, *Counterpart*, *The Bureau*, *Killing Eve*, *Patriot*), alternate realities (*Twin Peaks*, *Buffy the*

Vampire Slayer, True Blood, The Leftovers, The Man in the High Castle, Stranger Things, Lodge 49, Undone), and secret or remembered pasts or closeted identities (Six Feet Under, Big Love, Mad Men, Nurse Jackie, Sneaky Pete, Rectify, Orange Is the New Black, The Handmaid's Tale). In these serials, secret lives might be kept from a variety of actors, from other family members to neighbors to the state, and might straddle the above categories: in *The Americans*, espionage *and* murder; in *Counterpart*, espionage *and* an alternate reality; in *Killing Eve*, espionage *and* closeted desire. Likewise, those lives might take shape in relation to a range of established genres: *The Sopranos* owes its greatest debt to the gangster film; *Dexter*, to serial killer narratives; *The Americans*, to the cold war thriller; *Mad Men*, to postwar suburban fiction and soap opera; *The Man in the High Castle*, to science fiction (fig. 0.1).

The black-market melodrama has provided the genetic material of TV's own second life—and in the process fundamentally transformed how we think about "quality" television.[4] The *New York Times* called *The Sopranos* "the greatest work of American popular culture of the last quarter century."[5] Brett Martin claimed that the "twelve- or thirteen-episode serialized drama" that sprang from HBO's mafia story became "the signature American art form of the first decade of the 21st century."[6] Once the lowest of the low, TV came to be esteemed as never before. Jennifer Egan said her Pulitzer Prize–winning *A Visit from the Goon Squad*, optioned by HBO, was inspired by Marcel Proust's *Remembrance of Things Past* and *The Sopranos*.[7] TV's newfound prestige had far-reaching effects. Top-shelf Hollywood talent decamped into TV production, as media companies shifted resources from small- and medium-sized films to serial TV, which continues to anchor monthly subscription services. The rise of Netflix and the transformation of pay-cable channels into streaming services has only heightened TV's importance. While it appeared for a moment that big tech might swallow TV, there's a case to be made that the opposite happened. Don't look now, writes Michael Wolff, but Netflix has become a traditional studio, and "the digital industry . . . reverts, like cable before it, to its pure distribution function, and seeks out the highest-value products it can provide its customers, which, in the media business, is the extraordinary variety, the quite astonishing

0.1. The black-market melodrama.

inventiveness, and cultural primacy of television."[8] This book explores that primacy in the context of longer narrative traditions and broader industrial contexts, while nevertheless tracing TV's quality renaissance to a single genre. Indeed, we might think of the black-market melodrama as a meta-genre that integrates diverse generic forms into a recognizable and often reflexive brand of quality TV (my conclusion defines the genre in part by the self-consciousness with which it considers the nature of the TV medium and TV quality in a moment ostensibly characterized by the convergence of film and television).

As we've begun to see, black-market melodramas use a single dominating trope to integrate their antecedents. Secret second lives allow characters to "awake," as *Breaking Bad*, *Killing Eve*, and *Undone* all put it, from the slumber of their first lives. We awaken too; meth makes for more exciting drama than does high school chemistry. And these melodramas can be adrenaline-fueled romps—seemingly far in spirit from the domestic listlessness that defines the genre. But if we're watching closely, the thrills can feel forced, self-consciously futile efforts to hold at bay a creeping tedium. And indeed, more often than not, the fantastical becomes again mundane and life beyond the family becomes another version of it. However torqued up, the genre tends to produce a hall of mirrors, in which, say, Soprano's work in the mob becomes an echo of rather than a world apart from his home life, each "family" now a distorted reflection, an allegory, of the other. At its baroque fringes, the genre transforms that doubling into identical twins and murderous doppelgängers. But core instances of the black-market melodrama created in the two decades following *The Sopranos* tend to reiterate a key point: work beyond the white middle-class household has become indistinct from work within it, such that there can be no escape from one separate sphere into another. What begins as escape must end in allegory.

Secret second lives are not themselves novel. What is perhaps new—confining ourselves for the moment to the genre's sociological content—are the conclusions about the white middle-class family produced by the genre's allegorical doublings. *Mad Men* makes obvious reference to John Cheever, Richard Yates, and John Updike, and it's hard not to compare the black-market melodrama's disgruntled male protagonists to the bored white men of postwar novels who escape their families into secret affairs. But the stakes feel higher and the problems more intransigent. Across the genre, family has become unavoidable and damaging in equal measure. "Who is society?" Margaret Thatcher famously asked. "There is no such thing! There are individual men and women and there are families."[9] Black-market melodramas confirm that neoliberal dogma. Some kind of family is the individual's last best hope—the only remaining collective. And yet family no longer sustains. Dramas like *Big Love* and *Peaky Blinders* include portraits of fierce family loyalty. But by and large, and especially in core instances like *The Sopranos*, *Weeds*, *Breaking Bad*, *The Americans*, and *Ozark*, white families eat their own.

The genre commits to family, but despairingly—with different degrees of Lauren Berlant's "cruel optimism." Along the way, it undermines once-sacrosanct stories about why family matters, how it sponsors the good life, and how it functions as a "haven in a heartless world," to recall Christopher Lasch.

The closer we look at black-market melodramas, in fact, the less they look like TV elaborations of this or that established film or literary genre and the more they look like testosterone-infused soap operas, directed at men who work from home in new ways but lacking the soaps' historical consolations. Soaps were first addressed to women consigned to housework and tended in their commitment to romance to confirm a pernicious fiction: women's domestic labor wasn't labor at all but an expression of love. The black-market melodrama looks for but cannot find its own solution to the maintenance of separate spheres. Depressively realist, it sets no store in romance, nor manages to believe its own often fervently espoused clichés about the sanctity of family. Instead, the genre makes impossible any reconciliation of individual and collective interest. It identifies selflessness as family life's only possible justification even as it casts its families as entirely bereft of that value. In their final conversation in *Breaking Bad*, Walter White prepares to offer Skyler a version of the line that repeats across the genre, "All the things that I did, you need to understand. . . ." She stops him: "If I have to hear one more time that you did this for the family. . . ." And so finally he comes clean: "I did it for me. I liked it. I was good at it" (5.16). White's confession exposes one of the genre's key fault lines: it cannot imagine a collective other than the family, and it cannot imagine a meaningfully collective family.

The fact that so many of the genre's families run businesses makes it hard to think of them as havens from the market. "A family is like a small business," says *Ozark*'s Martin Byrde. He echoes microeconomists like Gary Becker, who asks us to "imagine each family as a kind of little factory" producing "human capital" while guided by altruistic bonds.[10] But Byrde's family isn't like a business; it is a business. And it doesn't produce human capital; it launders money. Forced on the run in the first season, the estranged husband and wife come together in a fight for survival. They learn to work side by side rather than apart, but under new auspices. "We are not husband and wife anymore," he tells her. "We are just business partners" (1.2). Across the genre, similar conditions transform once-sacrosanct family values, love and altruism foremost among them. Home is no longer where the heart is—it's where the work is. On *Peaky Blinders*, Grace Burgess tells a rival for Tommy Shelby's affections, with whom he has been working, "There is business and there is love." The rival asks, "Is there?" (2.6). The black-market melodrama knows no such distinction and casts intimacy as fundamentally shaped by economic calculation: "When relationships become a ledger of profit and loss," writes Jax Teller's father in *Sons of Anarchy*, "you have no friends, no loved ones, just pluses and minuses" (2.5).

Black-market melodramas offer few alternatives to that ledger. One of the genre's precursors, which dominated primetime during the 1980s and 1990s, was the "workplace drama," which, according to Thomas Schatz, "posit[s] the workplace as home and work itself as the basis for any real sense of kinship we are likely to find in the contemporary urban-industrial world."[11] If individual episodes followed characters to where they slept, it was generally not to anchor us in domestic life—paid work had subsumed that life. But rarely did that feel like a loss; these programs were often about high-minded professionals working earnestly on behalf of the public interest rather than profits. On *Hill Street Blues*, *St. Elsewhere*, *ER*, and *The West Wing*, say, newly integrated workplaces housed heroic men and women defending the greater good. Well-meaning state guardians, they tried to work a little harder and talk a little faster, to save the welfare state and, above all, the white family in whose name it acts. *Hill Street Blues* begins with a precinct roll call that identifies the theft of Social Security checks as the first priority of the assembled boys in blue. The black-market melodrama, on the other hand, tends to feature not professionals but predatory managers working at cross-purposes with the welfare state. Moments into *The Sopranos*, Tony reads a newspaper whose headline announces the bankrupting of Medicare. Minutes later, he is perpetrating insurance fraud.

Evening soaps of the 1980s like *Dallas* and *Dynasty* had featured similarly calculating leads. Here too, business imperatives occluded otherwise sustaining public values and private ties. But these programs were not about middle-class life or its pieties. Nor were they allegorical in the way that I describe, mainly because they did not turn on secret second lives. Rather, in *Dallas* and *Dynasty*, or, more recently, *Empire* and *Succession*, "family" and "corporation" form what Jane Feuer calls a "single representational unit."[12] Ideologically, black-market melodramas and corporate-family melodramas are secret sharers. Both genres capture a resurgent right-wing populism that has represented, in Melinda Cooper's words, "an insurrection of one form of capitalism against another: the private, unincorporated, and family-based versus the corporate, publicly traded, and shareholder-owned."[13] That said, black-market melodramas eschew the corporate-family melodrama's triumphalism: they are about downwardly mobile (rather than rich and powerful) families whose businesses are in illegal informal economies rather than state-recognized formal ones. Gangster films inform my genre more meaningfully than cold war thrillers, serial killer narratives, and science fiction (all of which might feature second lives), not because of their conclusions about criminality per se, but because their black markets allegorize more everyday informal economies. The genre is a rogues' gallery of unsavory white families committing capital crimes (often against people of color, we will see). But black-market melodramas divide the world into legal and illegal spheres, I argue, less to study criminality writ large than to capture a white middle class that increasingly must straddle formal and informal labor markets.

The genre's maniacally industrious white families feel precarious even when manifestly affluent and tend to think that to "just keep going" means to "just keep working"—away from the state's prying eyes. That secrecy is an incipiently reactionary response to what feels like the state's hostility to white middle-class life. Characters tend not to articulate that hostility; but the serials themselves often attribute it to the undoing of the Keynesian compact between state and industry and, ultimately, decades of deindustrialization. More specifically, the genre's black markets express the retreat of the "breadwinner" or "family wage" that once organized a gendered division of labor within white working- and middle-class families between male waged and female unwaged work. When historians note the undoing of the family wage, they typically stress the concomitant rise of two-income households. But whether men or women, the genre's leads rarely support their families with a state-recognized income and rarely work for the giant concerns still common to broadcast TV: corporations, hospitals, police forces, etc. The black-market melodrama instead captures the white household in extremis, scrambling collectively in some off-the-books illegal enterprise. As I argue below, the genre thus anticipates the rise in the US of the "mass industriousness" that sociologists identify across the underdeveloped world. Versions of that industriousness already thrive in the shadows in "the cities of the North," notes Adam Arvidsson, who recalls Fernand Braudel's claim that "despite almost half a millennium of increasingly sophisticated capitalist institutions, there [has] remained 'a sort of lower layer of the economy,' a competitive economy different from what he considered 'true capitalism.'"[14]

This book was finished during the COVID pandemic, when "life with the housebound white-collar workforce," as the *Washington Post* put it, realized globally a nightmarish version of the domestic entrapment that was already the subject of black-market melodramas.[15] The melodramas below evoke the "presence bleed" and "partial presence" experienced by knowledge workers whose salaries obviate time-sheet surveillance and who have been able, since the advent of the internet, to work flexibly from domiciles that might feel, as a consequence, a lot less like home.[16] Wherever you go at the end of the day, someone asks Philip Jennings in *The Americans*, "is 'home' the right word?" (2.5). Another black-market melodrama organized by Cold War spy conventions, *Killing Eve* finds a character asking, "Home? What do you mean, 'home'? Where is that exactly?" (2.4). In both serials, home is nowhere and everywhere, a purgatory, less somewhere you go at the end of the day than an oppressive condition you cannot escape. And in fact, black-market melodramas tend to question the meaning of "home" mainly on behalf of those lucky enough to have them. But these programs are not solely about the travails of remote white-collar work. More fundamentally, they evoke deindustrialization's upheavals across the middle class, as once-secure career work bleeds into casualized, outsourced, and frequently off-the-books proletarian work. In this growing sector, formal waged and salaried work is no longer adequate to the family's survival and no longer fully distinct from the range of informal work with which a growing number of families now supplement their state-recognized incomes. Indeed, however ostensibly racy, these melodramas are all in their way preoccupied with housework, by which I mean both traditional housework and a more encompassing category of what Ivan Illich called "shadow work," which for me includes above all the unwaged or otherwise off-the-books labor required to reproduce, or sustain, newly industrious households.[17]

The black markets to which these shows turn seem to save their toxic male leads from that reproductive labor, just as they seem to save the programs themselves from becoming soap operas. To this extent, they are symbolic antidotes to what Maria Mies called the "housewifization" of male labor, in which men are "forced to accept labor relations which so far had been typical for women only. This means labor relations outside the protection of labor laws, not covered by trade unions and collective bargaining, not based on a proper contract—more or less invisible, part of the 'shadow economy.'"[18] But ultimately, these serials don't save their leads from that fate (figs. 0.2 and 0.3). Having invented second lives that promise to free anxious men from domestic enmeshments by transporting them to a world well beyond the home, black-market melodramas reveal those lives as escapist reveries doomed to rude awakenings. Over time, and no matter how hyperbolic the masculinity on offer, one putatively separate sphere becomes a distorted echo of the other—or a "chiral" image of the other, to quote a *Breaking Bad* chemistry lesson. A doubling subtly different from the kind in *Dr. Jekyll and Mr. Hyde* and even *Twin Peaks* results. Walter White is not split into a good and bad self; he is given two personae, one at work and one at home, that become allegories of each other, above all, in the labor each performs. It is not coincidental but essential that White's second life finds him forever "cooking" (meth), "cleaning" (money), and raising a second son (Jesse Pinkman).

As *Breaking Bad* should make clear, besieged white privilege defines the genre. Individual melodramas typically feel purgatorial because they describe the collapse of home and work. But the genre's white families

0.2. *Breaking Bad*: Mr. Clean at work.

0.3. *Ozark*: Marty Byrde scrubs blood.

also fear they have entered a racial limbo between white and nonwhite. Black markets consequently promise escape from closely related versions of grayness, insofar as they are narratively propulsive, exciting, and, not least, racially consolidating. Black-market melodramas are persecution fantasies in which the retreat of the state-sanctioned family wage—never fully available to any but white workers—takes shape as a state actively impeding white families and subjecting them to conditions long suffered by those on whom white wealth historically has relied. In fact, these dramas are often thinly concealed revenge fantasies in which white families brutalize the minority populations toward which they fear they are falling. *Breaking Bad*, for example, worries that its aptly named lead has become in his precarity less white than he should be—too akin, for example, to the off-the-book Latina workers who toil above him in Gus Fring's laundry facility. It dreams its black-market dream to save White from that kinship, even as it leaves scores of dead brown bodies in his wake.

The genre's murderous white leads are no more incidentally racist than they are incidentally misogynist. In *Fargo*'s third season, a character notes the "number of people living on the streets," and adds, "there is an accounting coming. Mongol hordes descending . . . they are coming." He asks a seemingly successful businessman,

> What are you doing to insulate yourself and your family? . . . You think you're rich. You've no idea what "rich" means. "Rich" is a fleet of private planes filled with decoys to mask your scent. It's a banker in Wyoming and another in Gstaad. So that's action item one, the accumulation of wealth, and I mean wealth, not money. What's action item number two? To use that wealth to become invisible. (3.4)

The genre's commitment to white invisibility is fundamental, and diametrically different, for example, from the longing for official recognition that Lauren Berlant identifies in *La Promesse* and *Rosetta*. In those films, "the informal economy . . . where you don't exist on the identification papers the state recognizes, where you are always paid under the table if at all," frustrates "the possibility of achieving . . . the social density of citizenship at the scale of a legitimate linkage to the reciprocal social world."[19] In black-market melodramas, white families use their invisibility from the state to reassert their racial privilege, by recommitting to the exploitation upon which their class's wealth has long depended. From *The Sopranos*, *Breaking Bad*, and *Sons of Anarchy*

INTRODUCTION

0.4. *Weeds*: Nancy Botwin works at gunpoint.

to *Weeds* and *Ozark*, white families destroy the minority characters to whom they worry they are too proximate. Black markets provide an arena in which white families take what they consider theirs, more often than not, from more vulnerable populations unprotected by the law. And yet, even as agents of exploitation, these families fret the prospect of a racialized subservience, intimated not simply in White's proximity to Latina laundry workers, say, but in his subservience to Gus Fring and Mexican drug cartels (fig. 0.4). Cartels loom on *Weeds*, *Sons of Anarchy*, and *Ozark* as well, reminding entrepreneurial white families who, ultimately, they work for.

This bad-faith fantasy (in which white victimization justifies a renewed racial exploitation) suffuses even the genre's outliers. Racialized hordes drive the white family from its home and into a threatening world in both *Game of Thrones* and *The Walking Dead*. Neither of these is a black-market melodrama—not exactly. But they reproduce many of the genre's key features because, as I will show, the genre has influenced a much wider field of TV. *True Detective* is not a black-market melodrama either, at least not exactly, but the procedural cites the genre at every turn. "You ever been someplace you couldn't leave, and you couldn't stay, both at the same time?" asks an unemployed father, as he explains his inability either to free himself from or put himself "back in [the] old story" (3.2) that is his family. *Weeds* and *Nurse Jackie* were among the first black-market melodramas to ask versions of that question from women's points of view. *Orange Is the New Black* and *The Handmaid's Tale* are less recognizably a part of the genre; but they too extend its core concerns as they insist that this is what home *really* is and always has been: a prison for the women forced to work there. These are powerful correctives, even if, here too, white protagonists blithely confuse their interests with those of the racially oppressed, and in so doing wreak havoc on them, their good intentions notwithstanding.

Quality TV made by and about African Americans sometimes bursts this narcissistic bubble while engaging black-market melodramas in surprising ways. In *Queen Sugar* and *Atlanta*, even fractured families allow for the pooling of resources and the dividing of labor, and they provide kinship ties in a racist world that knows no other kind. *Queen Sugar* treats the Bordelon farm as the basis for a renewal through work; its family competes successfully because it draws on robust family bonds. But this industrious household is more vulnerable to state violence than the genre's white families. And however subject to renewal, the Bordelons remain at risk of slipping back into new versions of slavery and sharecropping. Like *Queen Sugar*, *Atlanta* traces its purgatorial feel to mass incarceration and the Black family's exposure to state violence. The Black family, it makes plain, has never enjoyed the fantasy of separate spheres that the white family has. In *Atlanta*, separate spheres are all but inconceivable, because there is no work to oppose home life and the looming threat of prison. Like many black-market leads, Earn Marks is without a wage. But he is also without money, and if he too commits to playing gangster, that role provides none of the compensations it does in *The Sopranos*, *Weeds*, *Breaking Bad*, or *Ozark*. Earn is homeless as the leads in those programs are not. Homophones tell the tale: unable to "earn" and socially dead, he retreats at night to an "urn," the storage facility that houses his worldly remains.

Nothing that follows argues for the value of *Atlanta*—or any serial—solely on the basis of its sociological insights. Certainly black-market melodramas aren't valuable only because they show us something of the world beyond our screens. *Big Love* asked its liberal viewers to identify with a family they might otherwise have disavowed; but it's not clear the drama told them anything all that new about polygamy. Nor did we need *The Sopranos* or *Breaking Bad* to experience entitled white men chafing against their imagined feminization. Better to say the genre explains the origins of its personal and familial crises in deindustrialization and the lost family wage. Indeed, we might value it for the subtlety with which it mediates (or allegorizes) economic life. This book is a study of compound mediation, insofar as I explore the different interests and constraints (as they emerge in specific writers' rooms and media corporations, for example) that pressurize TV melodramas and determine their necessarily tendentious accounts of economic and social life. Often, a given lead family allegorizes multiple interests and constraints, and refers not just to one but to many collective agencies.

But the genre is also melodrama, it is important to note, which means it is as influenced by longstanding narrative conventions as by contemporary reality. These shows are frequently well-made, and critics have exhaustively described just how literary and cinematic they can be. Nevertheless, this TV is melodrama, above all else. There is now a rich body of work on melodrama, produced by the likes of Thomas Elsaesser, Peter Brooks, Christine Gledhill, and Linda Williams. The pages below rely on that work, if selectively. I do not systematically demonstrate the many ways in which my serials are melodramas. There's much to be said about their relatively novel use of music, for example, a topic I scarcely broach. Rather, I am more narrowly interested in how the black-market melodrama's longings for a lost domestic idyll, neatly separate from paid work, produces what might be called "allegorical melodrama."

The epithet captures the hybridized aesthetic values on offer as black-market melodramas fitfully reconcile an up-market, historically male literary prestige long contemptuous of women and family life, on the one hand, to the gendered, allegedly lowbrow sentimental entertainments from which much TV springs, on the other. That reconciliation recalls Douglas Sirk's subtle Brechtian ironies but my genre rings a change on the intensely symbolized Hollywood family melodramas of the 1950s, which, Elsaesser notes, produced dynamic correspondences between mise-en-scène and emotional states.[20] Notable exceptions aside, black-market melodramas tend not to use mise-en-scène as richly as Sirk's films; relatively little serial TV does, given production time constraints. And yet they do ask what if anything separates a given home's insides from its outsides, in ways that activate melodrama's gothic inheritance. Early nineteenth-century stage melodramas were "subsumed by an underlying Manicheanism," writes Brooks; they put audiences "in touch with the conflict of good and evil played out under the surface of things." A "moral occult" infuses "the banal and the ordinary with the excitement of grandiose conflict," he adds, such that "the ordinary and humble and quotidian" reveal themselves to be determined "by the play of cosmic moral relations and forces."[21]

Along with *Twin Peaks*, which I discuss in the last chapter, *Buffy the Vampire Slayer* should be credited with literalizing this implicitly allegorical structure and making it available for a new kind of TV: the vampires and demons that terrorized Sunnydale's high schoolers were the moral occult made real; they allegorized the travails of ordinary teenage life by extrapolating that life to its felt cataclysmic proportions. And of course Buffy herself lived a secret second life, fighting one kind of demon at night and another during the day. Black-market second lives take their cue from those earlier melodramas but refuse their supernatural schemata and the moral binaries they buttressed. Chastising her for taking Soprano as a patient, Jennifer Melfi's embittered ex-husband declares, "Sooner or later you're going to get beyond psychotherapy, with its cheesy moral relativism. You're going to get to good and evil. And he's evil" (1.8). But get there we never do. Soprano is evil enough, to be sure, but we are asked to like him, however ambivalently, along with the many antiheros to follow, in a way that forestalls melodrama's Manichean drive. "Moral gray areas: learn to accept them, swim in them" (7.7), says a crooked cop on *Weeds*. "Allegorical melodrama" captures the herky-jerky manner with which these alternately schematic and sensational, clever and heartfelt shows ask us both to identify with and distance ourselves from their charismatic but repugnant leads (or the classes they exemplify). Allegory, we might say, provides the analytic distance that melodrama seeks to collapse in the name of what Brooks calls "moral legibility."

That legibility has never been assured. As Brooks makes clear, nineteenth-century melodramas often feel urgent—and extravagantly intense—precisely because they fear they cannot convincingly capture the strong, clarifying feelings that they seem too insistently to stage. The same is true of the mode's moral certitude. Melodrama restores moral legibility via sensationalizing bodily registers—by generating virtue from scenes of suffering, for instance. But its notorious "excess" stems from an intuition that legibility will prove elusive. *The Wire* is not a melodrama, Fredric Jameson argues, because it manifests a "reign of Cynical Reason" that vitiates distinctions between good and evil.[22] But melodrama has long insisted on those distinctions precisely because or when they seem impossible. And the fact that black-market melodramas feel amoral—when turning to the likes of Soprano, White, and Botwin—represents not melodrama's transcendence but its intensification, as programs stage efforts, ever more frantic because impossible, to produce moral clarity. The serials explore melodrama at its limits, above all, by attributing their moral ambiguity to the fact that the domestic idyll for which they long is now irrecoverable—as if to say, with obscene perversity, that good and evil are indistinct when men's work beyond the home is indistinguishable from women's work within it.

Those Were the Days

US TV about white family life has always been nostalgic. Andy Griffith said *The Andy Griffith Show* invoked a simpler time: "Though we never said it, and though it was shot in the '60s, it had a feeling of the '30s. It was, when we were doing it, of a time gone by." *The Waltons* said it by taking viewers to the Great Depression and a still more rural environment. And of course, TV nostalgia for an earlier version of the family is famously explicit in *All in the Family*. Archie Bunker prefigures the many difficult TV men to come, and the comedy's theme song offers a checklist of longings integral to the black-market melodrama:

> Boy the way Glen Miller played,
> Songs that made the hit parade,

> Guys like us we had it made,
> Those were the days.
> And you knew where you were then,
> Girls were girls and men were men,
> Mister we could use a man like Herbert Hoover again.
> Didn't need no welfare state,
> Everybody pulled his weight,
> Gee our old LaSalle ran great,
> Those were the days.

Here, in short, are the social givens that would prove elusive in the melodramas that followed *The Sopranos*: white male privilege ("Guys like us we had it made"); stable boundaries between home and work ("you knew where you were then"); clearly demarked genders ("Girls were girls and men were men"); and US industry in full gear ("Gee our old LaSalle ran great"). What is revealingly distinct here is the longing for a day *before* the welfare state; prominent among the irrecoverable realities longed for in black-market melodramas, on the other hand, is the welfare state, and the Keynesian or Fordist compact between state and business that codified the family wage.

"Nostalgia. It's delicate and potent," *Mad Men*'s Draper tells a room of clients and fellow admen, one of whom rushes weeping from the room. "In Greek, 'nostalgia' literally means 'the pain from an old wound'" (1.13). Draper is nostalgic for an earlier moment in his family's life. But the scene's deeper truth is that the drama is itself an expression of pain and longing, insofar as it conjures—as perhaps only *Peaky Blinders* and *The Man in the High Castle* also do among black-market melodramas—a world defined by manufacturing. Draper does not himself work in a factory; but his job, advertising, requires the selling of industrial products. Analogously, if more ominously, when the Nazi John Smith in *High Castle* says, "There's a feeling in the air. A kind of nostalgia, for a past that never was" (4.8), we might view the drama itself as a tortured and deeply disturbing expression of nostalgia. *High Castle* gives us hygienically separate spheres: its good Nazi men work for the fatherland in offices while its dutiful wives toil at home. Those homes define the genre's simultaneously spatial and temporal nostalgia. Science fictional and historical premises aside, the black-market melodrama's nostalgia is typically pain (*algos*) born of a failure to return (*nostos*) to the patriarchal middle-class white home that was integral to an expanding US manufacturing base.

One of the curious facts about US TV is that, by and large, relatively few of its protagonists have worked in manufacturing. Laverne and Shirley worked in a bottling company; Roseanne worked at Wellman Plastics; in *Grace under Fire*, Grace worked in a refinery. Evening soaps like *Dallas* and *Dynasty* were about the oil industry. But these were the exceptions, and when TV protagonists held industrial jobs, those jobs often seemed an afterthought. Bunker was a foreman at Prendergast Tool and Die, but the series explored his moonlighting as a taxi-driver before it took us to his day job. What defines the TV below, then, is not its dearth of visible manufacturing work per se, which never defined US TV, but its tendency to produce allegorical melodramas of deindustrialization that long for the gendered division of labor that postwar industrial production had enabled. Quality TV generally is often nostalgic for both family and industry. In *True Detective*'s first season, Rustin Cohle, whose name conjoins rusting steel and coal as industrial atavisms, has lost his family. In *Succession*, family replaces lost industry. Logan Roy tells his family, "Most things don't exist. The Ford Motor Company hardly exists. It's just a time-saving expression for a collection of financial interests. But this exists, because—Family. It's a family. We are a family" (2.10). Family is the last redoubt against deindustrialization—a saving remnant that holds the line against change. Neither program is a black-market melodrama proper, insofar as neither features a second life. But neither would have been possible without the genre.

The black-market melodrama first appears in outline in *Twin Peaks*, which begins with the closing of a mill. In its opening moments, Laura Palmer's corpse washes ashore, as if an emblem of the labor expelled from the mill—and an object lesson in what unemployed fathers do when forced to stay home. Though shorn of the Manichean moral order important to its supernatural predecessor, *The Sopranos* begins on a similar note: Tony opens his therapy with the claim, "the best is over," and thereby invokes, in part, a lost industrial New Jersey, testified to by the abandoned factories past which this murderous father drives in the title sequence. When plants close, family becomes dangerously inescapable. Soprano's lament anticipates Frank Sabotka's in *The Wire*: "We used to make shit in this country" (2.11), and even Raylan Givens, delivering *Justified*'s last line and explaining why he did not shoot Boyd Crowder: "We dug coal together" (6.13). But Soprano's lines find a better echo in *Hung*'s opening voiceover, when Ray Drecker announces, "Everything is falling apart, and it all starts right here in Detroit, the headwaters of a river of failure. Thank god my parents aren't around to watch the country they loved go to shit. They were proud Americans. They had normal jobs and made a normal living" (1.1). For Drecker, there is no way back; he becomes a sex worker to support his broken family. Nor is there a way back for Elizabeth and Philip in *The Americans*, which concludes with the couple contemplating Moscow at night. What if we had never left? Wonders Elizabeth. "I probably would have worked in a factory. Managed a factory" (6.10). Here, industrial labor represents the road not taken, less a life lost than one never lived.

Amanda Lotz and Brett Martin are just two of those who have written extremely well about the "masculinity in crisis" that defines recent TV. But these and other critics sometimes study gender and the media as if they exist in a vacuum, and Lotz herself acknowledges the need for a more substantial accounting than she herself provides: "Interesting, and still unexplained in my mind, is the impetus that stimulates stories about men's struggles. Some sort of catalyzing event remains elusive, so that these preponderant themes and stories of struggle seem instead to be an organic bubbling to the surface of largely unconsidered and unspoken challenges for men."[23] Naming that impetus is important, if tricky. It's likely foolish to point too confidently to any genre's ultimate determinants. Genres are too complexly determined, too temporally distended, and too flexible in their evolution to allow for simple origin stories. And yet, it is possible to identify key inflection points in generic histories. There were gangster films before the Great Depression, for example, but the genre reinvents itself in the years immediately following the crash. And from *Scarface*, *Little Caesar*, and *The Public Enemy* to

The Godfather and *Goodfellas*, the genre has been preoccupied with both a crisis of access to the family wage and that wage's inadequacies. The black-market melodrama is similarly preoccupied, if from the vantage of long-wave deindustrialization (rather than a sudden depression). Deindustrialization is the "impetus" that drives the genre, as it longs for the family wage that structured a now lost manufacturing boom. The family wage began to disappear in the early 1970s, as I explain in chapter 3, but it is not until the end of the last millennium that its erosion reaches an inflection point for a class ready to pay for cable TV and becomes in the process the basis for a new kind of melodrama directed to that class.

The family wage is an artifact of industrial capitalism; it reflects a world, as Nancy Fraser has it, in which "people were supposed to be organized into heterosexual, male-headed nuclear families, which lived principally from a man's labor market earnings. The male head of the household would be paid a family wage, sufficient to support children and a wife and mother, who performed domestic labor without pay."[24] From the start, the family wage cast a nostalgic eye on an earlier version of the family. It emerged during the second half of the nineteenth century in England, where it was used to inculcate in the working classes the gendered division of labor—and domestic ideology—that a rising bourgeoisie had borrowed from the aristocracy over the previous centuries. Women had performed wage work earlier in the century, typically at lower rates of pay. But the family wage ideal did not emerge until the second industrial revolution, when working-class women were systematically excluded from factory work.[25] Later, during the 1930s, the family wage was written into US welfare practice, which afforded heterosexual white men, and few others, an income adequate to the reproduction of their families, which were supported in turn by the unwaged labor of wives and, depending on class, the waged labor of frequently nonwhite women.[26]

The family wage sent white men to work and kept women at home, where they performed the putative labors of love that made the family a separate sphere insulated from the market. The separateness of these spheres had always been a tenuous fiction. Marx noted, "The bourgeoisie has torn away from the family its sentimental veil and has reduced the family relation to a mere money relation."²⁷ That might seem an odd claim, since the bourgeoisie is often understood to have produced the veil in question (in melodrama and sentimental fiction, for example). But the remark nicely captures the contradiction long ingrained in separate spheres. The agricultural household (or *oikos*) had been an economic enterprise (and had for centuries defined dominant notions of economy) for landowning classes before the rise of the bourgeoisie; it was only during the seventeenth and eighteenth centuries that a more urban English middle class, possessing mobile capital more than land, began to ape the agricultural gentry's gendered division of labor, and it was only during the nineteenth century that that class began assiduously to shun the overt presence of money matters at home and to hold up the married woman as "an angel in the house" who served, in Fraser's words, as a "stabilizing ballast for the volatility of the economy."²⁸ Later, as the middle class was itself proletarianized, with the advent of large-scale and then state-managed capitalism, the angel in the house became an individuated fantasy of privacy; when the middle class itself begins to work for a wage and salary, we see the emergence of what Eli Zaretsky calls "personal life."²⁹

The United States sponsored a famously sentimental version of domestic ideology. Alexis de Tocqueville claimed that the lessened presence of the gentry in the young nation produced a stronger separation of male and female spheres and a more potent domestic ideology. "In no country," he declared, "has such a constant care been taken as in America to trace two clearly distinct lines of action for the two sexes and to make them keep pace one with the other, but in two pathways that are always different." Tocqueville's thesis about "the circle of domestic life" has generated robust debate. And since the 1970s, critics like Ann Douglas, Lara Wexler, Gillian Brown, Richard Brodhead, Lori Merish, and Lauren Berlant have produced rich accounts of US sentimentality and domestic ideology, while reminding us, as Linda Kerber puts it, that the language of separate spheres is "vulnerable to sloppy use."³⁰ Cathy Davidson finds the term "both immediately compelling and ultimately unconvincing." It fosters a "binary thinking" that flattens the complexity with which women in particular negotiated the conflicting claims of home and work.³¹ It's worth repeating that separate spheres have always been less a fact about the world than a political imperative about how it should be ordered.

In the decades following the Second World War, broadcast TV played a crucial role in disseminating that imperative. The Big Three (ABC, CBS, and NBC) constituted from the start a state-sponsored system that existed in the service of an expanding manufacturing base. They received their broadcast rights from the state and disseminated domestic ideology while selling industrial products.³² The broadcast schedule, in turn, was built from the ground up around the family wage and the rhythms of the breadwinner's nine-to-five work week. As Nick Browne puts it, even

> the position [and content] of programs in the television schedule reflects and is determined by the work-structured order of the real social world. The patterns of position and flow imply the question of who is at home, and through complicated social relays and temporal mediations, link television to the modes, processes, and scheduling of production characteristics of the general population. . . . Television establishes its relations to the "real," not through codes of realistic representation, but through the schedule, to the socially mediated order of the workday and the workweek.³³

Writing in the early 1990s, Browne would have witnessed the increased popularity of HBO, a subscriber-supported cable network that didn't advertise commodities and whose intermittent, repeat programming broke with the rhythms of the work week. And, of course, HBO played a crucial role in the black-market melodrama's codification. But Browne directs us to the real or at least more generalized wellsprings of our story: we cannot understand how the black-market melodrama—or TV as a whole—addresses "who is at home," and in so doing rings a change on separate spheres, without first grappling with fundamental changes in the working day and the composition of the labor force. In the conclusion, I revisit Raymond Williams's account of broadcast TV's crucial role in the colossal social reorganizations required by postwar industrial production. So too, I add, cable, satellite, and now streaming media have been in their way adaptations to deindustrialization. Those distribution systems offer casualized viewing for a casualized workforce whose daily rhythms are no longer organized by the family wage.

Informal and Industrious

Neither cable nor streaming, nor any particular media network, nor yet the media industry as a whole, caused the larger changes in question. A narrowly industrial study of the black-market melodrama might trace its origins to the rise of cable and HBO, which first launched in 1972. But much more meaningfully, the early seventies are almost exactly when the family wage began to erode (which erosion coincided with the emergence of second-wave feminism). The drivers of this change were falling rates of industrial profit and a seismic retooling of the US economy, as we will see in chapter 3. Women began to enter the workforce in greater numbers, and men and women both began to work longer and more intermittent hours, sometimes holding multiple jobs, while confronting flat wages, rising reproduction costs, and work's casualization. The rise of the two-income household affords one (if only one) way to mark the consequent erosion of separate spheres (such as they were). In 1980, the number of US households with children supported by two incomes reached parity with the number supported by one; by 1990, the ratio of two- to one-income households had reached roughly 2:1, where it has remained since.[34] But that statistic is misleading, insofar as white working-class families were forced to rely on dual incomes before affluent ones and nonwhite families never enjoyed the family wage to the degree that white families did.[35]

Nonwhite families have been particularly hard hit by the rise of "dual labor markets" since the 1980s.[36] In developed nations like the US, labor markets have become progressively divided between a shrinking core of career work in finance, marketing, and logistics and a growing sector of casualized, outsourced, and frequently off-the-books proletarian work. That second, more disposable stratum has employed women and minorities at rates that Fordist industrial production had not; the first stratum of career work has remained more segregated along racial and gender lines, thus effectively preserving white male privilege under new auspices. The black-market melodrama arose so long after the onset of deindustrialization and the rise of the dual-income family, we might hazard, because white male privilege eroded later in the economy's career-oriented core than it did, say, in service work or casualized factory production.

We might also account for the genre's late arrival by way of the 1996 Personal Responsibility and Work Opportunity Reconciliation Act (PRWORA), which completed what Melinda Cooper calls "the wholesale reinvention of the American family" that neoliberals and new social conservatives began in the 1980s. Family would be "as central to the formation of a post-Keynesian capitalist order" as the Fordist family had been to "welfare state capitalism," Cooper writes, as a function of the state's newfound commitment to disciplining the poor on behalf of the rich. Though cast as a defense of the nuclear family, the act's workfare policies revived an older poor-law tradition by subjecting minority women in particular "to new forms of unfree labor *outside the home*"—frequently in affluent white households. The act "brutally reinstate[d] the historically racialized obligations of domestic servitude" while also placing "the labor of all other low-wage service workers under the shadow of workfare."[37] So too, it shifted responsibility for key forms of care from state to family even as it shifted deficit spending to families newly burdened with "responsibility" and, of course, debt. The rich, meanwhile, reaped the benefits of cheaper labor, asset appreciation, and tax laws that consolidated the family's role as an instrument of intergenerational wealth transfer.

This transformation of welfare helps explain why in black-market melodramas state authority—in the form of the FBI, DEA, etc.—is not so much diminished as rendered hostile to the now besieged family. And in general, the genre's rapacious white families fear being confused with those PRWORA was designed to police; the genre learns from a refashioned welfare apparatus that white middle-class households survive not by appealing to the state but by evading it. And that lesson has force because, at bottom, black-market melodramas anticipate the white middle class's increasing dependence on the informal labor markets that have long defined much of the developing world.

The category of informal labor came to prominence under the influence of the UN's International Labour Organization (ILO), Aaron Benanav notes, and was part of its effort, starting in the early 1970s, "to develop a globally operational concept of unemployment for use across the 'developing world.'" The category seemed preferable to "disguised unemployment" or "underemployment," because less normative in implication and more sensitive to the various modalities by which individuals worked outside the wage relation. It was an effort to sidestep a problem implicit even in the word "developing," which was itself an alternative to the term "third world." Assigning numbers to regions of the globe produced an implicitly colonialist hierarchy. But the word "developing" suggested a linear narrative whose happy ending would be adequate and implicitly Western levels of industrial production. The historical irony, Benanav notes, is that the ostensibly less-developed world "turned out to occupy the leading edge of an incipient global tendency," especially after the onset of deindustrialization in ostensibly developed Western nations. The category of informal labor, he adds, registers that "a sizeable fraction of the global labor force has found itself caught in liminal spaces between unemployment and full employment, with little hope of leaving those spaces." Over time, he adds, more and more of the developed world would find itself caught in these liminal (and "non-developing") spaces.[38]

As Benanav notes, the ILO report that defined informal markets made no distinction between licit and illicit goods (and therefore, between black and gray markets). He adds that the ILO based its original sense of informal markets on families whose members worked at a variety of jobs and in the absence of bookkeeping.[39] These often-extended households relied on "casual employment, kinship or personal and social relations rather than contractual arrangements with formal guarantees." And "insofar as family members were not paid, there was no need to distinguish between those who worked and those who did not. Instead, work was spread throughout a given household and over the course of a given day."[40]

In turning to families that are similar if not exactly like these, black-market melodramas make hay with "liminal spaces between unemployment and full employment"—as well as between home and work. Missing in these spaces are what Benanav thinks are missing in the informal sector generally: "the real abstractions, or divisions within individuals' lives, that work for wages instantiates: between labor-force participation and non-participation, between waged and unwaged work, between employer and employee, and between levels of labor productivity."[41] The absence of those abstractions and divisions gives the black-market melodrama its often gothic, purgatorial cast; in the genre's uncanny spaces, neither domestic nor yet not, informal labor comes to seem both an alternative to and also a new kind of housework. The genre's many homes are thus haunted by versions of the "world underneath," the name Alejandro Portes and Manuel Castells give the informal economy: from black markets to "the upside down" in *Stranger Things*, to a dimension literally beneath this one in *Counterpart*, to the purgatory signaled even in the title *Mr. Inbetween*.[42]

Economists debate the size and importance of the US informal economy.[43] It is certainly not now the case that the US white middle class depends on informal labor to anything like the degree that proletarianized, nonwhite populations do. Nor do labor-intensive family businesses characterize that class. But the black-market melodrama matters not because it opens a transparent window on the work in which white middle-class families now engage, but because it anticipates that work by allegorizing it in a revealing light. And as the genre anticipates deindustrialization's middle-class consequences and the white family's dependence on emergent labor forms, it draws out the gendered expropriation upon which that family has long depended. It reveals for instance that the developing world has *always* been present in the middle-class family, as a version of the "predatory patriarchal division of labor" that Maria Mies links to "housewifization," which names linked processes in the developed and underdeveloped world. Women are consigned to housework in the former and informal labor in the latter, she argues, the better to preserve men's exclusive access to the state-recognized formal economy in each.[44]

That said, black-market melodramas describe the retreat of the state-recognized industrial economy; and they conjure a future in which white middle-class families reproduce themselves with labor-intensive, nonspecialized housework, broadly conceived. As Ruth Schwartz Cowan put it in 1983, "The housewife is the last jane-of-all trades in a world from which the jacks-of-all trades have more or less disappeared; she is expected to perform work that ranges from the most menial physical labor to the most abstract of mental manipulations and to do it all without any specialized training."[45] Cowan's vanished world returns in black-market melodramas in which housework assumes a new generality and becomes more than the gendered counterpart to waged labor. The genre conceives of housework broadly, in other words, as "industrious" off-the-books labor in liminal spaces "between labor-force participation and non-participation, between waged and unwaged work, [and] between employer and employee."

The genre's industrious housework recalls preindustrial labor paradigms. The term "industrious revolution" was first used in 1967 by Hayami Akira to describe the labor-intensive family agriculture that emerged in Japan after the freeing of the peasantry. Since then, historians have described different industrious families at the heart of different forms of household production that ran alongside capital-intensive industrial production. In 1994, Jean de Vries described an industrious revolution that ran from the mid-seventeenth- to early nineteenth-century Europe and (he thought) paved the way for the industrial revolution. His industrious households produced specialized goods for the market while becoming increasingly dependent on market-supplied goods that they once produced themselves.[46] Kaoru Sugihara and Ken Pomeranz later placed a different industrious family at the heart of the "the Great Divergence" between East Asian and European economies that began in the sixteenth century. Where subsequent European development depended on capital- and resource-intensive production, East Asian economies, faced with limited land and natural resources, developed labor-absorbing technologies and institutions, chief of which was the industrious family itself. China and Japan, Sugihara argues, engineered "the full absorption of family labor" by prizing a family whose members could "perform multiple tasks well." In this dispensation, "it was important for every member of the family to try to fit into the work pattern of the farm, respond flexibly to extra or emergency needs, sympathize with the problems relating to the management of production, and anticipate and prevent potential problems."[47]

The "general background of technical skill" that Sugihara thinks important to this labor model speaks to the codification of informal labor. The first UN report to describe "informal enterprises," for instance, singled out "small scale" family operations in "'competitive markets' with 'ease of entry'" that used "'labor-intensive' technologies."[48] And though originally used to describe para-industrial household production, the industrious paradigm has encouraged speculation about the economic arrangements toward which Western economies seem now to tend. De Vries identified "a second industrious revolution" in the latter decades of the twentieth century, which, with the first, bookended roughly 150 years of industrial production and the nuclear family that lay at its heart. He noted a return to "the intensification of work and suppression of leisure" within the family and the "greater permeability" that characterized it as a result of the "greater labor force participation" of married women. The second industrious revolution "is reminiscent of its eighteenth-century predecessor," he wrote, because "it occurs in an environment of stagnant or declining individual real wages and salaries; [and] it is characterized by a rise in demand for market-supplied goods that minimize the addition of domestic 'value added' (chiefly time) before ultimate consumption."[49] Though interested in a different version of the phenomenon, Pomeranz added that two-income families that contracted out child-raising and food-making were "a logical conclusion of sorts" to de Vries's first industrious revolution.[50]

Giovanni Arrighi invoked Sugihara and Pomeranz on the industrious family when he described the capitalism with Chinese characteristics that he thought was converging with Western capitalism in the early twenty-first century. For Sugihara, East Asia's industrious revolution was a "miracle of distribution" that differed from the West's more properly industrial "miracle of production." The former distributed a higher overall standard of living to a greater number by mobilizing the industrious family, state agencies, and intra- rather than international trade; the latter depended primarily on wage labor and led, ultimately, to "the explosive growth in the number of transnational corporations" that "has become the most critical factor in the withering away of the modern system of territorial states as the primary locus of world power." The convergence between Eastern and Western capitalism, Arrighi speculated, suggested a way out of our present global accumulation crisis, which he described in *The Long Twentieth Century*, and which now confronts us, in addition to much else besides, as work's casualization, flat wages for those who receive them, the immiseration of those who don't, the welfare state's defunding, the ascent of finance capital, and the waning of US global hegemony.[51]

The black-market melodrama will not tell us if Arrighi's convergence is truly in the offing. But it does register the white middle-class household's newfound exposure to necessity and the seeming immanence of the less-developed world within it. "I'm starting my own hedge-fund," announces Sanjay Patel on *Weeds*. "Do you know that there are amazing opportunities to be had in the exploitation of emerging third-world countries?" He's standing in the gutted kitchen of a home in white suburbia, in which he, Nancy Botwin, and Conrad Shepard have been growing their first crop of marijuana. Conrad berates him for looking so far from home. "There are thirty-seven billionaires in this country and forty million living beneath the poverty line. Wake up, 7-Eleven, this is the fucking third world" (2.11). It matters, of course, that they've transformed an affluent suburban home into their grow-house; the genre's homes suffer what we might call domestic border crises: they have been penetrated not simply by the market but by the less-developed world. "We all know what's going on down there," Hank Schrader tells his DEA team in *Breaking Bad*, referring to El Paso. "We sure don't want it going on up here" (2.2). It's too late for such sentiments; later, Marie decides not to join Hank in El Paso because "It's third world enough around here" (2.7). Deictics like "there" and "here" appear throughout the genre, as characters struggle to shore up the family home against what de Vries calls its "greater permeability." But White's meth production brings the third world home—literally, in season 3, when the Salamanca brothers cross the Mexican border and find their way into his bedroom.

Black-market melodramas organized by Cold War spy conventions tell this story in a different way. Nicholas Brody's return home from Iraq in *Homeland* as a terrorist registers the white middle-class family's newfound exposure less to third world informal markets than to blowback from US global power. In *Mr. Robot*, an intergenerational family melodrama between Elliot Anderson and his dead father gets entangled with China's ascent. And yet, even when turning to geopolitics, the genre makes familiar points. *The Americans* uses the USSR as *Breaking Bad* did Mexico: as an object lesson that captures "the development of underdevelopment" not in the global periphery but in the semiperiphery that ostensibly developed nations now become. The drama's goal is less to consolidate distinctions between the US and USSR than to draw out the domestic consequences of Reagan's revolution.

Like *The Americans*, *Killing Eve* allegorizes wetwork and housework, as Eve Polastri, working for MI6, hunts Villanelle, a Soviet-trained assassin who lives luxuriously in Western Europe's glittering capitals. The melodrama stages a return of the Cold War repressed (in which Russians and Eastern Europeans invade and transform a now-decaying West) as a return of the sexually repressed (in which gay desire drives an endless love-hate *pas de deux* between the drama's doubled leads). But if Villanelle is Eve's double, Eve also has a more elusive doppelgänger, "the ghost," a "considerate assassin" (2.4) who works undercover in a low-wage, immigrant-staffed cleaning service (figs. 0.5 and 0.6). The ghost is a Korean-born, downwardly mobile alternative to Villanelle's high-end contract work. Almost nothing is made of Sandra Oh's ethnicity through the first two seasons, and her Korean heritage struck some as "refreshingly incidental"; the serial felt as if "from some future date where colorblind casting is expected."[52] Small recompense: while Eve speaks Korean only once in the first two seasons, she does so just before contacting the considerate assassin, whose empathy (like Eve's) contrasts with Villanelle's lack of same, and whose cover clarifies both the gender norms that Eve and Villanelle flee and the convergence of low-wage service work and seemingly elite knowledge work. By the third season, that convergence is all but explicit: Eve is still sleuthing,

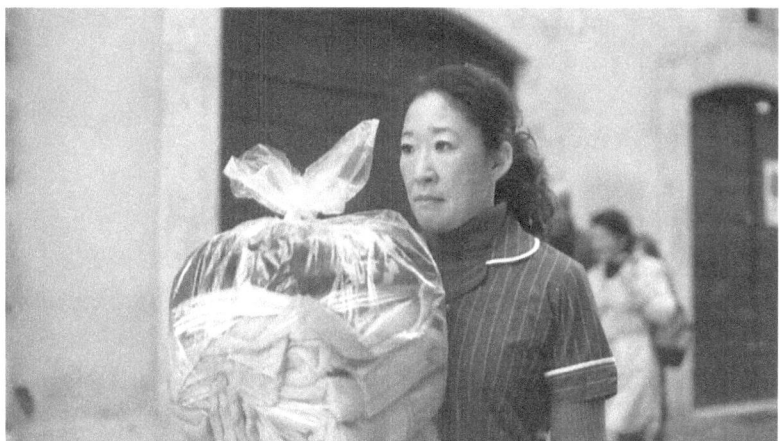

0.5. *Killing Eve*: Eve Polastri under deep cover.

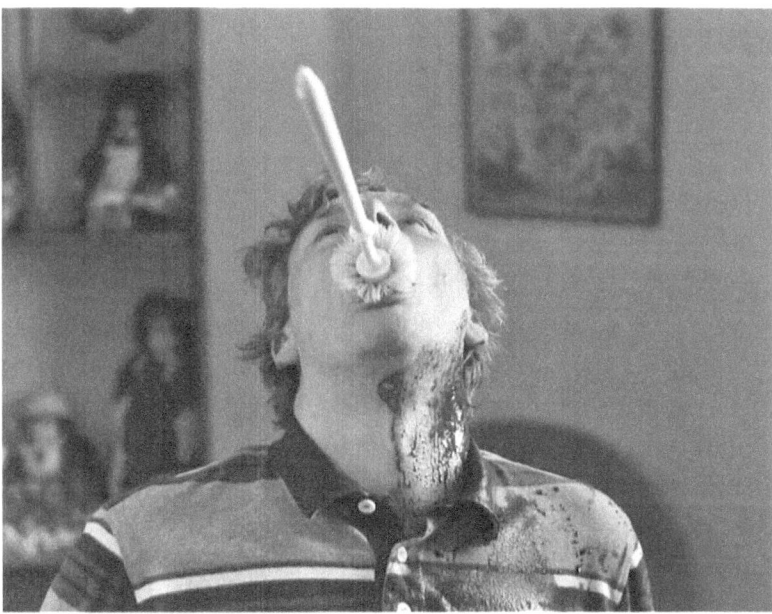

0.6. *Killing Eve*: The return of the repressed.

but no longer paid for doing so; instead, she labors in the kitchen of a local Korean restaurant.

Allegory, Melodramatic and Otherwise

Black-market melodramas might seem mainly interested in what Joel Fineman calls the "allegory of allegorical desire."[53] In other words, they might seem mainly to allegorize their own literary need to produce ever more allegory and ever more interpretation. Like quality TV generally, the genre promotes suspicious reading. Dana Polan compares *Sopranos* fans to "medieval exegetes of religious allegories who would devise ever more complex systems of interpretation."[54] Characters often instruct one another (and the audience) in how to read figuratively; AJ struggles with Robert Frost's "Stopping by the Woods on a Snowy Evening" and asks Meadow, "What does it mean?" She replies, "What does snow symbolize?" He doesn't know and when she tells him white symbolizes death, he replies, perplexed, "I thought black was death" (3.2). And there is a surprising amount of chatter about allegory itself in quality TV. On *Orange Is the New Black*, Nicky tries to speak "allegorically" to a guard who, uncomprehending, asks why she invokes Al Gore. On *Halt and Catch Fire*, one character chastises another for using "metaphor" rather than "allegory" (3.4). On *Legion*, a voiceover recounts the Allegory of the Cave as we watch primitive troglodytes evolve into smartphone addicts still unable to grasp unmediated reality (2.8).

But a receptivity to suspicious reading does not itself distinguish the black-market melodrama. More distinctive are its allegories of deindustrialization and the erosion of separate spheres. In *Lodge 49*, for instance, the alchemist lodge named in the title is an escape from grief over a lost father, intermittent work, poor health, and mounting bills that have led two siblings to share costs and live together. The lodge offers a version of the secret second life. Explaining its appeal, Sean Dudley recalls standing over a full-length mirror and feeling "like I was looking down into the sky. . . . It was like there was this whole other world just right below us. And I wanted to jump through. That's how I felt when I walked into the lodge" (1.1). We jump through with him, into a self-consciously allegorical world. Now a member, he contemplates an "allegorical picture" of an "allegorical golden book" while relating the secret society's "allegorical history" (1.2). His spectatorship allegorizes ours, as an escape from what a character calls "the epoch of postindustrial capitalism" (1.6). Here and across the genre, that escape is into the past. When exploring a closing factory, for instance, Dudley discovers he longs to "make it like it was in the golden age again" (1.7). A locus of allegory, the lodge is the "other world" in which characters try to recapture that age.

Such recuperative gestures exemplify one (if only one) kind of allegory. Fineman describes allegory as a self-consciously frustrated "journey back to a foreclosed origin."[55] Walter Benjamin and Paul de Man offer related accounts in which allegory tries and fails to capture some lost wholeness (for Coleridge, it aims for the "organic" but achieves only the "mechanic"). I frequently rely on Benjamin, who explains that failure in historical terms rather than structuralist (Fineman) or poststructuralist (de Man) ones. For Benjamin, seventeenth-century allegory is the product of failed restoration (and more generally of the loss of the king's divine right).[56] The black-market melodrama is allegorical in this sense when it pines for but fails to restore the ostensibly organic relation between family and work that has been foreclosed by deindustrialization. Notwithstanding his efforts to maintain gendered and raced segregations, Soprano's work family and home family are "mechanic" allegories of each other because the drama believes there is no longer any whole that separate spheres in their difference can together form. "That which the allegorical intention has fixed upon," writes Benjamin, "is sundered from the customary contexts of life: it is simultaneously shattered and conserved."[57]

To see black-market melodramas as allegories is to discover in them systems of occulted meaning relatively uncommon on broadcast TV during the first years of the new millennium—exceptions like *Lost* and *The Good Place* aside. But however consciously placed there, these systems do not somehow elevate our programs above a more banal throng of popular fare. Benjamin's version of allegory and melodrama share affinities as theatrical modes, though one is courtly in origin and the other demotic. Each yearns to recover some sacred vestige. For Benjamin,

INTRODUCTION

allegory longs for the king's second body, infused with divine right. Distilled into a marketable form in the wake of the French Revolution, melodrama replaced the deposed king with a fantasy of home and hearth, to vouchsafe an otherwise elusive innocence and, ultimately, to invest family life with a sanctity and good-versus-evil grandeur that its everyday realities consistently belied. Black-market melodramas are similarly backward-looking, knowingly quixotic efforts to restore an imaginary nuclear family thought to thrive during the glory days of US manufacturing.

But the genre's knowingness also points us to the present: insofar as the genre longs for separate spheres from within an ongoing deindustrialization—and from within particular corporate contexts—it evinces a synchronic rather than diachronic type of allegory. Often associated with corporate and ideological "symptomatic" readings, this kind of allegory, to which I now turn, allows us to unearth a given drama's determining origins in the present (rather than a distant past about which the drama is nostalgic).

In a sixth-season sequence, Soprano lies dying in a hospital bed, lost in a coma, his stomach an open wound. The sequence picks up on Soprano's MRI in the first season, and his therapy sessions, all of which ask: what, if anything, lives within this golem of a man? In this moment, the drama is itself an open wound, as one level of reality bleeds into another. Meadow and Carmela hover over Tony, watching as the audience might; in his dreams, he dimly perceives them, as he looks up into a light that seems both the light above his hospital bed and the set's camera lights (fig. 0.7). His dreams condense analogously related separate spheres. In them, he is Kevin Finnerty, a mild-mannered traveling salesman. Finnerty's problem is not that he cannot escape his family, but that he cannot return to it. He is stranded far from home and follows a beacon to a large manse nestled in trees that rustle ominously in the wind, a nod to *Twin Peaks*. He's greeted outside and told, "Your whole family is in there, they're waiting for you. You're going home." We catch brief glimpses of the family within, through the half-opened front door. But Finnerty is stopped because he carries his briefcase. "You can't take

0.7. *The Sopranos*: "Please don't leave us, Daddy."

0.8. *The Sopranos*: "You can't take business in there."

business in there" (6.3), the gatekeeper says. Only in death will Soprano find a truly separate family sphere (fig. 0.8).

There are other levels of espial at stake. In the hospital, Soprano is presided over by one "Dr. Plepler," named for the then-head of HBO programming Richard Plepler. It is Dr. Plepler's job to peer into Soprano's wound and determine if the plug should be pulled, as it was Richard Plepler's to determine if it was time to end the drama itself. In this moment, then, the drama stacks its separate spheres and different levels of mediation almost literally, as different kinds of audience look into the drama from different levels of reality, each motivated by a different set of pressures. Soon after awakening, Soprano is accosted by Evangelicals, who tell him, "God wants you to love him directly, without the intercession of any human agent" (6.4). He treats them with derision. The previous episodes have done nothing if not stage the multiple human and inhuman agencies that have interceded to keep Soprano (and his drama) alive.

The black-market melodrama allegorizes a range of similarly occulted agencies, often the corporate agencies responsible for a given program's production and distribution. It matters in *Six Feet Under*, for instance, that the Fishers fight the mortuary conglomerate Kroehner, whose name is close enough to "Chronos" to evoke Time Warner, and "kroner," to invoke the fiscal constraints imposed by Time Warner. So too it matters in *Big Love*'s first season that Bill Henrickson fights to retain control of Home Plus, which received financing from the shady Roman Grant. In black-market melodramas, small family firms that obliquely invoke HBO are forever struggling to remain independent from the larger corporate entities in whose shadows they operate. To miss how those besieged units allegorize the ones producing the television in question is to overlook a crucial dimension of the genre. But this level of allegory is not definitive, and I try throughout to emphasize the more systemic relations of which individual industries, studios, and even transnationals are but contingent forms of appearance. J. D. Connor's and Jerry Christensen's corporate allegories tend to insist on a film's origins in local rather than generalized dynamics.[58] I'm interested in corporate allegory as well, but ultimately I find the systemic more generative. And so rather than tie off local readings with gestures to particular corporate contexts, I endeavor to show how those contexts themselves mediate architectonically "deeper" forces, to quote Fredric Jameson, which become apprehensible only when allegorized. Allegory in this sense joins "a particular and a universal" in a "self-undermining" way, as Jameson has it, and a critic's "insistence on allegory is an insistence on the difficulty, or even impossibility, of the representation of . . . deeper and essentially relational realities."[59]

To put matters no doubt too schematically, "deindustrialization" names for me the generalized forces that drive the black-market melodrama, even as specific local agencies—from individual corporate balance sheets to industry labor relations to the federal deregulation of the media industry—mediate those forces. That use of deindustrialization amounts to a necessary shorthand: the deep forces that drive *it* are complexly and dynamically relational, which is why, for Jameson, they are beyond direct representation. That's not to deny that there are richer accounts of the economic processes in question than those offered here; far from it. It's simply to say that when I refer to complex processes as if they constituted a single legible event, "deindustrialization," I signal, unavoidably, the limits of this study's explanatory machinery. Some such limit is inevitable. And in any event, what interests me most is how the genre coordinates the multiple local agencies that mediate the forces thus named.

For example, the black-market melodrama emerged on the heels of two legislative acts, each passed in 1996. These two acts structured different aspects of the US economy's deindustrialization and, as a consequence, different aspects of the genre. We have already encountered one, the PRWORA, which recommitted the state to regulating nonwhite families on behalf of the white family's preservation. The other was the Telecommunications Act, which deregulated individual communications industries—newspapers, books, radio, TV, film, etc.—and created a global media industry hungry for finance capital, which had freed itself from industrial production in the developed core in the face of declining profit rates. TV scholars have written extensively about the impact on the media industry of the Telecom Act and, for example, the 1993 repeal of financial interest and syndication rules that prevented networks from producing their own content.[60] I've spent less time on those topics than I might have, not because they are unimportant to black-market melodramas—they are manifestly important—but because those regulatory changes are illustrative rather than definitive mediations of the deeper dynamics that drive the genre. On the whole, this is not a book about Hollywood or how it works, and I tend to eschew the meso-level industrial sociology that sometimes dominates television studies. That said, it's worth adumbrating the Telecom Act's generic resonance, if only to explain why I do in fact spend time below talking about specific studios and media corporations.

In the act's wake, the media industry consolidated into a handful of leviathan transnationals, which farmed out production in post-Fordist fashion to "families" of laterally arrayed, ambiguously autonomous units (some of which were formally internal to those corporations, many of which were not). Intent to explore the limits of that autonomy from its parent company Time Warner, HBO first produced (or contracted to produce) risqué, loss-leader programming about heterodox families struggling to maintain *their* autonomy.[61] And in fact, as the genre evolved, protagonist families often worked off-the-books for or in the shadow of a more potent if distant authority (*The Sopranos*: New York mob families; *Breaking Bad*: Madrigal Electromotive; *The Americans*: the KGB directorate; *Ozark*: the Navarro cartel). These semiautonomous, quasi-post-Fordist families—contracting for entities that do not acknowledge them, while managing similarly disposable workforces—evoke the decentralized production centers on which post-Fordist Hollywood came to rely (before Netflix money changed the system yet again, in ways that are beyond the confines of this book).

As we've begun to see, black-market melodramas stress the representational affinities of families and firms. It is no accident that firms speak of themselves as families (even if, here too, Netflix is an interesting exception: CEO Reed Hastings likes to insist the company "is a team, not a family").[62] However different the sense of belonging and kinship each offers, families and firms think themselves sustaining collectives even as they police the legal and moral boundaries that distinguish them from potentially similar units. That policing becomes acute when firms, say, cease to profit as they once did or when their boundaries begin to break down. Equally so, economic reality can lead families to think themselves corporations. Capitalist dogma encourages the comparison; for Randy Martin, neoliberalism models "domesticity along the lines of the modern corporation."⁶³ Black-market melodramas stress that formulation's reversibility and use family and corporate life to express each other.

That mutuality is an ideological mediation of the real economy. For David Harvey, the subcontracting on which post-Fordism or "flexible accumulation" depends

> opens up opportunities for small business formation, and in some instances permits older systems of domestic, artisanal, familial (patriarchal), and paternalistic ("godfather," "guv'nor" or even mafia-like) labor systems to revive and flourish as centerpieces rather than as appendages of the production system.... [Meanwhile,] the rapid growth of "black," "informal," or "underground" economies has also been documented throughout the advanced capitalist world, leading some to suggest that there is a growing convergence between "third world" and advanced capitalist labor systems.

This is a useful account of how we witness in deindustrialization's long tail a resurgence of broadly familial forms of economic production. But this is also a useful account of why "family" in black-market melodramas is so ideologically overdetermined as an allegorical register, why it is, in fact, ground zero of the genre's multifarious allegory: the abstraction applies flexibly to any number of failed collectives—whether organized around biology or corporate law—in which, as Harvey puts it, "class consciousness no longer derives from the straight class relation between capital and labor, and moves onto a much more confused terrain" dominated by "a kinship or clan-like system of hierarchically ordered social relations."⁶⁴

Luc Boltanski and Eve Chiapello tell a related story in which changes in the nuclear family have run alongside changes in the firm, informing how we think of each in the process. They elucidate three phases of capitalism. The first forms during the nineteenth century around the family firm, which is run as a family and in which employees have face-to-face relations with owners. During this phase, Hegel would theorize the corporation as the natural counterpart to the family (even as Coventry

Patmore would describe the married woman as "The Angel in the House" and Charles Dickens would declare in *Great Expectations*, "the office is one thing and private life is another").⁶⁵ The second phase takes shape in the middle of the twentieth century as shareholders become more distant and as publicly traded firms, detached from the fates of individual families, embrace cadres of now salaried managers. This phase reaches a zenith under state Fordism, which provides male workers a family wage and embarks upon a denigration of family bonds at work, in the service of bureaucratic norms that keep family and professional interests distinct. This was the scaled-up, corporate workplace version of separate spheres gender relations: (masculine) work and (feminine) home were to be kept rigorously separate.

The third phase, with which the black-market melodrama is preoccupied, follows deindustrialization and the bankrupting of state Fordism and reintroduces personal and familial values to the firm without actually reestablishing the biological family as a locus of value and meaning. Organized around ideologies of adaptive connection, and underwritten by the internet, this new phase conceives of firms as independent production units arrayed around a hub of marketing, finance, and logistics. The post-Fordist firm is now a loose amalgam of related families, in other words, rather than a hierarchically managed single family (Boltanski and Chiapello repeatedly use the mafia to illustrate closed versions of the "networks" that dominate this phase). And within each corporate unit, newly personalized work relations collapse the wall between home and work that was important to state Fordism. In the third phase, Boltanski and Chiapello write, "the distinction between private life and professional life tends to diminish," such that "it then becomes difficult to make a distinction between the time of private life and the time of professional life, between dinners with friends and business lunches, between affective bonds and useful relationships, and so on." So too it is difficult in capitalism's third stage to separate family time from firm time. That separation "is deemed deleterious inasmuch as it separates dimensions of life that are indissoluble, inhuman because it leaves no room for affectivity, and at the same time inefficient because it runs counter to flexibility and inhibits the multiple skills that must be employed to learn to 'live in a network.'"[66]

That endless work is industrious in all the ways that I have described, because it deploys "flexibility" and "multiple skills" within a "network" with no obvious outside and, more basically, because it raises fundamental questions of "affectivity" and social purpose, with which I now conclude. Over and beyond its tendency to allegorize the transformation of labor markets and the corporation, the black-market melodrama asks whether the stories that the white middle-class family has long told itself are still meaningful (if ever they were). The genre longs for and even supplies larger social wholes. As it moves from the mafia in *The Sopranos* to the polygamous family in *Big Love*, the biker gang in *Sons of Anarchy*, and the Soviet Union in *The Americans*, to take a few examples, it invokes collectives more encompassing than the nuclear households from which it seeks escape. As Jameson noted long ago about the mafia film, however ideological in nature, such collectives are always implicitly utopian. But the genre's lingering heteronormative biases, no less than the depressive realism to which it subjects those biases, overcome its utopianism, as one drama after another reveals the bankruptcy of communal life within and beyond the family. Generic offshoots like *The Walking Dead*, *Orange Is the New Black*, and *Game of Thrones* don't overcome so much as scale up this problem (which is perhaps why that last drama ends in unconscious farce). Nominally about tribal, queer, and feudal families, respectively, these dramas explode their traditional families and begin again with what seem like new kinds of community. But they cannot cease to pine—both for the families left behind and for a nuclear family that they can neither quite recall nor yet cease to allegorize.

CHAPTER 1

The Gangster Mourning Play

The Sopranos' title sequence begins with a welter of moving signs and symbols. It places us in the passenger seat of Tony Soprano's SUV as he drives home from New York. We register names and titles—the credits themselves—as we scan the ceiling of the Lincoln Tunnel, the dashboard, a ticket machine for the turnpike, the unlit and then lit cigar in his mouth, the Statue of Liberty, a graveyard, a butcher shop, a pizzeria, row houses, and finally Soprano's tree-ringed home upon a hill. Then a silent pause, as we move into the pilot episode and more languorous scenes of reading. The camera locates Soprano through the legs of a bronze statuette of a naked woman (fig. 1.1). We track his perplexed scrutiny of her upper half from behind her legs, and then from his point of view zoom slowly in on her face and arms, crossed behind her head. A door opens and Jennifer Melfi admits Soprano into her office. He takes a seat, and after some resistance to her questions, begins to explain the source of the stress that caused him recently to black out. We hear a voiceover as we watch a flashback: "The morning of the day I got sick, I'd been thinking. It's good to be in something from the ground floor. I came too late for that. I know. But lately, I'm getting the feeling that I came in at the end. The best is over." Melfi interjects, "Many Americans, I think, feel that way." He continues, "I think about my father. He never reached heights like me. But in a lot of ways, he had it better. He had his people. They had their standards. They had pride. Today, what do we got?"

CHAPTER 1

1.1. *The Sopranos*: Tony considers art.

With these lines, Sopranos inaugurates an allegorical narrative as potentially endless as a psychoanalytic talking cure. In his voiceover, he displays the "self-conscious and sacralizing nostalgia in response to authoritative but in some sense faded origins" that Joel Fineman claims has long characterized allegory, "that mode that makes up for the distance . . . between the present and a disappearing past, which, without interpretation, would be otherwise irretrievable and foreclosed." Since at least the first century, he adds, literary allegory has functioned as "a journey back to a foreclosed origin"; it is a "vivifying archeology of occulted origins and a promissory eschatology of postponed ends" that typically begins with longing for a lost golden age. But if vivifying, never completely so: unable to restore the loss that animates it, allegory turns on itself and becomes an "allegory of allegorical desire," that is, a search for the origin of the desire to search for occulted origins in the first place. This is why, for Fineman, psychoanalysis represents the culmination of the allegorical tradition.[1]

The proper object of Soprano's psychoanalysis, in this account, is the drive that produces it, rather than, say, his mother. The title sequence might be said to represent that drive. It tracks our emergence from watery depths—in Soprano's SUV—as a visually jarring and only belatedly stabilized surfacing from sleep. As we "woke up this morning," in the words of the theme song by Alabama 3, our field of vision moves from the disorienting blurred lines of the tunnel's roof, seen as if lying on our backs in bed, to the solidity of the family home, in or in proximity to which we fully awaken. Soprano's emergence from the tunnel is also a natal emergence from mom (the theme song chronicles a morning awakening that is also a birth). And so when considering the "something" that Soprano has failed to enter at the ground floor, or the thing his father had that he did not, we must consider Livia Soprano, especially given the pilot's inaugural camera angle, which captures Soprano's transfixed gaze from between the legs of the statuette. Soprano will later tell Melfi that mothers are "the vehicle that gets us here. They drop us off and go on their way.... And the problem is that we keep trying to get back on the bus, instead of just letting it go" (6.19). But if Livia is Soprano's bus, she's not the lost origin that defines all else. Over many seasons we come to recognize less her singular significance than Soprano's inexhaustible drive to tell stories about her, such that she can be routinely invoked and overcome, returned to and then left. She is a pretext for the imperative to narrate ceaselessly. Something similar is true of Soprano's relation to home and family: he will be forever returning to and leaving them, stuck in an endless commute whose repetition evokes our weekly viewing rituals.

Seen this way, Soprano's voiceover suggests a formal as well as a personal transition, one tied to our experience rather than his. Maybe the title sequence itself is the best that is over, not because of its quality or because it solves a psychoanalytic puzzle (that cigar in Soprano's mouth!), but because of its structural primacy: it provides the metaphor that Fineman thinks all allegory aims, in its properly temporal dimensions, to extend metonymically in time, as narrative. The title sequence transpires as if out of time, and eventuates in a single, structuring metaphor, which is also a single structuring contradiction. For most of the sequence, Soprano's SUV seems a vehicle in search of its tenor, which it appears in the end to acquire. Having moved up from the depths of the Hudson, over the surfaces of New Jersey, and then up again to the hill on which he lives, Soprano arrives at his house, which signals "family" in an obvious way. But this word names home *and* work, domestic as

CHAPTER 1

well as business arrangements, Soprano's nuclear family as well as his mafia Family. A workplace drama about the mob and a domestic drama about daily family life refer to each other, each a vehicle for the other's tenor. So, for example, it's unclear if Soprano is coming from or going to work. The best that has just ended in the pilot cannot really be, in the title sequence, his workday. He *seems* to move from work to home, such that he arrives at the end of the day at the heights that mark his success. But the clock on his dash reads "10:22," which indicates that we move in "the world turned upside down" signaled by the theme song not from work to home but from home to work. "Woke up this morning," repeats the chorus, "and got myself a gun." The speed with which the singer gets his gun (is he still in bed?), no less than the grim look on Soprano's face when he exits the SUV, suggests that home is work (rehashing home life is a labor; moments into his first therapy session, he says, "back to work"). And the title sequence ends after he leaves the SUV but before he enters his house. Soprano is stuck in a perpetual commute, unable fully to arrive or depart.

That commute transpires in an eternal present: the title sequence seems to take place *now*, in the moment of the drama's reception, rather than in the past of a completed action, as is the case for the narrative proper. Nevertheless, the title sequence gestures to a lost origin formally as well as thematically. Like the tunnel with which it begins and the HBO static logo from which it emerges, the sequence is a station between the narrative proper and more elusive extradiegetic sources, to which it can only gesture. And within the sequence's diegesis, names blur into view from the left of the screen, briefly come into focus, then speed off to the right, mimicking Soprano's perception of the billboards and road signs past which he moves. As "the credits," the sequence tells a story about where *this* story comes from by attributing names to work roles.[2] But the rush of language, no less than the talking cure that follows, are linguistic enterprises that compete for attention with what lies beyond them: the ruined landscape of industrial New Jersey, littered with factories, many shuttered. The competition is for more than our attention alone. Are those shuttered factories themselves a kind of author? Might they not be one expression of the agency that drives Soprano and even those responsible for creating the drama? *The Sopranos* asks those questions, I will suggest, as part of a sustained reflexive inquiry into its creation.

New Jersey's ruined landscape had not changed much by 2020, when David Chase penned an extra *Sopranos* scene, in which characters respond to the coronavirus. The drama had been from the start about a kind of home quarantine, in its preoccupation with the inescapability of family and in its relentless conflation of work and nonwork. The new scene toys with those themes. "We're not doing well with the quarantine in our house," says Carmela. "It's making me face the music that this is a dysfunctional family. But it's keeping my husband in, which is good." Tony was a philandering cheat. But in a sense, he had always been kept in, confined to a recurrent movement from family to Family, his toxic bluster a response to that confinement. Responding to *his* quarantine, Johnny Sack says, "It used to be part of our thing, going to the mattresses. But this?" Sack invokes a trope inherited from *The Godfather* and, further back, the British spy novel. As Michael Denning has it, the "safe house" where one goes to mattresses is "a place that is neither office nor home," and a "disquieting" reminder that "not all houses are safe."[3] Certainly in *The Sopranos* no houses were.

Soprano's response to the virus is the most telling: "The president might have a point," he says. "Let's get business and manufacturing going again—by Easter, May Day, whatever the fuck."[4] From first to last, *The Sopranos* had been about deindustrialization. The title sequence makes this clear when surveying, for example, the Hydro-Pruf Factory, an abandoned superfund site, or Newark itself, a one-time manufacturing hub whose waterfront Soprano and Sack try to develop into a leisure playground (the two discuss that scheme in the ruins of the abandoned Chemical Compounds Inc. factory [4.13]). These relics are a version of the graveyard past which he drives—and, as such, signposts of the drama's allegory. "In allegory," Walter Benjamin writes in *The Origin of German Tragic Drama*, "the observer is confronted with the *facies hippocratica* of history as a petrified, primordial landscape." That is particularly true in baroque tragic dramas, or "mourning plays," that relish the "untimely, sorrowful, [and] unsuccessful," and that dwell on ruins and graveyards as remnants of a transient human history. Allegories need not invoke actual ruins or graveyards; they are themselves "in the realm of thoughts, what ruins are in the realm of things."[5] They partialize and render lifeless once-living relationships. By these lights, ruined factories only incompletely gesture to the loss that drives Soprano. He stumbles in explaining himself to Melfi because the best that is over is no one thing, but an imagined way of life. Certainly he doesn't long for the factory floor itself. Rather, the relics past which he drives mark the end of the postwar manufacturing boom that made possible the particular shibboleth for which this golem of a patriarch is most nostalgic. Ultimately, Soprano's lament is for an imaginary white nuclear family, supported by a male breadwinner and set safely apart, a haven from a heartless economic world. The drama will struggle to resurrect even the ideological pretense of that family, which has been ruined and lost to time.

What follows plumbs the drama's multiple origins. The first section explains how, in its debts to gangster films, and in its preoccupation with nuclear family dynamics often overlooked by those films, the serial codified the black-market melodrama. I then read *The Sopranos* as a latter-day instance of Benjamin's mourning play, a bombastic precursor to stage melodrama that explains the crime drama's melancholic allegories and, specifically, its authorial reflexivity. My final section reads a season-three sequence that encapsulates *The Sopranos*' fascination with deindustrialization, financialization, and Time Warner's transformation early in the new millennium.

"You Don't Give, You Take"

When Soprano says "the best is over," he refers to a number of recent and impending endings: the traditional values according to which the mafia once did business; the mafia's influence; Tony Jr.'s ignorance of the family's business; Soprano's marriage; the millennium; and above all, a decades-long industrial expansion. But the drama also understands itself as a belated instance of a lapsed genre. "I thought the Mob was expired as a movie form before we ever started," Chase declared.[6]

Most accounts of the gangster film echo Robert Warshow's. The gangster is a tragic urban outsider whose rise and fall "rejects the qualities and demands of modern life." Warshow's terms became only slightly less broad in the hands of subsequent critics. Fran Mason thinks gangster films respond to "the threat of the modern." Richard Pells reads the genre as "a parody of the American Dream"; the gangster is a "psychopathic Horatio Alger embodying in himself the classic capitalist urge for wealth and success"; he is "a reproach to both the principles of the marketplace and the reigning values of American life." Ron Wilson calls the genre "a distorted vision of the American success story" and notes that "the earliest film images of gangsters emerged in the 1900s as a result of concerns over industrialization and urban life" and "fear of modernity and technology."[7] This is all right as far as it goes, but critics are more useful when they note the genre's appeal during moments of economic crisis. C. L. R. James, for example, claims that the gangster film was the first Hollywood genre to respond systematically to the crisis of the wage precipitated by the Great Depression, which is "the primary event which made Americans begin to realize that the ground under their feet was unsure."[8]

Many of the most storied gangster films were made during acute economic upheavals. *The Public Enemy* (1931), *Little Caesar* (1931), and *Scarface* (1932) are mostly about the roaring 1920s but were produced during the first years of Great Depression. And while there are many mob movies about the prosperous postwar years—including *The Godfather* (1972) and *The Godfather II* (1974)—few now iconic ones were produced in the 1950s and 1960s. The genre is instead reborn during the recessionary 1970s, when Frances Ford Coppola begins his famous cycle and Martin Scorsese makes *Mean Streets* (1973). These films struck a new note and anticipated the black-market melodrama. Depression-era gangster films tend not to be nostalgic. The neon sign that calls to Tony "Scarface" Camonte in *Scarface*—"The World Is Yours"—spurs him to look forward rather than back. In *Little Caesar*, Rico Bandello wants to be "somebody"; there is nothing to look back to, except anonymity and irrelevance. But later mob films look back longingly to industrial booms. In *Godfather II*, Hyman Roth crows to the underworld captains gathered before him in Havana: "We are bigger than U.S. Steel!" It was one thing to be bigger than U.S. Steel in 1959, when the film is set, and another to be bigger during the "Steel Recession" of the mid-1970s, when the film was made. During these years, unemployment was higher than at any time since the Great Depression. U.S. Steel was particularly hard hit. In 1943, it employed 340,498; in 1980, only 75,000; and in 1988, 20,000.[9]

Gangster films are often both nostalgic about and contemptuous of waged employment. As C. L. R. James has it, the genre is driven by despair that "there is no certainty of employment" and, at the same time, that what employment there is allows for no upward mobility: "the man on the assembly line, the farmer, they know they are there for life." The genre thus finds waged life both insufficiently available and promising. Not incidentally, gangsters almost invariably want to be entrepreneurs rather than wage workers ("do it first, do it yourself, do it often," as Camonte puts it). Moreover, they don't earn, but take: "what they want, they go for," as James puts it.[10] Tom Powers (*The Public Enemy*) rejects wage labor even when he has it—as he does the gender roles that waged life supports. Gwen tells him, you're not like the "nice" and "kind" men that most women like; "You're strong. You don't give, you take." Only taking, the gangster is a "social problem," as the film's final title puts it. Above all, he is at odds with the working day detailed in the film's opening sequence, which begins with faceless masses flooding city streets on their way to work, before cutting to overhead shots of Chicago's stockyards and then, after a slow dissolve to a blowing whistle, to workers streaming home and to neighborhood bars. Powers knows no such rhythm. And he wants neither family nor wife. "Tom ain't the marrying kind," says his friend Matt, with whom he thieves. When Matt gets engaged, it's as if he's betrayed their shared commitment to theft. "Matt's decided to take something lawful, a wife," declares a mutual friend.

It would be possible in the years to come, if not exactly easy, to hear the genre asking what it means for the gangster to take lawfully *from* a wife. Early hoods rarely had families; they were case studies in misogyny and sexual pathology. Post-*Godfather* gangsters often do have families, but they still reject the working day—and they still take. As Henry Hill puts it in *Goodfellas* (1990), "to us, those goody-good people who worked shitty jobs for bum paychecks and took the subway to work every day and worried about their bills were dead. I mean, they were suckers. They

1.2. *Goodfellas*: Karen visits Henry Hill in prison.

had no balls. If we wanted something, we just took it." Karen Hill adds, "We weren't married to nine-to-five guys." What they did, "none of it seemed like crimes. It was more like Henry was enterprising and that he and the guys were making a few bucks hustling." She adds, our husbands "were blue-collar guys." The gangster's is a working-class refusal of the wage on which his class typically relies. His wife, meanwhile, struggles to maintain the family in isolation. "Nobody is helping me," Karen tells Henry, a crying child on her lap as she visits him in prison, smuggling in goods with which he will enhance his standing. "I am alone" (fig. 1.2). It was appropriate that Lorraine Bracco played both Karen Hill and Jennifer Melfi, for Soprano offered his therapy confessionals, in part, on behalf of a genre that never knew what to do with the gangster's wife. *The Sopranos* broke that pattern, and though hardly feminist in a consistent or even heartfelt way, it would transform the genre's relation to gender by juxtaposing Soprano's multifarious illegal activities beyond the home with his legal expropriation of Carmela's labor within it. One set of abuses, the drama would insist, double the other.

Some form of symbolic doubling had long defined the gangster film. There are only two kinds of people, Paddy Murphy says to Tom Powers: "right and wrong." The wrong kind, the film makes clear, undermine family and its virtues. Thomas Elsaesser adds that Powers is a

CHAPTER 1

1.3. *Public Enemy*: The Powers family.

"contradictory social formation" who holds together otherwise "discrete traits." Secondary characters represent traits condensed in Powers, and produce an array of "binary oppositions, complementary pairs and mirroring doubles" (fig. 1.3).[11] New Hollywood gangster films produce more narratively embellished doublings, while generally sticking with this Manicheanism. Christopher Kocela, for example, identifies a "split" in these films "between a weak, 'good' family and a strong, 'bad' family, each defined through its relationship to the American Dream."[12] But it's useful to add that Scorsese's films don't just pair weak and strong families; they often elaborate whole parallel lives around these pairs. "It was like he had two families," says Karen of Henry in *Goodfellas*. She means he has numerous relatives. But she also learns that Henry has a secret girlfriend, and it's common in post-Scorsese gangster films for mobsters to have not simply intimacy "on the side," but a whole second life kept secret from their wives. In *The Departed* (2006), Billy Costigan's second life is even more elaborate. He goes undercover in the Boston mob, utilizing his capacity for class masquerade. "You were kind of a double kid, I bet, right?" Sean Dignam asks him. "One kid with your old man.

One kid with your mother. Upper middle class in the week, and then dropping your 'r's and hanging out in the Southie projects with daddy the donkey on the weekends." Costigan replies by quoting Hawthorne: "Families in America are always rising and falling, am I right?" As a child, Costigan's familial fortunes rise and fall each week, as he splits his time between maternal civility and paternal illegality. Later, as a cop, he'll be asked to choose in an analogous way between two father figures, one, effeminate and legal (Captain "Queenan"), and the other, a macho crook (Frank Costello, who repeats the genre's core mantra: "Nobody gives it to you, you have to take it").

Soprano splits his time differently, as he moves between his legal domestic family and his illegal work Family. When he and Meadow visit Bowdoin College, they confront a Hawthorne quote: "No man can wear one face to himself and another to the multitude, without finally getting bewildered as to which one may be true" (1.5). "Allegory," Angus Fletcher tells us, derives from the combination of *allos* (other) and *agoreuein* (to "speak openly, speak in the assembly or market"); put another way, allegory is speech kept secret from the market.[13] In black-market melodramas like *The Sopranos*, work lives like Soprano's are a kind of secret allegorical speech, hidden from the state. And while some of the genre's protagonists are bewildered because they do not know which face is truly theirs (*The Americans*), more consistently, they are bewildered by a congruence between home and work—which no longer correspond to "good" and "bad" spheres. *The Sopranos* inherits what Ron Wilson calls the New Hollywood "dualism" between "the blood family and the Mafia family."[14] But the dualism is now more elaborated and even less morally black-and-white than it once was. Soprano's two families echo each other in countless ways. Most revealingly, each pays empty lip service to noneconomic values: family in its commitment to love, and Family in its commitment to loyalty and honor. Those values prove shabby pretexts, as each family suffers at Soprano's ruthlessly instrumentalizing hands.

Throughout, an illegitimate secret world of work doubles a legitimate familial one. For example, Tony does not kill Tony Jr. and Meadow because he does not need to; Christopher and Adriana are their stand-ins, recipients of the contempt and desire that lurks just beneath the surface

CHAPTER 1

of his home life. Thus could David Remnick observe of *The Sopranos*, "The Mafia life is not so much the central subject as it is the intensifying agent. The conventions of the Mob heighten the conventions and contradictions of a modern family."[15] That heightening sometimes makes it seem as if there are not two families but one. "There's barely a boundary between family and Family for Tony," argue Matt Zoller Seitz and Alan Sepinwall.[16] But that is to confuse the literal and the allegorical: Tony's two families, as well as his home and work, do seem to collapse, but less because they are identical than because they share so very much.

Soprano works beyond his home and insists on separate spheres. He leaves each day for strip clubs and butcher shops and navigates a male arena off-limits to his family. That arena is preeminent. "Once you enter this Family, there's no getting out," Soprano tells Christopher Moltisanti during the ceremony in which he is "made." "This Family comes before everything else. Everything. Before your wife, your children, your mother, and your father" (3.3). Of course Soprano also jealously guards the integrity of his household, which he conceives of as a near-timeless realm. He tells Meadow, who debates sexual ethics at the breakfast table, "Out there it's the 1990s, but in this house it's 1954" (1.11). With that, he pastoralizes the home and renders it timeless in the way that, for Jeanne Boydston, nineteenth-century middle-class reformers did, as they theorized American separate spheres.[17] His vision is implicitly racist, insofar as he longs for a day when white girls never dated Black boys (as Meadow does, to his horror). And if 1954 represents the archaic (if at that moment desegregating) pasture to which he would confine "Meadow," he and Carmela can only produce that confinement, and their home's autonomy, with naked force. Their domestic pastoral arrives at the point of a gun. In the pilot, Carmela and her priest discuss the virtues of *The Godfather* and *Goodfellas*. Carmela stops the conversation after hearing a noise. The home's perimeter, it seems, is being breached. The priest stands by, shocked, as Carmela retrieves an AK-47 from a fake column (the Soprano interior is fin-de-siècle baroque). Having stormed outside, Carmela trains the AK on a drunk Meadow, sneaking back into the house. Right at the start, then, *The Sopranos* depicts family life as a separate sphere organized by brute violence.

There are in fact boundaries between Tony's two families. It is because of those boundaries, rather than in spite of them, that one family can allegorize the other. *The Godfather* films prove instructive. Meadow's confinement evokes Kay Adams-Corleone's in *Godfather II*, but with a significant difference. In *Godfather*, Vito Corleone wheezes, "A man who doesn't spend time with his family can never be a real man." By *Godfather II*, Michael lives and works with his family on a gated compound. This doesn't lead to quality family time. Michael holds his wife and children captive and by the film's end, after he murders Fredo, he estranges them completely. He opts to play the feudal lord, not the loving family man. Coppola's *Godfather* films are not that interested in the nuclear family's cherished myths. Rather, the agricultural estates of the Sicilian Mafiosi to which they take us, no less than Michael's gated compound, evoke Max Weber's *oikos*, an extended noble or quasi-noble household organized around agricultural production. That household knew no distinction between production and reproduction, or between work and home; it was not a separate sphere but a site of production organized around what Weber called the family's "want satisfaction."[18]

The size and scale of family in *The Godfather* supports an allegorical system crucially different from the one in *The Sopranos*. For Fredric Jameson, the mafia in Coppola's film allegorizes big business and its antithesis, the archaic, preindustrial family. On the one hand, "the ideological function of the myth of the mafia can be understood as the substitution of crime for big business, [and] as the strategic displacement of all the rage generated by the American system onto this mirror-image of big business."[19] Jameson paraphrases Brecht: the mafia substitutes the crime that is the robbing of a bank for the crime that is the founding of a bank. On the other hand, that displacement—crime for big business—exploits longings for a now foreclosed precapitalist family. *The Godfather*'s "fantasy message" inheres "in the family itself, seen as a figure of collectivity and as the object of a Utopian longing, if not a Utopian envy." The ethnic group projects "an image of social reintegration by way of the patriarchal and authoritarian family of the past."[20] We forgive the mafia because we envy its extended family and kinship structure (Jameson's well-neigh magisterial "we" is a WASP collective romanced by Italian American ethnicity).[21]

The nostalgia Jameson attributes to *The Godfather* is similar to the nostalgia Vincent Pecora attributes to Tennyson, Yeats, Balzac, Forster, and Proust (the subject of a *Sopranos* joke), each of whom romanced a noble "archaic household" lost with the advent of industrial capitalism. Pecora's modernists laid claim to the aristocratic prestige they associated with those households. Disillusioned with separate spheres, they conjured archaic households to claim their ostensible nobility for their own literary inventions; thus did the enchanting modernist text become "the nostalgic negation and overcoming of contradictions structuring the modern household, contradictions that were primarily economic in origin."[22] That claim clarifies Remnick's, that *The Sopranos* reveals "the contradictions of a modern family," and a key difference between *The Sopranos* and the *Godfather* films. No doubt Soprano would jump at the chance to be Michael Corleone, mob nobility by any measure; what penny-ante suburban mobster wouldn't? But Soprano also wants to be a nuclear family man, beloved by his wife and children, who are at the drama's start soon to fly away like so many migrating ducklings. He wants the "good" family to which, according to Kocela, the mobster's "bad" family is typically opposed. That's why he's in therapy, after all. But that good family and the domestic contentment it ostensibly provides is long since off the table. Where *The Godfather* and Pecora's modernists romanticize a preindustrial, archaic family from within the hegemony of the industrial (and its nuclear family), *The Sopranos* romanticizes the vanishing industrial nuclear family from within the event horizon of deindustrialization; that family, to recall the opening voiceover, is the best that is now over. That family itself does not vanish, of course; but the myths that once sustained it become increasingly implausible. Foundational to the industrial family's domestic ideology, we have seen, is the assumption that men support their families by working for money, while women support them with a love and solicitude that keeps crass capitalist instrumentality at bay. *The Sopranos* skewers that ideology unsparingly.

Domestic bliss and the good life are off the table, from Soprano's perspective, because Carmela has violated their marriage contract, whose terms are these: he will labor daily beyond the home and support her, in exchange for which she will cook, clean, and nurture; neither will think of her activities as work; they will agree she performs them out of love, which love will distinguish family life from the ugly world without. Carmela breaks the contract, to his mind, because, like his mother, she cares too much about his money. Why, he bitterly asks, does she forever worry about her financial future or what she can buy with his earnings? He's been sleeping with a Russian woman, Svetlana, who manages a home-care nursing business. She's had to "fight and struggle," he berates Carmela, whereas you only spend. Carmela spits back, "Who the fuck wanted it like this? Who the fuck pissed and moaned at just the idea of me with a real estate license? . . . Who knew that all this time you wanted Tracy and Hepburn?" (4.13). What Tony wants, at bottom, is her dependence. "The only reason you have anything," he berates Carmela, "is because of my fucking sweat" (5.9).

The couple's tacit contract is a farce, needless to say; their marriage is as exploitative as any black-market business (family mirrors Family). Tony steals what they have from those who sweat for a wage, even as he steals Carmela's unwaged labor. He wants her reliant on his stolen money and sweating on the family's behalf. She knows as much. "All I do is make sure he's got clean clothes in his closet and dinner on his table" (3.7), she tells a psychiatrist. But she's willing to acquiesce. She could stomach the tedium, she often tells Tony, were he only more loving. Indeed, if *The Sopranos* is less morally Manichean than its generic precursors, it is so in part because of the time it spends exploring Carmela's complicity in Tony's criminality. She frets that complicity, even as the male authority figures around her send her back into Soprano's lethal embrace. Carmela's priest tells her, "Your husband has good in him. What you have to do is learn to live on what the good part earns" (3.12). This is an unwitting parody of Marx on the working day; it asks her to imagine a moral boundary within Tony, rather than one within his workday between the time he spends producing surplus value for his employer and earning money to reproduce himself and his family. Carmela must live on what the good part earns in the way that married women with no direct access to the wage must live on the earnings of the latter part of their husband's working day. Soprano does not himself work for a wage and cannot divide his day between work and nonwork: he takes from "family" all day. And yet, his round-the-clock taking feels to him like a struggle with an engulfing domesticity. The drama generates most of its pathos—and bathos—from that perverse inversion. "If one family doesn't kill him, the other one will," announced HBO's marketing campaign.

But why, given his daily tyranny, is he so endlessly discontented, so broodingly melancholic, and so subject to fainting spells? Carmela does see the good in him. And she does make sure he's got clean clothes in his closet and dinner on his table. Why doesn't that satisfy our distempered petty lord? Perhaps because he sees, with his instrumental eyes, that what he has from Carmela, he pays for. His is a melodrama, at bottom, because he is consumed by sentimentality about the domestic life he wishes he had had, and might still now have, free of charge. His longing for Gary Cooper and Tracy and Hepburn is a longing for the uncompensated maternal solicitude (and labor) that he believes once attended a man's wage—even if, he finally acknowledges, nothing like this was true for his parents. Certainly he never received that solicitude from his mother. Just after Livia dies, Soprano tears up watching *The Public Enemy*. Elsaesser thinks Powers is driven by his "fear and desire of being smothered and re-absorbed by a resurgence of primal maternal solicitousness"; *The Public Enemy* becomes "hysterical" as it holds at bay that fear and desire, which "excess" makes it a melodrama.[23] But Soprano longs for that primal mother. He feared being smothered—literally. When alive, Livia was cold and remorseless; this Medea tried to kill him. He cries not because his mom was like Ma Power, but because he wishes she had been.

Soprano is in therapy, in part, because he intuits his childhood was other than it might have been. And to quote Lauren Berlant, his tears evidence "a sentimental account of the social world as an affective space where people ought to be legitimated because they have feelings and because there is an intelligence in what they feel that *knows* something about the world."[24] To riff on Berlant, Soprano's tears express a petulant "male complaint"—about the absence of the ostensibly selfless love he should have received from his mother and should continue to receive from Carmela. And for Soprano, "the unfinished business of

THE GANGSTER MOURNING PLAY

> A half belief is s the outcome of
> The criminal's sentimentality r
> In a few cases a criminal is so
>
> reveals itself

1.4. *The Sopranos*: Interpretation's end.

sentimentality" is less "that 'tomorrow is another day' in which fantasies of the good life can be lived," than one in which the material bounty that he already enjoys will be rendered richer still by his wife's nurture. He supports her with his hard work, doesn't he? His complaint, to riff on Berlant, is that, for Livia and Carmela, love should be the gift that keeps on giving, while for him, it should be "the gift that keeps on *taking*."[25] To quote Silvio Dante, for Soprano, "sadness accrues" (1.1), as if interest on lent money. An inveterate loan shark, he collects mercilessly, and yet feels wounded that he must collect at all.

Initially, Melfi thinks his tears testify to an inner life worth saving. But she decides they reveal nothing but sociopathy. In the penultimate episode, we see from her point of view increasingly large close-ups of a psychiatric journal (fig. 1.4). She reads about the criminal personality's excess sentimentality—toward children and pets, above all. For this personality, she reads, therapy is just "another criminal operation." Soprano has been conning her for years, she now accepts; therapy has been good for business. As the camera zooms in, Soprano's character emerges in its irredeemable flatness, with "stiff, puppet-like effect," to anticipate our turn to Benjamin. A version of the spatial arrest that is for Benjamin integral to the mourning play calls psychoanalysis to a halt: Melfi ends her treatment of Soprano just before the drama ends.

The Don's Two Bodies

In his study of *The Sopranos*, Dana Polan claims that "little sense of meaningful tragedy can be wrought from its farcical, trivial, confused characters and the fallen world they inhabit."[26] The literary mode that best describes the drama, he thinks, is the picaresque. But Polan also thinks the serial displays what Edward Said and Theodor Adorno call "late style": "nonprogressing cyclicity, repetition, irony toward affirmative forms of aesthetic expression, and what Said refers to as 'intransigence, difficulty, and unresolved contradiction.'" Late works, Polan notes, depict "an experience that is depressive, claustrophobic, repetitive and uneventfully downbeat to the point of deadness." For Adorno, late style "leaves only fragments behind, and communicates itself, like a cipher, only through the blank spaces from which it has disengaged itself."[27] As it happens, these passages represent in part Adorno's consideration of Benjamin's *Tragic Drama*, which is, among much else, an account of Greek tragedy's transformation into something more baroque.

David Simon insisted *The Wire* was Greek tragedy and noted that the reason "the show may feel different than a lot of television" is that "our model is not quite so Shakespearean as other high-end HBO fare. *The Sopranos* and *Deadwood*—two shows that I do admire—offer a good deal of *Macbeth* or *Richard III* or *Hamlet* in their focus on the angst and machinations of the central characters (Tony Soprano, Al Swearengen). Much of our modern theater seems rooted in the Shakespearean discovery of the modern mind."[28] This section considers *Hamlet*'s significance to *The Sopranos* in Benjamin's terms—for *Hamlet* is, to Benjamin, an exemplary mourning play.

Benjamin thinks the baroque mourning play is distinct from Greek tragedy, which focuses on a "speechless" but morally self-possessed hero as he engages in a struggle between human time and mythic time (the latter anticipates what Benjamin would later call "messianic time"). In mourning plays, by contrast, mythic time is inaccessible.[29] These plays capture the triumph of historical time and a newfound similarity between human and natural history. Having been abandoned by the mythic and the divine, human life has become "merely creaturely," confined as it is to a "primordial landscape" bereft of meaning: hence the mourning play's characteristic melancholy.[30]

Allegory is for Benjamin a forced, stagey effort to endow a fallen world with some transcendent meaning. He lingers over the intensity with which characters examine stage props—as Hamlet does Yorick's skull. Characters do so as if in "mourning," he writes, which "is the state of mind in which feeling revives the empty world in the form of a mask and derives enigmatic satisfaction in contemplating it." The prop becomes "allegorical under the gaze of melancholy"—and in that way dead. The actor who holds the prop "causes life to flow out of it" such that "it is now quite incapable of emanating any meaning or significance of its own; such significance as it has, it acquires from the allegorist."[31] Born from "an appreciation of the transience of things," the mourning play "embraces dead objects in its contemplation, in order to redeem them." And redeem them it does; for Benjamin, allegory in general raises up and renders meaningful an otherwise mundane object. But that process cannot but reveal its contrivance; it finds in a world of dead objects no significance except that which the allegorist has placed there—and thus only "soulless materiality."[32]

Soprano himself is the melodrama's most soulless stage prop, replete with contrived meaning.[33] The Sopranos have been in "the meat business" ever since Tony's father took over Satriale's butcher shop (and because their business is turning the living into meat). And meats, we learn, figure what Tony could not, when young, process about his father's criminality. As a child, he sees his father remove Mr. Satriale's pinkie as partial payment for gambling debts. That evening, he watches Livia become excited by meats brought home from the shop ("probably the only time the old man got laid was meat delivery day" [3.3], Soprano tells Melfi). Years later, encounters with meat trigger his blackouts, which grow more frequent. One might expect these insights to produce character development. But Soprano's "delving," as he puts it, doesn't reveal anything but that, like his mother before him, he is dead flesh animated by greed (which is not the only reason the FBI calls his home "the sausage factory" [3.1]).

For Benjamin, mourning play characters appear in similar manners for specific historical reasons. The petty rulers who people these plays are bereft of meaning (and in need of allegorical redemption) because the post-Reformation world seemed similarly bereft to dramatists. Specifically, mourning plays register the waning of the divine right with which kings were imagined to rule (as well as the doctrine of good works by which their Catholic subjects lived). They thus register a crisis in the doctrine of the "king's two bodies," which attributed to kings a concrete and tangible body, on the one hand, and an ineffable and divine body, on the other. A king's authority derived from his second body, the body of his office, which derived in turn from God. Ernst Kantorowicz would later describe the twofold nature of the "crown as fiction": "there was a visible, material, gold circle or diadem" and "an invisible and immaterial Crown—encompassing all the royal rights and privileges indispensable for the government of the body politic."[34] The earthly crown rendered tangible the otherwise ineffable afflatus, or immutable *Corona non moritur*, that descended from God, just as the king's earthly body did the body of Christ. (A contemporary of Benjamin's, Otto Rank applied related terms when producing his account of the literary doppelgänger, which is a second self that renders otherwise fragile bodies and egos immune from the ravages of time.)[35]

The mourning play registers the aftereffects of the Reformation's rejection of the divine right of kings. Writing during the counterreformation, Benjamin's largely Lutheran dramatists "felt bound in every particular to the ideal of an absolutist constitution." But their plays cast doubt on the Eucharistic corporatism on which that ideal rested, never so much as when they turn to rulers ill-suited to their office. The mourning play's "kings and princes appear with their crowns of gilt paper" to a "stiff, puppet-like effect," which makes "the rulers of the baroque stage" seem like "the kings of playing cards." The nobility no longer seems noble, and royal accoutrements ("Crown, royal purple, scepter") reveal themselves to be only stage props. Kings and princes are themselves stage props, most especially when the royal personage "falls victim to the disproportion between the unlimited hierarchical dignity with which he is divinely invested and the humble state of his humanity." His "actions are not determined by thought but by changing physical impulses" that bespeak a world governed by "the deadness of its concrete tangibility."[36] Thus dead, the prince cannot convincingly embody sovereignty. As a consequence, court "plotters," as Benjamin calls them, fill the mourning play; they conspire and scheme to acquire power, which no longer requires a divine warrant.

These terms are surprisingly relevant to mafia films, particularly those in which plotters, typically mob captains, undermine a given boss's shambolic nobility. *The Godfather* is the touchstone for all such stories, insofar as it recounts Vito's efforts to stem the narcotics trade, which he thinks will destroy the quasi-feudal, noneconomic code by which the mafia conducts itself. After *The Godfather*, mob bosses no longer pretend to that code and have lost all claim to the "God" in the honorific "Godfather." These bosses fall victim to Benjamin's disproportion only when they bother to ape hieratic dignity at all. In Mario Puzo's novel, Michael describes his father's authority: "They call it business. OK, but it's personal as hell. You know where I learned that from? The Don. The Godfather. If a bolt of lightning hit a friend of his, the old man would take it personal. . . . That's what makes him great. The great Don. He takes everything personal. Like God."[37] Vito is like God because his august and vengeful persona brooks no distinction between the personal and impersonal. Soprano takes everything personally, but he's nothing like God and is less like the regal Vito than *Goodfellas*' buffoonish Tony DeVito. Annie Leibovitz's mock re-creation of Leonardo da Vinci's *The Last Supper*, in which Soprano takes the place of Christ, does not contradict so much as accentuate that fact.

Soprano is the melancholy suburban prince on Prozac, as he confronts the disproportion between the ideal and the reality of family. The results are a neo–mourning play that is also high melodrama. Mourning play and melodrama share key features, in fact, even as they speak to potentially different audiences, the one incipiently popular and the other aristocratic. In Peter Brooks's account, melodrama is "a form for a post-sacred era" in which, according to Stephanie Hilger, "the story of the nation is no longer the tale of the king's two bodies, one physical and the other immortal, but the narrative of a young citizen who has only a material body, and whose physical vulnerability represents the state of the nation in synecdochal fashion."[38] Alive to that vulnerability, melodrama committed to a sensationalizing didacticism. It first became a coherent form on the illegitimate stages of Paris, where, facing a ban on spoken dialogue, individual plays communicated story with many of the mourning play's histrionic props and devices, from music, tableaux, and ostentatious placards to dumbshows. Like mourning plays, melodramas were often pointedly schematic. In Christine Gledhill's terms, their "personae, bearing the brunt of emotional trauma, become personalized metaphors for particular states of being and moral identity, at the same time playing roles—villain, victimized heroine, and absent hero—designed to make the wheels of the drama turn."[39] These personae were of course self-consciously allegorical, and while it's right to stress the different affects deployed by each stage form, melodrama and mourning play, both were nostalgic efforts to revive a faded authority. Where mourning plays turned to regional courts, melodramas turned to home and hearth and, as Brooks has it, conjured the family home as a space of lost innocence, the better to make legible an otherwise occulted moral order.

Soprano's self-aggrandizing sentimentality—his "male complaint"—generates family melodrama as it invokes home and hearth back in the day. But *The Sopranos* shades to mourning play more than traditional melodrama, we might say, when it confesses it cannot breathe life into that faded vision. Put another way, the drama makes manifest what is always latent in melodrama: that endowing everyday realities with grandiose emotional stakes cannot but seem contrived and finally unequal to the elusive need that sets melodrama in motion. Again and again, Tony gestures to a collective belonging in which neither he nor the drama really believes. When he declares "the best is over," he's offering what is already an empty cliché. The drama does relish sentimental moments. But it also exposes those moments as incapable of grounding any meaningful moral order. Trapped in Vesuvio's as a storm rages without, Tony toasts his family: "Someday soon, you'll have families of your own, and if you're lucky, you'll remember the little moments, like this, that were good" (1.13). He is sincere, and we can almost believe the drama believes it; but AJ will quote the line back to him, sarcastically, in the drama's final scene, and Tony has by then forgotten he ever said it.

Some of this might seem indistinguishable from a postmodern "waning of affect," just as the drama's reflexivity might seem generally postmodern. But in noting Soprano's inability convincingly to claim traditional melodramatic affects, I'd stress the fit Benjamin identifies between the mourning play's setting and theme and the specific reflexivity thus generated. His baroque drama is reflexive in a particular way because it is located in a postsacred court that is peopled by "plotters" whose tireless schemes the play likens to its own. As Samuel Weber puts it, "The sovereignty of the tyrant is replaced by the *mastery* of the plotter," an author stand-in who "exploits mechanisms of human action as the result of forces over which there can be no ultimate control, but which can therefore be made the subject of probabilistic calculations. The contingency of such calculations turns the 'intrigue' into something closer to a game or to the exhibition of a certain virtuosity." Weber adds, "The plot is replaced by plotting, in a staging that demonstrates its own artifices."[40] If the mourning play casts itself as a *spiel* akin to plots devised by court schemers (a game of thrones, let's say, given *The Sopranos*' influence on HBO's next monster hit), the courts in question evoke the court theaters in which mourning plays transpired: the two are linked sites of contrivance in which "nothing can ever authentically take place."[41] That affinity is famously revealed in the play within the play, typically performed at court by a traveling troupe.

With this we turn to *The Sopranos*' invocations of Shakespeare and *Hamlet*. An undead Shakespeare appears just offstage in *The Sopranos*, in what amounts to a play within a play. During the finale, Tony halfheartedly watches *The Twilight Zone* in the living room of a vacation home that he's converted into a safe house. This is an uncanny space in which henchmen sprawled languorously on chairs and sofas double the family Tony hoped might use the property. "The television industry today is looking for talent," we hear. "They're looking for quality. They're preoccupied with talent and quality, and a writer is a major commodity."

CHAPTER 1

The lines come from the last hour-long *Twilight Zone* episode, "The Bard," which depicts a hack writer pressuring his agent to place him on a show about black magic (the exasperated agent responds by emphasizing the importance of talent and quality). The writer raises Shakespeare from the dead and the Bard writes a script that lands the hack his show. But Shakespeare gets no credit, and appalled by how sponsors mangle his prose, he returns to the grave. Better to fester than to work in TV. Shakespeare is revived once by the struggling hack and a second time by David Chase, who conjures the playwright as a ghost to whom he confesses the nature of his ambition—and the limits of his talent. If from the perspective of the drama's countless appreciators Chase was responsible for the industry's newfound demand for quality as a branded property—for showing, in effect, just how major a commodity a TV writer this good might become—from his own famously abject perspective he was a sinful poser violating the origins he pretended to esteem. To be sure, *The Sopranos* is not Shakespearean in any consistent way. Indeed, for the bard we might just as easily substitute Coppola or Scorsese, or even "cinema." Chase thought his drama inherently benighted if only because it was TV and at too great a distance from any number of more noble wellsprings.

Originally, *The Sopranos* was to focus on a TV producer like Chase.[42] In this conception, on- and off-screen plotters would have been transparently aligned. "If there's anybody that people would have less sympathy for than a mobster," Chase said, "it would be a TV producer."[43] That's presumably because producers exploit talent as mafiosi do. "You're supposed to be earners," he tells his capos. "That's why you've got the top-tiered positions" (4.1). The analogy between top-tiered mobsters and writers is close to explicit in the first season when Moltisanti, frustrated he's not yet a capo, sets out to write a screenplay, "Made Men." (Chase's captain Matthew Weiner, who worked as a staff writer on *The Sopranos*, made good on Moltisanti's ambition while riffing on his title and extending his conceit: Weiner insisted *Mad Men*—about Don Draper rather than "the Don of New Jersey" [1.1]—allegorizes the TV industry.) Typically, Moltisanti is the site of the drama's most overt reflexivity:

"Where's *my* arc?" (1.8), he complains, when not being given his due in the newspapers for a caper. Tom Stoppard would be proud.

Moltisanti never writes "Made Men," but he does produce a film whose premier functions like the dumb show and "The Murder of Gonzago" in *Hamlet*. In the first season, Soprano is Hamlet at war with his mother and uncle, who conspire against him (*Sons of Anarchy* adopts the same conceit). But Soprano does not play Hamlet for long. After his uncle no longer poses a threat, Tony becomes Claudius. (It matters that his kingdom is peripheral: he does not live in Rome, Chase noted, but "the provinces," which is where the German princes in most mourning plays live, exiled from the centers of true power.[44] The mourning play is a self-consciously minor, peripheral genre that speaks in turn to Chase's sense that *he* was, when creating *The Sopranos*, exiled to the lowbrow backwaters of TV, in which he'd never approximate the Coppola and Scorsese gangster films he so revered; not for nothing does Tony live in New Jersey.) And by season 6, having ordered the death of Adriana, Soprano faces a threat from his nephew, the brooding Christopher. He perceives that threat only after the premier of *Cleaver*, Christopher's "*Saw* meets *Godfather II*" film within a TV serial. Soprano initially resists acknowledging the significance of the film, in which a young mobster kills his one-time boss. "It's a movie," he tells an alarmed Carmela. "It's fiction." It's a "revenge fantasy!" (6.14), she corrects him, in which he plays Claudius to Moltisanti's Hamlet.

The *Cleaver* premier takes place in a large theater that looks suspiciously like a giant TV room, filled to capacity with a very extended Family. Indeed, it might have premiered in Soprano's TV room, since the implicit joke throughout is that *Cleaver* is trashy in just the way *The Sopranos* is. For Weber, the TV room is a contemporary equivalent of Benjamin's theatrical court, in which "nothing can ever authentically take place": "the reality of television" is that "far and near are no longer mutually exclusive, but rather converge and overlap" in a way that "strongly resembles" what the *Tragic Drama* "described as the 'court' that emanates from all allegory." Allegory "brings with it a court," Benjamin writes; "the profusion of emblems is grouped around a figural center, which is never absent from genuine allegories"; a simultaneous "Dispersion" and "Collection . . . name the law of this court." Tracing "television's" etymology to "seeing at a distance," Weber adds that "like the allegorical court, television brings the most remote things together only to disperse them again . . . in the private space of the home."[45] *The Sopranos* marks the resulting inauthenticity with branded props: Tony watches Warner Bros.' *The Public Enemy* on TV; Moltisanti watches Warner Bros.' *Key Largo*; confined to home and slipping into dementia, Uncle Jr. watches HBO's *Curb Your Enthusiasm* and mistakes Larry for himself. These gestures recall Benjamin's claim that where "the Renaissance explores the universe, the baroque explores libraries"—in this case Time Warner's media libraries.[46]

Mourning plays were lost in a hall of mirrors, trapped in their own fictiveness, Benjamin argued. Carl Schmitt's *Hamlet or Hecuba* rejects that claim and Benjamin's argument that *Hamlet* specifically is unable to refer to anything authentic beyond itself. *Hamlet* is tragedy, Schmitt argues, and not simply *play*, because it contains "an ineluctable reality that no human mind has conceived—a reality externally given, imposed and unavoidable." In part, that reality is James I: Hamlet is a stand-in for the Scottish king as he contemplated the dilemmas he would face when ruling England. "The play within the play" in *Hamlet*, "is something other than a look behind the scenes." Rather, it is an echo of "the real play itself repeated *before* the curtains," present to the audience in urgent fashion.[47] Something similar might be said about *The Sopranos*. *The Godfather* allegorized John F. Kennedy, a figure of fascination for many gangster films.[48] And though *The Sopranos* was not a concerted political allegory in the way that *The West Wing* was, Soprano does evoke Bill Clinton, to whom the drama often refers (Hillary Clinton understood; she reshot the final scene as a campaign commercial).[49] But we might ask, in the spirit of Benjamin's analysis, what measure of authenticity does *not* appear on this TV stage? Put another way, what do we fail to see in Soprano's creaturely body, as it gropes for political significance? Perhaps, an absence of the quality that Schmitt discerns in Hamlet's body.

Schmitt's second reason that *Hamlet* is not a mourning play is that the audience sees in Hamlet's body not just James, but England's invention of capitalism. He acknowledges that James knew nothing of "the transition to a maritime existence that England [would] achieve." But a more modern audience discerns in the monarch's implied presence an "extraordinary quality, a kind of surplus value" that points not simply to "the great appropriation of the sea . . . [and the] new global order" that England would oversee, but to "the Industrial Revolution," which "caused a much deeper and more fundamental revolution than those on the European continent."[50] By this admittedly twisted logic, if *The Sopranos* is a mourning play, it is so in part because, unlike *Hamlet*, it cannot capture that extraordinary quality, that surplus value, except as a mystical quality lost in a now irrecoverable industrial past.

The Sausage Factory Floods

When Hyman Roth brags, "We're bigger than U.S. Steel," he celebrates his syndicate less as a version of than as an alternative to heavy industry. It matters, in obvious ways, that the alternative is illegal, but certainly the mafia also allegorizes legitimate business, as Jameson says. The problem is that "big business," his term, is far too broad. It's worth recalling Jameson's invocation of Brecht, which likens the mafia to banks, specifically. Roth's claim, that the mafia is bigger than U.S. Steel, might thus be read as allegorical of the financial sector's ascendant dominance over manufacturing. *The Sopranos* teases a version of that dominance. During a flashback, Soprano's dad sleeps with a newspaper on his chest. The headline reads: "Pistons Misfire, but Will Bullets?" The newspaper is dated 1970, the start of deindustrialization (which I analyze in chapter 3). If ostensibly about basketball, the title also asks whether the mafia might somehow fill the void left by manufacturing's retreat, as a surrogate for finance.

The mafia had been active in the US since the 1870s but began to receive national attention after 1919, with the onset of Prohibition. The first great wave of Italian immigration to the US began in the 1920s, soon after Mussolini rose to power, and coincided with Prohibition, which provided lucrative profits to syndicates that could manufacture and supply alcohol in cities like Chicago, New York, and New Orleans.

After 1933, with Prohibition repealed, the mafia continued to work a host of illegal activities, from gambling and extortion to narcotics and loan sharking, in which the press was particularly interested. Figures like Lucky Luciano had been drawn into lending at the start of the Depression, when the unemployed especially found it hard to secure money via banks. Syndicates became shadow banks catering to those unable to land official loans. Gangsters named the business "the Shylock racket" and newspapers commonly equated gangsters and bankers.[51]

As important as loan sharking was to the mob, it was not its primary source of income. The mafia had from the start fed on legitimate manufacturing and organized labor. C. Alexander Hortis reports that, between the 1890s and 1950s, when New York "built things" and "Lower Manhattan was the center of skilled manufacturing in the Atlantic world," the New York crime families enriched themselves by "skimming profits" from informal subcontracting and piecework in the garment and food industries especially. The mafia began to exploit unions in the 1940s and tended to prey on craft unions affiliated with the AFL rather than industrial ones affiliated with the CIO.[52] And they are famously associated with the Teamsters, the trucking union whose pension fund served as a mob bank—financing the growth of Las Vegas, for example. But as industrial profits began to dry up, the five families found their profits elsewhere, as did capital generally. According to Robert Fitch, deindustrialization hit New York earlier than it did the rest of the country; between 1899 and 1956, the city housed 15 percent of all US manufacturing jobs; but during the next two decades, as New York lost 250,000 manufacturing jobs, it began to transform itself into a capital of global finance.[53] By the 1990s, New York crime families had followed the city's lead, and in 1996, when Chase began to write, *Business Week* ran a series of articles about the mob's push into Wall Street and how its "boiler rooms," "chop houses," and "bucket shops" were perpetrating fraud on a staggering scale. As the magazine later put it, "Although organized crime had participated in a smattering of stock scams years before, never had 'wise guys' actually established and run brokerage firms. In the 1990s, firmly encamped in lower Manhattan, the six New York area crime families took a hefty chunk of the $10 billion-a-year trade in grossly overpriced microcap stocks. By the end of the millennium, Wall Street had become a leading mafia cash cow."[54]

This is *The Sopranos*' mafia. "I wanted to tell the story about the reality of being a mobster," said Chase. "They sit around eating baked ziti and betting and figuring out who owes who money. Occasionally, violence breaks out—more often than it does in the banking world, perhaps."[55] Or in the investment banking world. Tony describes himself as a "labor leader." But his dealings are a compendium of activities that point with different degrees of explicitness to 1990s-era finance: high-stakes gambling, stripping and flipping houses, setting interest rates, and loaning money. The serial also takes up stock fraud, in Moltisanti's pump-and-dump of Webistics equities. The first episode of season 2 begins with an unnamed Asian American pretending to be Moltisanti during an exam that credentials Moltisanti as a broker. In a subsequent episode, two of Moltisanti's goons beat a broker who fails to push Webistics. "The script is not far-fetched," said Securities and Exchange Commission enforcement director Richard Walker of the plotline.[56]

The Feds unsuccessfully investigate Soprano's relation to the stock scheme. Season 3 begins with FBI agents assessing that failure. They sit in what looks like a TV writers' room: ten agents listen to a recording of Soprano, as the camera moves from close-ups of various mob "actors"—pinned on what looks like a story board—to diagrams detailing the relations between them, to the agents following a transcript that looks an awful lot like a TV script. The conversation doesn't give them the incriminating information they need, however, so they decide to focus on Soprano's garbage business, which means bugging Soprano's home. The Feds now spring into action as a production crew, staking out the home. Once inside, they broadcast a live feed for agents who follow remotely. The FBI are here writers and audience: they produce and watch family TV—making jokes about *Mr. Rogers' Neighborhood* as they go. This first foray is preparatory: they're surveying the basement to determine where best to place a recording device on a subsequent visit, which is delayed unexpectedly. On the first visit, when the camera passes by a 120-gallon water heater, an agent watching remotely says, "Look at the brown water, right there, freeze it. . . . That baby's gonna blow." And it does, just as the

CHAPTER 1

1.5. *The Sopranos*: Representing "what went down."

agents prepare to install the bug. (Season 3 turns on another burst pipe: in the next episode, Livia Soprano suffers a fatal stroke.)

About to enter the house for a second time, the agents see Carmela and Tony rush home. Trying to ascertain the cause of their return and not yet aware that water has flooded the basement, one agent tells another, "It must be a crisis with one of the children." But it is not that kind of crisis. As the FBI agents prepare to install the bug, but before they enter the house, we're offered an aerial shot of downtown Manhattan (fig. 1.5). There is nothing that directly explains the shot, but there are clues. Just *before* his water heater bursts, Soprano asks a henchman to check one of his stocks. It's doing great, he's told; better than yesterday. Just *after* the water heater bursts, two FBI agents read a newspaper. "Red-hot telecoms take beating," announces the headline. "Deutsche Telekom, Nokia and WorldCom lead the latest decline." More clues: struggling to learn "what went down" in the basement, as one agent puts it, the FBI knock on a neighbor's door and ask if she was affected by yesterday's "shortfall," hoping to prompt a reaction. What has gone down, presumably, is the stock market. When Soprano offers the drama's opening lament, during the serial premier on January 10, 1999, the dot-com bubble was already inflated. It would by then have been too late "to get in at the ground floor," as he puts it. At the start of season 3, the dot-com bubble bursts, in tandem with Tony's water heater, which allegorizes overheated equities, cashed out as liquidity. We cut not just to downtown, then, but to Wall Street, where the dot-com bubble had burst nine to ten months before the episode aired—exactly when Chase and his writers were writing it.[57]

This financial allegory is part and parcel of the labor allegory adumbrated above, in which men confront the erosion of their family breadwinner status and, by implication, deindustrialization. Moving between the stakeout and the Soprano family, the episode also takes us to a picnicking Lilliana and Stasiu Wosilius. Lilliana is the Sopranos' maid, and her husband, an unemployed engineer. He is bitter that he relies on her wage, that his talents are wasted, and, specifically, that his naturalization instructor failed him on a quiz for misidentifying the meaning of the phrase "Stop Men at Work." Rather than read it as a call for attention in a construction zone, he read it as an imperative to produce unemployment: "How do we know it doesn't mean 'stop all men who are working'?" That imperative might be said to have been implicit in the dot-com bubble and the New Economy, invested as both were in tech and automation.[58] But if that feels too broad a register, we might see in the sequence now before us a more specific rebuke of Time Warner's efforts to merge with an internet provider, which merger was an emblematic expression of fin-de-siècle financialization.

The media industry was a prime beneficiary of finance capital in the '80s and '90s; it consolidated on the backs of borrowed money while chasing New Economy dreams. Announced ten days into the new millennium, the AOL–Time Warner merger culminated that trend. AOL purchased Time Warner in a massively leveraged deal worth $165 billion, still the largest merger in US history. It was by all accounts an epochal affair. *USA Today* called it "one of those rare events that seems to change the world overnight." Tom Brokaw announced "a whole new universe created overnight."[59] *Business Week* thought it heralded "a new world order" because "the digital will prevail over the analog, new media will grow faster than old, and the leaders of the Net economy will become the 21st-century Establishment."[60] Time Warner CEO Jerry Levin echoed *Business Week* when he offered what had become a typical account of the transformation at hand: "We were emerging from not just old media but from an analog world into a digital world," he said, "and philosophically people were beginning to understand that the digital world was a transformational universe."[61]

In 2000, AOL was a young internet service provider with a giant user base. It packaged email software and basic content with dial-up broadband; during the 1990s, it had built its customer base by mailing out millions of CDs to prospective clients. Time Warner was what would soon be called an "old media" company: among other holdings, it had film and TV studios, book and magazine imprints, and cable networks like HBO, CNN, and TNT. The logic behind the merger was this: heavily reliant on the low bandwidth twisted copper wires that make up telephone lines, AOL needed a network of coaxial cables the better to deliver internet access to customers. And threatened by the likelihood of readily available free access offered by its competitors, and therefore by the prospect that its wildly inflated share price would come crashing to earth, it needed to buy a corporation with established revenues—ideally one with a library of content deep enough to allow it to continue to justify its access fees. The largest media conglomerate on earth, Time Warner had steady revenues and the nation's second largest network of cable lines, as well as extensive holdings in TV, film, music, and print. It had been chasing hazy dreams of interactive TV for years but had failed to establish any significant presence on the internet; its executives, Levin above all, felt they needed to make a bold move in digital. As AOL's Steve Case put it, "The basic bet is that convergence is going to happen, and it's not just about the TV. It's about knitting together the PC, the TV, the telephone, and the stereo to allow people to be entertained in better ways, to be educated in better ways, to communicate in better ways, to change people's lives."[62]

The basic bet was also that the convergence of diverse business units under the aegis of one conglomerate would create something greater than the sum of its parts. The assumption partook of a certain mysticism, a version of which we encountered above. Defining the doctrine of the king's two bodies, Kantorowicz gives credit "to the Romans for having invented the idea of corporations" before noting that the doctrine descended from Roman corporate law. As he saw it, a legal fiction of corporate personhood had gradually displaced the legal fiction of the king's second body, sponsoring a secular and healthily democratic equivalent of kingly afflatus.[63] In this spirit, we might understand "synergy"—the goal of the giant merger—as corporate afflatus, a magical something that made a given corporate person more than the sum of its parts.

As *Fortune* put it when discussing the merger, *synergy* "is one of those marketing words that's bandied about to make mergers sound good. In truth, nobody knows what it means." Alec Klein adds, "'Synergy' was the raison d'être of the merger," even if few knew how to bring it about.[64] The mundane hope was that scale might eliminate redundancies. Different units might share advertising costs and engage in cross-promotion. Wanting to secure an ad deal with Victoria's Secret after the merger, AOL asked HBO if it would air a Victoria Secret's fashion show (HBO was incensed); AOL also asked if Mel Gibson could record the voiceover that greeted AOL subscribers when they logged on (Time Warner execs struggled to convince AOL execs that actors weren't regular employees of their company). As it happened, the behemoth's many fiefdoms would remain stubbornly siloed, opting to pursue their own ends rather than a single company strategy. But even if those units had been cooperative, the hoped-for synergy could not fully have materialized, for it named something more miraculously additive, an elusive quality that made a corporate person come alive. "In reality," argues James Phills, when discussing the merger, "synergy is as elusive as the Easter Bunny—it sounds real but is no more than a fairy tale."[65]

Media and tech companies sponsored an even more grandiose version of this fairy tale, one in which "communication" became not simply a primary product, but the template for all postindustrial production. In this fantastical vision, communication was a magic trick that conjured value from nothing, an endless stream of rabbits pulled from the mouth of a hat. *Wired* evangelists like Kevin Kelly thought the web would reshape "the geography of wealth" on behalf of a "new economic order." Kelly wrote his *New Rules for the New Economy* in 1999, during the run-up to the merger, and it's easy to see how Time Warner execs glimpsed, in jeremiads like his, a tantalizing prospect. For Kelly, "communication—which in the end is what digital technology and media are all about—is not just a sector of the economy. Communication *is* the economy."⁶⁶ Legerdemain like this stressed capital's liberation from the traditional factory and its relocation to new kinds of virtual factories lurking in media networks. Talking was producing and producing was talking. The internet would bring this marvelous world about. Alvin Toffler had coined the term "prosumer" in 1980, and within eight years, terms like "pro-ams" (Paul Miller), "commons-based peer production" (Yochai Benkler), "crowd sourcing" (Mark Robinson), and "produsage" (Alex Burns) would enter popular usage, each an effort to describe the participatory affordances of "Web 2.0," which would collapse the difference between passive consumption and active production. Citizen journalism, blogging, posting, video sharing, fan fiction: the beauty of it all was that even as this churn made media companies money, "consumers" would think they acted out of love, that they were sharing enthusiasms rather than working. (These breathless anticipations sounded a familiar note: taking place mainly at home, produsage was an unwaged activity engaged in for love rather than money.) In 2000, media companies were still trying to figure out how to monetize produsage. Neither the technology nor the vision was fully in place. A version of the convergence that drove the AOL–Time Warner merger would happen later on streaming services like Netflix. And social media platforms would later find a way to leverage produsage, if mainly by refining advertising's dark arts. But these developments were far more modest than those anticipated by the merger and were, in any event, still some years away. In fact, in the months and years following 2000, the big merger became an object lesson in the limits of synergy, produsage, and the New Economy generally. This was the case, in immediately concrete terms, because of how AOL had tweaked its books. The "productivity miracle" that the US seemed to experience on the back of the internet during the '90s was in many ways the product of accounting gimmicks. In 1995, the year Netscape's IPO kicked off a frenzy for tech stocks, and the year the Reverse Plaza Accords reinflated the dollar and, according to Robert Brenner, ended a brief reinvigoration of manufacturing, Allan Greenspan claimed that "in an economy in which the value added is increasingly software, telecommunications, and various means of conveying value to people without the transference of a physical good," businesses should consider money spent on "intellectual services" as capital investments rather than expenses.[67] Advice like this was at the core of Enron's accounting fraud—and AOL's, which ran afoul of the SEC in 1996 by amortizing advertising costs many years into the future, in the way that manufacturing firms were allowed to amortize the costs of factory equipment. That turned out to be only the visible tip of AOL's accounting fraud, which it concealed up to the moment the papers were signed on its purchase of Time Warner.[68] And moments after the papers were signed, in February 2000, the dot-com bubble began spectacularly to burst, bringing the new company down with it. Hobbled by debt, AOL Time Warner would write off a $100 billion loss two years later; AOL's stock eventually fell to less than 10 percent of its peak price, which fall is written into *The Sopranos*.

Even the drama's 1999 pilot anticipates the merger. Just before he kills a competitor threatening the family business, Christopher mistakes his rival's name, Emile, for "Email." He kills Email and then gleefully butchers his body, framed portraits of Hollywood gangsters looking down at him from the wall (he'll later dig up Email's grave, and, playing Hamlet, contemplate the moldering corpse). Also in the pilot, Meadow declines to leave the house with her mother, preferring to surf the web. "You've got mail!" bleats her computer, as Carmela frowns. These are anticipations of the star-crossed merger, versions of which had been kicked around Time Warner for the better part of the decade (the actual deal was announced less than one year later). The second season aired six days after the companies announced their merger. Writing the third season's first episode, Chase watched the merger announced and, quickly thereafter, its dazzling collapse. The bursting of Soprano's pipes winks at that collapse. "What went down," on this account, was not just the stock market generally, but AOL Time Warner's stock specifically. In the third season, the merger now an achieved reality, AOL makes a telling appearance. On first entering the Sopranos' home in the scene discussed above, a federal agent rifles through their mail. He picks up and briefly contemplates one of the countless CDs with which AOL wooed subscribers.[69] It will be as if that CD and the company behind it explain the disastrous effervescence of liquidity that later thwarts the operation.

It had been an article of faith within HBO that the merger was misconceived. HBO CEO Jeffrey Bewkes was vehemently against it. At a meeting discussing the merger's synergies, he is reported to have shouted, "This is bullshit!"[70] He was right. The merged companies were worth far less than the sum of their parts. As if to acknowledge his wisdom, after the merger decisively failed, he was made CEO of the bankrupt AOL Time Warner. He quickly began breaking up the debt-crippled behemoth. But if Bewkes was on record against the merger, the record had been diverse. He had green-lit *The Sopranos*, which was from the start a dissenting argument, one that cannily likened Soprano's efforts to stay independent from New York not simply to Chase's efforts to stay independent from HBO, but HBO's efforts to stay independent from Time Warner, and, as a consequence, independent from the internet users the company seemed too keen to woo. Exhibit A was Soprano's nominal employment in "waste management": the internet might be a superhighway, but if it promised new ways to monetize the consumer's attention, from HBO's mandarin perspective, Time Warner's merger with AOL risked confusing the "quality" the network was bringing into homes with the digital garbage the merged company would bring out of them. HBO was a premium network committed to literary, authored fare, over and against the internet's fan-driven drivel. AOL Time Warner would, in pursuing synergy, end up in waste management and, along the way, undermine HBO's claim to distinction.

As Bewkes saw it, Time Warner didn't need AOL, because it was already using its coaxial cables—to deliver HBO. *The Sopranos* suggests as much: surfacing from the Lincoln Tunnel, Soprano emerges in the title sequence as if from underground cables that ferry the drama from Manhattan, where HBO is headquartered, to an affluent suburban home, where it is consumed. And yet the drama and title sequence are haunted by the prospect that consumers do more than simply consume—that they also participate in the creation of meaning. That might sound familiar; in Benjamin's terms, the drama is haunted, as allegory always is, by the possibility that readers and viewers (and English professors) don't discover meaning so much as make it—there being nothing actually there. That problem is also inherent in psychoanalysis, if in a different way, and it is worth noting that Melfi's circular, lens-like office suggests an affinity between collaborative dream-work and TV watching (if not exactly as "psychoanalysis in reverse," as Adorno put it). After Soprano first steps in, Melfi tells him it does not matter where he sits, because they together drive their conversation. Maybe he's not such a Philistine after all, when questioning the validity of this shared journey. The title sequence anticipates that skepticism and transforms collaborative interpretation into something more ominously uncanny. As he drives home from New York, the camera sits next to Soprano; the point of view is ours; it belongs to the audience. He drives with a determined look on his face; surely we are only passengers. But after he stops in front of his home, the camera jumps quickly outside the SUV, before he has so much as cracked his door, as if to suggest a more empowered if occult agency. Who knows what awaits him in that house?

CHAPTER 2

The Informal Abject

Housework and Reproduction in Weeds *and* Orange Is the New Black

Showtime's *Weeds* recounts the adventures of Nancy Botwin, a widow who deals pot to maintain her family's affluent suburban lifestyle. The first seasons are set in Agrestic, a planned community filled with sanctimonious soccer moms and man-child stoners. A bullying Christianity rules the roost. But the satire felt "revolutionary," as Diane Shipley had it, because it skewers the vision of motherhood that is Agrestic's true religion.[1] For Ginia Bellafante, *Weeds* "thrives as radical comedy because it challenges one of our most preciously held assumptions: that parenthood is ennobling, rewarding work; that it grounds us and makes us marginally better people. Even *The Sopranos* didn't dare to do that." Bellafante thought that while *Weeds* was "a quiet indictment of haplessness and poor discipline, both personal and parental," it nevertheless challenged "our cultural images of maternal perfection," and relished "notions of maternal animosity."[2] Allesandra Stanley called *Weeds* "a *Desperate Housewives* for smart people."[3] ABC's drama about Wisteria Lane premiered one year before *Weeds* and each turned on a suburban mother jealously guarding a secret. Suzanne Walters and Laura Harrison thought each an indictment of the "new momism" described that year by Susan Douglas and Meredith Michaels in *The Mommy Myth*. The new momism holds mothers "to impossible standards"; it asks them to be self-sacrificing at home and ruthless at work; "hip, relaxed, spontaneous and . . . sexy" with husbands and "as vigilant as Michael Corleone's bodyguards" with kids. Above all, it dictates not "subservience to men" but "subservience to children."⁴ Yet *Weeds* abjures the "ironic detachment" with which *Housewives* assesses "female travails from a cold distance," as Suzanne Leonard has it.⁵ And while both are serialized comedies, *Housewives* evokes afternoon soap opera, while *Weeds* evokes *The Sopranos*.

It's tempting if not exactly right to say that being a black-market outlaw gives Botwin the freedom to reject the gender norms that render ABC's housewives so desperate. Walters and Harrison think her "unapologetically non-normative" in her "radical departure" from the new momism.⁶ But Botwin is hardly unapologetic; she routinely calls herself "the worst mom ever" and at one point confesses, "I love my kids more than anything. But sometimes, I think what it would have been like if they had died when [my husband] died. What it would be like to not have to worry. What it would be like to be only responsible for me. And free. How nice that might feel. How horrible is that? I'm an awful, horrible person" (2.7). Eventually, critics agreed, not knowing what to make of Botwin's odd mix of self-recrimination and racketeering. Bellafante lost patience and called her "a 40-year-old girl shunning responsibility and never wrinkling," an image of "parental fecklessness and narcissism."⁷ Emily Nussbaum called her "a shoe-craving manipulative MILF."⁸ Rarely was Botwin accorded the complexity of "antiheroes" like Soprano and Walter White, neither of whom, it's worth noting, worried all that much about being "an awful, horrible person."

Botwin is self-abasing in ways those difficult men aren't, which begins to suggest the recalcitrance of the gender norms she seems to indict. In many ways, she is a study in abjection, which Julia Kristeva describes as the queasy, unmooring experience of a confusion between self and other. The abject, Kristeva writes, is a "sudden emergence of uncanniness" that threatens one's perceived boundaries. It is what "disturbs identity, system, order. What does not respect borders, positions, rules. The in-between, the ambiguous, the composite." Kristeva locates the origins of the social abject in primitive efforts to distinguish humans from animals; individuals are abject, typically, because of their inability as children to produce stable boundaries between themselves and "the mother as other."[9] These terms recall *The Sopranos*—whose title sequence chronicles Tony's weekly birth—and are particularly relevant to *Weeds*, if from mom's point of view: Botwin is most abject with her children, to whom she feels both excessively and insufficiently attached; she's frequently paralyzed, for example, by the need both to flee and to draw them more closely in. Recent work on comedy influenced by Kristeva will shed light on why it makes sense to consider *Weeds* a comedy at all—and even why comedies and dramedies headlined by women have had more Emmy success than similarly headlined quality dramas. But ultimately, this chapter uses abjection to describe material rather than psychoanalytic relations. Abjection has emerged as a significant term in Marxist feminist accounts of sex work and reproductive labor generally, often referring to those denied access to the wage.[10] Relatedly, this chapter reads Botwin's abjection in light of the "boundary struggles" that for Nancy Fraser mark a contemporary "crisis of care." Brought on by shrinking social surpluses and the defunding of the welfare state; flat wages and rising costs of living; and above all, the erosion of the Fordist family wage and the concomitant emergence of the dual-income family, Fraser's crisis manifests as capitalism's inability to guarantee "a key set of social capacities: those available for birthing and raising children, caring for friends and family members, maintaining households and broader communities, and sustaining connections more generally." As those capacities become strained, borders between once seemingly distinct realms break down and "actors struggle over the boundaries delimiting economy from society, production from reproduction, and work from family."[11] The erosion of boundaries between work and family, above all, accounts for Botwin's abjection.

Black-market melodramas like *The Sopranos* and *Breaking Bad* capture the "peculiar relation of separation-cum-dependence-cum-disavowal" that for Fraser characterizes boundary struggles.[12] Soprano and a host of similarly toxic male leads wage an equivocal, back-and-forth struggle over the line between work and family, alternately fleeing and returning to their families, hoping and failing to discover a truly separate sphere of work to which they can daily remove themselves. *The Sopranos*, for instance, generates considerable abjection along the

CHAPTER 2

way; Dana Polan notes its fascination with "bodies that turn ill, that decompose, that lack control and grotesquely expel the substances of the interior (blood and brains, vomit, urine, and feces) into the world, that buckle under pressure, that give into bloated excess, and so on."[13] Something similar might be said of *Weeds*. Nancy vomits repeatedly, as does hard-drinking neighbor Celia Hodes, who slurs, martini in hand, "I don't vomit from drinking; I vomit when I think about my life" (3.11). In a season 4 sequence, Celia sneezes blood on those near her. In season 2, a dog eats two of Andy Botwin's toes. In the third season, a sabotaged sewer line spews feces over an assembled crowd (3.9). *Weeds* also generates a less grotesque if more telling abjection, one that explains the pathos over reproductive labor that animates the comedy's male-centric cousins.

On *The Sopranos* and *Breaking Bad*, work and home can allegorize each other because they are nominally distinct. Soprano and White have jobs that take them daily from their families. They don't need their children dead to feel free of them; they leave them daily. They do so, it hardly needs saying, because they are not their children's primary caregivers. But Botwin's pot business and family are not even nominally distinct; her family staffs her business and she cannot distinguish one from the other. Soprano and White cannot escape broadly familial dynamics. Botwin cannot escape her actual family; her work life *is* her home life, as it is for countless women who don't in fact sell weed. Marxist feminists associated with Wages for Housework, we will see, thought it impossible for homemakers to distinguish work from family. In her study on the automation of household labor, Ruth Schwartz Cowan argued, similarly, that "the houseworker" cannot know "where the activity begins and where it ends, what is essential and what is unessential, what is necessary and what is compulsive."[14] Botwin's business allegorizes that miasma, and round-the-clock parenting in particular. But not only parenting and literal housework: as the comedy progresses, Botwin's business assumes new meanings in relation to new boundary struggles. Turning to the US-Mexico border in season 4, for example, and to the drugs and sex workers that traverse it, *Weeds* places "domestic" labor—understood in alternately familial and national terms—in unsettling proximity to the oversees labor from which it is anxiously distinguished. Botwin's abjection now captures an unmooring intimacy between housework in developed nations and informal labor in underdeveloped ones, which intimacy this chapter explains with Maria Mies's groundbreaking account of "housewifization."

The final sections of this chapter turn to *Orange Is the New Black*, also created by Jenji Kohan. One of Netflix's first hits, the women's prison melodrama allows me to refine categories derived from Marxist feminists in the previous sections. *Orange* uses unfree prison labor to allegorize housework, I argue, and to comment on gendered reproductive labor generally—in often startlingly trenchant ways. That commentary becomes especially sharp in season 3, after a for-profit corporation assumes control of Litchfield Prison, previously a state-run facility, and begins paying select inmates a wage. That wage, moreover, transforms the drama's handling of black markets and informal labor. And it is only after Litchfield's privatization, I argue, that *Orange* begins to understand itself as a black-market melodrama proper.

This Is Not Your Mommy Talking

Traditional housework has been one of TV comedy's enduring subjects. "The idea that female spectators were also workers in the home," reports Lynn Spigel, "was, by the postwar period, a truism for broadcasting and advertising executives." Ads conjured a housewife who could do housework "in a state of 'utopian forgetfulness' as she moved freely between her work and the act of watching television" (or not moving at all, in the case of a stove with a TV set above the oven window).[15] Ads could be less utopian: the first spot on *The Ozzie and Harriet Show* begins with a closeup of a sink; "Dishes, dishes, dishes," intones a commercial spokesman. "Three times a day of every day of your life. Sometimes, does the sight of another stack of dirty dishes make you want to . . . ?" (fig. 2.1). We cut to an angry woman smashing a stack. "A new Hotpoint dishwasher," reassures the spokesman, will "save you over an hour of tedious work every day" (1.1). The savings were illusory: as Cowan demonstrates, the automation of household labor rarely resulted in less housework. And as

CHAPTER 2

2.1. *The Ozzy and Harriet Show*: "Dishes, dishes, dishes."

Roseanne's pilot made clear, even when women entered the workforce, they frequently were (and are) expected to perform what Arlie Russell Hochschild dubbed "the second shift": as Roseanne juggles work and family, Dan procures a Viking figurehead for his boat. He is himself a slothful figurehead: "I put in eight hours a day at the factory and then I come home and put in another eight hours. I'm running around like a maniac," she complains, "and you do nothing" (1.1).[16]

Some early sitcoms worried TV would keep women from their appointed tasks. On *The Honeymooners*, Ralph Kramden complains, "We've had that set three days now, and I haven't had a hot meal since" (1.1). Others made men unequal to those tasks: on *I Love Lucy* and *The Jeffersons*, husbands discover themselves unable to perform chores. Often, sitcoms pretended chores were not really work; and when families employed help, hired workers seemed intimates. On *Leave It to Beaver*, June Cleaver hires a white girl to work around the house. Gripped by what his dad calls "the chivalrous spirit," Wally does her work; waged exploitation becomes a "kitchen romance" (4.23) in which Wally becomes

88

the maid's servant. On *Gimme a Break!*, Nell Harper insists she wasn't hired by her racist boss, but volunteered to honor his dying wife (1.1). It wasn't unusual that this ostensibly working-class family could afford a housekeeper, presuming she was paid; on *All in the Family*, Gloria and Mike live with the Bunkers because Edith doesn't want them to live alone until they can afford a maid (1.1).

Traditional housework is crucial to the black-market melodrama, but in a different way. In part, the genre worries that housework and paid managerial work have become the same. In *Leave It to Beaver*, the maid frees June from one kind of work but subjects her to a new kind of worry; "One load is off my mind," she says, as if she were a washing machine, but "another one is on it." Black-market melodramas only sometimes recognize that work. "You are a house cat," Betty Draper's father tells her on *Mad Men*. "You are very important, and you have little to do" (3.5). But though Don Draper sells to house cats like Betty, his work mirrors theirs; when he's not tomcatting around, he's supervising "the little ones" (2.1) at the office—in ways that evoke Betty's supervision of their children and Carla, the Black maid.

As I argued in the introduction, the genre's secret work lives seem for a while to free men like Soprano and White from the homes to which they feel confined, in the same way that Draper's affairs seem to free him. Typically, black-market secret lives are ugly extrapolations of what men's work must become to preserve separate spheres decades into deindustrialization and the collapse of the family wage. Alternately, a drama like *Big Love* envisions what home life must become to preserve properly separate spheres. The dynamic is the same: the secret second life consolidates gendered distinctions between work and home. Bill Hendrickson seems a traditional breadwinner and then some; he supports three wives and seven children, after all. But the genre never really establishes separate spheres. Bill's life is no revanchist idyll, for instance. His first wife Barbara returns to "work outside the home" (1.5) and Bill will garnish her wages because his home improvement store is struggling. The store's name, Home Plus, echoes his scaled-up industrious family, and it is hard to tell where work and home begin and end. The frequently frantic Bill considers managing his three wives a "full-time job" (1.2), which is to say a job that echoes and competes with his job managing Home Plus. Both jobs echo those of the equally harried Barbara, who manages Bill's two other wives even after she returns to work. Hendrickson's business and home life have always been entwined. He secured seed money for the store by taking in his second wife as "collateral" (1.5) on a loan from a sect that trades in underaged girls. And his third wife was an employee at Home Plus. The drama anoints Bill a latter-day patriarch, then, even as it produces an enmeshment of home and work that makes separate spheres the thinnest of fictions. The first black-market melodrama to take up this problem from a woman's point of view, *Weeds* produces an even more profound enmeshment.

Showtime was the first cable network to air multiple variations of the black-market melodrama, with female leads no less, in both thirty- and sixty-minute formats. Longer versions included *Dexter*, *Homeland*, *Shameless*, *Twin Peaks: The Return*, and *Roy Donovan*. Each explored some version of the genre's secret second life. *Shameless* spent the most time exploring what felt like endless housework. It followed the ne'er-do-well and chronically destitute Gallagher clan, nominally headed by the deadbeat drunk Frank, but held together, in fact, by Fiona, the oldest daughter. All family members contribute to the "squirrel fund" that pays the bills. When Carl, the youngest, doesn't, Debbie, ten, upbraids him: "You're almost nine and you're going to have to start pulling your weight" (1.1). The division of family labor is pointedly gendered. Frank works a series of cons in which he impersonates other people. At one point, he generates a shadow version of his biological family. He names homeless kids after his own, cajoles them into earning for him, and thus produces "Gallagher 2.0" (7.3). Fiona abjures Frank's hustles and those of her boyfriend, a car thief and drug dealer. Responsible for the family, she cannot risk black markets. Instead, she burns through low-wage jobs that echo her unwaged housework: waiting tables, cleaning houses, tending children, and running a laundromat.

Showtime's thirty-minute varietals included *Weeds*, *Nurse Jackie*, and *The United States of Tara*. In *Nurse Jackie*, Jackie Peyton hides a pain killer addiction while working in an ER. She starts popping pills because her newborn daughter won't stop crying and, even years later, she prefers the hospital to home. Her marriage unravels. At one point, she visits a divorce lawyer during work hours; her supervisor berates her: "Family can't get in the way of work. If I'm focused on my kid, I'm not focused on my work. Home is home, work is work. Keep the boundaries clear" (4.7). This is hardly news to Jackie but keeping those boundaries clear is a struggle. She's getting divorced because her husband has discovered her affair with the hospital pharmacist. And of course her job echoes her work at home: for Jackie, there is nothing but nursing, during the day and then during her second shift at home. That said, *Nurse Jackie* shares as much with workplace dramas like *ER* as black-market melodramas, and not just because Jackie works for a state-recognized wage in a hospital. It spends far more time at work than at home, which can seem an afterthought. *Weeds* on the other hand is a paradigmatic black-market melodrama and preoccupied with housework from first to last.

"I wanted to do an outlaw show" like *The Sopranos*, creator Jenji Kohan explained; "from there, I needed to find an outlaw and a crime."[17] Kohan found these in Botwin and the weed business, respectively. Botwin lives a generically typical second life, initially hiding her dealing from her family and then over many seasons from assorted rivals and federal agencies. As in other black-market melodramas, that secret life precipitates a gendered transformation. When alive, the Jewish Jonah seemed more solicitous of the children than the WASPy Nancy. In old videos, we see him tending Shane, her youngest, while Nancy opts to sleep in: "Daddy made it all better" (1.2), the comedy suggests, not mommy. After Jonah dies, and Nancy starts earning, she's masculinized more decisively. She acquires a domestic helpmate, Jonah's brother Andy. "I'm family," he says. "Look, the way I see it, you're in way over your head here. You've got a house, you've bills, you're a mommy, dealing is a full-time job. You need some help" (1.4). And Andy does help; he cooks and tends the kids and does as Nancy asks. At one point, she tells him to cater a party on little notice. "I don't remember volunteering my services," he replies. "Maybe I have plans tomorrow. Maybe I have a playdate." Slapping his ass, she says, "You live here for free. You eat my food. You wipe your ass with my toilet paper. I don't have to ask you shit. Get in there and finish frying your eggs" (3.6). Nancy replaces Jonah as the household's breadwinner and makes his more feminine brother her housewife.

But Nancy is not consistently masculinized—and not really freed from housework. A reluctant mom, she is also a reluctant gangster. When running her business, in the first seasons especially, she tends to be reactive and passive; hers is no Heisenberg fantasy in which an overweening ego anticipates every contingency. Rather, she seeks her "Mr. Big," to recall *Sex and the City*.[18] She seems to find him in a cartel boss, Esteban Reyes, and is thrilled when he puts her over his knee and spanks her. The regressive scene eroticizes Nancy's passivity by allowing her to play child rather than parent. The redress is temporary, and not simply because, in season 5, Reyes rapes her: on the whole, and though she wishes it otherwise, playing gangster does not free her from mothering. In fact, it often requires playing mom: when she arouses suspicion crossing the border on a cartel errand, for instance, Guillermo Diaz berates her for her "check my shit out Technicolor slut suit"; he tells her, you're "supposed to be the All-American Mom" (4.3). However much housework Andy does, and however successful in business she becomes, she must be that All-American mom. That means taking responsibility for not less than everything. Faced with one of the many situations that make it impossible to do right by both her business and her family, she exclaims, "It wasn't my fault," before reflecting and then adding, "Actually, it probably was my fault, in a grand sense. Everything is my fault. It's all my fault" (4.5).

On the face of it, Nancy conceives of her pot business as an escape from that responsibility—into something riskier and exciting. Obviously enough, *Weeds* is a wish-fulfillment fantasy in which a mild-mannered soccer mom escapes her anesthetizing suburban routines into vivifying adventure. But Nancy's fantasy is an impossible one, no matter how dangerous her life gets. Having introduced herself to another dealer, Tusk, as "the suburban baroness of bud," she asks him, "how do you keep your business separate from your family?" (1.6). She doesn't want her kids to know she deals and she wants a life to which they have no access. But the children quickly discover her secret and as her business scales up and absorbs friends and family into one industrious unit, she confronts a fateful confusion of spheres. "We don't shit where we eat or eat where we shit," she tells Silas, who wants to grow weed at home.

"Either way, words of wisdom" (4.2). But the family is at this point mired in shit. Silas has wormed his way into the business, as has Andy; Lupita the maid moves into weed sales; Nancy's CPA, Doug Wilson, crashes on her sofa and with Andy starts a coyote smuggling service; Shane remodels the family's new home with the low-wage labor that Doug and Andy smuggle out of Mexico; Nancy's frenemy Celia works the register in the family's front business.

To recall Cowan, in *Weeds*, it is hard to know where housework "begins and where it ends." That's true above all of Botwin's parenting. Even as a gangster, she is unfree in the way that victims of the "new momism" generally are, above all because her industrious household makes it impossible to distinguish parenting from running the family business. She resists when Silas asks her to hire his girlfriend, not wanting further to mix family and business. She relents and when Silas later asks her to fire his now ex-girlfriend, she refuses, because the ex earns too much. "This is not your mommy talking, this is your boss," she says, explaining herself. Then, waving a hand before her face, her demeanor now softened, she adds, "As your mother, I'm sorry it's not working out between the two of you" (3.11). The device is felicitous, but Nancy does not really keep the personae distinct. One role is not replaced by so much as added to another, and then subsumed under a broadened aegis of motherhood. The mother-manager of a scaled-up household, Nancy struggles frantically to nurture her business and her children while assuming responsibility for whatever transpires beneath her growing tentpole.

That tentpole subtly changes the allegory common to black-market melodramas. Being a mom and running a weed business, the comedy never stops reminding us, demand similar kinds of oversight. And insofar as they require the same oversight—Nancy's family makes up part of her workforce—it can be hard to see one activity as allegorical of the other. They are simply the same. It's therefore tempting to say that Botwin's abjection registers allegory's failure, since for Kristeva, the abject springs from an inability to sustain subject-object distinctions; it is "the place where meaning collapses."[19] But this would be to overlook the richness of the comedy's central metaphor, "weed," which sustains the comedy's allegory of Botwin's abjection.

CHAPTER 2

"You see it as drugs, to push, like it's merch," a pot fanatic tells Silas. "But it's not dead. It's alive. It's ancient. It knows things. The plants pick you. But you have to be ready. It is a battle. You control them or they control you . . . they take you down" (8.5). Most obviously, the plants are children, who take down and control too-pliant parents. That much becomes clear, late in the game, when Andy's girlfriend speaks of not wanting "to grow" her own children (8.10). But throughout, Nancy's weed business gestures to parenting. In season 7, she returns to that business as if ordered by a judge, who tells her she will gain custody of her youngest child, Stevie, only by returning to what worked for her in the past. "Be the Nancy who raised Silas" (7.5), he says, which she takes to mean, "return to dealing." And in the comedy's final moments, we will see, she gives up Stevie and her weed business together, in the same moment.

Weeds are a metaphor for dirt as well as children, and for cleaning as well as parenting. "I've always loved getting clean," declares a sudsy Piper Chapman in the first line of *Orange*, as she luxuriates in a tub. "I love baths, I love showers; it's my happy place." The line reminds us that *Orange* descends from soap opera (as virtually all serialized TV does). It also anticipates Chapman's horror when, exiled from her space of domestic innocence, she's incarcerated. To her, prison is dirty not just because it's unhygienic but because it troubles the boundaries on which she's based her sense of self; this is to invoke dirt as Patricia Yeager does, as an abjection-inducing disordering of once-pristine borders and distinctions.[20] Blemishes that mar otherwise pristine lawns and garden beds, weeds evoke a similar abjection in *Weeds*. But if weeds are like dirt, they are also, obviously enough, drugs, which makes "getting clean" a complicated metaphor (fig. 2.2). We might think of Agrestic's "little boxes on the hillside" as pillboxes that contain "mother's little helpers." Pot recalls the midcentury association between valium and housework not because it helps Nancy tolerate housework but because it codes the male leisure that housework produces. In its first seasons, no Agrestic women smoke. Andy, Doug, and Dean Hodes partake together for hours, acting like children. Nancy and Celia mainline stimulants: the former, iced coffee, and the latter, Diet Coke. To recall the Rolling Stones, "'Men

2.2. *Weeds*: Nancy Botwin's dirty secrets.

are different today' / I hear every mother say / they just don't appreciate that you get tired." Agrestic's mothers get tired producing the free time in which men smoke weed. Moreover, Nancy's business produces *her* as a leisure object: Snoop Dogg names the family's proprietary varietal "MILF weed"; this is another new momism fantasy, in which mothers work a "third shift" to stay alluring.[21]

Agrestic's women do have help. Families like the Botwins don't typically pull invasive plants from their lawns or garden beds. Nor do they typically clean their own homes. More often than not, they hire Black or brown women to do their dirt work. Seen this way, "getting clean" produces a different kind of dependency—and a different kind of abjection, when white families lose their ability to pay for racialized labor (as the Botwins do), and, to their horror, become themselves racialized. Downwardly mobile from the start, Nancy struggles to pay Lupita, and eventually loses her; her weed business signals that loss and her newfound kinship with the Black and brown labor on which towns like Agrestic depend. Lupita discovers Nancy's secret in the linen closet, appropriately enough, and then refuses to work, demanding pay for her silence. Andy picks up some slack, but Nancy in effect takes over, selling a product that

CHAPTER 2

2.3. *Weeds*: Botwin hits bottom.

Weeds associates with cleaning services. During the first three seasons, Nancy buys from Heylia James, an African American woman whose pot business is fronted by a cleaning service, Tidy Up Inc. (1.2).

Heylia does not herself grow. Growing is reserved for men, Conrad and Silas, and though Nancy's last name evokes "botany," it's her married name; she never herself "husbands" (from the Old Norse, *husbondi*, for "master of a house and . . . tiller of soil").[22] When she does produce her own product, it's hash, not weed. And the manner in which she produces it makes clear that Heylia's front business is more than an incidental joke—and that Nancy's pot selling is akin to working for a maid service. When the now on-the-lam and broke family cross a picket line to find work in a Seattle hotel, Nancy sells her credentials: "I manage people really well" (6.3). She tends to float up organizational structures, hiring underlings while assuming executive functions. But season 6 makes clear how tenuous her upward mobility is. The hotel clerk looks Nancy up and down and hires her as a maid (fig. 2.3). It is in that capacity that she first makes hash—in the hotel's industrial dryer. In *Breaking Bad*, Gus Fring fronts his superlab with a laundry facility. The episode in which Fring reveals the lab to White, by taking him beneath a giant dryer (3.5), aired four months before the episode in *Weeds* in which Nancy first makes hash in her hotel's dryer. Later, Nancy and her team take another cue from Walt and Jesse, and make hash in an RV, again in its dryer (6.8).

Wages for Housework

There is no conflict in *Weeds* between pot's ability to refer to parenting and paid housework. Needless to say, women often perform both kinds of labor. At the hotel, for example, Nancy cleans rooms while still raising her kids, as countless US women do (women of color working for white families, more often than not).[23] Still, we need more generally to account for the relation of both waged and unwaged "reproductive" labor, on the one hand, to "productive" labor both within and beyond the US, on the other.

Marxist feminists associated with the International Wages for Housework Campaign of the 1970s sought recognition that housework was work rather than an expression of an essential feminine nature or love. In the words of Silvia Federici, "We have cooked, smiled, fucked throughout the years, not because it was easier for us than for anybody else, but because we did not have any other choice." The demand that that housework be waged was meant to "expose the fact that housework is already money for capital, that capital has made and makes money out of our cooking, smiling, fucking." And it was in her words "the first step toward refusing to do it."[24] Federici also likened the paid "second job" that houseworkers sometimes take to housework proper, since it "reproduces our role in different forms": such jobs "are mere extensions of the housewife's condition." As "nurses, maids, teachers, [and] secretaries—all functions for which we are well trained in the home," we lose the ability "to see where our work begins and ends."[25] Black-market melodramas like *The Sopranos* and *Breaking Bad* express similar sentiments even as they fret a generalized feminization of labor.

But "feminization" is too blunt an instrument to assess the relation of housework to reproductive labor generally; it does little to account for the objective material relations that produce gender. More useful than Federici in this regard is Mariarosa Dalla Costa and Selma James's *The Power of Women and the Subversion of the Community* (1973), which argued that housework was "indirectly waged labor." *The Power of Women* explains how the isolated working-class housewife—"always on duty" and subject to an "unending" workday—props up the male wage on which she is dependent.[26] Capital relies crucially on her labor even as it renders her dependent on her husband's wage. As Kathi Weeks notes, for Dalla Costa and James, the family is

> a distributive mechanism through which wages can be imagined to extend to the nonwaged, underwaged, not-yet-waged, and no-longer-waged. As a privatized machine of social reproduction, the family serves to keep wages lower and hours longer than they would be if the general assumption were that individuals needed either to be able to secure commodified equivalents to the goods and services produced within private households or to have enough time outside of waged work to produce the goods and services themselves. Although the family continues to serve as a crucial element of the wage system, it remains a hidden partner, its role concealed by those all discourses that naturalize, romanticize, privatize, and depoliticize the institution.[27]

Housework, or domestic work, is the engine of that hidden partnership, and is "the production of waged slavery via unwaged slavery." Above all, for Dalla Costa and James, "domestic work produces not merely use values but is essential to the production of surplus value." They do not clarify exactly how domestic work contributes to the production of surplus value. They claim "capital does not want ... to destroy the position of the housewife as the pivot of the nuclear family," for example, and note the family's role in stabilizing unrest: "The family, this maternal cradle always ready to help and protect in time of need, has been in fact the best guarantee that the unemployed do not immediately become a horde of disruptive outsiders."[28] But later theorists would fault them for not sufficiently debunking the fiction that the family was a maternal cradle, for example, or a separate sphere, and for not showing precisely how housework reproduces "labor power," a worker's capacity to labor.

Maya Gonzalez takes issue with passages from *The Power of Women* like these: "*where women are concerned, their labor appears to be a personal service outside of capital.*" Gonzalez thinks this "leaves open the question of dual modes of production—one capitalist and the other domestic." Dalla Costa often evokes the home as a space apart; and "it is not clear," Gonzalez adds, if for her the "feminine labor of reproduction is capitalist in nature, that is, a performance of living labor in the creation of a *commodity's* use-value, or if it is merely a holdover from traditional family formations found in older modes of production."[29] Gonzalez is equally wary of Federici. "To us," Federici recalls, "it was immediately clear that the circuit of capitalist production . . . began and was centered above all in the kitchen, the bedroom, the home—insofar as these were the centers for the production of labor-power—and from there it moved on to the factory, passing through the school, the office, the lab."[30] For Gonzalez, claims like these risk defining reproductive labor in relation to the domestic spaces in which it ostensibly transpires. Gonzalez prefers Leopoldina Fortunati's *The Arcane of Reproduction*, published in the wake of Wages for Housework, because it locates "the hidden abode of reproduction" not in kitchens, bedrooms, and homes but, more conceptually, in the second of the two circuits that Marx took to be inherent in the wage relation: M-C-M' and C-M-C.

The first of these circuits produces value: a capitalist uses money (M) to purchase labor power and uses that labor power to produce a commodity (C) whose sale realizes a surplus (M') beyond the cost of the commodity's production. In the second circuit, a worker sells his labor power and with the money gained purchases lodging and commodities, like food, with which he reproduces his labor power. But that is a deceptively simple abbreviation of a complex process, Gonzalez notes: "Between each moment of 'the buying and selling of labor-power,' there is a sphere of use-value creation—of the making (and maintaining) of labor-power." For Marx, "hidden" productive processes convert money into money prime. A capitalist cannot make a coat unless other capitalists have produced cotton, shipped it to mills, converted it to linen, and transported the linen to coat factories. And the coat-making factory doesn't simply combine materials as if in a vat. There are numerous intermediary stages to the process, mediated by waged labor, none of which are visible to the coat's purchaser. Fortunati is invaluable,

Gonzalez argues, for her reminder that similarly hidden reproductive processes convert commodities into labor power.[31] Food does not itself replenish labor power any more than cotton itself makes coats; food is a use value activated by the reproductive labor of shopping and cooking, for example. Seen this way, it does not matter in what spaces a given kind of work transpires; reproductive labor designates the maintaining of labor power rather than the maintaining of homes.

Crucially, for Fortunati, reproductive labor has a "non-direct" relation to the wage. Prostitution and housework are for her "the main sectors, the backbone" of the reproductive process because, though one is paid for and the other is not, both are supported by male workers from wages paid by capital. "In the case of housework," she argues,

> the relation does not appear to be between the woman and capital, but between the housewife and the male worker, thus it appears as a relation which is intended to satisfy reciprocal individual consumption and not the work relation it is—a relation of production. In prostitution too, the relation does not appear to be between the woman and capital, but between the prostitute and the male worker. In this case too, prostitution appears to be a relation which is intended to satisfy reciprocal individual consumption and not . . . a relation of production. Thus both these relations posit themselves as non-directly waged relations of production which take place between woman—as houseworker or as sex-worker—and capital, through the mediation of the male worker.[32]

These terms clarify moments in *Weeds* and *Orange* that liken housework to sex work. But taken on their own they don't account for what Gonzalez calls "the growing integration of the sphere of social reproduction into that of production"—in the manufacture of laundry machines or TV dinners, for example, or in the use of wage labor to clean other people's houses.[33] Reproductive labor does not always have a nondirect relation to the wage. It can be waged directly. As a consequence, in "The Logic of Gender," *Endnotes* argues that "cooking, looking after children, [and] washing/mending clothes," say, must be evaluated not based on the "concrete characteristics" of the work or the "actual place

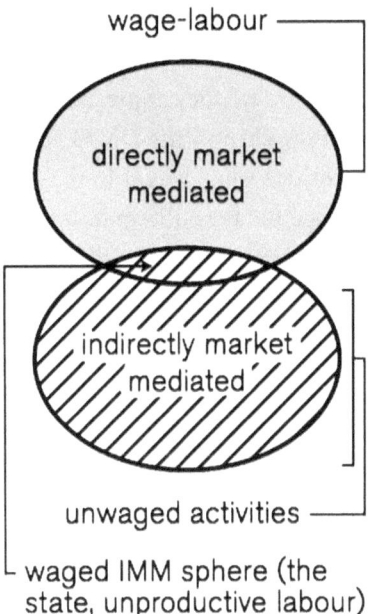

2.4. *Endnotes*: "The logic of gender."

in which it occurs," or even simply if they are paid for, but on their relation "to exchange, the market and the accumulation of capital." It thus distinguishes between "two spheres": "(a) the *directly market mediated* sphere (DMM); and (b) the *indirectly market mediated* sphere (IMM)." Reproduction in the IMM sphere can be waged, when state organized, or unwaged, as housework. But in the DMM sphere, reproductive labor takes place "under directly capitalist conditions" that require steady rates of return, "the uniformity of the laboring process, and of the relationship of those who produce to what they produce" (fig. 2.4).

"The growing integration of the sphere of social reproduction into that of production," then, involves the shift of specific jobs from the IMM to the DMM sphere. But inevitably, *Endnotes* argues, the market refuses to absorb certain IMM jobs, because doing so is not cost effective; this is the case for childcare, above all, insofar as it cannot be automated or sped up (at least not yet). And jobs that are "outside of market relations" because they "cannot be subsumed or [are] not worth subsuming,"

Endnotes adds, are "the abject." *Endnotes* uses the word broadly, and briefly, and with less specificity than it might. Still, the use is revealing. The "ugly face of gender today," they argue, is that women are relegated to the abject even as they earn in the DMM sphere: "If many of our mothers and grandmothers were caught in the sphere of IMM activities, the problem we face today is different. It is not that we will have to 'go back to the kitchen,' if only because *we cannot afford it*. Our fate, rather, is *having to deal with the abject*. Contrary to the IMM activities of the past, this abject has already been to a large extent denaturalised. It does not appear to those performing it as some unfortunate natural fate, but more like an extra burden that one must deal with alongside wage-labor."[34]

That double bind is in many ways like the one that Maria Mies attributes to women in underdeveloped nations. Mies defines historical processes of "housewifization" that forced third world women into a dual role, performing unwaged housework on the one hand and paid, under-the-table informal work on the other. Women in underdeveloped economies are abject, Mies might have said, because even as they generate informal income, they are forced to perform the unwaged IMM activities that reproduce their husbands' labor power. But for Mies, first and third world women are relegated to the informal economy specifically. The underdeveloped world is for Mies the "invisible underground foundation" of the global economy; but so too, developed and underdeveloped worlds share an informal underground: if "capital and waged labor form the visible economy" in each, " 'above the water,' [and] counted in the GDP," then women doing unpaid housework, on the one hand, and women engaging in "income generating activities" as they also perform housework, on the other, together form an international underground. For Mies, housework *is* informal labor. Reciprocal processes relegate women to the informal, and if those processes work differently in each world, they nevertheless exclude women in similar ways from the "so-called formal, modern sector," which is maintained as such precisely to subordinate women.[35]

For Mies, Wages for Housework's "domestic labor debate . . . did not include other areas of non-wage work which are tapped by capital in its process of accumulation. This is particularly true of all the work performed by subsistence peasants, petty commodity producers, [and] marginalized people, most of whom are women, in the underdeveloped countries."[36] In these and other cases, and "whether in use value or commodity production," women's work is "obscured, does not appear as 'free wage labor,' is defined as an 'income-generating activity,' and can hence be bought at a much cheaper price than male labor." The significant distinction is between the male worker's state-recognized wage and the female worker's informal labor, *both in underground economies and as housework*. Denied access to the wage, women are "reintegrated into capitalist development in a whole range of informal, non-organized, non-protected production relations, ranging from part-time work, through contract work, to homeworking, to unpaid neighborhood work."[37] And even as they contribute decisively to their families' incomes, they are forced as housewives to "deal with the abject."

In underdeveloped economies, abject labor is less "denaturalised," to again recall *Endnotes*, than never naturalized to begin with. The rise of separate-sphere gender relations in the first world, Mies argues, depended on colonialism and later on an international division of labor that outsourced industrial production to former colonies. "The emergence of the Dutch housewife," for example, "and the stress on family and homemaking 'back home,' was not just a temporal coincidence but was causally linked to the disruption of families and homes among estate workers in the Dutch colonies." Capitalism did not destroy the European family, she argues, against Engels and Marx; "on the contrary, with the help of the state and its police, it created the family first among the propertied classes, later in the working class, and with it the housewife as a social category." Colonialism was pivotal to the naturalizing of that category. Ideologically, it linked women and the colonies themselves; both were feminine because available for expropriation. In Europe, women's labor was seen as "a natural resource, freely available like air and water," akin to the colonies. And in the colonies, women's labor was kept invisible, even or especially when that labor brought in essential income.[38]

"Without the ongoing exploitation of external colonies—formerly as direct colonies," Mies writes, and "today, within the new international division of labor—the establishment of the 'internal colony,' that is, a nuclear family and a woman maintained by a male 'breadwinner,' would not have been possible." For Mies, this process is ongoing: "housewifization" names the continued "externalization, or ex-territorialization of costs which otherwise would have to be covered by the capitalists." Published in 1986, *Patriarchy and Accumulation on a World Scale* does not fully account for the rise of the dual-income family in developed nations; and so we must qualify its account of how, as the once third world undergoes industrialization, and the once first world, deindustrialization, "the dual model according to which Third World labor has been segmented is reintroduced into the industrialized countries."[39] But trends in female labor force participation in underdeveloped nations have largely born out Mies's claims.[40] And it is reasonable to speculate that even when receiving a formal wage, first world women are haunted by the prospect of a specifically third world informality, which prospect, Mies would insist, is already immanent in their relegation to housework, and to what *Endnotes* considers the abject. The fourth season of *Weeds*, I'll now suggest, describes that haunting in a revealing way.

Abjection; or, The Brain in Drawer Problem

Mary-Louise Parker said of *Weeds*, "I never treated it as a comedy. I thought it was a drama. They're the same thing; life is life, and you shouldn't play things for tears or laughs. It's somewhere in between."[41] Pamela Adlon plays it the same way on *Better Things*, also about a single mom. The program has no secret second life and thus lacks the elaborated allegorical dimension with which this book is concerned, but it is even more focused on parenting and abjection than *Weeds*. Throwing up repeatedly because of stress, Sam Fox finds her way to a doctor, hoping to get sleeping pills. She breaks down and describes "the mountain of mom shit" that she daily navigates:

> soccer-club signups and dance classes and tutors and tuition payments and parent-teacher conferences and schools and camps that I have to get them into and mean-girl issues with my youngest at school and birth

control with my oldest and cruelty from middle daughter and then there is my own mom who is driving me nuts and I'm pretty sure she has a mental disorder or something and my middle daughter is hitting puberty hard and I am definitely going through menopause and yet I still get my period and I have a beard and two mortgages and so yeah . . . it's a lot. And some mornings I just lay in bed in my room and stare and the ceiling and I say, I just can't do it anymore. I just can't. I just can't. I just can't. I can't. I can't. (3.5)

Adlon has twice been nominated for an Emmy for outstanding lead actress in a comedy series and Parker was nominated four times. Neither won, but comedies fronting women have found at least some Emmy success—in ways that dramas fronting women have not. Between 2000–2019, only two such dramas won Best Drama (*Homeland* in 2012 and *The Handmaid's Tale* in 2017). During that same period, comedies with a female lead won nine Emmys for best comedy (*Sex and the City* in 2001; *30 Rock* from 2007 to 2009; *Veep* from 2015 to 2017; *The Marvelous Mrs. Maisel* in 2018; and *Fleabag* in 2019). The two most recent of these might be considered "dramedies," but whether we use that term or not, it's clear enough that genre-troubling comedies with women leads have done better than have women-led dramas (reclassified as a drama by the Emmys in 2015, *Orange Is the New Black* is an exception). We need no elaborate machinery to explain the run-of-the-mill misogyny that relegates men to adventure and action and women to humorous self-abasement. But the abjection I've been elaborating does allow for further distinctions. The comedies and dramas treated in this study are all melodramas. But broadly construed, sixty-minute black-market melodramas tend to drive more single-mindedly toward affective legibility while embracing masculine affects that disavow their soap opera origins (and the soap's traditional viewers). *The Sopranos* and *Breaking Bad* are funny and represent abjection, but they typically rely on suspense to sustain narrative continuity and are in most ways generically recognizable. By contrast, whether classified as comedies or dramedies, the single-camera thirty-minute programs now under consideration tend to stress affective illegibility and, in *Weeds* and *Better Things*, gender that illegibility as a function of their interest in "women's work." And typically, though they can of course be serialized, these harder-to-classify programs utilize epigrammatic set pieces to encapsulate abjection in everyday life rather than represent crucial stages in suspenseful narrative sequences.

Insofar as the abject names a state of indiscrimination and disorder that troubles boundaries, classical comedy cannot really be abject, at least not in the end, since it disorders only to reorder and reconcile. In that sense, *Weeds* cannot be a classical comedy; and in fact, except for the briefest of moments at its end, *Weeds* refuses to stabilize the relation of family and work, above all. And yet recent work on comedy draws on Kristeva to explain why an abject indeterminacy might be considered central to a now-dominant strain of comedy. Uneasy or discomfiting humor, in these accounts, is a key feature of stand-up comedy. Typically, this work draws on John Limon, who calls abjection

> a psychic worrying of those aspects of oneself that one cannot be rid of, that seem, but are not quite, alienable, for example, blood, urine, nails, feces, and the corpse. . . . When you feel abject, you feel as if there were something miring your life, some skin that cannot be sloughed, some role (because "abject" always, in a way, describes how you *act*) that has become your only character. Abjection is self-typecasting.

Abjection is a psychic purgatory, a self-loathing that leaves one stuck in indeterminacy. For Limon, stand up is a stagey, self-objectifying effort to overcome that morass. "All [of] a stand-up's life feels abject to him or her, and stand-ups try to escape it by living it as an act." That act would convert pain to laughter but can never be at an end; self-typecasting must be ongoing; "comedy is a way of avowing and disavowing abjection," which can be "stood up" but not surmounted. "Reality itself, in the way of the abject, keeps returning to the stand-up comedian, who throws it off in the form of jokes. Obliviousness is earned from moment to moment."[42]

Rebecca Wanzo adapts Limon's terms to the "postfeminist" TV identified by Lynn Spangler, Bonnie Dow, and Susan Douglas. Specifically, she identifies "the precarious girl comedy" as a genre that takes up the "new economic and interpersonal insecurity of the US middle class" and speaks to millennials "who have less and now expect less, who have internalized many of second-wave feminism's claims (but may not admit it), [and] who have embraced identities that are not tied to heteronormative and traditional models for women in love and work but feel disappointed by their limited options."[43] In these comedies of thwarted and unrealized desire, "women's bodies become a site of the modern mire of economic and intimate abjection." In *Girls*, for example, Hannah Horvath's "inability to recognize boundaries—existing in that in-between characteristic of abjection—makes her an abhorrent object to others who want to flee her attempts to draw everyone into an aesthetics of the abject."[44]

Nancy Botwin is too old and initially wealthy to be one of Wanzo's heroines; she displays nothing like Horvath's millennial wretchedness. But she does exemplify the abject aesthetics identified by Caetlin Benson-Allott, who thinks Jenji Kohan prepared the way for *GLOW* and *I Love Dick*, for example. Citing Wanzo, Benson-Allott argues those comedies depict "female protagonists hitting personal and professional nadirs that destabilize their sense of self" and "demand respect for their characters by figuring defeat, failure, and desperation as stages women must pass through to challenge patriarchal cultures." The programs are also egregious displays of white privilege; their "preoccupation with white female abjection" proceeds by "introducing and then shortchanging supporting characters of color," such that "an ongoing negotiation with white privilege" comes to depend on the "mockery of minority lives and pain."[45] It's here, I would add, that Kohan's influence is most visible.

In the first scene of *Weeds*, white women in a PTA meeting snigger at Nancy's fake purse. The gray-market knockoff troubles boundaries and reminds Nancy she pretends to an identity she cannot maintain. It is the sign of something that must but cannot be cast off (abject objects are always nonobjects, because they fail to concretize what must be cast off). We then cut to Heylia's kitchen, where Nancy seeks reassurance the purse looks real. She doesn't get it, but does get a stream of good-natured abuse, which she drinks in. Like *Orange*, *Weeds* relishes abasing its white lead before Black and brown women. Nancy's visits to Heylia's evoke a tradition of fiction in which alienated whites travel to Black

CHAPTER 2

neighborhoods (or countries) looking to access more authentic versions of themselves (at Heylia's, Nancy meets "Conrad," the handsome Black man with whom she will go native). But Nancy's submission to abuse is also a version of Benson-Allott's abjection. It expresses an otherwise impermissible contempt: punish me for my privilege so I can continue to enjoy it, indifferent to you. To recall Limon, "When you feel abject, you feel as if there were something miring your life, some skin that cannot be sloughed." Nancy submits to Heylia's crew so that she might wear them as a second skin, before casting them off as so much bodily detritus. "Why is it that every move you make digs my grave?" Conrad later asks her. "You open your big brown eyes, and I fall into shit" (2.6).

"I'm fascinated by people interacting with the other, forced to interact with people they'd never have to deal with in their day-to-day lives," declares Kohan. Those encounters—between "white people" and "non-white others," let's be clear—often result in mockery. And it would be a mistake to overstate the degree to which Kohan's white heroines change as a result (just as it would be a mistake to celebrate this generally conservative program for its indictment of gender norms). More relevant is that these encounters take place in "underground economies," Emily Nussbaum notes, which enact interpersonal abjection on a geopolitical scale.[46] Weed is, like Nancy's bag, an abject object, specifically, as a sign of a relation to parenting that Nancy cannot cast off. But it is also a sign of a relation to Mexico that the US cannot cast off. Conrad tells Sanjay, a distributor, "There are thirty-seven billionaires in this country and forty million living beneath the poverty line. Wake up, 7-Eleven, this is the fucking third world" (2.11). Clearly, "this" refers to the US; Conrad might also be understood to suggest Sanjay has been sleeping through the sixteen-hour, 7 AM to 11 PM workday to which the nation's destitute are subject. The presence in the US of the third world and Mexico in particular is both problem and opportunity, insofar as Conrad grows for Nancy a boutique strain more up-market than the "Mexican" grass she initially sells.[47] But the fact that he stands in Nancy's grow-house kitchen when he delivers the line is doubly apt: if Conrad's "this" indicates the US, it also indicates that kitchen, in a house very much like Nancy's: suburban kitchens, he suggests, are sites of third world informal labor. Like the black markets that litter the black-market melodrama, the kitchen is what world-systems theory might consider a "semiperiphery," which rubric designates not transition zones between developed and underdeveloped national spaces but littoral zones of contact and commerce between what Chase-Dunn calls "logistical" rather than "literal" boundaries.[48]

Season 4 takes this spatial conceit in a different direction, by likening a tunnel beneath the US-Mexico border to Botwin's birth canal and, more broadly, her capacity to perform reproductive labor. Season 3 concludes with Botwin burning down her Agrestic house, fueling flames set inadvertently by Guillermo, as he tried to drive away Nancy's competitors. She burns the house because it never felt like "home" (3.14); she would be free of it. She longs for a new start and seems to find it when Guillermo gives her "what the world would call a normal boring job," which is managing a store:

> I wake up in the morning, get dressed, drive myself to work, put on a nametag, take my brain out of my skull and place it in a drawer. I spend the next nine hours smiling at people pretending to be interested in their happiness. Tolerating the company of my coworkers, staring at the clock. At the end of the day, I take the nametag off, open the drawer, reach for my brain, plop it back inside, walk to the employee parking lot, drive myself home. And it's really, really, really great. (4.5)

The job promises legitimacy in the formal economy and the restoration of distinctions between home and work. And while it echoes Nancy's mothering (it's in a maternity store), it requires "pretend" care work that makes no real claim on her brain or heart.

Her return to normalcy proves fleeting. Botwin doesn't wonder why Guillermo pays her a fantastic sum to manage a store near the border. But she soon learns it sits atop a tunnel through which a cartel smuggles guns and drugs. Her nine-to-six job, it turns out, asks her to place her brain in the drawer in ways she does not initially imagine. She protests half-heartedly and then becomes involved with Esteban Reyes, who runs the smuggling. As she grows dependent on him, emotionally and

CHAPTER 2

for his weed, she discovers he also traffics sex workers across the border. Nancy identifies with the drugged women who come through the tunnel, captive as she now is to Reyes (who drugs *her*, at one point). There is no effective difference between her coupling and their sex work, *Weeds* suggests. But she's also in part responsible for that sex work. Knowing this, she tries to look the other way—but cannot. She experiences crippling headaches and, at the beach, hallucinates a woman she saw emerge from the tunnel.

Identifying Botwin with both sex worker and cartel boss, *Weeds* rings a change on Mies's interest in how "the enslavement and exploitation" of women in the underdeveloped world became "the foundation of a qualitatively different type of enslavement of another set of women" in the developed world. On the one hand, Botwin's affluence depends on the subjugation of the sex worker; on the other, she is a slave to her children, the comedy suggests, in the way the sex workers are slaves to Reyes. The tunnel is beneath a maternity store, after all, which in addition to likening women to permeable borders casts the sex workers as born into the US as children from a birth canal. Doubling anatomical and political boundaries, *Weeds* captures the abjection described by Letitia Alvarado, who speaks on behalf of Mexican immigrants: "At times we are called into the life of the nation, invited to provide labor and to vote with our strong family values, while at other times we are central to xenophobic discourses that seek to expel or remove Latino traces from the national body." What results is abjection in "the social material realm," in which "a normative national identity" requires "the casting out of other undesirable bodies whose own interiority is diminished."[49] But in Botwin's case, the emphasis is on *trying* to cast those bodies out (of mind): however much she would place her brain in a drawer, they return as impingements on her liberal conscience.

Untroubled by her conscience, Celia replaces Nancy at the store. Celia is properly abject: addicted to coke, she sneezes blood on whoever is near. The border crossings mount and the comedy kicks into madcap gears. El Andy plays Moses, feeding Mexicans matzoh as he leads them out of the desert and into the Promised Land. An ethical coyote, he's celebrated as a folk hero. Doug falls for a Mexican woman he sees trying to enter the country illegally; he dreams of making her his wife, which dream casts her as a version of the sex worker. Andy smuggles her out, but Doug reports her to the INS after she picks Andy over him. Botwin, meanwhile, deals with her children, who haunt her in a manner that evokes the smuggled women.

Just before her hallucination, Botwin makes two discoveries. The first is that Silas has been growing MILF weed and sleeping with a single mom Nancy's age—a woman who is like the mother he'd like to fuck, in other words. The second is that Shane has been masturbating to pictures of her, Nancy. The comedy racially launders each transgression. Snoop Dogg named "MILF weed," recall, which weed will be the source of years of tension between mother and son. Shane, meanwhile, hides his photos in Sammy Davis Jr.'s autobiography, *Yes I Can*. The Jewish African American is cast as an intimate other, both endogamous and exogamous to the family's psychosexual dynamic. Botwin lectures her sons on their Oedipal attachments. The presumably sequential lectures are edited so we do not know to which of her two boys she speaks in any moment. It's a little "quirky," she says, as we cut between their reactions, to fantasize sexually about your mother, or to have sex with a "stand-in" for her. "According to Freud, a lot of people want to have sex with their mother, or with substitutes for their mother" (4.9). That's normal, she adds, while insisting, if not in so many words, that they stop trying to return to her tunnel.

To speak of stand-ins and substitutes, of course, is to speak of allegory, which *Weeds* deploys in farcically typological fashion. Where Andy liberates as Moses, Nancy enslaves as a Pharaoh. Her children should not want to return to mom as they do. But she is herself enslaved also. Later in the day on which she speaks with her boys about their attachments, she bends over the washing machine, exhausted, and asks Silas if he has any clothes she might launder. She would reduce the tension between them and replace an inappropriate maternal role with a more ostensibly appropriate one. She is a homemaker again, ostensibly desexualized; at the same time, thus prostrated and ready to service her men, she becomes akin to the sex workers rather than a party to their exploitation. She is back in a recognizable role, that is, one that allows the comedy to stabilize after its more frenzied (and abject) churnings.

CHAPTER 2

Moments like these subtend black-market melodramas: housework is the mundane truth, the ultimate referent of the genre's allegories. Over its eight seasons, *Weeds* would de-sublimate that truth, by transforming weed from an illegal to a legal object. Already legal for medicinal use at the comedy's start in 2005, pot would not become legal for recreational use in California until 2016, four years after the comedy ended. But *Weeds* anticipates legalization. For seven seasons, Nancy sells a black-market good. For much of season 8, she and Silas work for a pharmaceutical firm that makes medical marijuana. And when the comedy ends, we have jumped to an unspecified future in which cannabis is legal. HBO's *The Deuce* tracks pornography's legalization in a related way. David Simon explains, "Everything was in a brown paper bag under the counter, and then suddenly the interpretation of the law changed." That change produced "an interesting allegory. Here's a moment where something isn't a legal product and then suddenly it is. Let's follow the money and see who gets paid."[50] In *Weeds*, Nancy gets paid; finally legit, she sells her business to Starbucks. The trope recalls the *Godfather* films, which, to quote Fredric Jameson, "work themselves toward the light and toward thematic or reflexive foregrounding." In the first film, the mafia "served as a substitute for business." Over the next two, the mafia "transforms" into "business itself, just as 'in reality' the need for the cover of legitimate investments ends up turning the mafiosi into real businessmen."[51] The Botwins work toward the light, as if from a tunnel, not because they change their product but because the law changes around them.

And yet the serial's dénouement is not simply that Nancy gets paid or goes legit. It's that weed's legalization marks a signal change in her relation to parenting—as if the drug's entrance into the formal economy disables its ability any longer to allegorize parenting. In the comedy's last episodes, Stevie, the only one of her children still to live with her, announces his resolve to attend boarding school. Nancy is distraught. Andy consoles her: "You're free. You did your job. Now you're done" (8.13). For eight seasons, Nancy's children have been ineradicable weeds; they have sprung up around and encumbered her. What then does it mean to be free of them? Martin Shuster celebrates *Weeds* for showing that family is "the hope of an oasis, of something that might then grow into a world."⁵² But the promised oasis in the last moments is the loss rather than birth of children. And rather than speculate about Nancy's interior state—for what does she actually hope in this moment?—I note that being free from the "job" that was parenting means being free from the job that was weed. She only now decides to sell her business, which she had resisted doing. Thus divested, Nancy shares a farewell joint with her family. It's the first time she's smoked with them. She's able to do so, presumably, because weed has just become a leisure object rather than a symbol of her labor. Also, perhaps a fetish rather than an abject object: "A fascination with what is detachable may be fetishistic," notes Limon, "if its object is a distraction from what one fears to lose, what one fears one has never really possessed. A fascination with what is detachable may be abject if it concerns what one fears cannot be lost, what will always return."⁵³

Not So Crazy Eyes

In season 6 of *Orange Is the New Black*, Suzanne "Crazy Eyes" Warren is in the supermax facility to which she and her circle from the lower-security Litchfield Prison have been sent following season 5's riot. She's been hearing voices because she has come off her meds and, in this instance, speaks to an imaginary parent. "I made my bed," she says. "Can I watch TV now? Nope. May I watch TV now? Yes! Thank you" (6.1). Suzanne sits down on the floor in front of the glass door to her cell and looks into the camera, which captures her through the glass. She lifts an imaginary remote and clicks through a series of vignettes, each of which focuses on the inhabitant of a neighboring cell, and each of which uses an entertainment trope to encode a past trauma: Nicky Nichols delivers jokes in a dog outfit while discussing being "interfered with" as a pup; Freida Berlin alludes to her suicide attempt while doing card tricks with the king of hearts, "the suicide king." Each cell is a separate channel, and we are aligned with Suzanne's eyes as we surf them (fig. 2.5). *Orange* typically aligns us with the WASPy Piper Chapman; she is the drama's "Trojan horse," as Jenji Kohan put it, the white persona through which the drama smuggles in a more interesting cast of Black and brown

CHAPTER 2

2.5. *Orange Is the New Black*: Solitary TV.

characters. But in this hallucinatory sequence, the camera aligns us with Suzanne, in what the drama considers an act of blackface: as Freida does her tricks, she unearths the king of spades and declares, "Kind king of David wears his spade suit." Penned by Kohan (from the tribe of David), the drama here puts on a suit of darker skin, Crazy Eyes'. A version of that darkening is of course implicit in the drama's title: Chapman's orange prison suit marks her confinement with a heavily nonwhite prison population; long associated with Protestantism, orange now captures the racialization of downwardly mobile WASPs. The drama's title might simply have been "White Is the New Black."

Looking through Suzanne's Crazy Eyes, the audience sees the supermax and even Litchfield as a "stand-in," as Botwin puts it when speaking of Freud, for a different space. *Orange* is fascinated with a range of similar substitutions. Season 3 finds two inmates testing a hypothesis that any verb and noun when placed in the right combination can refer to sex: "I'd butter your toast. I'd feed her dog. I'd zip his sweater. See? It doesn't matter what you say, as long as it's 'I'd blank your blank.' " Not all inmates are able to think figuratively. Later, during a Wicca ceremony, a priestess intones, "And ye shall be free from slavery. And as a sign that ye be really free ye shall be naked in thy rites." A delighted inmate begins to undress, and the priestess says, "Wait, don't do that. It's metaphorical naked" (3.1).

Nor can all the guards think figuratively: inmate Nicky Nichols tries to speak in code to John Luschek about drugs. "I'm speaking allegorically," she says. He replies, confused, "You want to talk about Al Gore?" (3.2).

Orange speaks allegorically in the next episode, as one of the guards offers an improv class as therapy. "I took acting at high school," enthuses an inmate, "and we learned about masks, musicals, and chlamydia dell'arte." During the class, Piper and Alex Vause work through relationship issues by pretending to be a consumer and owner in a fruit market. The skit's premise is that Alex is returning a "piece of bruised fruit." After an inmate objects, "You're never supposed to start an improv with a transaction," the skit begins:

Alex: This fruit is defective . . . it's all nasty and bruised up.

Piper: Well, it's organic fruit. So if you don't like my produce, you can take your business elsewhere. . . . It's fruit, so get over it.

Alex: I am over it.

Piper: You're obviously not. You're not over anything.

Alex: You get what you pay for. When are you gonna realize that you don't get to do whatever you want because it makes you feel good?

Piper: . . . Do you think that this is what I want? To be here in this, um in this grocery store? I'm sorry I sold you the fruit. And, yes, fine. I will admit it. I knew it was bad. I did. But I wanted my power back, too. Because I wanted you back. Because I missed you and I missed your patronage. So, I sold you bad fruit so you would come back into my store. And I know it was wrong, and I'm sorry. But I'm also not sorry, because it is so good to see you, customer. Would you, maybe, like another piece of fruit? (3.3)

The substitutions are straightforward. Alex is angry that Piper contrived to have her sent back to prison so that the two could be together. Returning bruised fruit thus amounts to a rejection of the sexual intimacy that Piper extends after her return. But in so theatrically likening prison intimacy to a market exchange, the scene both anticipates Litchfield's transformation later in the season into a market-mediated institution and suggests that, even before that change, Litchfield is an indirectly market-mediated theatrical space. In the improv sketch, the drama wonders where exactly the characters are, if not "um, in this prison." They are in a space akin to the tunnel beneath Nancy's maternity store, I'd suggest, insofar as prison serves *Orange* as a self-consciously allegorical and even televisual space that draws forth similarities between first world domestic labor and third world informal labor. *Orange* is not quite as faithful to the black-market melodrama as *Weeds* is; but it's animated by similar problems.

When we see through Suzanne's eyes, we encounter a different answer to the question of where, figuratively, the inmates are. The answer—a family home—is surprisingly familiar to quality TV. On HBO's *Oz*, the Oswald State Correction Facility causes inmates to feel both as if "there's no place like home" and that there's no refuge from "families," which, narrator Augustus Hill exclaims, "determine who we are, determine what we're not. How we relate to other people is based on the way we relate to the members of our families. No wonder the world's so fucked up" (2.5). An exile from but also an extension of the fucked-up families that drove inmates to crime, *Oz* is a nightmarish mirror of the heteronormative family. In the second episode, an inmate prepares to marry remotely, by enacting the ceremony on both sides of the prison's walls. "While you'll be here," a guard explains, "and your fiancée will be at your local Baptist church, you'll both be exchanging vows at the same time and each of you will have someone standing in for the other person" (1.2). That is true of *Oz* generally, which like *Orange* uses prison to double or stand in for domestic life. *The Walking Dead* conflates prisons and domestic spaces more literally. The second season ends with the dead overrunning the plantation-like southern manse in which Rick Grimes and his band of survivors have been holed up. This drama's dead are always incipiently Black, racist specters of what drives the white family's downward mobility and what the white family risks becoming. Fleeing from their overrun farm, it is as if the band is both driven off by freed slaves and themselves those slaves. They head north in a perverse, white-flight inversion of the

Great Migration, finding their way, appropriately enough, to a prison. Only this prison does not subjugate racialized surplus populations—as US prisons do. It protects an extended family and its soon-to-be-born white child from those populations. "Baby will be here in a few days," Rick says. "Time to get the house in order," replies the pregnant Lori. They do so in a cell block. "Home sweet home" (3.1), says Glenn Rhee, as the team enters it for the first time. They linger for as long as they can, before continuing their odyssey to Washington, DC, which they will seem never to reach.

Rectify works a similarly southern gothic terrain, paralleling Daniel Holden's life in prison and his life at home in overt ways. And as we'll see in the last chapter, *Queen Sugar*, also set in the South, chronicles not simply the daily struggles of released inmate Ralph Angel Bordelon, but also the looming transformation of the Bordelon sugar farm into a prison. For this African American family, there is no safe space outside of prison, not because domestic life is tedious, but because even private property proves to be subject to manipulation by the carceral state. And then there is *The Handmaid's Tale*, which, if not about an actual prison, does shed considerable light on *Orange*.

In addition to sharing an actor (Samira Wiley), the two dramas share with *Oz* flashbacks that move from extreme to everyday versions of family life. In *The Handmaid's Tale*, flashbacks take us from the fundamentalist state of Gilead to life in Boston before the coup that created it. The flashbacks romanticize Boston (if we could go back to the good old days, we would appreciate the freedoms capitalism gave us) and temporarily release June from an oppressive home, which is more horrific than is typically the case in the genre: she is ritualistically raped to provide a wealthy couple a child. But June has a second life, as a secret agent in the resistance. That second life does not reestablish separate spheres, as secret lives in black-market melodramas typically seem to do, so much as it fights the severe reimposition of those spheres. But like many black-market melodramas, *The Handmaid's Tale* is a white persecution fantasy. The drama subjects its white lead to the forced surrogacy common to the slave plantation system.[54] And for Sophie Lewis, *Handmaid* "neatly reproduces a wishful scenario at least as old as feminism itself. Cisgender womanhood, united without regard to class, race, or colonialism, can blame all its woes on evil religious fundamentalists with guns." At the same time, "supposedly nonracist, universalist concerns about quality of life slip, easily, into competitive latter-day imperial worries about being overtaken [and] overrun"—by brown migrants from nondeveloped nations who procreate faster than do white citizens.[55] (Relatedly, for Mies, "the rhetoric on integrating Third World women into development means precisely this: obfuscating women's work as producers for capital by defining them as housewives and not as workers, and by emphasizing their behavior as 'breeders' of unwanted consumers.")[56]

Where June is confined in a home that feels like prison, Litchfield's inmates are confined in a prison that often feels like home (if not in a good way). "You're home" (1.3), Red Reznikov tells Nicky after she returns from solitary confinement. "It's like family" (2.3), Lorna Morello Muccio tells a new inmate. Daya, Flaca Gonzalez, and Maria Ruiz debate whether inmates really do form a family (3.3). Sometimes, as with Aleida Diaz and Vee Parker, biological and adoptive mothers serve time alongside their daughters. Sometimes, prison provides a surrogate family that rectifies a familial deficiency, as with Nicky, who finds in Red the caring mother she never had. And *Orange* can be quite sentimental when depicting inmates coming together in nonnormative, queer families that are often more sustaining and caring than the families they knew on the outside. But Litchfield families are precisely not "families we choose," in Kath Weston's memorable phrase. Inmates don't choose to be in Litchfield and they generally join groups because they need protection. Typically, incarceration echoes an earlier imprisonment, which is why the flashbacks feel less a release from claustrophobia than another version of it. Litchfield subjects its inmates to an only more explicit version of the abuse they received in their families. Growing up, Poussey Washington suffered a stern military father; at Litchfield, the unforgiving Desmond Piscatella, chief prison guard, causes her death. Often, biological mothers deliver the formative abuse. Yvonne Griggs notes both the "foundational" importance *Orange* gives "prison 'families' or 'tribes'" and the drama's "ongoing preoccupation with mother/daughter relationships." *Orange* is a recognizable "family melodrama," she adds, because of its handling of these often abusive relationships.[57]

If Litchfield replicates formative family dynamics, it also evokes the housework to which many of the women were subject. Inmates cook and clean in "institutional support" jobs that echo the domestic work they did on the outside. "Who else is going to do it?" says Morello to Piper after they meet. "We do everything around here" (1.1). Morello points out Claudette Pelage, who ran a maid service before killing a client. "Watch out for that one," she says. Sometimes, inmates commit with gusto to support jobs, as do Red and Gloria Mendoza, who battle for control of the kitchen. But mainly, they're trapped in a nightmarish version of the housework they did on the outside. That's evocatively the case for Alex. Nicky walks into the laundry room with Piper, where Alex folds sheets. Nicky pretends to be a repairman making house calls; Alex pretends to be a southern homemaker. "My husband isn't home," she says, "and he's got the checkbook. Hopefully there's some way I can pay you?" (1.8). Housework and sex work converge, in a personal way: Alex's mother worked four jobs raising her; we don't know what the jobs were, but we know that Alex becomes a drug smuggler to avoid her mother's fate. Reality now intrudes. Piper starts fixing a dryer as Alex tells her they're forced to launder not just the inmates' but the guards' clothes. Trying to help, Alex climbs in to work on the dryer from the inside. Piper steps away and Tiffany Doggett locks Alex inside (fig. 2.6).

Where exactly is Alex trapped? Inside a dryer, for one: we need not pretend that, in addition to whatever else it might be, the dryer is not a dryer, or the prison is not a prison. If *Orange* often suggests prison is more than it seems, it still renders its environments with a straightforward visual realism. And while the melodrama hardly treats prison with the seriousness it deserves, it does sporadically communicate prison's crushing literalism: no matter its own flights of figurative fancy, the inmates themselves remain immobilized behind bars. When turning to other programs, it's worth keeping housework's literalism in mind, even while noting how frequently it becomes allegorically laden. At stake in the black-market melodrama is the massive growth of reproductive rather than productive labor at all levels of a deindustrializing

CHAPTER 2

economy. But even as housework figures that growth, it must still be taken for what it is. In *The Americans*, Philip and Elizabeth set up their spy center in the laundry room. In *Weeds*, Botwin makes hash in a laundry. In *Breaking Bad*, White hides his cash in his laundry room, which he uses to clean his blood-stained money (fig. 2.7). Later, he launders his money another way, via a car wash, converting ill-gotten cash into taxable income. Money laundering represents both White's conversion of informal into formal gains, and, implicitly, the melodrama's reciprocal, allegorical conversion of mundane legal into fantastical illegal work. That conversion is implicit in the fact that when cooking for Fring, White toils beneath a laundry; in *Breaking Bad*, meth production is thinly disguised reproduction. And throughout the genre, laundries are emblems of the genre's own allegorical launderings—its capacity to change one thing into another while disguising or cleaning evidence of that conversion. And yet laundries are also literal sites of the specifically gendered reproductive labor thus laundered.

Better to say, then, that Alex's confinement in the dryer figures nested imprisonments, some of which are enforced by metal and concrete, some of which are not. Litchfield holds her, but she is also imprisoned by "gender," "family," and decisively, labor regimes that relegate certain kinds of bodies to certain kinds of work. These nested imprisonments are

2.6. *Orange Is the New Black*: Laundry lockup.

120

2.7. *Breaking Bad*: How not to launder money.

not incidentally related: the drama can allegorize "home" with "prison" because both spaces house coerced labor external to the wage relation but nevertheless integral to capitalist accumulation. TV itself is another containing space that matters here. *Orange* suggests that Alex is trapped in a staged enactment—she seems, in looking out from her dryer, to be looking out from a TV. However earnestly *Orange* treats prison, and however intelligently it links incarceration specifically to a gendered division of labor generally, it cannot resist conceiving of its space reflexively, such that Litchfield's transformation into a for-profit facility tells the story of the program's own genesis as a quality melodrama.

Private Prisons, Black Markets, and the Quality Turn

The United States has the world's largest prison population, at just under 2.2 million.[58] The NAACP estimates that African Americans and Hispanics make up 32 percent of the nation's population but 56 percent of its prison population. African American men make up 34 percent of the male prison population and are incarcerated at roughly five times the rate of white men, while experiencing massive sentencing disparities for similar crimes. African American men represent about 12.5 percent of the nation's illicit drug users, for example, but 33 percent of those incarcerated for such use, while serving consistently longer sentences. Women make up roughly 9 percent of the US prison population and Black women are imprisoned at roughly twice the rate of white women.[59] In general, according to the Sentencing Project, the number of female inmates in US prisons rose 1.5 times faster than the number of male inmates; an increase of 646 percent between 1980 and 2010.[60]

These numbers indicate the staggering scale of US mass incarceration. But they tell only part of the story. They don't, for example, explain the prison system's relation to the economy as a whole. Prison is no more a space apart from capitalism than is the nuclear family. Rather, it is an "internal colony," to recall Mies on the first world family, that for centuries has been integral to capitalist accumulation. As Genevieve LeBarron notes, "Prison labor systems have instantiated shifts in power and production during at least three crucial moments of capitalist history—all times of considerable ferment in the conditions, power, and composition of working populations—with devastating consequences for labor in the so-called free market." By "compelling deviants and the racialized poor into deeply unfree forms of labor exploitation, prison labor has underpinned and reinforced the racialized and class-based social relations central to specific forms of capitalist order."[61]

The early nineteenth-century prison-contracting system produced the first for-profit prisons in the US. "Through the contract system," LeBarron writes, "states sold their property right in convicts' labor to some of the period's largest corporations in exchange for substantive revenues—often up to 150 percent the costs of carceral administration." Faced with brutal punishment if they didn't work, "inmates toiled for private companies who built factories inside of state and federal prisons." As in all phases of US prison history, the impact of prison labor extended far beyond those imprisoned. For R. Petchesky, the "penal-social laboratory" of the contracting system shaped "the essential function of management in industrial capitalism"; "the total economic, spiritual, moral, and physical domination of laborers required by the factory system found its prototype in prison industry." More basically, prison labor kept total labor costs down, both because it was cheaper than ostensibly free labor and because capital used the prospect of imprisonment to discipline vulnerable populations into accepting poor wages for poor conditions.[62] In this, the convict lease system was unparalleled. In effect legalizing slavery for those convicted of crimes, the Thirteenth Amendment inaugurated a second system of prison labor in the South, where states leased Black male prisoners to capitalists who frequently worked the men to death. Those convicts were both cheaper and more productive than wage laborers: LeBarron estimates they did between 30 and 50 percent more work per hour than free labor.[63] In addition to being massively profitable, the lease system extended racial subjugation by other means; as such it was only a particularly naked example of how US mass incarceration has terrorized Black men above all with arbitrary captivity and death.

The New Deal ended the for-profit use of prison labor for a while. But at the dawn of the neoliberal revolution, for-profit prison labor returned with a vengeance. The Prison Industry Enhancement Act and the Percy Amendment, both passed in 1979, allowed private companies to move production into prisons (175 have done so since). And by 1983, it was legal to require federal inmates to work forty hours a week. This "acceleration of unfree labor," LeBarron notes, "has not been disconnected from the overall functioning of the economy but rather has been deeply imbricated in the very production of it." That's been powerfully the case since 1979: "Just as the convict lease system violently entrenched a social order based on white supremacy into the post-emancipation money economy, and the industrial prison contract system disciplined human bodies into the forms of factory labor that were fundamental for the new industrial capitalist system," the state now uses private prisons especially "to coercively impose the forms of labor discipline necessary to the neoliberal order."[64] Heather Ann Thompson adds that "by the dawn of the twenty-first century, federal prisons had come to rival the nation's largest private corporations in terms of the sheer number of products manufactured and services offered." Those prisons are "the new American sweatshops—low-cost workplaces where employers could exploit a contained and more docile workforce and avoid the tariff and transportation issues of sending their manufacturing or service tasks to China or India."[65]

In 2016, 8.5 percent of the US prison population was in private prisons. From 2000 to 2016, that number increased five times as fast as the total prison population (over the same timeframe, the number of people detained in private immigration facilities increased by 442 percent).[66] Conditions in these prisons are almost invariably worse than in state institutions. The company that takes over in *Orange*, the Management and Correction Corporation (MCC), is a thinly disguised Corrections Corporation of America (now known as CoreCivic), which is the largest US prison corporation and which, according to the Sentencing Project, "manage[s] over half of the private prison contracts in the United States with combined revenues of $3.5 billion as of 2015."[67] In 2018, a *Time Magazine* reporter went undercover in a CoreCivic facility and was told, during an outbreak of violence, "Our job was simply to shout the words 'stop fighting,' thus protecting the company's liability and avoiding any potentially costly harm to ourselves. Our [real] job, after all, was to 'deliver value to our shareholders.'"[68]

Orange's tone changes after MCC's takeover in season 3. It becomes darker and more somber. But it's not the case that the melodrama becomes more politically pointed. Its intermittent earnestness notwithstanding, *Orange* does not on the whole render either state-run or for-profit mass incarceration with real seriousness. On the other hand, it does use MCC's takeover to offer a sophisticated account of the genre with which it would affiliate—the black-market melodrama. Privatizing the prison becomes an occasion for increasingly self-conscious generic positionings, above all, as the program explores the black markets that grow up around the prison's newly available wage labor. Specifically, MCC's takeover allows *Orange* to announce its debts to earlier black-market melodramas, like *Breaking Bad* above all.

There have been women-in-prison films since before the Hays Code, and rarely have they taken prison seriously. As Griggs notes, the films and later TV programs that made up the genre were typically low-budget sexploitation or soft-core pornography that subjected "fallen" innocent women to titillating sexual abuse. She adds that, however much *Orange* parodies the genre, it is as faithful to it (and melodrama generally) as it is to the Piper Kerman memoir on which it is based. The genre's stock characters become more nuanced, and rather than focus on hardened criminals, *Orange* takes up low-level offenders serving time, typically, because of a drug-related offense. And rather than focus on a dominated innocent or anticipate a "return to the heteronormative familial fold," it produces queer relationships more varied and sympathetic than are typically found in women-in-prison dramas. But, Griggs adds, *Orange* is in other ways utterly recognizable as a women-in-prison story, for example, in how it divides Litchfield into families headed by a symbolic mother, each of whom runs a black-market business: Red, Vee, Maria Diaz, etc. Each is a "'mother figure' whose leadership of the tribe is predicated on more than personal gain"—as is generically typical. Piper is an exception; her business uses "a purely capitalist model . . . seldom seen in the genre." As is rarely the case, "Fealty to her criminal enterprise is dependent solely on material reward."[69] Put another way, Piper's atypical racket shadows the directly market-mediated labor that arises within the now for-profit prison.

As a state-run facility, Litchfield houses what *Endnotes* would consider indirectly market-mediated labor. The prison's support jobs are waged ($0.10/hour) but cannot be said to reproduce labor power (unless we understand that labor as sustaining the inmates for labor after their release). But on taking control of Litchfield, MCC begins paying some inmates to sew at $1/hour. The work takes place in the directly market-mediated sphere, broadly conceived, such that prison cooking and cleaning now reproduce labor power. The drama captures that change, as it tracks Red's return to the kitchen, which she secures by offering sexual favors: a woman is robbed of her "currency," she explains, except "one coin . . . the one she was born with. It may be tawdry and demeaning, but if she has to, she will spend it" (3.6). Red offers to spend her coin so she might secure the admittedly limited power that comes from kitchen work. Big house housework and sex work refer to each other, in ways that do and don't accord with Fortunati, for whom housework and sex work are "united, but juxtaposed and interdependent": the former "produces and reproduces" labor power while the latter "sexually reproduces" it.[70] There is no exact equivalent at Litchfield of Fortunati's "fundamental [reproductive] exchange": "between woman and capital, mediated by the male worker."[71] But inmates who receive MCC wages assume new power relative to those who don't, to whom they distribute some of their wages. And when Red returns to the kitchen, she confronts a changed form of labor. MCC has outsourced most of the food preparation; cooking now requires the releasing of sludge from plastic bags. The kitchen's labor has been automated as, say, a premade TV dinner automates dinner preparation. Indeed, we might think of the sludge as a figure for the socially necessary labor time that mediated the food's waged production—or, perhaps, for the labor power that kitchen work can now be said to reproduce. In this spirit, as MCC takes over, Daya prepares to deliver a child, as if to figure what Fortunati calls the "*commodity* contained *within* the individual: that labor power which as capacity for production has exchange value."

What I would stress, however, is that the arrival of for-profit labor all at once produces an allegorically complex informal economy. MCC pays inmates a wage to produce intimate apparel for the Whispers Corporation (CoreCivic used prison labor to produce intimate apparel for Victoria's Secret). But no sooner does undergarment production start than Piper begins to smuggle panties from the factory floor and hire inmates to wear them, so she can sell them for a premium on the outside to men who want to smell female prisoners. "I need your vag sweat," she tells an inmate. Sweatshop labor produces at its margins a different kind of sweating, which figures in turn a variety of Red's sex work: Piper's employees spend their "one coin" as workers whose sexual odors earn payment in ramen noodle spice packets (now in demand because prison food has become flavorless). Heterogenous work arrangements compound, in ways familiar to black-market melodramas. Wanting new workers, Piper stands upon a table and proclaims:

> Sisters! We may be incarcerated, but our panties will travel the world, and in that way, long after we are gone, our smell, our smell will linger in some gas station in Toronto, in some office cubicle in Tokyo, and in that

way we are known, and in that way we are remembered. Do you want to be remembered? Then sweat profusely and fart with abandon and make a reek. Make a reek my sisters! Make a reek to last one thousand years! (3.8)

Piper evokes a pride in craftsmanship and a hope for immortality typically associated with art and, indeed, she might as well be speaking directly to the drama's writer's room. Her panties are what her brother Carl calls "premium artisanal shit" (3.12). And Piper's business, Felonious Spunk, allegorizes "premium artisanal" TV production, while disguising it in blackface.

Piper's racket is not the only one in Litchfield, even if, as Griggs says, it's the only one run on "a purely capitalist model." More importantly, it is the only one that exports goods beyond the prison; the others import contraband. From the start, Chapman is a stand-in for the program's writers, who sell salacious prison stories to an up-market audience. In season 2, she smuggles out stories to NPR. Yet it's not until season 3 that that reflexivity finds common cause with the gangsterism requisite to black-market melodramas, when she smuggles out soiled panties that point to the drama's own salacious "whispers." Her workers' reeks concretize both underground labor and the "quality" that distinguishes *Orange*, not just from the generic—the too general—but also from low-end women-in-prison stories. *Orange* thus takes itself to be an underground artisanal product dependent on the formal economy to which it is an informal alternative. As we will see in the next chapter, *Breaking Bad* repeatedly analogizes itself to White's artisanal meth as a high-end elicit good you can't find on ad-supported TV . And as Chapman starts her business, *Orange* begins referencing *Breaking Bad*. Piper's personality changes radically. She becomes ruthless, dumps Alex, takes up with a hot coworker, and gets a tattoo, "Trust No Bitches." Assessing it, an inmate tells her, "You are not Walter White yet" (3.13). Chapman won't be fully there until next season when, hardened and indifferent to anything but profit, she falls in with white supremacists (White works with Uncle Jack's neo-Nazis). Piper's white-power workforce wears her intimate apparel (only Aryan reeks will do) and protects her from rival gangs. But so callous to her employees does Chapman become that her bodyguard gives her up to the Dominicans, who hold her down and brand her arm with a swastika. Now she is Walter White.

If we're feeling charitable, we might read that branding as an acknowledgment of the white supremacy implicit in *Orange*'s decision to focalize its narrative through Chapman. We don't need crazy eyes to view those stories as disturbingly exploitative. But it's more likely that the branding is a version of the insider baseball that suffuses *Breaking Bad*. In *Oz*'s pilot, an Aryan Brother tells his cellmate, "I'm gonna brand you myself"; you are "my livestock," he adds, "your ass belongs to me." The cellmate belongs to the Aryan as the characters belong to HBO: the drama's title sequence shows a needle tattooing the show's logo onto what is presumably an inmate's arm, as if to liken the carceral ownership of network and penitentiary. Piper's swastika suggests a similarly oppressive corporate overlord. But Red quickly rebrands her, adding four bars to the swastika and thus transforming it into a window. The window looks like Microsoft's logo, but the tech giant probably matters less than tech per se, and certainly less than the color here at stake: originally Chapman's antagonist, but now her protector, Red evokes Netflix, whose brand, of course, is bold red. *Orange* was made by Lionsgate Television, but was rebranded a Netflix Original (it was the third Netflix program to be thus billed, in 2013, and it was the longest-running Netflix Original when it ended in 2019). "All the information in the world is in wires, right?" (2.7), an inmate asks in season 2. Chapman's family nickname, "Pipes," suggests the conveyance of those wires (while evoking the tunnels in *The Sopranos* and *Weeds*), just as her business suggests Netflix's capacity to move product through them. Piper sells her panties over the internet. "The World Wide Web, man, it's some fast shit," says Carl, as they discuss how quickly the panties sell. "I hear it's the latest thing" (3.9), Piper replies.

CHAPTER 3

AMC's White-Collar Supremacy

Breaking Bad, Mad Men, *and* Halt and Catch Fire

In the last season of *The Sopranos*, AJ Soprano explains to his father that he hopes upon returning from a tour of duty in Afghanistan to fly helicopters for Donald Trump. The offhand remark has since seemed prescient, for while *The Sopranos* appeared in the final days of Bill Clinton's administration and later struck many as a fittingly dark expression of George W. Bush's 9/11 presidency, still later it seemed to anticipate Trump's presidency. As pundits called out Trump's mafia leadership style, critics noted that he and Soprano were each an "unsettled white man raging against the erosion of his power," as Brett Martin put it in a *Vanity Fair* article titled "How Tony Soprano Paved the Way for Donald Trump." And as the Trump presidency ended, Joanna Weiss added in *Politico*, "These past five years" were like "a prestige cable drama, the kind built around a powerful antihero" who was "simmering with rage." Viewers had binged Trump as they had these dramas: his "fiercest hate-watchers and biggest fans followed his moves and tweets the way addicted viewers do: incapable of looking away, driven to rehash and recount every sordid moment."[1]

Weiss thought the endings of these dramas might predict "how the Trump show ends." Martin saw admonitions: "TV's difficult men didn't invent Trump, but he is what they were warning us about." *Breaking Bad* might be said to have issued a particularly clear warning: its aptly named lead lives in a border state and allies with neo-Nazis in a desperate bid to restore the privilege that he feels is his right. But Martin's formulation is too self-satisfied by half: it assumes that this implicitly liberal drama wanted to warn "us," smart appreciators of smart TV, about an outcome we might have prevented, whether by dint of our brains and good intentions or, even, a decision to watch another kind of TV. In point of fact, *Breaking Bad* implicates its white liberal viewers in Walt's suppurating resentments by tapping into a specific class animus: that highly educated technical-managerial elites no longer enjoyed their pride of place in a fading US Empire.

Some thought *Breaking Bad* conservative right off the bat. David Segal dubbed Vince Gilligan, its creator, "TV's first true red-state auteur" because of his emphasis on personal choice and the battle between right and wrong. Jonah Goldberg said the drama deserved "special respect from conservatives," because it detailed "the fragility of civilization" and the need for "binding dogmas to constrain us even when our intellects or appetites try to seduce us to a different path."[2] These are useful correctives. But conservatives who hold forth about right and wrong or civilization do not really matter to Trump's Republican Party. Bad-faith defenses of US industry and the working class do, and though written before the 2016 election, Malcolm Harris's "Walter White Supremacy" proves apt. "Besides the War on Terror," he writes,

> there aren't a lot of other scenarios in which it's possible to root for the particularly American cocktail of meritocracy, the little guy, the good guy, and the white guy, all at the same time. Put it this way: A show about a small American toy manufacturer laying waste to the villainous and inferior Mexican industry would be such a transparent and reactionary play on post-NAFTA anxieties that no luxury advertiser would dare sponsor it.[3]

Harris is right that White's story might have been told as one of US industrial might regained. As he battles Gustav Fring and a Mexican cartel, White plays out a fantasy in which American manufacturing trounces overseas competitors. While doing so, he dons a symbolic blue collar. But White's black-market good, methamphetamine, is not an industrial staple. On the contrary, as we will see, the drama considers it a version of White's cancer, insofar as it captures the metastasis of reproductive service work throughout the US economy. *Breaking Bad* is indeed an allegory about the fate of American manufacturing. But even as it confirms deindustrialization's inevitability, it peels back White's ersatz working-class resentments and discovers, beneath them, a seething cauldron of conflicting impulses and identifications. If one of *Breaking Bad*'s achievements is the subtlety with which it captures antagonisms between capital and labor, another is the intelligence with which it reveals intraclass affinities between affluent white elites that fancy themselves fundamental political antagonists.

Breaking Bad is a "working-class revenge fantasy," Travis Linnemann suggests, when White demonizes Elliott and Gretchen Schwartz, his ex-partners in Gray Matter Technologies, the biotech startup he left years ago because, as Gilligan has it, he felt "inferior" to Gretchen, "the girl he was about to marry" who "was so very wealthy and came from such a prominent family."[4] In the last episode, he leaves the couple in terror. Create a trust for my children after I am dead, he says, or one day,

> when you're going for a walk in Santa Fe or Manhattan or Prague, wherever, and you're talking about your stock prices without a worry in the world . . . you'll hear the scrape of a footstep behind you, and before you can turn around, pop! Ah, darkness. Cheer up, beautiful people. This is where you get to make it right. (5.16)

White is not himself a kale-eating beautiful person, he implies; he is a red-blooded white American in ways that these effete cosmopolitans are not. "Ah, darkness" indeed: as his season 5 alliance with Uncle Jack makes clear, White is a neo-Nazi manqué, Uncle Jack's double, pitted against a decadent miscegenation; "Gray Matter" signals both scientific knowledge work (brain tissue) and a corresponding racial ambiguity. It derives from a combination of "White" and "Schwartz" (black), the last name of Walt's original partner. Walt is bitter because Gretchen, with her German name, ends up with Schwartz, who is played by a diminutive

CHAPTER 3

3.1. *Breaking Bad*: White supremacy doppelgängers.

Jewish actor. *Breaking Bad* ends with White killing Jack's supremacists. But he has belonged among them all along, as he has dreamed of paradise regained (fig. 3.1).

If anti-Semitism is white nationalism's atavistic expression, violence toward Black and brown low-wage workers is its bleeding edge. Gretchen and Elliot don't bear the brunt of Walt's racial animus. He wreaks havoc on the Latino populations toward which he feels himself falling.[5] When he's not killing Latinos, he's getting them fired. White is as seemingly well intentioned toward Hugo Archilleya in season 1 as he is to Fring's undocumented laundry workers in the fourth; but he costs them their jobs all the same. He is indifferent to their fate; Curtis Marez notes that *Breaking Bad* "emerges from a world" in which white men, working class or not, "are used to commanding disposable raced and gendered migrant labor." But white men can no longer do so—certainly Walter cannot. Forced into moonlighting at the local car wash, he fears he has become equally disposable. And so he "displaces the conventionally Latino narcocorrido protagonist," as Marez has it, "by becoming a better Latino gangster than the Latino gangsters": he must replace Fring, so that he can command low-wage workers, rather than become one.[6]

In fundamental ways, Walt's whiteness tells us all we need to know about the sense of entitlement that drives that project. He thinks he deserves to command because he's white. But the drama's canny class dynamics complexify that racial privilege. White concatenates seemingly distinct class formations only to reveal key affinities between them. In part, he codes not simply a "little guy" factory owner, as Harris has it, but the kind of small family business owner who would figure prominently in Trump's GOP. As Melinda Cooper argues, "Trump projected the image of the plain-speaking businessman who had started off 'small' and made it 'big' in the non-college-educated world of construction." In point of fact, the GOP's new populism embraced small and big alike: "The family-based capitalism that stormed the White House along with Trump stretches from the smallest of family businesses to the most rambling of dynasties and crucially depends on the alliance between the two." Nevertheless, the small family business proved essential to the party's "binding dogma." Its "natural labor hierarchies and personalized property relations stood in contrast to the suspect anonymity of the modern corporation" and lent warrant to a counterfactual embrace of "blue collar," which term, Cooper notes, came to designate "an aspirational small business owner rather than a wage worker—a slippage that helps explain the strangely capacious understanding of the 'working class' that circulates on the American right today."[7] We might add that family businesses so effectively nurture blue-collar fantasies in part because they allow entrepreneurs to conceive of themselves as committed to familial reproduction rather than profit. Even when rich, White casts his pursuit of millions as an effort to ensure his family's survival.

At the same time, it's not only as a family business owner that White imagines himself allied to (if not exactly a member of) the working class. *Breaking Bad* draws out the affinity between "the natural labor hierarchies" at stake in family businesses (in which CEOs manage workers as fathers do their families) and the white-collar paternalism at the heart of the more impersonal "modern corporation" (in which highly educated elites manage workers ostensibly unable on their own to perceive and pursue their true interests). Integral to each ideology, the melodrama suggests, is an employer's or manager's bad-faith identification with the workers over whom s/he has power, which identification aims to transform that power from the stuff of raw exploitation into a benevolent and caring stewardship. It is when superimposing these two paternalisms that the drama most effectively implicates its ostensibly liberal viewers.

White's frantic rush to accumulate resources adequate not simply to his health care but to his children's education after he dies struck a broad chord, one that cut across classes and educational backgrounds. The pathos of providing for one's family invariably does. But it's nevertheless essential that White belongs to a scientific elite that would later fancy itself Trump's greatest antagonist. If *Breaking Bad* anticipates key aspects of Trump's appeal, it does so by chronicling the fortunes of a Cal Tech PhD whose doctoral work contributed to a Nobel Prize. White thinks he deserves his riches because he's flat out smarter than those around him and because there are no good salaried alternatives to those riches. An X-ray crystallographer devoted to pure research, then briefly involved in a startup, and later a teacher in a failing public school, he represents knowledge workers confronted with seemingly stark options: make it big as an entrepreneur or fall into the swelling ranks of a precarious underclass. White makes his choice. But he does so yearning for options that are no longer on The table.

Jesse Pinkman is the key to those yearnings. Walt needs his blue-collar bona fides, which Pinkman supplies. White's first batches of meth are white, but quickly become powder blue. Pinkman facilitates the change, if only as an object of White's uplift. The uplift is as comically absurd as it is revealingly contradictory. Pinkman is not working class in any obvious way. He's from a wealthy family. And if his off-white last name registers a feminization, his speech and dress register a corresponding racial hybridity. In part, White stays white by dominating a pink that feels too close to brown. Still, Jesse is essential to White's counterfactual amalgam of white and blue. Walt imagines himself defending Jesse's interests, as a father would a wayward son. As he does, his commitment to natural labor hierarchies bleeds into a different kind of paternalism. If *Breaking Bad* is a working-class revenge fantasy, it is also a working-class rescue fantasy, in which White saves Jesse from poverty and bleaches him clean, working by his side as an equal. We are the same, he says to him, saved by our dedication to science and the job. And in the third season, as he toils with Jesse In Fring's superlab, manipulating heavy machinery and making a magnificent salary, he appears content, as if for the first time. This is the life for which he's longed; would that he could inhabit these upper-middle rungs forever! He will become a proper capitalist, he later tells himself, running his own business in the final season, only because he must: Fring schemed his replacement with cheaper labor. Still, in an unguarded moment, White acknowledges his companionate idyll cannot last for other reasons. "I've lived too long," he tells Jesse; he had passed the "perfect moment" (3.10) to die.

He means he's missed his chance to be remembered well by family. But the line also suggests it's too late to turn back the clock to a moment when scientists and engineers labored alongside industrial workers on behalf of a state-sponsored national project. That alliance had been long in the making. It was implicit in the promise extended to the proletariat by the bourgeoisie at the start of the second industrial revolution, that efficiency, positivism, and rationality would deliver ever higher standards of living. Organized labor embraced that promise after the 1930s and pinned its hopes on modernization, even as the New Deal and Great Society deployed a "new" "professional-managerial" or "technical-managerial" class of experts to safeguard working-class interests (while disciplining workers on behalf of capital, Barbara Ehrenreich adds).[8] In many ways, these terms better describe White than "white collar," which I use nevertheless to register of his incipient white nationalism. The crucial point is that, even as he commits with vengeance to a right-wing vision of family capitalism, White longs for the class coalition that cemented the Keynesian state's "compromise toward the left," as Gérard Duménil and Dominique Lévy have it.[9]

In addition to longing for the Keynesian state's gender norms, *Breaking Bad* wants us to know that state won the Second World War, which the serial replays. It romances Detroit muscle cars, from its Dodge Charger product placements to its sequel, *El Camino*. And in its last scene, it lends the car industry a new kind of muscle. Ever the technical wizard, Walt has bolted a remote-controlled General Dynamics M60 machine gun to the trunk of his Cadillac DeVille. The rig evokes Detroit's transformation in the early 1940s from "Motor City" into "the Arsenal of Democracy" and allows Walt both to vanquish the Nazis and to liberate Jesse from their nefarious grip.[10] That wish-fulfillment fantasy—in which native ingenuity transforms a famous industrial project and saves the white working class from fascism—hardly restores the moral clarity for which this surprisingly earnest melodrama longs. The Los Alamos National Laboratory looms offstage to recall the specific scientific enterprise on which US power was built. After Walt decides to distribute as well as make meth, he meets his team next to a replica of the atom bomb dropped on Hiroshima. They discuss territorial expansion; White would open new markets by dint of his lethal expertise, as the postwar US state did. But there is no way to restore White's class or the patriarchal nuclear family that attended the bomb's dropping—or for that matter, US manufacturing. There is only lingering illness. Residual radiation from New Mexico test sites looms as a source of Walt's cancer and his son's cerebral palsy.[11]

The first section of this chapter reads *Breaking Bad*'s gender anxieties and allegorical doublings in relation to the lost family wage for which this and all black-market melodramas are implicitly nostalgic. The next reads an extended second season sequence in relation to the long-wave deindustrialization that looms so large in this serial and the genre as a whole. I then explain how the melodrama allegorizes not simply the rise of reproductive service work and scientific cadres within the technical-managerial class, but entertainment industry cadres within that same class. Subsequent sections elaborate the TV writing allegories that characterize AMC serials like *Mad Men* and *Halt and Catch Fire*. That last show returns us to the terms with which we started, as it chronicles the exploits of would-be entrepreneurs who fail haplessly upward into the larger organizations they had hoped to disrupt. In *Halt and Catch Fire*, tech is less a brave New Economy than a deluded one that imagines itself exempt from deindustrialization's generalized declensions. Characters scramble unsuccessfully to harness macroeconomic shifts over which they have no control, while dreaming of becoming their own brands. In this overlooked melodrama, *Breaking Bad*'s agonistic entrepreneurial consciousness becomes an engulfing corporate consciousness, as a cadre of cut-rate Walter Whites embark on one startup after another, hoping to leave their mark, but never quite managing to become more than cogs in the mediocre companies for which they work.

Double the Housework

The first sign of human life in *Breaking Bad* is a pair of pants floating through the air (fig. 3.2). From start to finish, the serial describes White's efforts to wear those pants. "I don't want him dicking you around tonight. You get paid till five, you work till five, no later." These are almost the first words that Skyler speaks to Walt, as he returns from a long day working two jobs. Dicked around by his boss at the car wash, Walt is later dicked around by Skyler, who has her own designs on his time. In bed that evening, she mechanically delivers a hand job while reminding him to paint the nursery. "What did you feel you had to run from?" a hospital psychiatrist later asks White, who has just confessed to having faked a "fugue state" to flee his family. As he answers, he stares at a watercolor of a nineteenth-century sailor rowing out to sea and away from his family: "Doctor, my wife is seven months pregnant with a baby we didn't intend. My fifteen-year-old son has cerebral palsy. I am an extremely overqualified high school chemistry teacher. When I can work, I make $43,700 per year. I have watched all of my colleagues and friends surpass me in every way imaginable and within eighteen months, I will be dead. And you ask why I ran?" (2.3). Alas, poor Walter, the fallen patriarch. Later, he will relax at the end of a hard day and watch a documentary on the elephant, "the largest land animal in all the planet," which "lives in a tightly knit matriarchal society led by the eldest female in the herd" (2.12).

Assessments of the drama's gender anxiety often describe it as the product of political factors. Amanda Lotz, for example, counts *Breaking Bad* as a "male-centered serial" that explores "men and masculinities in an era after substantial, yet incomplete, gains of second-wave feminism and the entrenchment of those gains after their contestation."[12] *Breaking Bad* does represent a crisis in masculinity and White is indeed toxic. But casting that crisis as a response to second-wave feminism simply inverts

CHAPTER 3

3.2. *Breaking Bad*: Who will wear the pants?

the conservative tendency that Cooper finds in Wolfgang Streeck, Luc Boltanski and Eve Chiapello, and Nancy Fraser, all of whom attribute the crisis of the family wage, for example, to second-wave feminism.[13] Laura Renata Martin provides more useful terms when describing deindustrialization's impact on the white working class. For her, working-class nostalgia is often nostalgia for white privilege not because working-class whites are less enlightened than white-collar ones, but because the mid-century manufacturing boom for which Trump voters are implicitly nostalgic employed a division of labor "between, on the one hand, the 'free laborer' . . . who has secured for himself a certain rate of exploitation and become accustomed to wages that allow him to reproduce himself with a certain degree of material comfort; and, on the other hand, the irregular worker whose status as racially or ethnically 'different' both allows him to enter into wage labor on the basis of this difference (as cheaper labor) and makes him expendable and surplus (always the easiest to fire)."[14] White's class and racial entitlements are entwined and inseparable from his longing for the family wage to which neither minoritized men nor women had consistent access.

The division of labor supported by the family wage is at least in theory at odds with the one supported by the family business, in which husband and wife might well work together. And indeed, whether he is working with Skyler or not, White longs for the cleanly separate spheres that the family wage entrenched. He wants a "firewall" between home and work, he says; the two must be kept as distinct as "church and state" (4.6). Toward that end, he is forever clarifying divisions of labor. "You cook, I sell," Jesse tells Walt. "That was the division of labor when we started all this" (2.5). Later, Mike tells Jesse and Walt, "Division of labor: I handle the business" (5.3). He will be the man in their partnership. Most tellingly, Walt says to Skyler, "This is a simple division of labor. I bring in the money and you launder it" (4.7). To be sure, laundering money is part of the family business. But White might just as well have said "spend" instead of "launder," so traditional is his vision, in which he makes the money and Skyler disposes of it. In that sense, he considers her laundering not really labor at all, in just the way that domestic ideology has long considered housework not really labor at all.

White's clarifications feel necessary because the divisions of labor in his household have become profoundly unclear, especially after season 2, when Skyler reenters the workforce and becomes, to all outward appearances, the only source of the family's income. To Walt, those appearances matter, and one reason he cannot answer the question often put him by Skyler—"how much money will be enough?"—is that money alone cannot give him what he wants. When the Whites work up a cover story that allows them to explain why they can pay for Hank's physical therapy, Walt simmers with resentment. "It cannot be blind luck or some imaginary relative who saves us. No, I earned that money, me" (2.11). He's not satisfied when they agree to say he won the money gambling, because the story makes his wealth a speculative windfall rather than something earned making (rather than selling) a product. Even after he begins distributing meth, he insists he produces what his lawyer Saul Goodman calls a "high-margin commodity" (2.11). At one point he stammers, "I—I'm—I manufacture. I am not a dealer" (3.1). Manufacturing meth promises to restore a division of labor in which he alone brings in earned money.

If White's meth production is a version of the sailor's escape, it is also one that, in his mind, restores the separate spheres for which he longs. His secret life ensures work and home will remain distinct—if only for a while. Like Soprano and Botwin before him, he lives two lives, one in each sphere, that become uncanny echoes of each other—which echoing suggests, ultimately, the impossibility of truly distinguishing one sphere from another.

In his public life, White is a mild-mannered and vaguely defeated family man. In his secret life, he is a ruthless gangster who provides for his family. A version of that double life might have been familiar to those who had not seen *The Sopranos* and *Weeds*. Evil twins began to appear on TV in the sixties, on the likes of *Bonanza*, *I Dream of Jeannie*, *Star Trek*, and even *Gilligan's Island*; in high melodramatic fashion, these programs split characters into good and evil components who then confront each other.[15] In the 1980s, evil twins found a home on soap operas like *All My Children*, and by the end of the 1990s, twins and doubles had become a mainstay of quality TV: on *The X-Files*, Dana Scully writes her dissertation on "Einstein's Twin Paradox"; on *Dexter*, Dexter Morgan discovers that the serial killer for whom he has been hunting is his twin; and visually identical versions of the same character appear on *Buffy the Vampire Slayer*, *The Sopranos*, *The United States of Tara*, *Orphan Black*, *Fargo*, *Westworld*, *The Leftovers*, *Mr. Robot*, *The Deuce*, and *Counterpart*, among others. *Twin Peaks* should be credited with transporting soap doubles into quality TV, while tapping into a longer tradition: *Twin Peaks* updates the gothic psychological fable, Len Gutkin notes, which had absorbed allegory's once Manichean moral terms. Released from the mind, and no longer simply aspects of character, as they are in the gothic fable, good and evil roam free as supernatural entities.[16]

Breaking Bad has no supernatural entities, but it is suffused with a gothic uncanniness. After White's diagnosis, and as he begins to cook meth, he tells Jesse, "I am awake" (1.1), as if from the long slumber of his life with Skyler. But by the fifth season, he's urging Jesse to think of their drug exploits as "nothing more than a bad dream" (5.11). Shortly after the finale, fans began speculating that White dies asleep in his car at the start of the last episode, rather than during his flawlessly executed strike against white supremacists. Fueling speculation, Sony Pictures released (and quickly retracted) an alternate ending in which White wakes up from a long dream as the family man Hal from *Malcolm in the Middle* (the role for which Bryan Cranston was previously best known).[17] These theories were more than rote invocations of a well-worn gimmick that appears everywhere from *St. Elsewhere*, *Newhart*, and *Dallas* to *Lost* and *Twin Peaks*. Rather, they were responses to what was all along the uncanniness of White's secret life, which need not be a literal dream to allegorize features of the life he means to escape. This mirroring both echoes and departs from the gothic fable, which Otto Rank described so well. Rank's doppelgänger produces a second self, ultimately, to guarantee immortality. Late Victorian fiction provides ample evidence of Rank's thesis, and *Dr. Jekyll and Mr. Hyde* is particularly apt, if only because it describes a meek chemist who conjures a fearless and brutal double (we are likely meant to hear both "high" and "Hyde" in "Heisenberg").[18] And yet, contra Gutkin's account of *Twin Peaks*, *Breaking Bad* largely empties its doubles of moral freight. To be sure, White the gangster behaves in ways that White the father does not. But the difference between these roles erodes over time; *Breaking Bad* lives in gray areas in which home and work—the former no longer morally superior to the latter—reflect on each other.

White himself provides the best account of his doubling. "The term *chiral*," he tells his bored chemistry class (fig. 3.3),

> derives from the Greek word "hand." The concept here being that, just as your left hand and your right hand are mirror images of one another, right? Identical, and yet opposite, well, so too organic compounds can exist as mirror image forms of one another all the way down at the molecular level. But although they may look the same, they don't always behave the same. For instance . . . Thalidomide. The right-handed isomer of the drug Thalidomide is a perfectly fine good medicine to give to a pregnant woman to prevent morning sickness, but make the mistake of giving that same pregnant woman the left-handed isomer of the drug Thalidomide, and her child will be born with horrible birth defects. Which is precisely what happened in the 1950s. So, chiral, chirality, mirrored images, right? Active, inactive. Good, bad. (1.2)

White at home and White cooking "don't always behave the same," to put it mildly, and it is possible to read the drama, as Gilligan sometimes did,

CHAPTER 3

3.3. *Breaking Bad*: "Identical and yet opposite."

as an account of a virtuous man turned evil ("good, bad"). But viewing Walt's chiral selves in this way misses how similar White's two selves become, which similarity is, in effect, the drama's core subject. Walt finds in Jesse, for example, a surrogate son upon whom he releases reserves of contempt stored up, we speculate, from life with Walter Jr. Indeed, White's "work" involves actively parenting Jesse; in basic ways, his job is the raising (and breaking) of a second son. Walt needs Jesse as worker and son; he can no more do without Jesse's labor than he can do without Jesse's fearful respect, and the tortured intimacy between them that is the drama's most harrowing creation. And so it goes for most of White's black-market activities, which are less alternatives to than versions of his domestic responsibilities, which, fantastically, seem themselves to have caused his cancer.

To wit, White's "two-handed" chiral compound is oriented to mirrored if contradictory forms of reproduction. Thalidomide has two versions, which alternately support and disrupt biological reproduction. The conceit is integral, which is why *Breaking Bad* begins by discovering something growing in Walt as well as in Skyler. Walt's MRI in the pilot recalls Soprano's in *The Sopranos* pilot, but also anticipates Skyler's sonogram in the second episode. His cancer is something like the chiral double of her growing fetus; toward season 2's end, Walt's oncologist cuts the cancer from his body one episode before Skyler's obstetrician delivers her child. That symmetry echoes the feminization captured, for instance, in Jesse's comic "Kanga-Man"; unaware of kangaroo anatomy, he gives his male super-marsupial a pouch. *Breaking Bad* discovers an analogous feminization, and even cancer, all the way up the food chain, as it were. White and Pinkman ultimately learn that in producing meth for Fring they have been working for Madrigal's food division. The drama reaches toward a global transnational to expand its frame of reference, it would seem, but instead everywhere discovers analogous forms of gendered, reproductive labor, broadly construed. Cancer grows in Madrigal's food division, in other words, *as* covert meth production, which is simply a more pronounced blight than are this once-proud manufacturing firm's food services themselves. Our first shot of Madrigal is of a test kitchen. A listless executive who will later kill himself prepares to taste new sauces. He is another version of Kanga-Man. And "Madrigal" itself derives in part from the Latin *matricalis*, for "maternal or primitive," and *matrix*, for "womb."

Analogously, White will seem even as a gangster to do little more than clean, cook, and launder. "For a show set in the dirty world of methamphetamine, *Breaking Bad* is obsessive about cleanliness," notes Harris.[19] In the pilot, White is humiliated when students see him washing

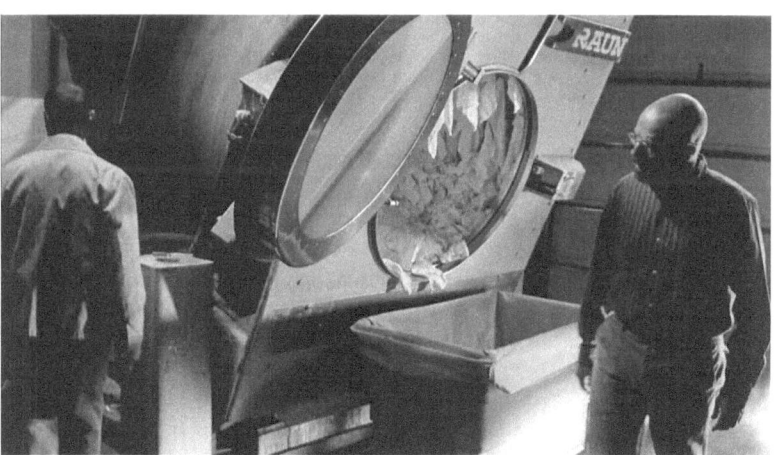

3.4. *Breaking Bad*: Down the rabbit hole.

cars. Later, having shaved his head, he will be known as Mr. Clean (after the Procter & Gamble cleaning product). He is forever scrubbing and cleaning, at home and at work. And, of course, his work is "cooking," in a series of locations that point back to the family home he only seems to leave: first, in a claustrophobic RV; later, beneath a laundry facility; and finally, in toxic family homes being fumigated for pests. The second is the most instructive. White first hides his cash in the wall behind his home's washer and dryer. His money comes from and returns to the laundry room. *Breaking Bad* is fascinated with laundries; it twice captures White in POV shots that place us inside dryers looking out. These shots anticipate the drama's most sustained conjunction of meth production and reproductive labor. Walt enters Fring's laundry facility and stops before a giant dryer. Fring presses a button and the front lowers, revealing a hidden passage (fig. 3.4). The two descend like Alice down her hole, into a state-of-the-art superlab whose location crystallizes the drama's core problem. Fring's lab appears industrial; its heavy equipment glistens. But while White seems to find in the lab an industrial cure to what ails him, he finds only a different version of the reproductive service work from which he would escape.

After gazing in wonder at the equipment, White expresses reluctance to work for Fring, with whom he has spoken only once before, while cooking with him in his kitchen:

> **Walt**: I have made a series of very bad decisions. And I cannot make another one.
>
> **Fring**: Why did you make these decisions?
>
> **Walt**: For the good of my family.
>
> **Fring**: Then they weren't bad decisions. What does a man do, Walter? A man provides for his family.
>
> **Walt**: This cost me my family.
>
> **Fring**: When you have children, you always have family. They will always be your priority, your responsibility, and a man—a man provides.

3.5. *Breaking Bad*: White's daily grind.

> And he does it even when he's not appreciated or respected or even loved. He simply bears up, and he does it because he's a man. (3.5)

Fring sweetens the pot. White will set his own hours; his will be a salary rather than a wage, which he will earn working flexibly while meeting production benchmarks. Why not bear up and be a man while keeping your own schedule? White likes this arrangement, for reasons I return to below. But the setup is less appealing to Jesse, who has joined Walter in the lab. He describes his job this way:

> One day pretty much bleeds into the next. Been working a lot. I got a job.... It's in a laundromat. It's totally corporate. Corporate laundromat. It's, like, rigid. All kinds of red tape. My boss is a dick.... I'm not worthy or whatever to meet him, but I guess everybody's scared of the dude. The place is full of dead-eyed douchebags, the hours suck, and nobody knows what's going on, so sounds kind of Kafkaesque. Yeah. Totally Kafkaesque. Majorly. (3.9)

The lie contains an essential truth. In conflating his high-end salary work and low-end wage labor, Jesse reveals the drama's beating heart.

CHAPTER 3

The secret life of the gangster collapses into the crappy corporate job—a racializing job, when considered in light of the Latina workers who toil for low wages above. White will battle Fring, his racial double, to hold the implications of that collapse at bay. But that battle is a generically dressed up version of the more prosaic fear that Walt cannot directly acknowledge, that he is no heroic manufacturer, and that his work is not so different either from the work done by Skyler or the Latina workers upstairs (fig. 3.5).

Meth and the Long Downturn

Federal authorities had been largely unconcerned with crystal meth before *Breaking Bad*'s premier, because it was consumed primarily by the white working class (and so not a pretext for policing minorities) and manufactured primarily in the US (and so not a pretext for overseas militarism). In September 2007, however, just before *Breaking Bad* aired, congressional subcommittees began decrying the role of Mexican cartels in the meth trade. Subsequently, lawmakers chronicled clashes between "mom and pop" small-batch meth production in the US and large-scale production both in the US and Mexico.[20] *Breaking Bad* chronicles similar clashes, as it romances the small family business over the international behemoth. In the first two seasons, White and Pinkman cook for distribution in Albuquerque; in the next two, they cook for Fring, who battles a Mexican cartel while distributing meth across the Southwest; in the final season, after Jesse teaches cartel chemists to cook, Fring destroys the cartel, and Walt kills Fring; finally, Walt and Jesse go into business with a rogue faction of the fast food division of Madrigal, with which Fring had been working all along, it turns out.

That widening frame (and the accelerating speed with which the melodrama progressed) came into focus during the Great Recession and its aftermath. *Breaking Bad* aired at the start of 2008, at the height of the financial crisis, even if it wasn't until its second season that the drama concertedly tapped into the ongoing fallout. That season's first episode ("Seven Thirty-Seven") finds Walt calculating what he'll need to leave his family when he dies:

Adjusting for inflation—good state college—adjusting for inflation, say $45,000 a year, two kids, four years of college, $360,000; remaining mortgage on the home, $107,000; home equity line, $30,000, that's $137,000; cost of living, food, clothing, utilities, say two grand a month? I mean, that should put a dent in it, anyway. 24K a year provides for, say, ten years; that's $240,000, plus 360 plus 137 . . . 737. $737,000, that's what I need.

These are middle-class ambitions: a good state college, the maintenance of a modest ranch home in a cheap housing market, etc. But these carefully laid plans are in ruins at the end of the season, which concludes with Walt's discovery that he has indirectly caused the midair collision of a charter plane and a commercial jet, debris from which will land on his home. The jet, as it happens, is a Boeing 737, and the repetition of "737" casts the crash as the collapse of his family's financial future. To us, that future is immanent throughout the season as black-and-white flash-forwards of agents in hazmat suits cleaning up Walt's mess; to the Whites, that future might have been immanent as crushing debt.

One morning, before the collision, as Skyler eats breakfast before leaving for her new job at Beneke Fabricators, Walt is under the house cutting furiously away at its foundations. "Are you going to work today?" she asks. He responds, "Skyler, there's rot." Their foundations are rotten in part, the scene suggests, because Skyler has reentered the workforce. Since his diagnosis, he has been teaching sporadically and earning money making meth. He provides for his family as never before but seethes with resentment that to all outward appearances, he has become a stay-at-home dad. The rot also registers the erosion of his breadwinner status another way: as a version of the $137,000 the Whites owe on their house. As Skyler talks to Walt, the radio recounts the fallout from the housing crash: "causing the housing prices to trend. . . . Foreclosures are being fueled by a spike in [inaudible]. The economy is rapidly deteriorating and unemployment is climbing. With Americans losing money over rising inflation and tight spending, the housing market is unlikely to rebound, spelling more pain for the economy" (2.10).

The immediate causes of the Great Recession are familiar enough: it was precipitated by a sharp rise in defaults on subprime mortgages that

CHAPTER 3

had been bundled as collateralized debt obligations and distributed to all corners of a heavily financialized global economy. It quickly became clear that much of the vast sums that banks had extended households would not be paid back. Hoping to thaw the resulting credit freeze, the Federal Reserve began to purchase mortgage-backed securities and treasuries while increasing the money supply. Season 2 registers that intervention in clever ways. Skyler's new workplace, Beneke Fabricators, is also eaten by rot. "We make things here," CEO Ted Beneke tells her, "and the people who work here are like family." But the business is going under and the family breaking apart, he adds, because "the economy's in the toilet [and] China's undercutting us at every turn" (2.11). Ted's language evokes Walt's excavations: he starts "undercutting" his house because brown "toilet" water indicates faulty plumbing. And Beneke drags Skyler into the toilet, as Walt does, if in another way: he's tricked her into perpetrating accounting fraud, to avoid paying taxes on his profits. That fraud in turn evokes the Fed's response to the "tight spending" mentioned on the radio: "Ted Beneke" suggests then–Fed chairman Ben Bernanke, who had months before the season's premier dropped the federal funds rate from 5.25 percent to 0.0 percent.

Walt's cancer recedes as he accumulates a giant cube of cash in a storage locker. It almost seems as if making meth, or the mountain of money he makes making meth, cures him. We might say, moreover, that he's cured as if by the magic of the Fed's quantitative easing. Doctors cut what is left of his cancer from his lungs just before he cuts the rot from his home's foundation, and just as Skyler starts working for Beneke. Cancer and rot leave body and house in tandem, as if a bad debt wiped off the books. This might seem to work only up to a point, insofar as it is Skyler, and not Walt, who receives money from Beneke/Bernanke. But ultimately, it matters little whether it is Walt's meth money or Beneke/Bernanke's fiat money that seems to cure Walt of his cancer. The cure is only temporary, regardless. Meth and Fed monies provide an illusory stay of deindustrialization's cancer, we might say. Meth isn't his cancer's cure, it's that cancer's objective correlative, in just the way that his giant cube of money is. And so it is no surprise that his cancer returns in the fifth season with the inevitability that attends long-wave deindustrialization processes that might be paused but not reversed by massive cash infusions.

Meth is well-suited to this particular allegory. Drugs had figured in black-market melodramas since *The Sopranos*, which begins with Tony going on Prozac; *Big Love* begins with Bill Hendrickson going on Viagra; *Nurse Jackie* begins with Jackie Peyton already hooked on pain killers. In *Weeds*, the Botwins grow and sell marijuana; in *Peaky Blinders*, the Shelbys produce and sell bootleg alcohol. Taken together, these drugs figure the programs themselves, as typically addictive substances supplied illicitly, tongue in cheek, by black-market cable and web providers. But each drug invokes particular contextual associations, and meth has strong historical associations with manufacturing and its declines. As Jason Pine notes, it and related forms of speed first emerged in the service of commodity production as "a vaccine for that great obstacle to boundless productivity: fatigue."[21] But more recently, and more pervasively, meth has been a poison for those expelled from production and made either jobless or reliant on low-end service work. Meth is thus the sign of a specific dispossession. For Dylan Mathews, "the rise of meth coincided with the rise of low-paying low-skilled service work, where people had to work multiple menial jobs to earn the same amount they used to earn in one manufacturing job, or other good-paying low-skilled positions."[22] Currently possessed of one of the smallest manufacturing sectors in the nation, trailed only by Hawaii and Washington, DC, New Mexico lost almost 25 percent of its manufacturing jobs in the fifteen years leading to *Breaking Bad*; halfway through this period, the state's meth usage rates had more than doubled.[23]

Those statistics usefully correlate local meth usage and declines in manufacturing. And in doing so, they clarify the economic processes and class conditions implicit in the drama. But they don't on their own tell us what deindustrialization is and when it became a generalized phenomenon across the US, and they don't on their own explain the relation between that generalized phenomenon and the Great Recession.

Robert Brenner dates the start of US deindustrialization, and "the long downturn," to 1973, when industrial profit rates began precipitously to fall, having begun to decline in the mid-1960s. The decline started, he argues, when once underdeveloped manufacturing sectors in Japan and West Germany began to catch up to US sectors and thereby produce a global manufacturing "overcapacity." Before China began "undercutting us at every turn," as Beneke puts it, Japan and West Germany did, by flooding markets with lower-priced goods. This made it difficult for US manufacturers "to secure the established rate of return on their placements of capital and labor."[24] US firms responded by cutting costs and suppressing wage growth, and by implementing the logistical efficiencies that David Harvey associates with "flexible accumulation."[25] Emulating Toyota, firms developed "lean," "just-in-time," or "post-Fordist" systems to coordinate globally dispersed supply and to manage workforces divided between well-paid workers in the core—in design, branding, and finance—and low-wage, casualized workers on the periphery.[26] But for Brenner, logistical innovations could not mitigate global overcapacity. Once US profit declines became severe, and the long downturn began, the only thing that achieved the "turnaround in relative costs that [firms] had been unable to achieve by way of productivity growth and wage restraint" was the dollar's devaluation.[27] That happened first in conjunction with the Reagan-Thatcher monetarist revolution at the start of the 1980s and later in the 1985 Plaza Accord, which

> set off ten years of more or less continuous, and major, devaluation of the dollar with respect to the yen and the mark, which was accompanied by a decade-long freeze on real wage growth. It thereby opened the way simultaneously for the recovery of competitiveness, along with the speed-up of export growth, of US manufacturing; a secular crisis of German and Japanese industry; and an unprecedented explosion of export based manufacturing expansion throughout East Asia.[28]

The reversal was short-lived. Ten years later, faced with distressed Japanese and German economies, and with what might have been the liquidation of Japan's US assets, the Clinton administration inflated the dollar against the yen and the mark. Signed in 1995, the "Reverse Plaza Accord" represented "a stunning—and entirely unexpected—about-face in the policy stance of both the US and its main allies and rivals, in much the same way as had the original Plaza Accord of 1985."[29]

Beginning in 1985, Brenner adds, the world economy would run according to a "hydraulic dynamic" in which "one leading economy or group of them took advantage of reduced exchange rates to undertake manufacturing-led, export driven expansions, but heavily at the expense of others with correspondingly increased exchange rates." This dynamic did not reverse the larger trend toward deindustrialization. Rather it dispersed the trend's effects spatially and temporally, such that the US manufacturing sector seemed for a while to recover only to lose its momentum and slip again into decline after 1995, at which point, because of the reinflated US dollar and the Fed's rate suppression, foreign capital flowed still more heavily into the US. The corresponding reduction in German and Japanese interest rates, along with the continued durability of the dollar as the world's safe-haven currency, drew global reserves into US markets, whether from Japan and Germany, so-called Asian Tigers, or new sites of production in Brazil, Russia, India, and China. In short, for Brenner, the US saved itself from its manufacturing decline "by its own debility," insofar as it operated as "a market of last resort" for "vast inflows of private and public monies from abroad."[30]

That capital influx elevated equities and housing markets, which encouraged corporations and households to assume even more debt, the better to float upward on what seemed an ever-rising tide. As Brenner has it, the purchase of American debt, or sale of credit, produced various "wealth effects" in the US: dot-com booms, consumption highs, asset-price run-ups in stocks and real estate—each bubble realized through ready credit.[31] The proximate cause of the Great Recession, and still with us today, this "asset-based Keynesianism" produced "the greatest wave of accumulation of debt in history," as firms refrained from investments in fixed capital and borrowed to pursue mergers and stock buybacks. In traditional Keynesianism, "demand is 'subsidized' by means of the federal government's incurring of rising *public* deficits, so as to spend more than it takes in taxes. By contrast, in [Alan] Greenspan's version, demand is increased by means of corporations and households taking on rising private deficits, so as to spend more than they make, encouraged to do so by the increased paper wealth that they effortlessly accrue by virtue of the appreciation of the value of their stocks, or other assets."[32]

Brenner's account has been subject to fierce debate.[33] Marxist political economists differ over why the crisis begins at all. Brenner's emphasis on overcapacity is subtly different from Harvey's on global overaccumulation crises "in which idle capital and idle labor supply . . . exist side by side with no apparent way to bring these resources together to accomplish socially useful tasks."[34] And for both Harvey and Arrighi, accumulation crises are cyclical structural tendencies that recur in the absence of global overcapacity. Moreover, Arrighi thinks Brenner too concerned with state agencies; while he confirms Brenner's overall picture, he faults him for failing to register the phases of financialization that for five hundred years have marked accumulation crises.[35] Identifying deindustrialization's exact inflection points is tricky, in any event. And it's important to remember that the term denotes macroeconomic tendencies, not local realities. Political economists tend to confirm Brenner's claim that US manufacturing entered into acute crisis in the early 1970s. Randy Martin, for example, notes that 1973 marked the first time that US "financial assets surpassed those of production."[36] But over the last five decades, deindustrialization has named an uneven process that can manifest differently depending on the timeframe, location, and industry in question. Robert Gordon measures "total factor productivity (hereafter TFP)" as "a measure of how quickly output is growing relative to the growth of labor and capital inputs." He echoes Brenner in noting the general trend: "TFP grew after 1970 at barely a third of the rate achieved between 1920 and 1970." But more locally, Gordon's account is almost exactly the inverse of Brenner's: it locates the last period of significant manufacturing growth in the years following the Reverse Plaza Accord: "the growth rate of aggregate U.S. productivity soared in 1996–2004 to roughly double its rates rate in 1972–1996."[37] Deepankar Basu and Ramaa Vasudevan locate a "sharp fall in capital productivity since 2000, after a period of fairly steady rise for almost two decades"; "Capital productivity increased through the 1990s," they conclude, "along with rising labor productivity and declining capital intensity."[38] The Federal

Reserve splits the difference between Brenner and Gordon: it has total industrial production rising to a new height roughly ten years before the 2008 premiere of *Breaking Bad*, falling sharply three years later, rising again, and then falling precipitously at the onset of the Great Recession—when *Breaking Bad* begins.[39]

These data points describe what might feel, on the ground, like a baffling sequence of revivals and declines. Deindustrialization does not begin and end in one moment; it names an uneven trajectory, which individual workers might or might not experience. Nor does deindustrialization necessarily entail an aggregate reduction in industrial employment. Brenner and Arrighi account for reductions in the relative rather than absolute allocation of capital to manufacturing, such that the sector's total number of jobs might grow, if more slowly than in other sectors. It is only at the level of class that an absolute increase in the overall number of manufacturing jobs might seem a loss relative to greater increases elsewhere in the economy.

Who Is It You Think You See?

In season 2, Ted Beneke, CEO of Beneke Fabricators, tells Skyler that his company used to "make things."[40] We never learn what the company made or if it was part of the manufacturing sector, which the Department of Labor defines as "engaged in the mechanical, physical, or chemical transformation of materials, substances, or compounds into new products." That definition likely would not include story "fabrication," like the writing of *Breaking Bad*, because of how the Department of Labor understands mechanical, physical, and chemical transformations. The definition likely *would* include the "molecular switches" produced by Gray Matter.[41] And the Department of Labor definition does recognize a "food manufacturing sector," which would include the fast food produced by Madrigal, for which Fring, White, and Pinkman all work.

But the proliferation of Los Pollos Hermanos franchises does not feel like a manufacturing boom. Madrigal is a "highly diversified conglomerate" that produces "industrial equipment, global shipping, major construction, and [has] a tiny little foothold in American fast food"

(4.7). That foothold houses the conglomerate's covert meth production, and I'd suggest that that clandestine operation figures the tendency of manufacturing firms, when faced with falling profit rates in their core operations, to diversify into (food) service, finance, and media businesses that grow like cancer at their and the larger economy's expense. Indeed, Madrigal is an electronics firm that diversifies into fast food in the way that similar firms have diversified into film and TV production. The analogy is more than casual.

When he cashes out of the meth business, White buries $60 million in the desert. He marks the site with GPS coordinates that lead neo-Nazis to the money (which they take) and to Steven Gomez and Walt's brother-in-law Hank Schrader (whom they kill). The coordinates also pointed to the drama's own production. Gilligan notes that "anyone who cared to Google [them] might be tickled to discover they actually lead to the show's specific studio in New Mexico."[42] The conceit is clever enough, insofar as Walt's artfully made meth figures this artfully produced program, we will see. But the studio is only a local contractor, *Breaking Bad* hints. When Walt and Jesse discover they have been working for the food division of a German conglomerate, they discover on the drama's behalf that Gilligan and his writers have been working for the entertainment division of a Japanese conglomerate that holds major stakes in electronics, gaming, and financial services. Madrigal Electromotive evokes Sony Corporation, the Japanese electronics firm that runs the Sony Group, which owns *Breaking Bad*. "Electromotive" forces are the basis of all electronics, and if "Madrigal" evokes "womb," it also evokes early modern vocal music and might thus remind us that "Sony" derives from *sonus*, Latin for sound.

The echo between the two conglomerates is fortuitous, given the turn to Robert Brenner above: Sony (Japanese) and Madrigal (German) nicely register the resurgence of Japanese and German manufacturing in the 1970s and 1980s and the corresponding onset of US deindustrialization. But Japanese transnationals were themselves eventually subject to deindustrialization's widening gyre, as manufacturing moved in bulk to still cheaper locales. And in any event, I wish now to pursue another avenue for linking the economic life in *Breaking Bad* to the economic life that produced and distributed it. White produces speed for New Mexico's dispossessed. But speed is also a key attribute of the drama, whose relentless, masterful accelerations turned viewers into addicts—able to overdose as never before, especially after the program hit Netflix before its fifth season.

Each successive season finds the serial moving faster in tandem with White. When it begins, White is working himself to death teaching and washing cars. A good boy, he never smokes. But he is short of breath and exhausted, both because of his overwork and because cancer grows within him. Later, when making meth, a breathlessness born from speed seems to save him—and make the program itself more thrilling. White's worry that he's lived too long, I claim above, expresses a class anxiety that there can be no restoration of the industrial might white-collar workers once so effectively leveraged. But it also expresses narrative anxieties that *Breaking Bad* will continue past its own natural ending. "Television is historically good at keeping its characters in a self-imposed stasis so that shows can go on for years or even decades," Gilligan notes. "When I realized this, the logical next step was to think, how can I do a show in which the fundamental drive is toward change?"[43] *Breaking Bad* does drive relentlessly toward change in its last seasons especially. And as it ramps up in tandem with White's ever more frantic production, it becomes frenzied, hopped up, as if afraid that despite its ferocious speed, it only stands in place. That temporal tension produces intensified melodrama, a mode, according to Linda Williams, that often feels both defeated and urgent. Melodramas acknowledge it is "too late" to restore the innocence of home and family for which they long; at the same time, they generate improbable "in-the-knick-of-time" solutions to their own acutely felt belatedness.[44] *Breaking Bad* performs this two-step: along with White's sped-up life, it promises to restore the familial, racial, and class authority that he's lost.

This analogy between (meth) speed and (TV) speed might seem too clever by half, or at least the kind of cleverness that has little to do with the serial's real substance. But *Breaking Bad* frequently teases just this analogy. In the fourth season, Skyler urges Walt to confess to the police. You are in over your head and in danger, she tells him. He walks away from her and then turns, as if a different person:

> Who are you talking to right now? Who is it you think you see? Do you know how much I make a year? I mean, even if I told you, you wouldn't believe it. Do you know what would happen if I suddenly decided to stop going into work? A business big enough that it could be listed on the NASDAQ goes belly up. Disappears! It ceases to exist without me. No, you clearly don't know who you're talking to, so let me clue you in. I am not in danger, Skyler. I am the danger. A guy opens his door and gets shot and you think of me? No. I am the one who knocks! (4.6)

In what is arguably the most famous scene in this or any quality drama, we are asked to defamiliarize the object before us. At issue is not simply Skyler's ignorance about what Walt has become, but also our own possibly too-literal understanding of the drama. I have suggested we read White as broadly emblematic, not simply of whiteness, or of patriarchy in crisis, but also, and more specifically, of a downwardly mobile technical-managerial elite nostalgic for the glory days of US Fordism, when that elite was integral to a national mission and allied to the white working class. But these terms might not adequately defamiliarize White, whose last name announces his racial representativeness loudly enough, and whose alliance with neo-Nazis trumpets one possible outcome of resentments like his. White also codes the particular managerial elite responsible for the drama's creation—namely, its writers.

As White reveals to Skyler who he secretly is beyond their home, we look up at him, from Skyler's point of view. He begins his speech framed within a door and his metaphor places him intruding into rather than living within a home; he is "the one who knocks" because he has left home and found riches and a lethal vitality that now endangers his family.[45] We feel he asks his question of us as well, especially since he challenges her to know the difference between what is inside and outside her house. Do we know the difference? As spectators looking in, we are outside their house, even if, in a more literal sense, the drama is inside ours. *Breaking Bad* is consistently interested in how and via what agencies we espy the White home. It offers point-of-view shots from inanimate household objects and through walls and floors: from the bottom of a toilet, frying pan, or bathtub, or up through a scrubbed floor. These uncanny shots defamiliarize the lifeless even as they identify viewers with otherwise innocuous contrivances and surfaces now rendered invasive. As if to stress this disembodied spectatorship, in the second and subsequent seasons, an eyeball once lodged within a teddy bear, which fell from the sky with the Boeing 737, floats about the household (fig. 3.6). In the scene before us, even as the drama's adherence to classical continuity conventions allows us to forget the space from which we watch, as White challenges Skyler to defamiliarize what she sees, and confront the reality that the extra-domestic danger she fears already inhabits her home, we experience a reciprocal recognition in which the drama acknowledges us as both inside and outside its world. The scene's shot-reverse-shot structure drives this home, and moves us between two subject positions, such that we are both the gangster who escapes and returns home and the unwitting wife and mother confined and at risk within the home.[46]

But the scene is industrially as well as formally reflexive. Even as it asks viewers to see themselves both as intruders and those intruded upon, it asks them look behind the curtains in another way. Walt asks, "Do you know what would happen if I suddenly decided to stop going into work? A business big enough that it could be listed on the NASDAQ goes belly up." He says, "could be," but might just as well have said "just was": White made his brag in August 2011, some six weeks after AMC Networks conducted its IPO and became listed as AMCX on the NASDAQ. White brags on behalf of Vince Gilligan, *Breaking Bad*'s creator, head writer, and showrunner. The brag was plausible: without the likes of Gilligan and *Mad Men* creator and showrunner Matthew Weiner, AMC might never have been listed at all. It was only because of the enormous prestige and popularity of their programs, after all, that AMC was able to generate buzz and raise its cable carriage fees, thereby increasing its economics prospects.

"I can create a network," Jesse tells Walt before the two go to work for Fring. "Look, we control production and distribution" (2.5). They do create a network, after a fashion, insofar as their product becomes central to Fring's operations. But they can't in fact distribute, given the resources (and violence) available to larger operations. They need Fring,

CHAPTER 3

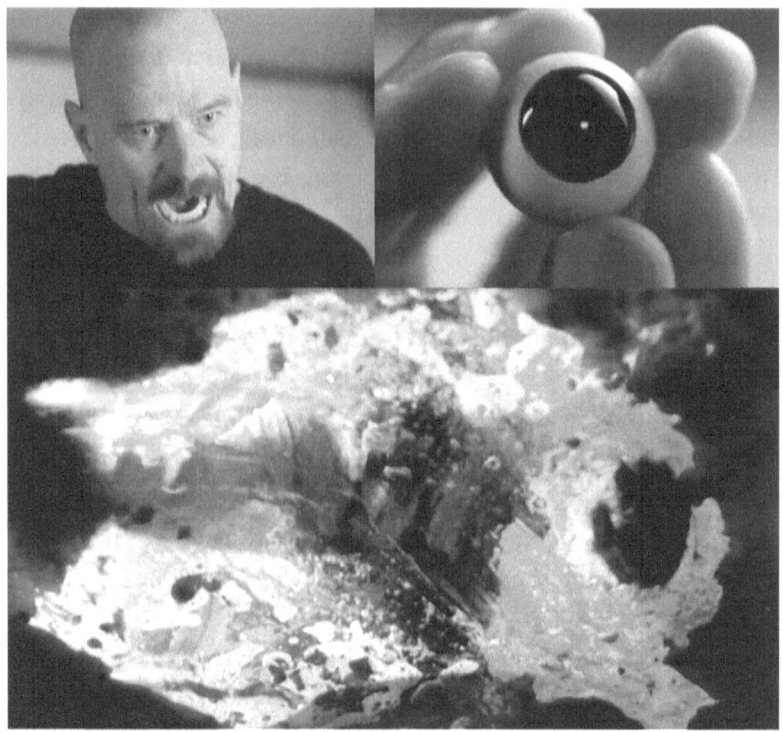

3.6. *Breaking Bad*: "Who is it you think you see?," How is it you think you see?, Who is it you think who sees?

just as Weiner and Gilligan (and Lionsgate and Sony) needed AMC to distribute their creations. But nor do "they" produce together as equals; Jesse is in no way Walt's equal. He is, in effect, only a staff writer, working beneath a more celebrated showrunner. Something similar might be said of Skyler. In "Bullet Points" (4.4), Walt helps her craft a plausible story. She has long dreamed of being a writer but struggles under his scrutiny: "I'm doing the best I can here Walt," she says; "maybe lying doesn't come as easily to me as it does to you." "Bullet Points" conflates marks left by a gun and a those left on a page: Walt is the consummate storyteller; his ability to lie convincingly is essential to his success as a gangster. Nobody spins yarns so quickly, except of course Gilligan. The inimitable purity of Walt's crank makes this essential point: nobody else can come close to doing what this guy does (except Jesse, in the final seasons). Walt's artistry allegorizes Gilligan's, and his exquisite meth, the drama's own addictive properties. At bottom, this is the story of a singular talent able to produce better TV than his hack competitors. And not just any TV, but up-market quality TV consigned to a commercial network. White will denigrate one competitor by telling him, "Yours is just some tepid off-brand generic cola. What I'm making is Classic Coke" (5.7). Three years later, *Mad Men* (also about a singular talent) ended with an extended homage to Coke's famous "I'd like to buy the world a Coke" ad. Perhaps even commercial TV could be great art, we hear the two dramas musing.

Coca-Cola owned TriStar Pictures before it was acquired by Sony, whose television division made *Breaking Bad*, and it is possible to see, in one of the drama's many reflexive gestures, a nod to the properly corporate nature of the authorship at stake in its demotic high art. When Jesse first sees the pure glass that Walt concocts, he explains, "You're a damn artist. This is art, Mr. White" (1.1). Walt is not just an extraordinary craftsman—he's akin to a poet, in fact. He deflects Hank's scrutiny by suggesting that the "W.W." in Gail Boetticher's journals refer to Walt Whitman, rather than to him. But the lie contains a truth: Walt's voice, which is the voice of an implied showrunner, contains multitudes, as so many leaves of grass. *Mad Men*'s Don Draper is similarly corporate. His real name is "Dick Whitman," which he conceals, as if to conceal his multitudes, the better to pursue accolades and wealth (even when others, like Peggy Olson, create the work that makes him famous). On the whole, *Breaking Bad* confesses in ways that *Mad Men* won't—that containing multitudes means subordinating and even breaking others. In one flashback, White catalogs the compounds that make up the human body and muses, "There's got to be more to a human being than that" (1.1). He hunts the trace element that makes up the soul, as Gilligan does the elusive elements that make art: the drama's title sequence highlights periodic table elements as they appear in the names of those who contributed to its creation; a showrunner catalyzes talents as so many chemical compounds, manipulating and combining, hiring and firing. Thus does he create a whole greater than the sum of its parts. If this is incorporation, as in the creation of a corporate person, it is also part and parcel with what White calls "chemical disincorporation" just before dissolving the body of a rival in a rubber vat. The showrunner is a poet/killer who assembles and disassembles as needs dictate. That is why Tony Soprano was an apt role model (*Mad Men* and *Breaking Bad* were not written to be commercial TV, but to land at HBO, which was, rather than Coke, their original object of desire).[47]

Draper is unlike Soprano and White insofar as he doesn't leave dead bodies in his wake. But like his gangster peers, he is a manager-poet whose "creativity," such as it is, requires command. He never really runs Sterling Cooper or (in season 4) Sterling Cooper Draper Pryce—jobs that surely belong to the formidable Joan Holloway. Nor does he want to run his firm's accounts (a role he explicitly rejects after the Hilton fiasco in season 3). But he embodies the fantasy that creating and managing a workforce are the same. "There was such depth and complexity" to *The Sopranos*, Weiner recalls, "and at the same time it was so commercially successful." *The Sopranos* made clear that "quality is a commercial decision"—and produced by those decisions. "I am of the persuasion," he added, "that budget constraints are very, very good for creativity."[48] In this vision, so congenial to management, quality derives from a version of the compromise at the heart of auteur theory, which attributed a given directorial style to its idiosyncratic, managerial negotiation of the demands made by genre on the one hand and studio on the other. As Andrew Sarris notes, "The auteur theory values the personality of a director precisely because of the barriers to its expression."[49]

Critics tend to trot out *auteurism*—however tired the concept—when crediting the likes of Jenji Kohan, David Chase, Weiner, and Gilligan for whatever artistry the TV in question seems to possess. And most of the dramas in this book imply that showrunners deserve that credit. On *Orange Is the New Black*, a guard responds to being told that all of the inmates producing a prison newspaper are assistant editors: "You mean like a TV show with all those names rolling by up front? They can't all be that important" (2.7). Certainly they have not all been equal, not since the early 1980s. *Hill Street Blues* is typically credited with giving "writer-producers," as Horace Newcomb and Robert Alley called them, a new importance, both by importing into prime time the developing serial narratives that had long defined daytime soaps and, the better to curate those narratives, by instituting a stable writer's room and a lead writer who would oversee the dizzying range of alternately creative and managerial decisions that go into making a serial. The work demanded of this position has changed, as television became more important in the media industry after *The Sopranos* and as showrunners became managers of "transmedia franchises" that, in the words of Denise Mann, "successfully mobilize a host of ancillary revenue streams, engender merchandising opportunities, and spawn multiple spin-offs, including digital content and promotions for the web."[50] Jason Mittell adds that the "authorship by management" celebrated in serial TV is different from the "authorship by origination" and "authorship by responsibility" celebrated in literature and film production, respectively. "Authorship by management," he thinks, resembles "the leadership and oversight that managers take in businesses and sports teams." He adds, "complex TV" encourages a compensatory "discursive production of authorship," as the imputation of a recognizably literary author to whom everyone from fans to industry insiders can attribute creative agency.[51]

And yet, showrunners do not own the product of their labors. Salaried employees, they are dispossessed of their copyrights (as White is dispossessed of the patents that enrich Gray Matter). That dispossession, along with no doubt heartfelt political sympathies, accounted for their decision to join the 2007–2008 writers' strike, which interrupted production of *Breaking Bad*'s first season. The strike was called by the Writers Guild of America, West, and the Writers Guild of America, East (hereafter WGA), and targeted the Alliance of Motion Picture and Television Producers (AMPTP), with whom the guilds negotiated a contract every three years. Writers wanted an increase in residuals for DVD sales and, above all, residuals on TV and film distributed via new media. Showrunners had not lined up with the rank-and-file during the guild's previous labor action. But the WGA persuaded them to honor the strike, in part because of their new prominence.[52] And numerous showrunners did, even as the studios used their participation to deride the labor action as "millionaires holding picket signs."[53]

CHAPTER 3

Rank-and-file WGA members had their own version of White's blue-collar nostalgia. The Hollywood writer's identification with labor was forged in the 1930s, when studios and even the Federal Writers' Projects treated writers as waged employees akin to those who staffed other craft industries. In the 1930s, at the height of the studio system, a Paramount Pictures writer quipped that the studios ran an "assembly line" because, in Ian Hamilton's words, they "doled out *dramatis personae*, one each to a team of five writers—the writer was then instructed to supply 'his' character with lines of dialogue but to avoid consultation with other members of the team: the idea, so far as anybody understood it, was that the producer would 'assemble' the five contributions, jigsaw style, into a final script."[54] Metaphors like these were central to Adorno and Horkheimer's account of the culture industry, which was, they argued, "weak and dependent" on "the most powerful sectors of industry: steel, petroleum, electricity, chemicals."[55] By their lights, all industries were industrial, only differently so. And whatever we think of this classification, it made a kind of sense, at least from the Hollywood writer's point of view, which looked as if across a vast gulf at studio management.

But the rise of the TV writer-producer and later showrunner would narrow that gulf. Insofar as most showrunners had been staff writers, it became possible to imagine the two categories as simply different stages of a successful career. Conversely, the increased importance of writers to TV production—both over time and relative to film production—afforded them an affluence that made it difficult to think of them as labor in a traditional sense. As John Caldwell, Vicki Mayer, and Miranda Banks have noted, there is a wide gulf in pay, status, and power between writers and below-the-line workers—or, indeed, between writers and the Teamsters who supported their action in 2007–2008.[56] Critics have brought much needed attention to the struggle of writers to wrest control, credit, authority, or recognition from those who determine the conditions of their work; but they have also made clear that that struggle often rests on writers distancing themselves from below-the-line labor.[57]

We seem to have traveled far from manufacturing, since we speak now of "labor" as salaried employees in a media industry that began to grow exponentially at precisely the moment that capital began to shift from manufacturing to finance. The media industry does not exist in its current form until the likes of Rupert Murdoch and Steve Ross began in the 1970s to leverage global capital to pursue conglomeration across a range of still relatively distinct industries: film, TV, publishing, broadcast, cable, etc. To speak of "labor" in this industry is important politically, since the term captures the structurally abject condition of those who can be hired and fired en masse, at the behest of ownership and management. But the term is also potentially misleading, and not simply because writers enjoy profit participation (residuals) and affluent lifestyles. Staff writers are labor, in legal terms, because their employers possess the contractual right to demand revisions. Writers benefit from the contractual protections negotiated by the WGA in the Minimum Basic Agreement (MBA). From Hollywood's earliest days, studios insisted that writers were "employees" because, under copyright law, the employer is deemed the author and therefore the legal owner of any "work made for hire" made by paid employees (17 U.S.C. § 201(a)).[58] And for decades, networks and studios have refused to relinquish the one corollary power that has been legally decisive: the right to demand revisions. As Erik Barnouw explained in 1962, "The right to demand revisions became by definition, and logically so, the essence of an employer-employee relationship."[59] According to the MBA, writers are employees because they are subject to the power of the network or studio "to direct the performance of personal services in writing . . . or in making revisions, modifications, or changes" to what they write (MBA Art. 1.C.1.a.(a)). By this definition, though they turned out for the strike, showrunners categorically are not labor—they "direct the performance of personal services in writing."[60]

Showrunners are management. To borrow from Duménil and Lévy, they are "*top management*," as "the *interface* between ownership and management." As the two have it, "the reliance on top management has been a prominent feature of neoliberalism"; to them, neoliberalism is defined mainly by capital's effort to wean top management of "sectional behavior" born from its identification with lower workforce echelons (precisely the identification to which White is initially susceptible).[61] This process has been important to the TV production pioneered by HBO, in part because, as Toby Miller notes, the studio-network has "wished to avoid the tight nexus that broadcast television had with a unionized workforce and job security." Miller thinks HBO "represents the disorganized, decentralized, flexible post-Fordism of contemporary cultural capitalism. It relies on a variety of workers, many of whom do not have tenure and benefits, who are employed by small companies even when they sell their labor to . . . [a] giant corporation."[62] The showrunner (and his or her boutique production company) is essential to this system insofar as he or she supervises a contingent labor force on behalf of a much larger media transnational (whether as network or studio).

A downwardly mobile white-collar worker, White believes he shares more with Jesse than with Fring, just as he believes his interests are the same as Jesse's no matter how aggressively he manipulates him. That twisted solidarity speaks to the showrunner's role in the writers' strike, not because striking showrunners acted in bad faith or wished their writers ill, but because, whatever their intentions, their interests were structurally at odds with those of their rank-and-file allies. As I noted above, *Breaking Bad* chronicles White's eventual drive to become ownership. He tarries with labor for as long as he can, because it suits him to do so, and in no way compromises his ability to earn. In season 3, he and Jesse make more working for Fring than they ever did on their own. Walt seems not to mind that Fring is making far more off of them in turn. But Jesse is rankled by what he takes to be their exploitation:

> **Jesse**: That is so messed up. Fairness-wise, I can't even—
>
> **Walter**: Jesse, you are now a millionaire, and you're complaining? What world do you live in?
>
> **Jesse**: One where the dudes who are actually doing all the work ain't getting fisted. (3.9)

The raised fist, adopted by Socialists and Communists in the early twentieth century as a sign of solidarity, is here an instrument of rape. But the arrangement suits White, in part, because it gratifies his working-class nostalgia. He gets to have it both ways: working side by side with Jesse, he's both rich and the dispossessed little guy. Pinkman sees it differently; indeed, White has control and power in ways that Jesse never does. Decisively, he has the brand: "Heisenberg" gets the credit as Big Blue's author, no matter who makes or distributes it. Jesse learns to make meth almost as pure as Walt's, and in the fifth season, Uncle Jack places him in chains and forces him to cook meth he will sell as Heisenberg's. In one scene, we cut between a sepia-toned memory and the cold reality of his

3.7. *Breaking Bad*: Jesse Pinkman dreams of craft labor.

3.8. *Breaking Bad*: Jesse Pinkman and the machine.

imprisonment: Jesse recalls making a wood box, while toiling as a slave (figs. 3.7 and 3.8). In one reality, he is a craftsman lovingly producing art; in another, a cog chained to a faceless machine. Throughout, Walt gets to be the craftsman, and Jesse, the cog. And after he kills Fring and begins making and distributing his product, White becomes both craftsman and owner. As such, he forges the chains that bind (as if chemical bonds): *that is his craft*. White's art *is* Jesse's subordination.

The Zombie Network

AMC might have taken note. White's singular abilities suggested the greater importance of the creative showrunner and his team than the network, which could not but seem a parasite. And *Breaking Bad* was about an outsized talent who almost always got what he wanted, which was autonomy, control, and credit. Certainly this is what Matthew Weiner wanted. The network's relationship with him became contentious in 2011 when he refused to shorten *Mad Men* episodes to facilitate the airing of more commercials. Though he eventually backed down, the drama's fifth season was delayed until 2012 and AMC agreed to pay him an unheard of $30 million salary over three years.[63] The dispute marked a turning point for AMC. Why pay the likes of Lionsgate and Sony (which produced *Mad Men* and *Breaking Bad*, respectively) for the right to distribute programs it could not fully control—programs that lionized producers over distributors, as if to add insult to injury? AMC Studios had begun producing programs in 2010, with *The Walking Dead*, and later that program allowed the fledgling unit to clarify who was running the show. The same year AMC Networks went to war with Weiner, AMC Studios fired Frank Darabont, *The Walking Dead*'s first showrunner. Some eighteen months later, it fired the show's second showrunner, Glen Mazzara, who had led it to the highest ratings ever recorded for a cable drama. This was unusual, to say the least; programs rarely belonged to their showrunners legally, but the industry typically accorded those figures noneconomic "moral rights" in them. Darabont eventually sued, claiming AMC had fired him "without cause, without notice, without explanation, and without any opportunity to cure."[64]

But AMC was undeterred. And in 2015, the year *Mad Men* concluded, it made AMC Studios a stand-alone unit.[65]

White and Draper are Promethean egos and fledgling entrepreneurs who want to be more than faceless organization men. But where *Mad Men* and *Breaking Bad* dramatize the ascent of irreplaceable talents, subsequent AMC Studios serials would embrace anonymity and collectivity as core values. In the wake of those two celebrated dramas, critics wondered what would become of AMC Networks. A scathing 2013 article in *Grantland*, "The Zombie Network," accused AMC of producing "quality simulacra" that "delivered the appearance of everything audiences have come to love about the Golden Age of Television without any of the value."[66] That was not entirely fair, if only because the network's in-house programming aimed very consciously to embrace quality simulacra. In *The Walking Dead*, Rick Grimes keeps the living one step ahead of a sea of lifeless clones—the dead themselves. Subsequent AMC Studios programming would embrace the clone and related knockoffs.

Take *Humans*, a coproduction of AMC Studios and Kudos, a British studio. It aired in 2015 and described a future in which humanity has mass-produced a workforce of robots ("synths"). As the title sequence and first season make clear, synths exist for one reason: to replace human labor (household care work, in the case of the drama's central synth). But four synths become conscious, and the first season recounts their quest to secure a program that will similarly awaken all synths. As one puts it, "Humanity is not a state. It's a quality." If "quality" names the elusive something that separates humans from synths—or, on *The Walking Dead*, the living from the dead—it also, and obviously enough, names the something that separates good TV from bad. The synths struggle to achieve that quality on behalf of AMC Studios—in a novel way. Their awakenings were the products of a dead white man (read: Weiner or Gilligan) whose brilliant programming none of them can themselves reproduce. But collectively, and after much effort, they do, and manage thereby to transform lifeless machines into living things—their self-less teamwork standing where a self-aggrandizing genius once stood. Equally concerned with cloning, coding, and originality, AMC's *Halt and Catch Fire* (*HCF*) turns on this dynamic.

CHAPTER 3

HCF follows four protagonists from the early days of the 1980s tech revolution in Texas to 1990s Silicon Valley. The four change employers many times and struggle to create their own companies—with decidedly mixed success. In many ways, the drama is about the unglamorous, day-to-day realities facing those who never make it big. In this way, it shares core features with black-market melodramas. It is about the conflicting demands of home and work as the two become confused and upend traditional gender roles. An engineer, Donna Clark eclipses her husband Gordon who, in a nod to *Breaking Bad*, develops brain cancer, as if because he's been displaced as his family's chief provider. And like most black-market melodramas, *HCF* registers the dissolution of putatively separate spheres. At one point, Gordon works from the family's rented apartment; they've sold the family house to fund Donna's startup. Bitter, he asks, "what the hell is home anymore?" (3.1). Also like *Mad Men* and *Breaking Bad*, *HCF* is a reflexive think piece on the talent-centered fusion of management and creativity in TV production. But this is no story of genius or entrepreneurial triumph; instead, it follows those who fail upward and who achieve what success they enjoy by dint of working collectively with others. Pointedly, *HCF* both emulates and rebukes earlier AMC dramas like *Mad Men* and *Breaking Bad*; the very fact that we resemble those shows, it declares, clarifies what they got wrong about creativity: as stories about creative talent come to characterize the AMC brand, it insists, they reveal themselves to be less expressions of personal vision, or talent, than impersonal surrenders to the properly generic agency of the corporation itself.

Like *Mad Men* and *Breaking Bad*, *HCF* is a backstage allegory. Its showrunner Jonathan Lisco reports that when he first read the pilot, "he realized the show wasn't, at its core, about technology. It was about what [its creators] had gone through to land it." Lisco was not one of those creators. Chris Cantwell was; he had worked in marketing at Disney before coconceiving *HCF* with Christopher Rogers. In setting out to write the drama, Cantwell wanted to know whether he was "a Disney suit or . . . a writer." He recalls producing an ad for *Toy Story 3* set in 1983. The ad's success caused him "to fantasize about being the first marketing exec in history to promote the content so well they asked him to make it."⁶⁷ That's a fantasy, presumably, because promoting and creating are different. But are they? Set the same year as Cantwell's ad, the first season of *HCF* frames this question with respect to tech rather than TV (and a different Steve Jobs toy).

A hardware engineer (Gordon Clark), a software engineer (Cameron Howe), and a marketer (Joe MacMillan) argue over which of them is the true author of the PC that they together produce. Surely somebody should get credit. "If you want this machine to stand out from every other machine on the floor," argues a Cardiff employee, "you got to stop talking about the machine and you got to start talking about the people that made it." But which people? The team's Don Draper, MacMillan thinks he should get the credit. But as if to recall Cantwell's metaphor, he's likened to "a thousand-dollar suit with nothing inside" (1.6). And he unwittingly spearheads the creation of an unexceptional, generic machine that does modest credit to Cardiff and none at all to his team. When he walks into a room and sees his first Apple Macintosh, and hears it say "hello" to a room crowded with candle-bearing devotees, he says, astonished, "It talks." This is the moment toward which the first season has been driving: it wants to create a distinctive object capable of corporate speech (as TV is). The many conversations on *HCF* about what it means to personalize Cardiff's PC, by giving it interactive software, for example, are invariably conversations about what it means for AMC Studios to constitute itself as a corporate person in the making of this drama. But MacMillan realizes when seeing the Mac (embedded in his last name) that he's been missing the big picture (he always does). He's helped Cardiff create a functional person, not a compelling one. "You tried to be good," an exec tells Donna in another context; "we just had to be good enough" (1.9).

To MacMillan, good enough is worth nothing at all. But the drama stands by the virtues of the well-made also-ran. And with good reason: it is itself an extremely modest if smart and well-made show, and it thrives in its middle registers, side-stepping the overheated moral stakes that sometimes characterizes black-market melodramas. It's not nothing, we hear it say, to be a machine that works. In any event, good enough likely suited AMC just fine. Because if one of *HCF*'s goals is to produce AMC as an author, by casting itself as the corporate speech that AMC utters, then another is to nudge media industry understandings not just of originality and creativity, but of the intellectual property laws that codify ownership.

Mad Men and *Breaking Bad* were often explicitly about IP. In the former, Draper takes credit and wins an award for Peggy Olson's work; when she confronts him, he says, "I give you money and you give me ideas." "But you never say thank you," she responds. "That's what the money is for!" (4.7), he yells. So it goes under the work-for-hire doctrine; if an employer pays an employee a wage or salary, the employer owns that idea. *Breaking Bad* is about a different kind of IP. Before the events in the serial, White sells his stake in Gray Matter for $5,000. The company becomes a $2 billion enterprise, on the back of his patents, which he's likely left with the company because of an "invention assignment agreement" during his buyout.[68] "It was my hard work. My research," he complains to Gretchen. "And you and Elliott made millions off it" (2.6). The episode finds him waxing bitter that GE compensated the inventor of the artificial diamond with a measly $10 bond. As if to drive the theft home, Jesse later witnesses an ATM machine crush the skull of an addict. Having burst his head—and pulverized the "gray matter" therein—the machine springs open and spews cash, one kind of liquidity producing another. That violent conversion of brains into money drives White. There are no copyrights or patents to be had in White's "big blue" meth, only extralegal remedies.[69] *HCF* describes a different kind of IP battle, while referencing that meth. It depicts a team that reverse engineers a generic version of a product made by a more prestigious company: IBM, which, the drama drops twice, came to be known in the early 1980s as "Big Blue." (Sony Pictures Television, it's worth adding, also has a blue-dominant logo.)

Intent on pushing Cardiff into competition with IBM, a marketer and engineer reverse engineer the IBM BIOS. The BIOS is an abstraction layer for hardware, a set of protocols through which programs and operating systems interact with the keyboard, display, and other input/output devices. And the BIOS is an essential ingredient in producing a PC clone that can run PC software. But how to steal IBM's IP without incurring liability? The engineer and marketer announce to IBM that

3.9. *Halt and Catch Fire*: Allegorizing corporate control.

they've reverse-engineered the BIOS. IBM lawyers descend on Cardiff. Left with no other way to save the company, a senior VP originally hostile to the project sets up a "clean room" in which engineers design an equivalent of the IBM BIOS without copying it directly and without any input from the two renegade employees who did so initially. Using this legally sanctioned technique, Cardiff circumvents IBM's copyright in its BIOS and designs firmware functionally identical to it.

With this storyline, *HCF* revisits the moment when companies like Columbia Data Systems and Compaq circumvented the copyright protection accorded computer operating systems in *Apple v. Franklin* (1983). In 1982, 85 percent of sold software was for Apple Computers, and 5 percent for IBM. By the next year, reports Russell Moy, "virtually every software company [was] giving priority to writing software for the IBM machine" because IBM had decided to implement an open architecture policy, which gave away Big Blue's trade secrets and allowed developers direct access to its code. That access allowed competitors to produce clones of the IBM BIOS, which, fatefully, IBM chose to secure with copyright rather than patent protection. Writing in 2000, Moy thought the successful cloning of the IBM PC led many to believe "the functional quality of software seemed to beg for parallel protection from the patent system."[70] And the question of whether software and algorithms might be patented rather than copyrighted speaks to a contentious and still evolving area of patent law.[71]

HCF applies these debates to the TV industry by understanding itself as an executable action—or, in terms borrowed from Alexander Galloway and Wendy Chun, as a practice designed "to do something to the world."[72] Put another way, *HCF* conceives of itself as an app subject to patent rather than copyright law. Patents protect the efficacious application rather than the singular expression of ideas. And by the drama's lights, industrial application is everything—ideas being common and everywhere available. The point is less that *HCF* would change copyright law (which of course it can't, and which showrunners do not own, in any event) than that it would adjust prevalent understandings of creative control (and moral rights ownership) that shadow copyright law. As the billboards that went up in Hollywood just after the *HCF* premier made clear, this drama is finally most interested in control (fig. 3.9). It takes its name from a machine code instruction that shuts down a CPU. And *HCF* isn't just *about* executable computer actions; it *is* one such action. It would shut down the prestige and power of writers and showrunners (like the fractious Matthew Weiner), stripping those figures of the moral rights that the vogue for quality drama might otherwise give them. Its clean room cleans out its writers' room. Nobody gets control except Cardiff and, by implication, AMC.

CHAPTER 4
Managed Hearts
The Americans *and* News Corporation

Homeland, *The Americans*, *The Man in the High Castle*, and *Counterpart* all feature a version of the secret life integral to black-market melodramas. In the first two, characters hide second lives from family or neighbors; in the second two, characters discover they have doubles in other worlds, and struggle to keep them secret from family members. In all four—and as is not the case in *The Sopranos*, *Weeds*, and *Breaking Bad*—second lives assume a geopolitical significance. Characters engage in international and even inter-world intrigue that seems for a while to preserve domestic autonomy. But for these dramas, "*domestic* has a double meaning," as Amy Kaplan puts it, "that not only links the familial household to the nation [or world] but also imagines both in opposition to everything outside the geographic and conceptual border of the home. The earliest meaning of *foreign*," she adds, "is 'out of doors' or 'at a distance from home.'"[1] In all four dramas, in other words, a version of the foreign underwrites the integrity of worldly, national, and ultimately familial space. But as secrets out, a given foreign outside becomes an uncanny mirror of a given domestic inside. As this happens, the family dilates, becoming in the process more than it was. This enlargement can feel radically ambiguous, promising either the dissolution of all noneconomic intimacies or conversely the extension of care and belonging to ever more encompassing groups.

CHAPTER 4

In *Homeland*, CIA operative Carrie Mathison and ex-POW Nicholas Brody have secrets: he is an al-Qaeda agent and she suffers from bipolar disorder. They become lovers and a threat to both the United States and the Brody household. Gary Edgerton calls the two "doppelgängers" "searching for meaning in the aftermath of 9/11"; they threaten even as they cast doubt on the moral authority of domestic spaces. Mathison elicited strong reactions. Alyssa Rosenberg thought *Homeland* "a defense of Carrie's emotionalism, turning it into a superpower rather than a feminine weakness." Sophie Gilbert thought she "embodies the ugliest stereotypes about women in the workplace: that they're hysterical, brittle, rude, entitled, inefficient, and governed by emotions rather than logic."[2] Either way, as a single woman in a male-dominated field, Mathison cannot defeat her enemies (coworkers or terrorists) without seducing them, and cannot save the nation without destroying the household in whose name it acts. And in fact, each of the dramas below sets its female lead against marriage and family as a function of her commitment to work and politics.

Nominally about counterterrorism, *Homeland* is a version of what Elizabeth Anker calls a "9/11 melodrama," which legitimates state power with "moral polarities, good and evil, overwhelmed victims, heightened affects, pain and suffering, grand gestures, feats of heroism, and the redemption of virtue."[3] But in the melodramas below, political parties, institutions, and ideologies morph into their seeming opposites. *Homeland*'s brainwashed sleeper agents borrow from Richard Condon's *The Manchurian Candidate* (1959), which was about an "all-American brainwashing," author Richard Condon insisted, that had less to do with Communism than capitalism. He dismissed the Manichean terms espoused by Cold Warrior Harry Truman, for instance, who insisted in 1947, "At the present moment in world history, nearly every nation must choose between alternative ways of life."[4] The following melodramas want but rarely find those clear alternatives and might be understood to represent a "geopolitical gothic" that cannot maintain stable boundaries between worlds, nation-states, belief systems, and ultimately, the domestic and nondomestic, broadly understood.

Richard Hofstadter famously described a "paranoid" style that "traffics in the birth and death of whole worlds, whole political orders, whole systems of human values."⁵ Those terms capture the totalizing impulses behind *High Castle* and *Counterpart*, both of which invent "whole worlds," it would seem, to overcome the nuclear family. Both allegorize some aspect of the Cold War, the former by describing nuclear brinkmanship between global superpowers—the Greater Reich and the Empire of Japan—and the latter by describing a unified Berlin that diverges from itself at the end of the Cold War. Both flirt with an emancipatory, antifamily politics. *High Castle* begins in the early 1960s, in a world in which the Axis powers have won the Second World War and divided North America between them. It lingers in Obergruppenführer John Smith's swastika-draped suburb. Aryan homemakers dutifully support their Aryan husbands on behalf of a genocidal agenda; these are separate spheres, triumphant. But not for long: Juliana Crain plays the part of Mathison, a lethal single woman tasked with the destruction of an all-American family. She's bewildered as she travels between worlds. "Nothing's fixed in place anymore," she says. "Nothing's solid. Like everything's just a reflection of a reflection.... It's like being suspended, each existence as real as the next" (4.5). That's what needed to defeat the Nazis and, by implication, the white family. As Hawthorne Abendsen (the Man in the High Castle) tells Smith, "You're caught betwixt, in between" (4.6). "You're damned," he later adds. "You'll wander forever between the worlds, lost!" (4.8). Smith thus becomes his opposite, a wandering Jew. As do we all: immediately after Helen and John Smith die, the portal between realities opens. Faceless masses stream through a gateway that seems like nothing so much as a giant screen. Cinema delivers the American Reich and its hygienic separations a coup de grâce. And why not? From the start, renegade film reels give hope to the oppressed by revealing alternate realities. But the ending remains ambiguous, if only because we experience this now-borderless world teeming with refugees from within a bunker, and as a kind of cinematic TV; worlds collapse into each other, but only on our screens.

High Castle ends by opening its portal, which it locates beneath the Poconos; its gateway is a weekend family getaway (fig. 4.1). *Counterpart* ends by closing its portal, which it locates beneath a futuristic Berlin. First- and second-world versions of this Berlin are divided as if by the

CHAPTER 4

4.1. *The Man in the High Castle*: Screening other worlds.

Berlin Wall: Dimension Prime is identical to Dimension Alpha but for the fact the former is still recovering from a devastating virus, released decades ago by the latter. Like *High Castle*, *Counterpart* explores the threatened integrity of dimensional rather than national space, even as it deploys its alternate reality to explore mundane domestic life. Struggling to recognize her home, a character searches for the word *uncanny*: "What's the word when everything's a bit off?" she asks. "You know, in a dream when you're in your home but it's not your home" (2.1). Prime and Alpha become uncanny mirrors of each other—mainly to render domestic intimacies unfamiliar and unsettling. That mirroring moots the portal's eventual closing. The virus escapes into Alpha just as the drama decides that individuals have no choice but to embrace the uncanny other within. In *High Castle*, Smith the traveling salesman is morally good. Hence Nazi Smith's final words: "It's unbearable. To be able to look through that door and glimpse all the people you could have been. And to know that out of all of them this is the one you became" (4.10). *Counterpart* looks closer to home and insists on acceptance rather than choice. Characters must embrace their doubles, even when they're morally dubious, in the name of their own "better selves": "We've been taught to believe that the existence of this other world is some kind of aberration of nature. But what if this is all nature's plan? And the real test isn't whether we can eradicate this other side of ourselves? What if it's about acceptance?" (2.10).

The world building required of their science fiction premises and the time they spend on geopolitical machinations makes it hard for these melodramas to attend closely to properly domestic life and the home's division of labor. Consequently, neither really allegorizes the convergence of waged labor beyond the home and unwaged labor within it, as core black-market melodramas do. The chief subject of this chapter, *The Americans* does. Also indebted to *The Manchurian Candidate*, this story of Soviet sleeper agents living in the US begins in 1981 and takes us to the start of glasnost and the beginning of the end of the Cold War. Like the serials just discussed, *The Americans* depicts a collapse of geopolitical barriers. But it also captures what seems a collapse of domestic labor roles. There are for Elizabeth and Philip Jennings no distinctions between work and home and, ostensibly, no traditional gender roles. They work side by side and Elizabeth is if anything the more dominant—even though, like Mathison and Crain, her worldly commitments set her against family life even as she and not Philip dutifully performs the housework that keeps their household running.

While always focused on the daily rounds of the industrious Jennings household, *The Americans* also thinks intelligently on the range of collectives that set their family in motion. The first sections explain why *The Americans* is a black-market melodrama, how it links espionage and housework, and how it sheds light on deindustrialization and the rise of what Arlie Russell Hochschild calls "emotional labor." The next sections link emotional labor's felt alienations to the drama's corporate allegory. Seen one way, the Jenningses' allegiance to the KGB captures the allegiance of oversees workers to transnational corporations that were beginning in the 1980s to move goods and services around the globe with greater ease. Seen another way, the two capture the future militants hiding in a proletarianizing US middle class. Neither way of seeing need prevent us from registering how the two allegorize media workers at Rupert Murdoch's News Corporation. The political implications of that allegory might have made it seem a stretch, at least before the 2016 US elections, when Russian intelligence services threw in with the American right. But as *The Manchurian Candidate* had insisted, Manichean belief systems reverse themselves with ease. And it is possible to glimpse in the drama's concatenation of left and right the utopian dimensions of a more encompassing ideological field. *The Americans* is fascinated by the occult capitalist agencies that drive its Communist characters. And as it encases its Russian dolls in progressively larger ones, the better to personify those elusive agencies, it discovers that its fantasies of personhood are not so personal after all, but incipiently communist.

The Russians Love Their Children Too

In *The Americans*, Elizabeth and Philip Jennings are KGB agents masquerading as an affluent couple in 1980s Washington, DC. They have two children, Paige and Henry. They are, in the words of the FBI, "supersecret spies living next door" who "look like us" and "speak better English than we do" (1.1). So deeply undercover are the Jenningses that it can be hard—for the FBI and, ultimately, for the couple—to know what separates them from ordinary white middle-class Americans (fig. 4.2). They do not speak Russian and are under orders not to discuss each other's pasts because, as the Soviet colonel who arranges their marriage explains to Elizabeth, it will be easier to remain undetected "if there is no other version of this man hiding away in the back of your mind" (1.1). Their children know nothing of their secrets, at least initially. And Philip and Elizabeth don't pretend to run the travel agency to which they commute daily; they actually run it. Philip doesn't pretend to love the Camaro he purchases on a whim; he really does. That degree of immersion makes it possible to claim that while the two are spies masquerading as Americans, they are also, in a less literal sense, Americans masquerading as spies.

According to the drama's creator Joel Weisberg, "*The Americans* is at its core a marriage story. International relations is just an allegory for the human relations. Sometimes, when you're struggling in your marriage or with your kid, it feels like life or death."[6] Critics echo this claim. Calling *The Americans* "one of the most multilayered dramas on TV," Joshua Rothman argues that its title "has many meanings"; its "implication is

4.2. *The Americans*: "Super-secret spies living next door."

that we are all, in some sense, undercover in our own lives. Parents who aren't spies nevertheless hide things from their children and each other; even people with nothing to hide (if such people exist) must find ways to perform their normality." Emily Nussbaum adds that the drama "is about life as kinky role play" just as it "is about human personality as a cruel performance, even (and sometimes especially) with the people we claim to love."[7]

"Cruel performances," Rothman and Nussbaum might have added, generate the pervasive sense of alienation and unreality experienced by the protagonists, who tend not to know when they are acting and when they are not. Elizabeth's ex-lover, who knows her secret, tells her, "Your marriage ain't real. Your husband ain't real. None of this domesti-shitty is real" (1.3). Elizabeth has ended their affair because she has begun to have real rather than faked feelings for Philip, with whom she has been living for years. She tells him, "I want us to be able to say what's true. I want us, it to be . . . I want it to be real" (1.7). Philip loves her desperately, but has just come from a sexual liaison, and so lies to Elizabeth. She discovers the lie and withdraws. The Soviet operative who handles the couple

CHAPTER 4

4.3. *The Americans*: "I want us to be real."

wants them disaffected. "If you start to think of your marriage as real," she tells Elizabeth, "it doesn't work . . . it's an arrangement" (1.8). This is also true for Philip, who is tasked with seducing and then marrying Martha, an FBI worker. Martha falls for him and, half aware she is being duped, asks him just before they wed, "Just please tell me one thing, is this real?" (1.9). Philip in turn develops what he thinks might be real rather than faked feelings for Martha, which jeopardizes his mission. But like Elizabeth and Martha, he's lost the ability to know when he's acting and when he's not. That lost capacity is a telling measure of the drama's interest in alienation, which I understand in relation not to the *New Yorker*'s anodyne humanism ("we are all . . . undercover"), but to what were in the deindustrializing 1980s new kinds of service work. There is no single code-key that unlocks every layer of this complexly allegorical drama. But some registers coordinate others with greater coherence, and below I give pride of place to the "deep acting" that Hochschild identified as constitutive of emotional labor (fig. 4.3).

It is tempting if ultimately limiting to say that *The Americans* allegorizes the pull of a higher calling on those for whom marriage or family is emotionally unfulfilling. Philip and Elizabeth are driven by a sense of mission and purpose that Americans superficially like them might seem to lack. As a Soviet agent with whom Philip works puts it, "Only honor and duty are real" (1.7). For Elizabeth especially, serving the Party amounts to an impassioned calling that endows what would otherwise be family tedium with vivifying meaning. That calling is often outright hostile to the family; for Elizabeth, the Party promises a worker's collective incompatible with private need. *The Americans* makes a good show of taking that promise seriously, as it critiques the family from a broadly Marxist point of view (fig. 4.4). We twice find Paige reading from Marx's *Capital* and at one point a North Vietnamese operative accuses them of jeopardizing their mission because of "petty bourgeois concerns" (5.13). The words sting because Elizabeth sees their merit. But the drama takes its family critique only so far; Elizabeth will chastise the operative that he needs a life partner, not to be happy, mind you, but to be more effective at his job. In general, Elizabeth is torn: she loves her family but is typically willing to sacrifice its happiness for Party ends.

Philip is not torn. It is in their love for their children and each other, he insists, that he and Elizabeth become more than simply Russian and ultimately real. He shows the audience not simply that "the Russians love their children too," to quote Sting, but also that there can be no love of country or party greater than love of family. To his mind, he

4.4. *The Americans*: "Old Nick" Marx.

CHAPTER 4

and Elizabeth become what they pretend to be in their love for each other and their children. "Maybe this is the perfect time for us just to think about living the life we've been living but just really living it. Just being *us*. . . . We *are* Philip and Elizabeth Jennings. We have been for a very long time. So why don't we get ahead of this?" We could defect, he tells her, "take the good life and be happy," because "our family comes first" (1.1). Over six seasons, the couple's time, energy, and affective investments are caught up in the struggle between Philip's familial commitments and Elizabeth's Party loyalties. That struggle frequently amounts to one between privation and self-discipline on the one hand and consumer bounty and self-indulgence on the other. "Don't you enjoy any of this?" Philip asks her, "this house, your clothes, all those beautiful shoes?" (2.8). Doing David Byrne, she replies, this is not my house, not my life. Over time, she becomes unsure. Three seasons later, Philip is still telling her, "We're allowed to have a life" (5.13), by which he means a private family life beyond their mission. Considering what she would lose upon returning to Moscow, she marvels at her shoe collection, "Goodbye Yellow Brick Road" playing in the background, and cries. She decides to stay.

When Elizabeth and Philip do finally return to the Soviet Union, the price is far steeper. During the third season, Paige discovers her parents are spies. That the older daughter rather than younger son learns the family's secret life is one of many nods to *The Sopranos*. Meadow Soprano rather than Tony Jr. first learns the truth about their family; Soprano will spend hours in therapy mulling the consequences of that discovery and worrying he will lose his children. In its gut-wrenching final moments, *The Americans* confirms a version of Soprano's worst fears: at the last minute, Paige opts not to return to Russia with her parents. That decision is a stinging indictment. Black-market melodramas often turn on conflicts between individual and familial interests. Declaring their "family comes first," Philip offers one of the genre's most recognizable taglines. He means it, but the genre typically debunks such sentiments, as it exposes the virulent self-interest lurking in pious invocations of the family's collective good. So too, black-market melodramas tend to expose the suffering that sustains the family's fortunes. Children discover the ugly realities upon which their class status depends. In *High Castle*, for example, the Smith's eldest daughter fatefully confronts her mother and forces her to acknowledge the genocidal horror upon which the family's fortunes have been built. "Everything we have," she says, "was bought with other people's lives" (4.10). In ways too ornate to rehearse here, that familial confrontation leads directly to the destruction of the Reich

"You grind people into dust," a federal agent tells Elizabeth. "Your hands are covered in blood" (1.11). As Philip and Elizabeth negotiate their days—getting up in the morning, getting the kids to school, having dinner at the end of the day—we experience the familial ordinariness that, for example, Walter White finds so dispiriting. But the ordinary depends on ugly realities. "We should have built that secret underground chamber in the basement" (1.1), Philip tells Elizabeth. He means a wine cellar, which would have come in handy, since in this moment the two are struggling to hide a dead body. In *Breaking Bad*, Skyler chides Walter for having expected to own something grander than their modest ranch home. Were you expecting a wine cellar? she asks. Ample though it is, the Jennings home is missing this refinement. Only now the couple jokes knowingly, as Communists attuned to the dead bodies upon which American affluence is built.

If *The Americans* tells "us" about "our own lives," then it does so by holding up an unflattering mirror to affluent white Americans who pay for cable TV (and perhaps read the *New Yorker*). But the affluence is not assured. Typically, black-market melodramas depict newly wealthy white Americans who think themselves precarious. Also typically, the genre's arriviste families scramble to sustain an endangered upward mobility while casting a nostalgic eye on humbler origins. As Elizabeth and Philip recall their privation growing up in the USSR, *The Americans* generates working-class solidarity among the nouveau riche. A good portion of the drama's alienation comes from the reiterated imperative to remember where you came from; as a rule, Elizabeth offers that admonition, reminding Philip that though they have a large home and many toys, they are not really of this world. One day they will leave it, when circumstances force them back to the USSR and, more allegorically, back

CHAPTER 4

into the US working class from which they came. Don Draper's secret origins in poor white trash and Bill Hendrickson's in a rural polygamous compound generate shame rather than solidarity, in *Mad Men* and *Big Love*, but their core anxieties are the same. While the Jenningses do not experience the money trouble that drives White to meth production on *Breaking Bad*, they are still haunted by downward mobility. And as a whole, the genre discovers that fear in a newly arrived managerial rather than professional elite. If you manage others, the black-market melodrama whispers, and don't work in the professions (which once dominated TV's workplace dramas), you are at greater risk of becoming the managed.

That prospect is inextricable from the genre's fear of state persecution; in the black-market melodrama, the white middle-class family, long a beneficiary of state violence, has become an object of it. During the second season, Elizabeth picks up her morning newspaper and scans the horizon (2.2). Along with a similar scene in *Breaking Bad*, the sequence quotes moments in *The Sopranos* when Tony walks to the end of his driveway, to pick up his paper while scanning nervously for the FBI. Like Tony, Elizabeth and Philip are on constant watch for the FBI, which, with the DEA, represents a state hostile to their class interests (fig. 4.5).

As they become subject to state power, the genre's white leads often brutally exploit the racial minorities toward which they fear themselves falling. Though its racial exploitations are not immediately economic, *Homeland* is instructive: Nicholas Brody returns from Iraq with a double, the African American Tom Walker; both work for al-Qaeda. But the two are hardly allies. Robbed of complexity and even subjectivity, Walker represents a terrorist threat more real than Brody's, and suggests, albeit too obliquely, that the nation's animus toward Islam has a more properly domestic referent (in a key sequence, Carrie discovers Brody has been signaling al-Qaeda by watching the fingering of a Black jazz trumpeter). Walker serves twice as a sacrificial object; Brody beats him almost to death to cement his bond to mastermind Abu Nazir and kills him later, in a racist exorcism that clears his way to run for Congress. *Homeland*'s title sequence warned us. It borrows from a sequence in the first film version of *The Manchurian Candidate*, in which the camera

4.5. *The Sopranos*, *Breaking Bad*, *The Americans*: Scanning for the Feds.

enters the sleeping mind of Colonel Ben Marco, returned home from an eight-year captivity in North Korea. A dreaming Marco moves from a real memory (in which his racially integrated platoon sits on stage and is watched by men and women from Red China and the Soviet Union) into a false one (in which his platoon sits before dowdy women at a New Jersey garden party). The dream rewrites racial and national difference as gender difference, subjecting the bored men to the gaze and control of a foreign power on the one hand and middle-class women on the other. In *Homeland*'s title sequence, we enter the sleeping mind of Mathison. The transpositions here set racial difference against national and gender difference. Images of Louis Armstrong and Colin Powell bookend images of Middle Eastern women in hijabs; the three images are followed by one of a helicopter gunship. African Americans are both feminized and cast as enemy combatants.

Good Communists, the Jenningses do not themselves persecute minorities; they enlist them. But the family's survival depends on a zero-sum racial logic: at one juncture, the couple leverages a Black domestic worker by poisoning her son and beating a family member; later, the couple evades the FBI because a Black militant in love with Elizabeth sacrifices himself on her behalf in a hail of gunfire. The violence makes sense of the fact that Stan Beeman, the FBI agent who lives next door, returns at the drama's start from working undercover with white supremacists. Hunting the Jenningses, Beeman hunts less overt supremacists; their politics notwithstanding, they thrive at the expense of raced populations.

In other ways, the drama represents a key evolution of the genre. Philip is not a toxic husband in the mold of Soprano, Draper, or White. On the contrary, it will seem as if he and Elizabeth have swapped traditional gender roles. He is nurturing, sensitive, and oriented to consumer goods and family; she is dispassionate, distant, and oriented to a historical mission. More importantly, though with crucial exceptions, husband and wife work side by side as equals, out of their home. The melodrama asks us to see this development as the expression of an enlightened foreign ideology and, simultaneously, the overwork besetting the harried dual-income family. But even when seeming to celebrate the family's new division of labor, *The Americans* treats the couple's relation to work in subtly different ways. As if to stress this difference, the drama ends by reimposing the gender norms it only seemed to overthrow. In its final season, to which I turn below, Philip runs their failing travel agency, as it struggles in the face of new challenges from the internet. Elizabeth works undercover as a nurse tending a dying cancer patient. He will try to learn, too late, to fire workers with an eye on the bottom line, while she will learn, perhaps just in time, who she really is—by caring for others and contemplating art. Depressively realist from the start, *The Americans* will leave the Jenningses utterly crushed by the End of History, the Soviet Union about to collapse, familiar gender hierarchies reestablished, and its reduced nuclear family, now bereft of children, still the only available form of collective life.

Broken with a Feather Duster

The first season begins with the speed-up that will consume the Jenningses. Reagan has just announced his Star Wars program, and the couple is told it will have to work faster than ever, since the clock on a new arms race is now ticking. Quite literally: in one plotline, the couple coerces an African American domestic worker to steal a clock from Caspar Weinberger's study so they can turn it into a surveillance device. The couple is itself surveilled by an always-ticking clock. After Paige discovers her parents' secret, they argue over whether she should join the KGB. Elizabeth wants her to; Philip doesn't. Ultimately, Elizabeth decides Paige is more suited to a nine-to-five desk job than fieldwork. She prefers this less to spare her daughter the sex work and violence required of field agents than to give her stable daily rhythms. "She'll have it better," Elizabeth says. "She will go to work in the morning and she will come home at night" (6.2).

That is an improvement over mom and dad's life because, for them, everyday rhythms do not apply. They work erratic hours, travel incessantly, and often go to work in other peoples' homes. Philip intermittently works/lives in Martha's home for years. The working day distends. At one point, Paige, Elizabeth, and her handler watch Mikhail Gorbachev

CHAPTER 4

announce arms talks with the US on TV; Paige asks them, Are you now finished with your jobs? "The work never ends" (6.8), replies the handler. Nor does it end for Beeman, who spends his every waking hour hunting for spies who happen to live next door. He has been leading his own double life; at the drama's start, he is returning from three years undercover and trying to transition back to family life and what his wife calls "the regular world" (1.1). But his world is not regular: like the Jenningses, Beeman is a busy bee; he "punches the clock, but the clock never stops ticking, never" (1.7). For the Jenningses, work does not necessarily eat into time they might spend with family, as it does for Beeman. Their problem is that work and family time are the same. They work together on multiple jobs involving diverse competencies, both at and away from their home, which is less a retreat from work than a work barracks for the team that is their family. When Paige joins that team and her brother goes to boarding school, their household becomes unambiguously a workplace. Wherever you go at the end of the day, a defecting scientist asks Philip, "is 'home' the right word?" (2.5). The KGB manages the family's every intimacy—by arranging their marriage and forcing them to recruit their daughter into wetwork, for example. Their employer controls their lives on and off the clock; but in truth there is no clock, just as there are no separate spheres.

As we have seen, the couple's work life is organized by a sense of mission as much as by a brute struggle to survive. Endless work thus renders acute a contradiction between the Protestant calling and the menial job. The drama elaborates a longstanding association, first explored by Michael Walzer, between Communism and radical Protestantism, such that the former represents a version of the higher purpose and calling that the latter sublimated into the career or vocation.[8] In so doing, the drama asks whether it is any longer possible to conceive of middle-class service work as the expression of a vocation. The Jenningses repeatedly exploit the conceptual transfers between Christianity and Communism—most obviously in their insistence that Paige attend the Reed Street Church (whose extra *e* hardly disguises its pastor's political sympathies). Paige joins in an act of teenage rebellion, and then moves to quit, but her parents drop their opposition to the church and now insist that she continue to attend to avoid arousing suspicion. For his part, after learning the Jenningses' secret, the pastor supports the family's espionage because he wishes to reconcile his activism to the Soviet Union's social mission.

We thus witness what Max Weber would have called an "elective affinity" between the pastor's anticapitalism and theirs, even as we confront a growing mismatch between the endless work that grinds the Jenningses down and the elevated ideals with which they justify that work. That mismatch emerges alongside but is not reducible to one between murderous means and noble ends. Elizabeth is forever reminding Philip, "this is the job," by which she means, all of this and worse is required by the Party and is in fact the substance of our work. And what a range of work it is: the two are flexible employees, as they become by turns sex workers, assassins, technicians, best friends, whatever "the job" requires. Over time, the sheer diversity and volume of this grunt work renders talk of noble ends beside the point. Elizabeth's ideological fervor is revealed to be less morally suspect than simply incompatible with the degrading labor into which they are forced, such that the melodrama captures the absurdity of trying to reconcile an older notion of the calling with both the low-end temp work toward which the white middle class feels itself falling and the unwaged reproductive labor of housework itself.

As we have seen, Elizabeth's love of country often stands against the love of family with which capitalist patriarchy has long explained the reproductive labor of women denied access to the wage. But the drama also superimposes those two callings while emptying each of its ostensibly higher purpose. Tradecraft often employs terms—like "housekeeping" and "dry cleaning"—that evoke gendered domestic labor (spy fiction's use of these terms stems mainly from John le Carré). In *Counterpart*, Emily Burton-Silk works in counterintelligence, which she calls "housekeeping." On *The Americans*, espionage allegorizes Elizabeth's place in a recalcitrant division of labor. At one point, she tells her handler that an informant will turn because he "could be broken with a feather duster" (1.12). The instrument is apt, insofar as it is Elizabeth rather than Philip who is accused of grinding people "into dust."

Her espionage codes housework far more frequently than his. Elizabeth has reason to be ambivalent about the claims of family. Her "secret

CHAPTER 4

underground chamber" exists not beneath the laundry room (where Philip wanted his wine cellar) but *is* the laundry room, which serves as the couple's headquarters. On *Breaking Bad*, White hides his laundered money, made by cooking meth beneath a laundry facility, in the wall behind his family's washer and dryer. Elizabeth and Philip have built a secret storage space into the wall behind their washer and dryer, in which they hide their spy gear. The couple spends a lot of time in this room decoding messages. But only Elizabeth does laundry there, and that mundane fact might be the drama's most important secret message.

It is in that laundry room that we witness the convergence of Elizabeth's many roles. She sublimates rage over her rape by a Soviet officer, the drama reveals, into a passionate defense of Mother Russia (holding a carving knife in her kitchen, she resolves to kill that officer, now hidden in her garage). And unlike Philip, she has a living parent in Russia, a mother who when raising Elizabeth was forced to exchange sex for food. Elizabeth's matrilineal bond to Russia is organized around the need to defend physically against men and drives her subsequent connection with Paige; the two grow close only during violent sparring sessions, as mother teaches daughter to fight. But it is in the laundry room that we witness Elizabeth at her most raw and vulnerable—when she accesses cassette tapes dictated by her mother. She leans against the back of the dryer and listens: "They brought me a picture of you this year, with your children. And husband. Your family is so beautiful. I look at it every day" (1.13). We close in on Elizabeth's tear-stained face, gentle piano lilting in the background. She's crying as she listens to a mother she might never see again (fig. 4.6). The scene is melodramatic and even soap operatic by design—and in a surprisingly complex way.

In *High Castle*, Japanese trade minister Tagomi travels between dimensions. In one scene, having traversed worlds to visit his family (now dead in his dimension), he watches TV. He flips through different channels; the first features a program in which a white woman sings a duet with her Asian American husband, played by a white actor in yellowface. She sings, "I run the boarding house"; he responds, "I run the laundry" (2.5). The gendered inversion tracks a racial one; in this reality, Japanese men are feminized, subservient partners. Tagomi moves on and, after

4.6. *The Americans*: The secret life of laundry.

watching a series of commercials, finds a news program. Though it contains no exact equivalent of this Orientalism, *The Americans* performs a version of this gendered channel hopping. The ideological competition between Philip and Elizabeth, between the claims of family on the one hand and work and history on the other, is at times a generic competition between soap opera and both spy narratives and the news. Black-market melodramas like *The Sopranos*, *Weeds*, and *Breaking Bad* admix soap and gangster film conventions. Genres collapse in tandem with separate spheres: family life is exposed as a gangster story, and gangster stories as family melodramas. But more simply, these melodramas embrace testosterone-laden secret lives to stave off soap opera's lowbrow cultural associations and to thereby become quality TV worth paying for. In *The Americans*, Elizabeth bears the weight of that disavowal while Philip safely relishes the down-market pleasures of family life and his children's affections. He plays the sensitive and emotive soul bent on self-actualization; she is tasked not just with the laundry, but with keeping

CHAPTER 4

at bay melodrama's unwanted emotional excess. Elizabeth often acts out male fantasy, dressing up and playing dominatrix, say, when eliciting information. But though she will play the happy homemaker next door, she finds it hard to be tender with her family. And while she is forever watching TV, she prefers the news. She is stymied by soap opera. "I'm just trying to understand," Elizabeth says to Paige, who has shown her a soap. Baffled, she stares at the screen and stammers, "It's not logical, it's emotional" (4.12). There is something she cannot see, but her blindness is born of more than subjective impairment. No matter its generic disguise, *The Americans* is, in addition to being quality TV, also quantity TV: an evening soap. And in Elizabeth's perplexity at the soap, we witness the program's simultaneous fascination with and disavowal of soap opera's historical orientation to women working at home. *The Americans* would ward off that orientation by dressing up the serial structures and familial intimacies of soap opera in something both political and sexy. Its Cold War narrative doesn't just require Elizabeth to dress in costume, in other words, it *is* that costume. Even so, the clothes must come off to be laundered; Elizabeth must do both her spy work and her housework, as well as the sex work that in many ways connects her work and family roles.

Nominating housework as the melodrama's key referent—the laboring body beneath the sexy clothes—does not vitiate its Cold War frame. As a champion of the Party's collective good, rather than her family's private good, Elizabeth echoes the postwar "momism that identified domineering mothers as the spearhead of Soviet infiltration" (a domination that Philip Wylie attributed to mothers "having lost the household functions of preindustrial women").[9] And of course the Cold War played out on any number of fronts, one of which was the interior of the family home. During their "kitchen debate" in 1959, Richard Nixon told Nikita Khrushchev that the US would triumph over the Soviet Union in part because of the luxuries of the suburban home, which was "designed to make things easier for our women."[10] They didn't make things easier, in fact, either for white middle-class women or for the nonwhite working-class women once employed in their homes, but now out of work.[11] Women were asked to see that increased workload as an opportunity; as

Betty Friedan put it, wives were told to consider "housework a medium of expression" for their "femininity and individuality."[12]

The first season ends with Paige, having begun to suspect that something is off, searching the laundry room for evidence that her mother is more than she appears. Elizabeth *is* more than she appears. But Paige is looking not for a spy but for her mother's "femininity and individuality," as she understands those terms. What part of my mother lives here, in the laundry room, in these machines and in these well laundered, neatly folded clothes? As she turns to the washer and the dryer and the clothes, hoping for clues, we listen to Peter Gabriel's "Games without Frontiers, Wars without Tears." *The Americans* eschews but does not escape tears, while dressing up "washboard weepies" (as soaps had long been known) in colder Cold War affects. But as we will see, pain suffuses its borderless world.

Managed Hearts

The same year HBO green-lit *The Sopranos*, Arlie Russell Hochschild's bestseller *The Time Bind: When Work Becomes Home and Home Becomes Work* (1997) described a hall of mirrors akin to the one that would be featured in black-market melodramas. She argued that men and women both were experiencing work as more rewarding and nurturing (and more homelike) and home as more tedious and demanding (and more worklike). Her claims might have been faulted for producing too normative and white a vision of family; for giving short shrift to the necessity that pressed workers into long hours; and for paying insufficient attention to the systemic dynamics that drove employers to extend the length and intensity of the working day. Nevertheless, her critical paradigm-shifting claims captured meaningful shifts.

Just as relevant to black-market melodramas is the concept Hochschild introduced in 1983: "emotional labor." This term names service work that standardizes and requires employees to self-manage their emotional displays. Insofar as it describes self-management, the term is sometimes distinguished from "affective labor" that produces affective states in others—as does therapy work, say, or most kinds of entertainment work. The distinction can be hazy (an employee is typically tasked with self-management precisely to produce affective states in others) but, overall, emotional labor is narrower in application than either affective or "immaterial labor," which can describe any labor geared to "the development of the social individual which appears as the great foundation-stone of production and of wealth," to quote Marx's "Fragment on Machines" (to which I return below).[13]

Published in 1983, two years after the events first chronicled in *The Americans*, Hochschild's *The Managed Heart* estimates that one-third of all US workers, "the great majority" of whom were middle class, were then performing emotional labor, a form of service work that was filling the void occasioned by the retreat of manufacturing jobs.[14] Her central case study is Delta Airlines and the "social engineering" with which it inculcates specific emotional displays in flight attendants: a welcoming smile, a gracious nod, and, in general, the sunny disposition of "southern womanhood." Emotional labor as such is hardly novel, she grants; what's new, rather, are systematic corporate efforts to standardize specific workplace emotions that are so deeply felt as to not be feigned. The "deep acting" protocols that most interest her, at Delta and elsewhere, demand "deceiving oneself as much as deceiving others. In surface acting we deceive others about what we really feel, but we do not deceive ourselves. . . . In deep acting we make feigning easy by making it unnecessary. At Delta, the techniques of deep acting are joined to the principles of social engineering."[15]

In part, Hochschild describes the early stages of what would be a widespread turn to employee self-management in service work. Some form of self-management was always integral to service work. But historians argue that by the end of the 1960s, service employees increasingly were exhorted to supervise themselves and so replace (costly) supervisors. This project, write Luc Boltanski and Eve Chiapello, involved "transferring constraints from external organizational mechanisms to people's internal dispositions, and for the powers of control they exercise to be consistent with the firm's general project."[16] Hochschild is interested in how the self-management that is deep acting produces a wholesale transformation of interior life. In deep acting, "display is a natural result of working on feeling; the actor does not try to *seem* happy or sad but rather expresses spontaneously, as the Russian director Constantin Stanislavski urged, a real feeling that has been self-induced."[17] And because the worker has been commanded to self-induce feelings, she becomes unable to distinguish between her own "feeling commands" and those of her employer. She "wonders whether her smile and the emotional labor that keeps it sincere are really hers. Do they really express a part of her? Or are they deliberately worked up and delivered on behalf of the company? Where inside her is the part that acts 'on behalf of the company'?" The alienation that gives rise to this type of question, she insists, is new. "Those who perform emotional labor in the course of giving service are like those who perform physical labor in the course of making things: both are subject to the rules of mass production. But when the product—the thing to be engineered, mass-produced, and subjected to speed-up and slowdown—is a smile, a mood, a feeling, or a relationship, it comes to belong more to the organization and less to the self. And so in the country that most publicly celebrates the individual, more people privately wonder, without tracing the question to its deepest social root: What do I really feel?"[18]

That question arises in an environment modeled on domestic space. Workers at Delta, Hochschild argues, experience a bewildering conflation of work and home that evokes soap opera specifically: "Airlines seem to model 'stage sets' on the living rooms seen on daytime television serials; the Muzak tunes, the TV and movie screens, and the smiling flight attendants serving drinks are all calculated to 'make you feel at home.' Even fellow passengers are considered part of the stage."[19] Airlines transform passenger cabins into sets by using blandly homelike settings that evoke "the idea of a private family and the feelings one would have there." But the idea is implausible. "The home is no longer a sanctuary," she writes, even as "the atmosphere of the private living room, which a young flight attendant is asked to recall as she works in the airplane cabin, has *already borrowed* some of the elements of that cabin." This echo chamber makes it still harder to distinguish between home and work since, in asking its flight attendants to truly experience prescribed emotions, Delta asks them to perform the "shadow labor" long demanded of housewives. "The emotion work of enhancing the status and well-being of others," she writes, "is a form of what Ivan Illich has called 'shadow labor,' an unseen effort, which, like housework, does not quite count as labor but is nevertheless crucial to getting other things done. As with doing housework well, the trick is to erase any evidence of effort, to offer only the clean house and the welcoming smile."[20] Housework is not itself emotional labor, Hochschild would later insist, when the term threatened to become too capacious.[21] Emotional labor is paid for and subject to corporate standardization. Nevertheless, it is denigrated because of its association with housework. Citing Richard Sennett and Jonathan Cobb in *The Hidden Injuries of Class*, Hochschild notes that, despite the often-middle-class nature of the work, Americans consider emotional labor of far lower status than industrial labor because of its associations with housework: "At the bottom end of the scale are found not factory jobs but service jobs where the individual has to perform personally for someone else."[22]

So many are the resonances between Hochschild's study and *The Americans* that it's plausible the writing staff was asked to read it. Elizabeth and Philip run a travel agency and Elizabeth will at one point impersonate a flight attendant. More basically, the drama understands spy work to produce a self-deception akin to Hochschild's deep acting. Tasked with playing parts, Elizabeth and Philip are chameleons. And as they play their parts, they are remade. They become a loving couple because the Party asks them to play one. Philip falls in love with Martha because he is told to pretend to fall in love; he becomes Stan's best friend because he's been told to. (In a workplace romance that echoed the drama, actors Matthew Rhys and Keri Russell, who play Philip and Elizabeth, respectively, fell in love and married, while playing a couple that fell in love and married while playing a married couple.)[23] All of which suggests it is not quite right to say, as Rhys does, that the drama's "scene of domesticity" is "an absolute lie."[24] It is a scene of managed emotional labor that converts work performance into interior reality.

And yet the question that Hochschild discerns in new workplaces— "What do I really feel?"—will not go away. Their emotional labor generates in the Jenningses inchoate yearnings. They imagine a more fulfilling species of intimacy beyond work, even as they dimly recognize that their bruising secret life only amplifies the everyday tedium to which it seems an alternative. The drama tracks their respective acts of self-management as they generate ineffable longings for something more authentic. For Hochschild, a longing for "'authentic' or 'natural' feeling" is a response to "the rise of the *corporate* use of guile and the organized training of feeling to sustain it. The more the heart is managed, the more we value the unmanaged heart." She adds, "One clue to the modern-day celebration of spontaneous feeling is the growing popularization of psychological therapies, especially those that stress 'getting in touch with' spontaneous feeling."[25] Philip turns to one of those therapies: hoping to live more authentically, he takes Erhard Seminars Training (EST). "It's hard—marriage," he has earlier told Stan. "You know, you love your wife, and then the day-to-day crap starts to creep in" (2.14). It is not clear which wife he means and what "the day-to-day stuff" is. But he takes EST classes because he longs for something more; and unrelentingly dark though it is, *The Americans* is surprisingly sincere when holding out hope that Philip and Elizabeth will slough off their emotional masks and find it.

Alienation and Personification

Marx's account of alienation, Fredric Jameson notes, turns on "the fourfold 'separation' of the worker from tools, from object, from other workers, and from species-being as such, or in other words from that productive activity that makes the human animal human." These separations culminate, Jameson adds, in "the new space of the factory inside which production is concentrated" and in which "those tools or instruments from which the laborer was initially separated . . . have now become something like ends in themselves."[26] Running alongside this development was "the spatial separation of the homeplace from the workplace," which, according to Wally Seccombe, turned on the "decline of various forms of commodity production in and around the household"; "the decline of subcontracting arrangements and family hiring, so that the great majority of workers were now hired and fired individually and paid in person for their work"; "the severance of all remaining paternalist ties to the sphere of subsistence, so that employers no longer had any direct jurisdiction over the lives of their employees off the job"; and "the complete monetization of the wage, so that workers received nothing but their paychecks in exchange for their labor power."[27]

Marx presumes but does not elaborate the separate spheres that came to define the nineteenth-century working-class family. He says little about the exclusion of women from factory work during the second industrial revolution and the concomitant production of a gendered division of labor in which a woman's unwaged labor reproduced her husband's labor power. But these developments are implicit in his account of home as an existential reprieve from work (rather than a physical domicile) that allows the male worker access to his "species being" (while his wife, we assume, does the housework). The worker, Marx writes, "feels himself only outside his work, and feels beside himself in his work. He is at home when he is not working, and when he is working, he is not at home." That much said, home is not a true reprieve any more than alienation is limited to waged work. The worker cannot clock out of alienation. Only communism can end that alienation, Marx speculated, as "the *positive* transcendence of *private property* as *human self-estrangement*," and as "the complete return of man to himself as a *social* (i.e., human) being."[28]

Though not limited to his working hours, the worker's alienation stems from his estrangement from the product of his labors. For Marx, "the worker is related to the *product of labor* as to an *alien* object"—a commodity that seems to possess those qualities that the worker has lost in its production:

> Whatever the product of his labor is, he is not. Therefore, the greater this product, the less is he himself. The *alienation* of the worker in his product means not only that his labor becomes an object, an *external* existence, but that it exists *outside him*, independently, as something alien to him, and that it becomes a power on its own confronting him. It means that the life which he has conferred on the object confronts him as something hostile and alien.[29]

This early account reemerges in different form in *Capital* when Marx describes the commodity fetish, which confronts the worker not as it expresses a "definite social relation between men"—one that might reveal the relation of his labor to the social totality of labor—but as "the fantastic form of a relation between things." The alien object that is the commodity assumes human characteristics even as the worker becomes more like a commodity. Personification and alienation are reciprocal processes, the former emerging as an effect of the latter. E. Urbánek describes this process as the "reification of persons and the personification of things."[30]

The commodity is for Marx an ersatz person, an alien power that appears to the worker as all that "he is not." We might say, at a higher level of abstraction, that the corporation is an alien power (in Timothy Brennan's terms, an "*imperson* of capital") that first confronts the alienated working class—amid increasingly collectivized production processes—as everything "*it* is not."[31] Armin Beverungen, Anna-Maria Murtola, and Gregory Schwartz note that the "socialism of capital"

> was used from the late nineteenth century onwards to denote the socialization of capital, i.e. the way in which the socialist threat of organized labor was suddenly confronted with the concentration of capital in the emerging modern corporation and with the abstractions of finance. While Marx . . . does not directly use the phrase "socialism of capital," he notes the rise of the joint-stock company, in which private property is conceptually transformed into social property, as stocks came to be held by a greater number of people in common.[32]

Corporations were a kind of bastardized socialism. In Marx's words, they expressed the "contradiction between the general social power into which capital develops, on the one hand, and the private power of the individual capitalists over these social conditions of production, on the other." This contradiction, he adds, optimistically, "contains the solution of the problem, because it implies at the same time the transformation of the conditions of production into general, common, social, conditions."[33]

Autonomist Marxists like Antonio Negri, Franco Berardi, Maurizio Lazzareto, Michael Hardt, and Paolo Virno think the problem all but solved. In an oft-debated section of *The Grundrisse*, the "Fragment on Machines," Marx speculates that the social cooperation and "general social knowledge," or "General Intellect," required of factory production might someday become a "*direct force of production.*" In *A Grammar of the Multitude*, Virno follows Negri in claiming that the General Intellect already has, and in the process realized "the communism of capital." This requires a new figure, one capable of personifying the collective agencies here at stake. Virno returns to the seventeenth century and finds in Hobbes an adequate term. For Virno, Marx's General Intellect creates "the multitude." That entity represents the many as it escapes state and corporate efforts to reduce it to the one, or any singular thing (including any one social class), and as it embodies the communism now immanent in "post-Fordist" capitalism. Whether the multitude is a personification at all is open to debate. What matters is that, for Virno, it names the collective agent of "the communism of capital" that arises as "capitalistic initiative orchestrates for its own benefit" "the abolition of that intolerable scandal, the persistence of wage labor" and "the valorization of all that which renders the life of an individual unique."[34]

Virno focuses on managerial labor in the developed core that "appropriates the special characteristics of the performing artist," on the one hand, whose performances lack any end beyond themselves, and the politician, on the other, whose performances require virtuosic communication. He's particularly interested in the culture or communications industry, which houses "the matrix of post-Fordism" because it specializes in the "'production of communication by means of communication.'" For Horkheimer and Adorno, the culture industry was "weak and dependent" on "the most powerful sectors of industry: steel, petroleum, electricity, chemicals." By contrast, for Virno, the culture industry is "exemplary and pervasive," as the "*industry of the means of production.*" It "produces (regenerates, experiments with) communicative procedures, which" then "function also as means of production in the more traditional sectors of our contemporary economy."[35] Virno says little more about the culture industry. Nor does he situate his account of post-Fordism generally relative to secular trends in global production, which in no way have eliminated "the intolerable scandal" of wage labor.[36] Indeed, his terms invalidate distinctions between the waged and the unwaged. He reduces labor to language use and social cooperation. He mystifies ownership and romanticizes distributed creativity.

Virno conceives of post-Fordism as Franco Berardi conceives of "semiotic capitalism," not as part of "that chain whose preceding links are . . . the worker by trade and the assembly-line worker," but as it "projects itself into" "the level of life forms, of cultural consumption, of linguistic practices," which is to say "into every aspect of experience, subsuming linguistic competencies, ethical propensities, and the nuances of subjectivity."[37] This produces a familiarly postmodern account of alienation. In "the domain of the postindustrial," Berardi writes, we witness alienation as "de-realization," which is "the social, linguistic, psychic, emotional impossibility of touching the thing, of having a body, of enjoying the presence of the other as tangible and physical extension."[38] *The Americans* pays predictable homage to this cliché, to be sure. And, in fact, Elizabeth and Philip are, in Virno's terms, both politicians and performing artists. But the two do not capture the communism (small "c") immanent in capitalism either by expressing "de-realization" or by representing (absurdly broad) "communicative procedures" already deployed by "the culture industry." Quite the contrary, the drama's utopian horizon takes meaningful shape only as we pass through not simply Soviet Communism (big "C"), but the specific private property structure known as News Corp (big "C").

News of the World

In the final season of *The Americans*, Elizabeth goes undercover as a care worker. She and Philip are estranged and no longer work together. He runs the family's failing travel agency; she tends the dying wife of a government official while spying on him. The wife is a painter and has been teaching Elizabeth to draw. At one point, in the episode "Harvest" (6.7), she asks Elizabeth to explain a sketch of clouds glimpsed through an airplane window. Elizabeth does not know why she drew the image. In response to her uncertainty, the artist tells Elizabeth how truly to see her subjects:

CHAPTER 4

> You don't know what you see until. . . . you need to bring yourself into it. If you don't, what is the point? But if you do, there's a moment when it's not you seeing it, it's I don't know, it's a something come [she gasps] something comes through. You need to bring all yourself to it. And then they'll let you get out of your own way. . . . I know, you have no idea what I'm talking about.

Elizabeth does understand. She is not just pretending to be a care worker; she brings herself to her role, gets out of her own way, and is made over. She seems when speaking to the artist not to be acting, but rather tranquil and wiped clean. Her undercover care work, the drama suggests, humanizes her, and is in part responsible for her decision to forswear hardline KGB factions wanting to overthrow Gorbachev. So too, what seems a humanizing experience with art allows her finally to commit to a life with Philip beyond spying. The scene reveals the drama's conservative imagination, insofar as it links Elizabeth's affective education to the gendered work from which her spying was from the start an allegorical escape.

But in other respects, her experience is not humanizing at all. What "comes through" when Elizabeth gets out of her own way is wholly ambiguous—as is the enigmatic "they" to which the artist refers. With echoes of T. S. Eliot, the painter suggests that only artists possessed of real personalities know what it means to give them up and thereby achieve the saving grace of impersonality. But her advice differs from Eliot's, insofar as she speaks while convulsed with a pain that she thinks essential to her art. "The more perfect the artist," wrote the poet, "the more completely separate in him will be the man who suffers and the mind which creates; the more perfectly will the mind digest and transmute the passions which are its material."[39] Conversely, the painter paints an untransmuted pain. Her room is a menagerie of agonized faces that scream from the walls as if from another plane of reality (fig. 4.7). If these are faces, they are incomplete personifications, tortured forms arrested on their way either to or from differentiation.

The scene echoes one in the first season, in the apartment of Gregory, Elizabeth's Black lover. His walls are lined with art, and on one occasion Elizabeth stands before a painting of two figures with red blots for heads

4.7. *The Americans*: "Something comes through."

and asks about the "red marshmallows" (fig. 4.8). It's easy to see why she's captivated: red replaces what is potentially personal about these figures, as it does for her and Philip, who have been tasked by a Red collective to perform but never accept American individualism. The blots make sense of moments leading to the scene with the artist. Elizabeth makes her sketch of the airplane window while returning from Chicago with Philip, whom she has enlisted in one last mission, the outcome of which requires him to remove the hands and head of a CIA agent with an ax. Philip pays a price for the grisly depersonalization. Elizabeth later finds him at the travel agency staring blankly into an empty computer screen; he's just fired workers and seems stunned as a result. She says, "I wanted to check on you; in the garage . . . your face" (6.7). He had lost his features in a way that evoked his victim. His expression was then as vacant as it is now; in a sense, his face was not there, like the faces in Gregory's painting. It is similarly missing as Elizabeth approaches him, and as he contemplates driving workers into the anonymous ranks of the unemployed, another version of the mysterious corporate "they" to which the artist refers. "In business," Philip earlier muses, "there's always this pressure about growth, that if you're not growing, you're not succeeding." And so he takes out loans and hires extra workers. But the

CHAPTER 4

4.8. *The Americans*: The red marshmallows.

travel agency doesn't grow, and when he tells Elizabeth he might have hired too many, she replies, "I keep forgetting their names" (6.4).

The moment with the artist is particularly enigmatic because *The Americans* refuses to decide whether the couple's true faces and names are obscured by their Communism or by their daily capitalist cosplay. But that choice is in some sense misleading, insofar as the drama's Communist collectives allegorize capitalist ones: the nuclear family on the one hand, and the corporation on the other. Indeed, we might understand the faces that line the artist's wall as personifications of the corporate agencies animating the drama, such that Elizabeth and Philip become News Corp employees, and the red marshmallows figures for the red not of the Communist but of the Republican Party, on behalf of whose class interests Fox News operates.

"There is an excitement, an electrifying sense of accomplishment, when you give Murdoch what he wants," writes biographer Michael

Wolff. "Every second spent working for Murdoch is a second spent thinking about what Murdoch wants. He inhabits you."[40] *The Managed Heart* takes up a similar haunting; it recounts workers wondering, "Where inside [me] is the part that acts 'on behalf of the company'?" Hochschild adds, "As workers, the more seriously social engineering affects our behavior and our feelings, the more intensely we must address a new ambiguity about who is directing them (is this me or the company talking?)."[41] To read *The Americans* simply as Murdoch talking is to commit any number of critical sins. It risks devaluing those who made the drama, for example, and dismissing their autonomy. Surely a serial this smart deserves more respect. Likewise, to read the drama as Murdoch talking is potentially to confuse the capitalist with the collective agencies he only personifies. But we are justified in proceeding provisionally with this thought experiment if only because for decades News Corp has seemed the expression of a single capitalist's vision in ways that other media companies have not. As Scott W. Fitzgerald notes, before it was spun off in 2013, it was "the epitome of the new corporate empires that have used their grasp of new technologies and overall financial and operational scope to escape the confines of the modern world of national cultural and nation states and to become sovereign entities in their own right: electronic empires."[42] But the publicly traded company was and is unusual for being a family controlled enterprise managed by a single man. And the nature of Murdoch's management has made it possible if not unavoidable to read News Corp as intentionally promulgating a coherent political program. To conceive of News Corp in these terms is to speak of ideology in the weak rather than strong sense; it has been first and foremost a news company because it has been driven by Murdoch's editorial position taking. Those positions are all too familiar: having attached his fortunes to Reagan and Thatcher in the 1980s, he spent the next decades proselytizing on behalf of state downsizing, union busting, upward income redistribution, and the raft of policies that have defined the political project of neoliberalism.

That said, we must also address "an ambiguity about who [or what] is [or has been] directing" *him*. Murdoch is a placeholder for or personification of the financial and class interests that speak through his company. Neither he nor his company is the definitive origin of the forces that drive the drama; ultimately, that production credit belongs to a global accumulation crisis in which, starting in the 1970s, mobile capital in the US sought better rates of return than could be found in manufacturing. As I have insisted throughout, in ostensibly developed economies, that accumulation crisis produced and still produces the erosion of the family wage and the rise of reproductive labor that *The Americans* and black-market melodramas allegorize. That crisis also remade the media industry, which sucked up vast sums of mobile capital (as debt). More than most media moguls, Murdoch navigated the crisis adroitly. He grew his corporation by leveraging the steady income provided by his newspapers (and his changing citizenship) into loans that allowed him to consolidate otherwise diverse assets (TV, film, music, etc.) into a single empire.

For David Harvey, neoliberalism's global elites "attach themselves to specific state apparatuses for both the advantages and protections that this affords them." He frequently cites Murdoch, who "may begin in Australia then concentrate on Britain before finally taking up citizenship . . . in the United States."[43] Murdoch was a lamprey fish, a parasite feeding off global capital as it encircled the world. And his personal mobility was an expression of finance capital's new mobility, as it moved strategically between different state accounting regimes. His relocations secured him credit on more favorable terms. In 1985, for instance, he assumed massive debt to purchase TV stations in the US. But because he was still an Australian citizen, and News Corp was listed in Australia, the debt became an asset for further leveraging.

> In the United States, preferred shares, the type that Murdoch is issuing to the television station bondholders, are considered debt; you *have* to pay their holders what you said you would pay them before anyone else; these preferred shareholders are not, like common shareholders, owners who are part of the fate of the enterprise. In Australia, however, preferred shareholders *are* considered owners—hence the value of their interest is not a balance-sheet minus but a balance-sheet plus. In the

United States, the television deal makes News Corp. worth $1.6 billion less; in Australia, this makes it worth $1.6 billion more, which Murdoch can borrow against.[44]

Subsequently, as Fitzgerald notes, Murdoch's political clout—secured in part by those TV stations—allowed him to move his company's headquarters to the US and to attain citizenship. This allowed him to buy more stations, because it allowed him to circumvent restrictions that limited foreign nationals from owning too much of a given media market. And when, because of this borrowing, News Corp "faced bankruptcy due to short-term debt in the early 1990s, the banking community in the three states in which News Corp. principally operated—Australia, the United Kingdom, and the United States"—was persuaded to permit "the restructuring of its operations in a manner that helped to assuage its debt concerns." This "reliance on the co-operation of three states," Fitzgerald notes, "was itself mediated through and dependent upon the neoliberal agenda of state restructuring in which these three nations had a uniquely linked relationship."[45]

These international adventures are woven into the warp and woof of *The Americans*. News Corp incorporated in Australia in 1980, one year before the events in the drama begin. Two years later, it initiated its purchase of 20th Century Fox, the Hollywood studio that would make *The Americans*. Murdoch's Australian citizenship threatened the deal. Riding to the rescue like a two-bit cowboy, Reagan helped him circumvent naturalization requirements to complete the purchase. But though Murdoch became a US citizen, the FCC later questioned the legitimacy of the maneuver, because Reagan pulled strings to get Murdoch his citizenship and because News Corp remained incorporated in Australia for years to come. This meant that even after the acquisition closed, working in the US for Fox would mean working for an oversees entity fronted by somebody pretending to be a US citizen. Elizabeth and Philip do something similar, and on behalf of a politics alien to those around them.

The Jenningses serve a Communist agenda while surrounded by American patriots. Workers at 20th Century Fox served a right-wing

CHAPTER 4

agenda while surrounded by Hollywood liberals. Two such workers were Dana Walden and Gary Newman, who became chairs of 20th Century Fox Television in 1999. It was unusual for a team of two to run a TV studio as equals, let alone a team made up of one man and one woman; the Hollywood press described the arrangement, predictably enough, as a work marriage.[46] And like Elizabeth and Philip, whose marriage is arranged by the Directorate, and who kick into high gear following the initiation of Reagan's Star Wars scheme, Walden and Newman shepherded *The Americans* to air during a tense moment in the history of News Corp, which green-lit the drama in 2012, as it was engulfed in controversy over its phone hacking in Great Britain. A Murdoch paper, *News of the World*, was exposed as spying, bribing, and extorting British citizens in the service of its parent company's interests. This was why it was a mistake to allow leviathans of this size so much power over the media, critics cried. Don't be silly, Murdoch replied, everybody does it. (Even the Communists next door; the Jenningses are endlessly phone hacking and extorting.) But the moment required the appearance of autonomy among News Corp's many units. Regulatory agencies needed assurance that media companies were not propaganda machines. Murdoch gave it; he split his company in two, during production of *The Americans'* first season. And in fact, the drama was itself a kind of assurance. How better to convey the autonomy of the newly formed 21st Century Fox than to produce a drama that seems to embrace Communism?[47] Who could accuse Murdoch of meddling with his fiefdoms when one of them was producing a story about sympathetic suburbanites working to bring down Reagan's America?

After the split, News Corp retained all publishing assets and 21st Century Fox retained all film and TV assets. The two resulting entities now allow us to recast the drama's allegory in less personal terms, such that Elizabeth and Philip stand not for Walden and Newman, but for two corporations, one permissive and one ideologically strict. In this accounting, the fully assimilated and liberal Philip is the Hollywood-oriented 21st Century Fox, and Elizabeth, never really at home in the US, and an uncompromising hardliner, is News Corp itself. She is forever chastising Philip not to drink the Kool-Aid and to remember they will return one day to their home beyond the US. And she is forever watching and decrying the lies peddled by US news outlets.

Given their seeming differences, we might say that Elizabeth and Philip are red and blue corporate marshmallows, rather than both red. What could be more "fair and balanced," to quote Fox News? But of course the network incorporates liberals into its news programs to subject them to a deeper ridicule, and News Corp's dramatic programming has been no different. On *24*, President David Palmer is endearing and full of integrity; but his choices are invariably wrong, and he's an unwitting puppet of the deep state that has been a Fox preoccupation at least since *The X-Files*, and that the network and its affiliates consistently associate with the left. While *The Americans* treats the Soviet cause with sympathy, it too exposes a problem with the deep state. More significant than the drama's position taking on Communism or phone hacking, in other words, is its embrace of the small flexible unit that must check the antidemocratic tendencies immanent in ossified managerial structures. That unit appears in a different form on *The X-Files*, *Buffy the Vampire Slayer*, *24*, *Dark Angel*, and *Homeland*—all produced by 20th Century Fox. In *X-Files*, *24*, *Homeland*, and *The Americans*, especially, a renegade intelligence team fights against a sclerotic cabal housed within an impersonal state bureaucracy; that team is often a "hacker unit," as Alexander Galloway describes Jack Bauer's team at CSU, which opposes the nefarious state within a state that houses it.[48]

Fox News and 21st Century Fox embraced the same mission, in other words, not by advancing the same policies but by dividing the world between deep state bureaucracies and renegade patriots working on behalf of noble ends forsaken by their bosses. On *The Americans*, the final season sets Philip and Elizabeth against a KGB deep state trying to stop Gorbachev. As with many Fox productions, the animating problem is straight out of James Burnham's *The Managerial Revolution* (1941), according to which Nazi Germany, the Soviet Union, and the New Deal all shared a baleful commitment to "bureaucratic collectivism." The political foe against which the right must rally, Burnham insisted, was a self-perpetuating managerial elite, and critics on the right to this day cite Burnham as a prophet of the deep state toward which the liberal state tends.[49] Communism on *The Americans* codes that state, because, as Fox News talking heads insist, all federal bureaucracies are socialist atavisms—not so different from Soviet bureaucracies. It matters, in this respect, that Philip and Elizabeth repair their intimate ties when fighting the KGB. Family is the best resource in the fight against state power. So too, it mattered that News Corp cast itself as a family business: Murdoch didn't sit atop a giant bureaucracy; he was the rebel father-in-chief on whom the patriot's resistance depended.

These terms allow us to understand Fox programming as part of a broadly cultural rather than narrowly political project. For Harvey, neoliberalism's global class restoration has meant "not the restoration of economic power to the same people," but the "reconfiguration of what constitutes an upper class."[50] News Corp spearheaded that reconfiguration in fundamental ways. Alongside its news, the corporation's scripted programming rendered class more nakedly economic by divorcing it from the "establishment" privilege that New Corp associated with state and professional authority and draping it in a self-consciously downmarket populism that rejected old-guard aristocratic pretensions. "Elite" came to signify not economic power, or inherited wealth, but the educational and cultural privileges that News Corp consistently attributed to deep state functionaries. That populism expressed in turn a political alliance between a new entrepreneurial elite (an important component of which were owners of family businesses) and a jingoistic working class whose nationalism would be increasingly at odds with the interests of the wealth to which it has been allied. (Donald Trump is the product of that alliance and embodies its contradictions in more or less obvious ways.)

For decades, News Corp's dramatic programming drove that populism—celebrating its parent company along the way. Chris Carter, creator of *The X-Files*, recalls screening his pilot for Murdoch. As the credits rolled, Murdoch stood and "applauded." It would have been easy for him to see himself on screen: "Fox Mulder," affixes the name of Murdoch's US film and TV holdings, "Fox," to a patronymic three letters from Murdoch's own. The intrepid FBI agent was from the start a corporate person, and he advanced his namesake's political ends, however elliptically. But again, "Murdoch" is here a vehicle for and a personification of a more fundamental class transformation, one expression of which was the Tea Party movement, which gave Inkoo Kang a new way of thinking about *The X-Files*. "When the tea party first arrived on the political scene in January 2009," she wrote in 2013, "I blamed Fox Mulder," who was "the angry but noble muckraker that Patrick Henry wannabes saw themselves as, while waving misspelled posters as their versions of 'the truth is out there' slogan—only in their case, the 'truth' was President Obama's Kenyan birth, his scheme to confiscate every gun in America, and his conspiracy to transform America into an atheistic socialist state *and* a radical Muslim theocracy." The drama's "peppering of scientific jargon gave the show a patina of educated respectability, but scientific knowledge was often derided as a crude and inadequate forensic tool. The greater value lay in Mulder's leaps of faith—or, to use today's parlance, his sense of 'truthiness.'" And so "when Fox Mulder was reincarnated on Fox News," she adds, "it was like discovering that my first love, who had seemed so sophisticated . . . was actually a skeevy, none-too-bright loser."[51]

All true, but with one qualification: Mulder wasn't reincarnated *on* Fox News; he was reincarnated *as* Fox News, which became a corporate person in his image. Murdoch grew News Corp from his tabloids, and FBI higher-ups on *The X-Files* repeatedly refer to Mulder's alien-abduction stories as tabloid fantasies that should be kept from the public. The perniciousness of that federal gatekeeping was the point. Launched in 1986, the Fox Broadcast Company became "the fourth network." But Fox News didn't launch until 1996, three years after *The X-Files* premier, when after years of battling Clinton's regulatory agencies, it became, with CNN, the second "extraterrestrial" alternative to broadcast news. In TV, "extraterrestrial" transmission refers to satellite rather than broadcast transmission. The allegorical truth was out there—it always is. But the more particular and instrumental "truth" that Mulder wanted to reveal, and that the Feds wanted to keep secret, was coming from the heavens, beamed in by what had always been Murdoch's favored TV distribution technology—satellites. As Elizabeth Jennings tells her son over breakfast, championing Soviet science as explicitly as she dares, "The moon isn't everything. Just getting into space is a remarkable accomplishment" (1.1)—even if, at that remove, everything below seems very much the same.

CHAPTER 5

Waiting for the End

Twin Peaks, The Wire, Queen Sugar, *and* Atlanta

We meet *Mr. Robot*'s Eliot Alderson in the same place we meet *The Matrix*'s Thomas Anderson: in a tech-firm cubicle. This black-market melodrama fantasizes an escape from office work. The grand hack for which Eliot later (mistakenly) thinks himself responsible—the destruction of consumer credit records held by the leviathan E Corp—will be referred to as "5/9." Ostensibly a reference to "9/11," the code also gestures to the hours of the day not spent at work. But in *Mr. Robot*, the working day has radically expanded, such that there is no difference between Eliot's nine-to-five and five-to-nine. He cannot distinguish between the two; he is on call permanently, whether as an office worker or, in his secret life, a guerrilla hacker. His endless work embroils him in a version of the geopolitical gothic discussed in the previous chapter; Eliot is revealed to have been not a self-authoring agent but a pawn of Chinese operatives. This is true even in relation to his intimate family relationships. As is the case for the protagonists of the melodramas in the previous chapter, his work problem is a family problem. Eliot aims to destroy the working day in large part because he thinks it destroyed his father. To do so, he resurrects his dad as an alternate personality within himself (Mr. Robot). By the second season, Eliot is in open conflict with his internalized father, whom he cannot expunge. By the third, their conflict has taken temporal form. Eliot tries to move forward, but Mr. Robot holds him back—literally, in the fifth episode, by seizing his body and moving him away from a computer terminal he tries many times to approach, which in effect rewinds the scene. Eliot appears looped in time, unable to move forward. The conceit literalizes the dead father's grip on his son, which prevents Eliot from getting on with his life.

The third season offers a range of loops and repetitions. Eliot's childhood friend Angela Moss wants to reach back into the past and save her mother from death. She will repeatedly replay footage of a terror attack she might have stopped, pressing buttons on her remote as if doing so will rewind history. Eliot later watches *Superman* (1978), in which Superman reverses the orbit of the planet to resurrect a dead Louis Lane. But though Angela and Eliot want to change the past, the drama cannot really imagine an alternate version of it—or the future. This conspiracy narrative confesses it cannot supply the epochal change of which Eliot first dreamed. Having thought himself capable of altering history, Eliot learns that, in fact, history repeats itself over and over again. That lesson speaks reflexively to the drama itself. At one point, an underground operative with whom he's been allied points his finger at a gathering of the ultra-rich on a balcony overlooking the street that he and Eliot occupy. "See, kid," he tells him, "that's been your mistake the entire time, thinking this whole thing's about your silly little plan. No, your revolution was only allowed to happen because it was bought and paid for by people like them. Face it, no matter how hard you try, that's always the end result." Witness a recurring reality beyond your agency, driven by a class (and TV audience) to which you do not belong. History amounts to the same old story, with the same protagonists. "Literally nothing can stop these shindigs," he says, "not thousands dead across the country, not a lifeless mistress in the guest bathroom" (3.7).

Moments like these aside, *Mr. Robot* is a representative instance of the "serial narratives" that began to appear at the end of the last millennium on nonbroadcast channels—first on cable and later on web platforms. A TV "serial" is "cumulative," Horace Newcomb explains, and produces an overarching story distinct from the episodic stories of a TV "series." Jason Mittell adds, a TV serial "*creates a sustained narrative world, populated by a consistent set of characters who experience a chain of events over time.*"[1] Serial narratives were common to film in the

1910s and radio in the 1920s; increasingly common to daytime soaps in the postwar period, serial TV narratives began to appear in the 1980s on primetime evening soaps like *Dallas*, *Dynasty*, and *thirtysomething* and on incipient "complex TV" like *Hill Street Blues*. Subsequently, 1990s programs like *X-Files* and *Buffy the Vampire Slayer* began to admix episodic and serial narratives. *The Sopranos* did the same, even if it is often seen as inaugurating the "twelve- or thirteen-episode serialized drama" that would become what Brett Martin calls "the signature American art form of the first decade of the 21st century."[2] Trisha Dunleavy builds on Martin by focusing on "high-end" dramas like *The Sopranos*, *Mad Men*, and *Breaking Bad*. These "complex serial dramas" "tell a complete story from beginning to end. Pursuant to this, their episodes are interrelated and interdependent, must be viewed in strict order, and the interpretation of new events in the narrative present is always informed by events of the past.... The high-end serial's 'overarching' story entails unavoidable change and an inevitable end."[3]

Contemporary scripted quality drama is indeed often serialized. But as *Mr. Robot* makes clear, it is not the case that all overarching stories advance purposefully toward an inevitable end. We might feel, as critics famously did with *Lost*, that the serial in question has no real plan and instead makes up its story as it goes. Alternately (or, in the case of *Mr. Robot*, additionally), a serial's cause-and-effect unfolding of "a chain of events over time" might leave us feeling that, in fact, beneath the changing sets and costumes, nothing really changes. Dana Polan characterizes *The Sopranos*, for example, by its "structure of stasis, repetition, and cyclicality," in which "characters seem to replay certain types of behavior again and again rather than move forward."[4] Still more basically, and moving now to more molecular narrative levels, whether or not it stresses stasis and repetition, a given serial will likely depict its chain of events unevenly, using suspense strategically to arrest and intensify its forward movement.[5] Melodrama depends on related kinds of unevenness. For Thomas Elsaesser, it captures an "exaggerated rise-and-fall pattern in human actions and emotional responses, a from-the-sublime-to-the-ridiculous movement, a foreshortening of lived time in favor of intensity—all of which produces a graph of much greater fluctuation, a quicker swing from one extreme to the other than is considered natural, realistic, or in conformity with literary standards of verisimilitude."[6] For Linda Williams, most forms of melodrama actively manipulate temporal flow and turn on a herky-jerky "give and take of 'too late' and 'in the nick of time.'"[7]

This chapter focuses on various kinds of stasis and repetition. Examples might involve local loops in which characters repeat the same action (Eliot at the computer terminal) or the recurrence of more abstract patters and problems (as in *The Wire*). The serials from which I take these examples do tell ongoing stories, but not necessarily "complete" ones that move inexorably to predetermined ends. Each bogs down in a different version of what Walter Benjamin called "petrified unrest."[8] Personal and historical events appear simultaneously dynamic and stalled, propulsive and yet incapable of true progress. In the case of *Twin Peaks* and *The Wire*, that dynamic sheds light on the genre that has been the subject of this study. Black-market melodramas, I claim in the introduction, often stall self-consciously, when their otherwise serialized, overarching plotlines get stuck in the nonprogressing, everyday rhythms of the family home. And throughout this study, I've said that these melodramas tend to attribute that stall to the fact that their male leads especially cannot enjoy the separate spheres for which they are mordantly nostalgic. Ultimately, these melodramas attribute their belatedness to deindustrialization and the lost family wage; they think themselves unable to move forward because they "came in at the end," to recall Tony Soprano's opening voiceover, or because they feel, like Walter White, that they've "passed the perfect moment to die." *Twin Peaks* and *The Wire* fit the overall pattern. *Twin Peaks* links the closing of a sawmill to the dilation of domestic space and the horrors that unemployed men commit in it, as if outside time. Also about the shuttering of factories, *The Wire* links Baltimore's deindustrialization to homelessness, hopelessness, and civic patterns fated to repeat themselves.

Queen Sugar and *Atlanta* attribute their petrified unrest to different causes. These programs share key features with black-market melodramas, even if they don't really belong to the genre proper. But their different emphases on Black rather than white families change the meaning of those features in fundamental ways (*Atlanta* is particularly useful, insofar as it sharply elucidates the limits of my genre's explanatory power). Neither displays the family wage nostalgia that defines *Twin Peaks* and *The Wire*. *Queen Sugar* picks up where *Twin Peaks* leaves off; it narrates the opening rather than the closing of a mill and pegs its hope for familial renewal on reindustrialization. But this melodrama about an African American family reclaiming land once worked by its ancestors as slaves discovers no renewal and attributes its inability decisively to move forward not to any confusion of home and work but to the living legacy of slavery—and to the purgatorial social death thus imposed. *Atlanta* is episodic magical realism rather than serialized melodrama. But it is also interested in wageless Black Americans kept frozen in place, as if out of time. The two programs generate distinct experiences of petrifaction: the former, as stasis within seemingly progressing storylines; the latter, in surreally nonprogressing storylines. But they share a deeper unrest and insist, even as they cannot move forward, that returning to the past holds few solutions to the problems of present. In the *Atlanta* episode "Teddy Perkins," we will see, that insistence powerfully reframes the corporate allegory in which this study has been interested from the start.

Soap Opera's Eternal Recurrence

The first shot in the *Twin Peaks* title sequence is of a wren perched atop a branch, which image dissolves into the Packard Sawmill and then the automated cutting of mill blades. There are no workers. The camera leaves the factory, enters the town, and moves to the Great Northern Hotel, perched atop a waterfall as the wren was atop its branch. The camera zooms in on the falls and, with an imperceptible shudder, the frame rate slows. We follow the cascades to a reflective pool beyond the base of the falls and, transitioning now to the pilot, into the house that sits beside these waters. Our first shot of this or any domestic interior is of Josie Packard seen through a mirror, which echoes the still waters beyond the house. She is a racial Other out of place and yet dominant within this home, which once belonged to Catherine and Pete Martell. So too she owns the mill but is conspiring with Ben Horne to destroy

CHAPTER 5

5.1. *Twin Peaks*: Laura Palmer washes ashore.

it. The mill is no longer profitable, and Josie wagers she can make more by burning it down than by running it, pocketing the insurance money, and selling the land to Horne. Laura Palmer's body washes up from the still waters beyond the Martell house, a figure for the jobs that will be lost (fig. 5.1). In fact, the body's appearance provides Josie with a pretext to close the mill.

"You can't do that to my workers!" yells Catherine. But Josie can and does. "The mill will shut down," she announces. "Perhaps you can spend the day with your families." We cut to Horne chasing investments for the country club he plans to build on the mill's land. He has no money of his own to invest. "Fluidity is everything," he will tell Josie, but "I can't summon up cash reserves that I don't have" (2.6). Laura's body emerges from a still body of water (as Packard's does from a mirror) as if both a symptom of and a solution to *Josie's* liquidity crisis; the water is still, we might say, because the mill no longer generates capital, and the body is dead, we might add, to register the mill's cost-saving expulsion of labor.

But if a necessary condition of the town's deindustrialization, Laura's death is also a figure for a timeless condition that exists less prior to than somehow beyond the narrative's historical framework. The titles invoke the mill less as an automated factory than as one never enlivened by labor. The machinery exists out of time, and it is as if the whole of *Twin Peaks* plays out within—even as it seeks to escape from—an interminable present in which the men have already lost their jobs and have already been consigned to a life at home from which they then dream an ugly release. *Twin Peaks* integrates daytime soap with detective genre conventions that move us from a mystery to its solution. But it is more accurate to say that it mires the linear form of detective fiction in a recursive and stalled narrative structure that it traces to soap opera on the one hand and deindustrialization on the other.

Quality serial TV comes from the soaps, I have argued throughout this study, notwithstanding the efforts of English professors to liken it to the novel. When the serial narratives that were for decades a staple of daytime soaps migrated to evening soaps, and then morphed into more seemingly serious fare, those narratives changed less than some would have it. Quality serial TV is still dominated by melodramas about family life and the kinds of work that define it. And most black-market melodramas possess "an infinitely expandable middle," as Dennis Porter says all soaps do. Likewise, they inherit the "clotural conventions" that Jane Feuer discerns in *Dallas* and *Dynasty*, for example.[9] Black-market melodramas deploy those conventions even as they disavow soaps as the lowbrow, too-feminine form from which they came.[10] But as they move between home and work, they discover an unsettling congruence between the two and a concomitant inability to produce fully serialized narratives.

According to Charlotte Brunsdon, soap operas capture "the sphere of the individual outside of waged labor," which is also "the sphere of women's 'intimate oppression.'"[11] Tania Modleski adds that soaps prepare women for the "interruption, distraction, and spasmodic toil" that characterize their unwaged domestic labor, which labor sustains and reproduces male labor power.[12] Soap seriality is for Michèle Mattelart a thwarted effort to flee the sphere of unwaged labor and gain access to what seems, from within that sphere, like the linear time of waged labor. Mattelart describes soaps as "a symbolic revenge on the triviality of everyday life, whose monotonous repetition is countered by the day-to-day episodes of the heroine's unusual adventures." Invariant and seemingly geared to the reproduction of what already exists, rather than the production of something new, unwaged housework calls forth a need for serial adventure. But the resulting narratives typically confine themselves to and provide narrative continuity in personal rather than properly social relationships. They are in that sense stagnant. And above all, for Mattelart, soaps remain stuck in nonindustrial time, which is to say, in the time of unwaged reproduction rather than waged production. As she puts it, referencing Nietzsche, sequential episodes try to break free from the "eternal recurrence" of housework, but fail to attain "the dominant idea of time as geared to linear industrial productivity."[13] Soaps thus heighten contradictions between the home's "eternal recurrence" (which they represent) and "the dominant idea of time as geared to linear industrial productivity" (which they limn negatively, as an unfulfilled aspiration). This rings a crucial change on Elsaesser's 1950s family melodramas, which substitute static tableaux for narrative progression. Lavish mise-en-scènes function as objective correlatives for characters unable to break free of psychoanalytically inflected impasses, he argues. Feuer adds that these films often figure "the disintegration of a capitalist ruling class family," such that psychological stasis counterpoints economic decline.[14] For Mattelart, soaps offer psychological dynamism as a "symbolic revenge" on a proletarian stasis rather than bourgeois decline; their escapist, "unusual adventures" placate a gendered workforce denied access to an industrial wage.

Mattelart's terms echo but also update work on the conflicting temporal regimes produced by capitalism's combined and uneven development. In his analysis of Russia's capacity for industrialization, Leon Trotsky argued for the nationally idiosyncratic nature of capitalist development—against the notion that all nations needed to industrialize just as England did. Nations might instead combine the old and the new unevenly, telescoping or compressing different features of capitalist production as needs dictated. Those combinatory processes, Trotsky added, might lead in turn to the mixing not just of industries or production techniques, but also of different daily rhythms that were dominant in different locales at different historical moments (hence Ernst Bloch's

Trotsky-inspired phrase, the "simultaneity of the non-simultaneous"). Moreover, for Trotsky, economic efforts to conjoin the industrial (hammer) and agricultural (sickle), above all, necessitated corresponding political and cultural efforts to integrate the lifeworlds and temporal experiences sponsored by each production regime.[15] In this spirit, Antonio Gramsci would distinguish between industrial production's daily, linear time accountancy and agriculture's longer-wave rhythms, which registered seasons more meaningfully than hours of the day.

These terms are useful, but potentially misleading, insofar they downplay how fundamentally industrial capitalism has always depended on what might seem archaic labor arrangements. For Harry Harootunian, capitalism often contains residual practices that generate "temporal unevenness, untimeliness, and arrhythmia." He tracks the "temporal interruption, unevenness, fracturing, and heterogeneity" that arises as capitalism places "practices from earlier modes alongside newer ones." For Harootunian, those earlier practices might be family agriculture, putting-out household production, or any version of unwaged reproduction. Capitalism remakes them to meet present needs, even as each practice retains an "archaic silhouette" and evokes daily rhythms at odds with those sponsored by industrial production. Prior to "the greater expansion of the wage form," he continues, there was "no sharp differentiation between domains of work, as such, and nonwork, since the economic was hardly distinguished from other realms of social activity." As the wage form expands, work and nonwork—or, in different registers, production and reproduction—continue to produce different rhythms, even as the wage tries to "eliminate the scandal of plural temporalities" and to "singularize time into a coherent narrative story."[16]

That scandal persists in and as soaps, Mattelart might have added. But she might also have added, along with Marxist feminists associated with the Wages for Housework movement, that calling unwaged reproductive labor "archaic" misses how fundamental it was and is to the most ostensibly pure forms of industrial production. English and American manufacturing relied from the start on the expropriation of women's labor. Mattelart's terms are useful, then, not because they register the persistence of the archaic with the properly contemporary, but because

CHAPTER 5

they explain exactly how soap opera captures an abiding and constitutive contradiction, lodged in the core of industrial capitalism, between the experience of waged productive and unwaged reproductive labor.

Black-market melodramas generate similarly equivocal if slightly different contradictions. Between, say, its recurring credit sequence, its relatively static vision of home, and its more fully if still fitfully serialized depiction of illegal work beyond it, a given serial amalgamates discordant speeds. And so rather than view black-market melodramas as the apotheosis of serialization—in which evening TV, suddenly like the nineteenth-century novel, manages finally to produce ongoing narratives that engage the world in a realist idiom, as soaps supposedly never did—we should read them as peppered with thematic and formal arrhythmias. In *The Sopranos*, Tony says to Meadow, "Outside there it's the 1990s, but in this house it's 1954" (1.11). More than just an expression of patriarchal revanchism, the line captures the drama's self-consciously fraught temporal integrations of home and work. Seemingly out of time, home life recalls a halcyon social order premised on tidy separate spheres (and white supremacy). Life beyond the home seems to march inexorably forward and, indeed, the drama serializes Soprano's work in ways it doesn't his family life. But as *The Sopranos* moves him daily between home and work, distinctions between the two become harder to make. And even as "outside" time grinds to a halt, Soprano strives to break free, psychoanalytically, from his mother's enduring hold and, more prosaically, from what he considers an engulfing domestic scene. It's appropriate that the mafia sponsors the resulting temporal unevenness. A repurposed archaism, it captures a coerced expropriation that evokes Soprano's expropriation of Carmela. Family unevenly mirrors family, and work unevenly mirrors nonwork, as the drama worries it cannot sustain its forward movement—or the wage's "coherent narrative story."

Twin Peaks is likewise about the loss of the wage's coherent story. "Spend the day with your families" indeed: that is the problem. After the mill closes, the family home becomes a lethally endogamous, gothic hall of mirrors. The father of the girl abducted and abused with Laura Palmer, Ronette Pulaski, works at the mill before it closes. And though

Leland Palmer is never himself employed there, after the mill closes, we find him at home during the day watching *Invitation to Love* when his niece Maddy arrives for Laura's funeral. Anticipating *The Wire*, this soap—which we'll see again and again—is about an apartment complex called The Towers, whose name evokes the twin peaks from which the town and drama take their names. Throughout, domestic space dilates, and time grinds to a halt in the face of twinned and otherwise recurrent events that give the lie to cause and effect. Just as the mill has always already expelled its workers, so too Leland has always already raped his daughter; there is no before and after within the Palmer home. So too, Leland will murder Maddy just as he did his daughter—tellingly, as the needle of the living room phonograph cycles back and forth within the lead-out groove of a Louis Armstrong LP. Family time is traumatic time, which is to say soapy, stuck-in-place time, and it opens a space for the supernatural, figured here in the transgenerational, palindromic entity "Bob" that drives Leland to violence.

"Tell Me, Jimmy, How Do You Think It All Ends?"

The Wire also turns on closed factories and, as it happens, its season 2 cold open represents petrified unrest in relation to a body of water that figures stalled capital in flight from industry. The camera surveys ruined factories along the periphery of Baltimore's Inner Harbor. The point of view is Jimmy McNulty's, as he and a fellow officer navigate the waters and recall when their fathers were let go from those factories. They spy a stalled pleasure boat, Capitol Gains, and set about towing it in. "Capitol" houses "Capital"; the factories lining the harbor were gutted and shuttered because, enticed by the prospect of better returns elsewhere, their owners decided against reinvesting in production on site, and instead sold off their land and assets. The owners thus realized capital gains. That process led to a decrease in cargo traffic heading into the port and eventually transforms season 2's underemployed dockworkers into an unemployed surplus population. "It is capitalistic accumulation itself," Marx writes, "that constantly produces, and produces in the direct ratio of its own energy and extent, a relatively redundant population of laborers, *i.e.*, a population of greater extent than suffices for the average needs of the self-expansion of capital, and therefore a surplus population."[17]

From first to last, *The Wire* is interested in redundant laborers driven into the informal economy of the drug trade. Barksdale corner boys aspire to promotions that will grant them percentages of their packages, rather than fixed salaries. "Coming off the clock," as they put it, represents a significant improvement in their standard of living. But they are selling drugs because their community was forced off the factory clock years before, when capital once located in Baltimore either invested in production elsewhere, transitioned into finance, or disappeared into profit taking and luxury good consumption. The drama's informal drug economy both shadows the formal economy (by absorbing castoff labor) and allegorizes it (by mirroring state-recognized businesses). In season 5, Gus Haynes asks his boss at the *Baltimore Sun*, then announcing layoffs, "How come there are cuts in the newsroom when the company is still profitable?" (5.3). But the question is not "if profitable" but "how profitable," and what to do with profits. "I've got too much money," Marlow Stanfield tells a lieutenant as we cut from the *Sun*. Stanfield sends that excess offshore. In neither the drama's formal nor informal economies do profits return in bulk to production, and, in the former, fiscal crises serve as pretexts to fire workers and enfeeble organized labor.

The cold open intimates the limits of this process. The vessel cannot make an adequate "return" (literally, to shore, and metaphorically, as "offshore" capital). The fact that its engine is dead suggests that eventually, and in aggregate, capital gains stall upon a sea of liquidity.[18] The cold open thus condenses allegorically the contradictory processes that animate the drama's social world, just as *The Wire* as a whole diagrams the local effects of what has been a decades-long decline in US industrial profitability (McNulty's dad was fired in 1973, the hinge year between boom and bust, when US industrial production, already having fallen off in the late 1960s, decelerated precipitously).[19] As this decline becomes acute, and as money runs out generally, managers of all kinds "find ways to do more with less" (5.3), as the *Sun* editor puts it. *The Wire* registers the manifold consequences of that imperative, as it reshapes Baltimore law enforcement, schools, city politics, and the lives of already precarious populations.

Did we need five seasons to learn the dynamics of this overaccumulation crisis? Alberto Toscano and Jeff Kinkle find it easy to "imagine [*The Wire*] going on endlessly, each season focusing on a different facet of the contemporary American city (the growing Hispanic population and informal workforce, the sex trade, sanitation, the emergency services, cleaners, pizza delivery guys, etc.)."[20] Yet they reject the notion that subsequent seasons would have told us anything more about the larger forces driving Baltimore's crisis. Lester Freamon and Cedric Daniels each speak a version of the drama's most famous line; as Daniels puts it, "you follow the drugs, you get drug dealers. You follow the money you don't know where it's going to lead" (1.8). But we know exactly where the money will lead, not because we know to whom or into what licit venture this or that bundle of cash will go, but because by the first season's conclusion, we have been provided a version of what David Harvey calls a "descent from the surface appearance of particular events to the ruling abstractions underneath." The season 2 cold open, discussed above, captures those ruling abstractions particularly well.

Toscano and Kinkle are interested in the necessarily partial nature of that descent: *The Wire* is about the "institutional and cognitive limits faced by anyone seeking to orient oneself in the realities of contemporary capitalism."[21] I'm interested in the narrative limits thus imposed. Adorno claimed in the 1950s that "every spectator of a television mystery knows with absolute certainty how it is going to end. Tension is but superficially maintained."[22] *The Wire* is a masterpiece of tension, but by the close of the first season, at the very latest, we have a reasonable sense of how subsequent seasons will end: McNulty is in the back of a courtroom, watching in despair, as he did at the start of the first episode; as new seasons unfold, different characters will be sent to jail, even as new ones spring up to replace them. These new characters will be placed in motion in turn by ruling abstractions that disallow the kind of change for which the detectives long. Neither groups nor individuals will alter the dynamics in which they are caught. Given to a naturalist pessimism,

CHAPTER 5

The Wire insists that all of its stories are ultimately the same, insofar as they reveal that neither individuals nor groups can change their larger environment.

Linda Williams stresses the drama's exhortation to redeem a fallen world; *The Wire* is an "institutional melodrama," she argues, because it is animated by a clear vision of right and wrong and by a corresponding impulse to seek justice via institutional means. But if, as Laura Mulvey notes, melodrama draws its "source material from unease and contradiction within the very icon of American life, the home," then *The Wire* enacts a still more contradictory melodrama, because of its inability to conjure the family home as "the space of innocence" (Peter Brooks) or "the good place from which one comes" (Williams).[23] Melodrama becomes "institutional" precisely because home is now everywhere and nowhere; and as melodrama becomes both ubiquitous and impossible (because unable to recall a space of innocence), its narratives become both serial and stagnant. Characters cannot but seek justice, and they cannot but fail to find it. This amounts not simply to melodrama, but to an exploration of its limits. The historical dynamics delineated in season 2's cold open render reformist agency irrelevant, after all, and as often as *The Wire* celebrates moral action (and character *bildung*, in the cases of Bubbles and Roland Pryzbylewski, for instance), it suggests the impossibility of real change. This is why Williams is only partly right to dismiss the drama's pretense to tragedy; however earnest in its reformism, *The Wire* also insists on what feels akin to fate and inevitability.

As on *Twin Peaks*, the male detective's inability to change ossified dynamics takes shape in relation to a tendentious vision of domestic life. FBI agent Dale Cooper would save the Palmer family from its recursive rhythms by dragging what haunts it into the light of historical time; in *The Wire*, home is what detectives idealize and long for after fleeing from it headlong, and what they return to after having failed to change anything. Members of the Special Unit feel called to a mission; they work feverishly in pursuit of historical stakes. McNulty and Kima Greggs especially think those stakes inimical to domestic life. But as they are rebuffed in their mission, family ties beckon. "You got to ask yourself how you want to live your day-to-day" (2.7), Freamon tells

Daniels. Home and domestic ties extend the promise of something more authentic. "This is life, Jimmy," McNulty's ex-wife tells him when speaking about their kids. "This is the stuff that matters" (5.5).

When McNulty briefly gives up "career cases" and takes a beat as a patrolman, he experiences happiness, we're meant to understand, as a function of days and weeks now clearly divided between his job and his life at home with Beadie Russell, who also works a nine-to-five. This is the moment at which the drama is most pointedly nostalgic, and in a white key. Williams avers that "we are never asked to believe that any past home represented a golden age. No one is trying to 'get back to the garden.'"[24] But *The Wire* is awash in nostalgia for industrial production's clearly separate spheres. And even if McNulty and Russell both work, they both "come off the clock" at the end of the day. Home is a haven because neither thinks about work when home—unlike detectives, who never stop working. For a while, McNulty enjoys this retrograde retreat from the technical-managerial class into family life (and an implicitly white proletariat). The problem, of course, is that he cannot sustain his domestic bliss, because ultimately he cannot stop working. And one of the key impulses that produces melodrama—McNulty wants justice—is the very impulse that destroys the sanctity of his newfound home.

"Tell me Jimmy," Freamon asks, "how do you think it all ends? The job will not save you. Cases end. You need something outside this." Like what? McNulty asks. "A life. It's the shit that happens while you're waiting for moments that never come" (3.9). The terms are manifestly contradictory; a life "outside" work, presumably lived at home, might save you, but you'll live that life waiting for something else. And of course waiting turns out to be the name of the game, at home and at work. When McNulty returns to career cases, he experiences a version of the endless tedium that detectives frequently associate with domestic life. Kima tells him at the start of the fifth season, "Every day, same shit." His reply, which repeats in different form throughout: "shit never fucking changes" (5.1). Fredric Jameson thinks moments like these reveal *The Wire*'s anatomy of boredom; Hua Hsu thinks the drama given to "extended periods of seeming stasis." Williams thinks the drama produces "the rhythm of certain situations felt again and again" and characters caught in a "trap of repetition."[25] On *Twin Peaks*, a signature combination of dread and monotony concatenates prosaic tedium and the ambivalent longing for the disruption—and even the destruction—of the domestic. We witness the costs of a life spent within that space in the drama's many broken women, confined to wheelchairs, missing eyes, lost to madness, and strung out with stress. *The Wire*'s dread and monotony, and its dread of monotony, feels very different, but is in the end surprisingly similar.

As we have seen, the drama attributes its repetition trap to deindustrialization, the generation of racialized surplus populations, and the concomitant proletarianization of the technical-managerial class, which simultaneously experiences downward mobility and the loss of clear demarcations between work and nonwork. When chronicling the immiseration of Baltimore's Black citizens at the hands of newly mobile capital and the quixotic hours and days of detectives struggling against the tide of history (and their own precarity), *The Wire* finds it impossible to allow the possibility of significant change (narrative or historical). Moreover, it generates a static melodrama made contradictory by its inability to invoke a domestic "space of innocence" that might serve as the basis for Baltimore's redemption. Homes and families remain, but characters do not leave them each day to engage with and change the world. Rather, they choose home or world, which amounts to no choice at all. The perceived loss of separate spheres, then, has led to two seemingly different but functionally similar outcomes; home and work have become indistinct even as they have become still more radically separated. As this happens, the domestic becomes simultaneously inescapable and unavailable. This is why "homelessness" emerges in the final season as such an equivocal and yet organizing metaphor. All are homeless when history grinds to a halt, even as all are stuck in what seems a newly encompassing domestic space. For Williams, the orange couch in the middle of the pit beneath the towers represents an outside workspace made into a home (fig. 5.2). We might also note the many times that detectives, asleep at their desks, are told to go home. But there can be no true home in such a world, the drama frets, just as there can be no true escape from home. McNulty speaks the drama's last line, "Let's go home," to a white homeless man, and that line certainly suggests the

5.2. *The Wire*: The couch.

utopian impulses with which our detectives have fought for a sustaining collective life. But calling Baltimore home can only be an act of despair. The homeless man will find no home; the city will remain dysfunctional. Making peace with that means giving up on reform and returning to homes and families that function as sites of empty consolation rather than renewal. Like Bubbles, who after much humiliation gains access to his sister's home, McNulty and Greggs beat a forlorn and conservative retreat, back into the families from which they fled.

"Farming Is Waiting and Waiting Is Farming"

On *Queen Sugar*, Charley Bordelon and her siblings have inherited land in Louisiana that their ancestors once worked as slaves. They stake their survival on harvesting the farm's cane and processing it in their own mill. But the ostensibly historical narrative stalls, palpably so in relation to a protracted growing season that takes up the first two seasons of the drama. Narrative time distends. The resulting admixture of anticipation and stagnation both promises and defers the arrival of significant change. Charley thinks the processing of cane harvested by

CHAPTER 5

5.3. *Queen Sugar*: Reclaiming the land.

Black farmers in her mill (the first in the state owned by a Black woman) augurs the end of a white "system of oppression" (2.3). Less radically, *Queen Sugar* anticipates a Black ownership class in the rural South. Prolonging the cane's growth dramatizes that class's arrival and, presumably by extension the end of some measure of white oppression. But it also forestalls the reality that the drama will never really represent the end of that oppression. And so at the close of the second season, the harvest now here, Charley asks for more time, one feels, on the drama's behalf. "This is the beginning of the end for your way of doing business," she tells a white landowner. "Maybe not next month or next year, but the end is coming" (2.16). The harvest that promises a new beginning now intimates a more far-off horizon (fig. 5.3).

As we have seen, quality TV often discovers that linking the events of one episode to those in another does not necessarily produce meaningful progression. A local conflict introduced and quickly resolved might produce the effect of progress and closure. A more substantive conflict drawn out over many years, as in *Queen Sugar*, can produce the effect of no progress at all, whether resolved or not. This is doubly true of not-yet-concluded TV that airs week to week, and not simply because its story and its telling might diverge. All narrative plays with differences between *fabula* and *sjužet* (the Russian formalists), *histoire* and *récit* (Gérard Genette), or "story" and "plot" (Peter Brooks). Equally so, different media generate different "*temporal autonomies,*" to borrow from Genette, in relation to a narrative's consumption. A given novel's story and plot might diverge both from each other and from the uneven rhythms of reading.[26] Watching TV and film can feel more akin to each other than to reading a novel. The speed with which we experience their narratives—however given they are to temporal compression or distension—is fixed, as is our total viewing time. We know how long watching a given film or episode will take. But when watching not-yet-concluded serial TV, we don't know how long the story will last, and so encounter another kind of temporal autonomy. The difference between binging a concluded series and watching it week to week might matter less here than the indeterminate time span of the program's initial run. Genette thinks of narrative "duration" as a function of how long the events in a story take relative to the time it takes to narrate them. But in not-yet-concluded serial TV, duration remains indeterminate because neither plot nor story nor our experience of either has a fixed end.

Though we might know the growing period for sugar cane, we have no idea during the first two seasons when *Queen Sugar* will arrive at the harvest, and not simply because we don't know when the plot will get there. We also don't know how long the plot will continue, and so our own experience comes to seem both structured (we watch in increments) and open-ended (we don't know for how long there will be increments to watch). This is complicated on *Queen Sugar* by the fact that harvest portends more than simply fall. It portends a new way of "doing business." Fall, not winter, is coming. And it might be coming for a very long time. In this context, "the season" takes on a radically ambiguous meaning.

When their episodes are not dropped all at once, as is common on Netflix, serial quality dramas in the United States often air in eight-to-thirteen-week increments that are more like seasons than the September to June arcs that once dominated broadcast. But no longer confined to a fall-winter-spring cycle that tracked with the school year, that TV now comes and goes in autonomous time horizons that seem both seasonal and detached from any calendar logic. *As the World Turns* proceeded in a famously deliberate seasonal fashion. As creator Irna Phillips wrote of her show, "As the world turns, we know the bleakness of winter, the promise of spring, the fullness of summer, and the harvest of autumn—the cycle of life is complete."[27] But in serial quality TV, time speeds up even as it slows down—contradictory rhythms sit atop one another; we can seem both stuck in and speeding through this TV, as we look toward an end we know is coming, but that might be coming for longer than we know. Distending seasons often capture these asynchronous rhythms. On *Game of Thrones*, we experience over eight seasons an epoch-defining transition from feudalism to a political system about which we know very little. The transition takes shape in relation to a single season within the story. It is fall, and winter has been coming for some time. And so a world-historical transition collapses onto a distended seasonal transition of uncertain duration, which duration amounts to the drama's own. On *The Walking Dead* we also encounter an endless season. Plant life proliferates as wildly as the dead; vegetation is all but unstoppable and has overcome civilization's remains. On this kudzu southern gothic, there are no seasons except growing season. There is no waiting for harvest; characters reap all year round. But harvest promises only more of the same: minimal sustenance and no more than a chance at survival. Here too, then, a distended season stalls an otherwise healthy cycle, as if to register that even the cyclical time of the calendar year can be misleadingly progressive. The narrative stalls even as it rushes forward; it promises progression but keeps us moving in place.

Queen Sugar nods to *The Walking Dead*, while stressing the racial dynamics implicit in the latter's temporal purgatory "Who does society say is disposable or trash?" Nova Bordelon asks a panel. "Who are the real-life walking dead? If not through physical death, then social death, economic death, or political irrelevance" (2.3). The South's Black underclass makes up this group, she insists. And *The Walking Dead*, she might have added, panders to whites who would stay one step ahead of that underclass: especially in its first seasons, the zombie melodrama brutalizes and replaces its Black male characters with frequency, the better to hold at bay the fear that Rick Grimes is already symbolically dead (and, for this drama the same thing, symbolically Black) because he is now truly out of work and deprived of the monopoly on violence he enjoyed as a cop. Relevant here are the zombies that schoolchildren imagine inhabiting abandoned row houses on *The Wire*'s fourth season. Those houses symbolize the symbolic death taking shape in domestic spaces still inhabited by the living, and the children's zombies are precursors of the walking dead that the children shortly become as they discover with only one exception that their high school education will consign them to Baltimore's killing corners.

Seen this way, Nova's more meaningful reference is to Orlando Patterson, for whom slavery "is the permanent, violent domination of natally alienated and generally dishonored persons." Above all, the slave is "socially dead"—not just because he is subject to death at a master's will but because he is "formally isolated" in his social relations and "culturally isolated from the social heritage of his ancestors." Slavery was a "relation of domination," he writes, in which slaveholders "annihilated people socially by first extracting them from meaningful relationships that defined personal status and belonging, communal memory, and collective aspiration and then incorporating these socially dead persons into the masters' world."[28] Patterson did not believe his account necessarily described the experience of all slaves. Nor did he believe social death described those not subject to chattel slavery. But a vital strain of Black studies has seized on his claim that slavery is defined neither by legal ownership nor by the forced imposition of certain kinds of labor but rather by social death, which it understands in a broader way. For Frank Wilderson, social death has three elements:

> One is gratuitous violence, which means that the body of the slave is open to the violence of all others. . . . The other point is that the slave is natally alienated, which is to say that the temporality of one's life that is manifest in filial and afilial relations—the capacity to have families and the capacity to have associative relations—may exist very well in your head. You might say, "I have a father, I have a mother," but, in point of fact, the world does not recognize or incorporate your filial relations into its understanding of family. . . . And the third point is general dishonor,

which is to say, you are dishonored in your very being—and I think that this is the nature of Blackness with everyone else. You're dishonored prior to your performance of dishonored actions.[29]

Taken together, these conditions enforce "the essential stasis of Black 'life'" over and against "the essential capacity for transformation and mobility that characterizes Human life." This means that "for Blackness there is no narrative moment prior to slavery," but also that there is no narrative moment after slavery: Wilderson identifies "a continuum of slavery-subjugation that Black people exist in [such that] 1865 is a blip on the screen. . . . the technology of enslavement simply morphs and shape shifts."[30]

Queen Sugar captures that morphing continuum in a range of ways. Confronted by a public defender's indifference to the fate of a wrongly accused teen, Nova asks, "So this kid's supposed to just live in limbo? . . . It's like purgatory for all of us" (1.12). Like the Black community generally, the Bordelons exist at the borderline or in the borderland between life and death. This is true for Ralph Angel in ways that it is not for his two sisters, each of whom has a job and a different relation to the police. Charley, a "High Yellow," to borrow the name of the drama's diner, has a white mother and is in the process of divorcing an NBA superstar. Already wealthy, her struggle will be to understand the rural working-class Black community to which her father belonged, while opening her mill. Charley's half-siblings born to two Black parents, Nova and Ralph Angel, represent that community in different ways. Uninterested in raising a family, Nova is at the start an activist journalist in love with a white cop. She is the mouthpiece for the drama's politics. Ralph Angel is the drama's object of uplift, as he struggles to gain a version of the nuclear family from which Charley and Nova are differently in flight.

A single parent, he must on his release from prison be saved from the too-feminine relation to parenting and domestic labor that awaits him. In part, that means reuniting with the mother of his son Blue. But the bigger challenge is securing a family and job (and a narrative that will take him daily from one to the other) in the context of a system that does not supply Black men with a wage adequate to even their own reproduction. One of the drama's ingenious strokes is to capture that challenge, and Ralph Angel's liminal status, by rendering him subject to two employment regimes. His father leaves the farm to him and not his sisters because he thought Ralph Angel needed it most. But even after he becomes an owner, Ralph Angel remains Charley's wage laborer, because the terms of his parole require a W-2. Two things at once, Ralph Angel has one foot in a carceral wage system and one in an ownership class, even as he is at permanent risk of falling out of that class and into prison, there being little for him in between. Given this, it hardly makes sense to supply him with the secret second lives that define black-market melodramas. The sugar crystals featured in the first season title sequence reference *Breaking Bad* and the illicit informal economies into which families are often driven on black-market melodramas. But while agriculture is sometimes considered part of the informal economy, it is not illicit, and ultimately *Queen Sugar* asks whether it makes sense, given the fact that Black men will never be legitimate in the eyes of a racist state, to draw distinctions on their behalf between the informal and the formal economy, or between unwaged expropriation (in families and prisons) and waged exploitation (on farms and in factories). Ava DuVernay created both *Queen Sugar* and the documentary *13th* (2016), and the two offer similar accounts of the prison-industrial complex and the effects of mass incarceration on Black men and the Black family generally.[31] Both argue that the state's systematic incarceration of Black Americans, and the corporate expropriation of unfree labor in predominantly Black prisons, represent a new instance of slavery and a key engine of capital accumulation (as I elaborate in chapter 2). And both suggest that there is no understanding wage labor for African Americans except in light of the always-implicit threat that their ostensibly free wage labor might in a moment be transformed into coerced prison labor.[32]

Even as an apparent capitalist who owns his own farm, Ralph Angel is a wage laborer one step away from prison. As such, he's subject to conflicting time accountancies. It's useful here to recall Gramsci's account of Italy's division into semiautarchic spheres, which Harry Harootunian summarizes:

CHAPTER 5

> Between the capitalist North and semifeudal South, there were two distinctly different forms of time accountancy, the former regulated by the workday based on quantitative calculation and averaging of labor time (abstract labor) and its everyday remainder (disposable time), the latter determined more by seasonal constraints and obligations of labor service that made it difficult to separate work from nonwork during certain times of the year.[33]

Part carceral wage laborer and part farm owner, Ralph Angel straddles a similar divide. He goes to work for a wage and then returns to his farm, where he also works. Others in his industrious family similarly combine waged labor with entrepreneurial endeavor. Nova works as a journalist but also grows and harvests marijuana in her front yard, which she sells to support her activism. And Aunt Violet, who seems not to have a job, has been paid all along by Darla's parents to raise Blue, it turns out. Later, echoes of *Mildred Pierce*, she turns her amateur pie-baking into a business.

Charley combines wage labor and farming differently than Ralph Angel. She is the family's true capitalist, even if she too suffers a fateful confusion of home and work. In the second season, she and her son move into and make a home in the factory she has just opened, which factory shares the drama's name, and which factory represents the drama's own hope that it might, pace Mattelart, escape the eternal recurrence of reproductive labor into something more properly linear because industrial (fig. 5.4). As she takes farmers on a tour of the rehabilitated sugar mill, she offers a lesson on industrial time accountancy: "They're setting up our eye in the sky room where we'll monitor all the parts of the process, which means we'll be able to locate and fix problems quickly. Add that upgrade to our short-retention clarifiers, which process in forty-five minutes instead of three hours, and our new spectrometers which analyze cane sucrose levels in less than a minute. And I hope I've been clear our focus is on efficiency." Monitoring, fixing, upgrading, and creating production efficiencies generally, Charley maximizes her extraction of "relative surplus value," as Marx would have it. But her foreman interjects, reminding her of a more agricultural time accountancy: "Your

5.4. *Queen Sugar*: The eponymous factory.

daddy used to say farming is waiting and waiting is farming." Charley shoots back, "My motto for the mill is another old saw: time is money. I keep my costs down, those savings go to you" (2.4). To you the viewer, also: Charley fights narrative as well as cost inflation; like the TV viewer, her "eye in the sky" can witness in forty-five minutes (the running time of each *Queen Sugar* episode) a performance that might otherwise take three hours. At the mill, soapy quantity TV is compressed into efficient quality TV. Charley needs that compression, the better to escape the oppressive agricultural rhythms of her father's life, which the melodrama consistently associates with soap opera.

When the Bordelons visit the lavish estate of the landowner whose family once owned theirs, Charley asks Nova if she's been there before. "To this museum of our enslaved ancestors? No. It's like going back in time" (1.3). We hear a repeating refrain: "don't look back, look ahead." The didactic use of music to clarify emotional states represents one of the drama's more obvious melodramatic gestures. More generally, the narrative frequently stalls in soapy renditions of the family's love lives. That soapiness is all but inevitable, by the logic I have been developing, because nobody in the family, not even Charley, can access what

CHAPTER 5

Mattelart calls "the dominant idea of time as geared to linear industrial productivity." Stressing home-work convergences, and, above all, the threat of violence that hangs over Black men, *Queen Sugar* suggests that stories about Black families must in some sense always recapitulate soap conventions, organized as those conventions are by failed efforts to reconcile the experiences of time at the core of ostensibly free productive labor and unfree reproductive labor.

The drama takes soap conventions in a new direction, by capturing petrified unrest that reflects both endless workdays and much longer timeframes. The family seems when working the farm always one step away from working it as versions of their slave ancestors. Indeed, the drama's avowedly historical narrative about the rise of a Black ownership class is forever jeopardized by the past that is always immanent in their land. Slavery haunts their farm as a historical dynamic that gets replicated at the moment its legacy seems to be transcended. Even as Ralph Angel farms on parole, always one mistake away from returning to prison, the farm threatens to become a prison. In season 3, the landowner with whom the Bordelons have been vying moves to acquire and lease the land surrounding their farm to a for-profit prison, whose arrival would be the return of slavery in a new guise and would thus bear the family back into the past. Recidivism here takes on a new light.

In this spirit, the melodrama's title sequence artfully conjoins Ralph Angel's difficulty moving forward after leaving prison with its own narrative difficulty doing the same. On much quality TV, the title sequence possesses an unspoken affinity with the home's everyday rhythms: it is what repeats and stays the same, day in and day out, unlike the narrative that follows. But this melodrama explicitly associates its cyclicality with soaps. The lightly psychedelic, kaleidoscopic visuals are self-consciously retro in their pairing of actor's names and faces; the action, rather, is in the music, which repeats in varying order four key lines: "dreams never die / take flight / as the world turns / keep the colors in the lines" (fig. 5.5). The dreams of characters *in* this drama, to take flight from a racial capitalism that would keep its colored citizens both segregated from whites and between the vertical lines of prison bars, are inextricable from the dream *of* this drama, both to keep Black themes and

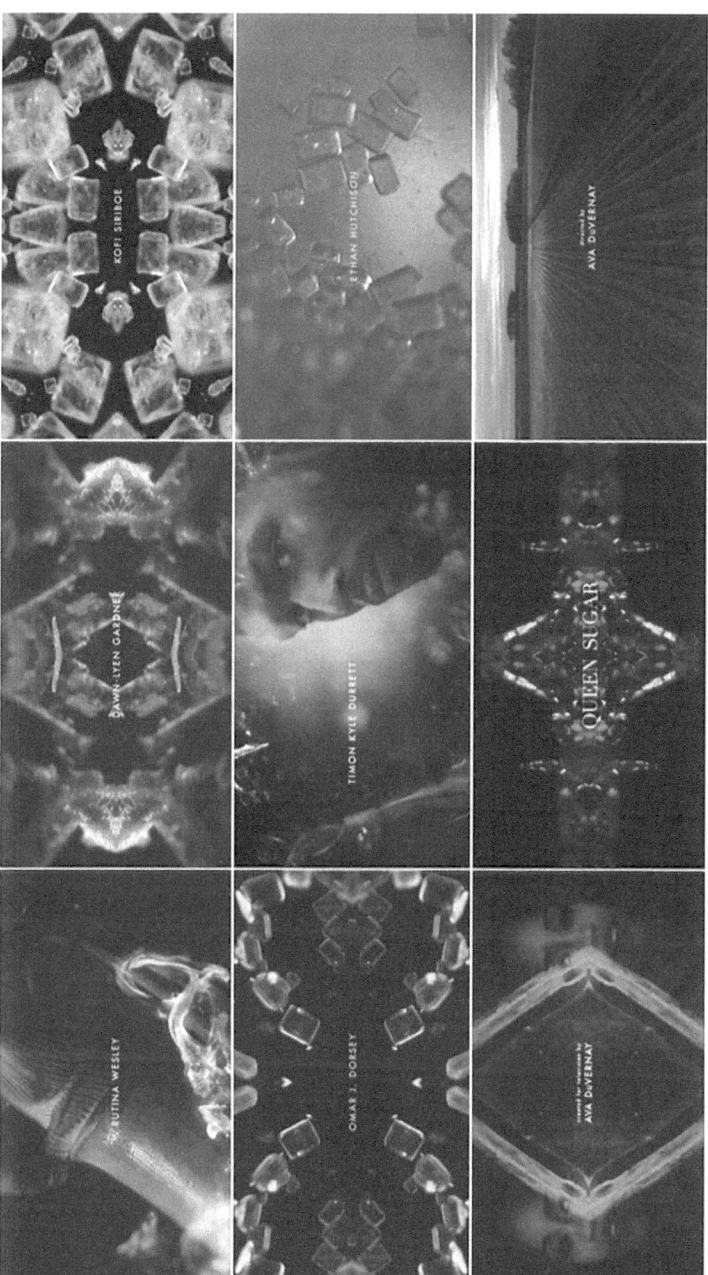

5.5. *Queen Sugar*: Title sequence.

values (colors) within its written lines, and to take flight on the strength of that writing from fare like *As the World Turns* (which flight would represent the opposite of coloring between the lines). Of course "as the world turns" signals both a famous soap and what feel like the invariant rhythms of daily life and taking flight from the former means discovering something historical beyond the latter. But the sequence of the core elements changes and takes on different meanings in light of their order: we might hear an imperative to take flight either *in* or *from* the soaps and daily life, depending on where "as the world turns" falls in the overall sequence, and how implicitly continuous, and productive of meaning, the elements of the sequence are taken to be: "dreams never die" means something different, say, if it comes before rather than after "keep the colors in the lines." The continued looping of the refrain is the point: there is no beginning or end of the ordering as it repeatedly turns back on itself.

Ultimately, the titles do not insist on any one set of meanings so much as constellate mutually implicated problems. *Queen Sugar* doesn't leave the soaps behind, in other words, so much as it returns again and again under changing circumstances to the problem of doing so. Even as the Bordelons seek escape from a racial "borderland" between life and social death, and even as Ralph Angel seeks escape from a borderland between ownership and labor, as well as one, lodged within that second term, between free and unfree labor, the drama stalls in "boredom" that characterizes both farming and domestic life. In the novel on which the drama is based, one of Charley's relatives declares, "Life does get daily": that in response to Charley's description of a moment in her past when she found it hard to venture from her home and into the world.[34] Similarly unable to break free from family and home, *Queen Sugar* derives real pleasure from the routines of everyday life: cooking a meal, setting a table, rejoicing in family when beset by the larger world. And yet those quotidian delights signal a problem. They come to feel imposed and too nakedly compensatory for ambitions thwarted beyond the home.

That speaks to TV generally, if in less pointed ways: this is a medium, after all, that keeps us complacent and stalled even when out in the world with mobile devices. Jameson thinks *The Wire* a form of "consolation" that assures us, as all TV does, that we are not alone. But it produces only "boredom and sterile or neurotic repetition or paralysis."[35] Melodrama specifically is not possible on *The Wire*, Jameson adds, because the drama manifests "the reign of Cynical Reason," in which distinctions between good and evil are vitiated and there are no "political consequences any longer" to "the corruption of the political generally, and its complicity with the financial system and its corruptions."[36] Williams disagrees, and I have suggested that each is right in part, insofar as *The Wire* manifests both traditionally melodramatic as well as traditionally naturalistic tendencies (on behalf a new kind of serial melodrama, the kind detailed in this book, that turns at its hollow core on vitiated distinctions between good and evil). *Queen Sugar* also commits to Cynical Reason. As the crop comes in, white landowners thwart the Bordelons at every turn and divide them from them the rest of the Black community. Charley tries to activate utopian longings in her fellow Black farmers but is forced instead to play the gangster. See in my mill a kinship alliance that might protect you from white capitalism, she tells them. But they forsake her, troubled by rumors about her motives. And so she pretends to ally with the corporation trying to destroy her; she will fight it from within, later, by selling her mill for a seat on its board. "You on some *Godfather* shit" (2.16), Ralph Angel tells Charley when he learns of her plan. With this, the drama swerves less toward *The Sopranos* than toward *Dallas* and *Dynasty*, which involve intricate boardroom machinations. The drama thus achieves a now familiar kind of quality, in which realpolitik conspires with half-hearted systemic analyses. "It's a game of chess," Charley tells her dumbfounded community-oriented lover. *Queen Sugar* offers a trenchant account of the stasis that governs Black life. But in other ways, it simply gestures to a vague anticapitalism. In the same moment Charley allies with her competitors, Nova finishes her opus, "Race, Land, and Trump's America." *Queen Sugar* does not reveal Nova's analysis; it is there, one feels, mainly to counterbalance Charley's machinations and to thereby elevate the melodrama. This works, if only for a while: the drama drags on, stuck in place, as the corporation that Charley sets out to destroy becomes just another dysfunctional family. Melodrama makes its eternal return.

CHAPTER 5

Earn/Urn

Atlanta's is a strikingly mundane magical realism; we get ghosts, footprints on ceilings, and invisible cars, but none of these spectral manifestations remove us from otherwise oppressive everyday registers. "Petrified unrest" usefully evokes the resulting affects, insofar as characters feel trapped, stalled, and not least, when confronted by a racist state, terrified. But *Atlanta* is only loosely serialized and captures its stasis less by stressing the halt of otherwise progressing narratives than by anatomizing the "dispossessive force" of racial capitalism, to anticipate my turn to Fred Moten. That anatomy produces powerful social analysis, while also mooting key categories to which the previous chapters have made recourse. *Atlanta* is not in obvious ways a melodrama, for example. It does not make legible or evoke coherent emotional states. Rather than generate what Jameson calls "named emotions" (fear, anger, love, etc.), it trades in nebulous affects, such that it is difficult to know what characters are feeling, or when the typically deadpan Earn is "earnest," rather than, say, simply flat or ironic.[37] For Jameson, the rise of ambiguous or hard-to-categorize affects, and the corresponding "waning of named emotions," is "a story that can be told as the gradual replacement of personification by a language of affective sequences, a substitution of the substantialism of names and nouns by the relationality of qualitative states."[38] *Atlanta* tells a version of that story powerfully, and I read it alongside black-market melodramas the better to shed light on its innovative if indeterminate "comedy."

At the start of *Atlanta*, Earnest Marks is selling credit cards on commission. He will later manage his cousin Alfred Miles, the trap star "Paper Boi." But his income is sporadic and less than he needs to contribute to his daughter Lottie's upbringing, and he is frequently homeless. The comedy does not use his predicament to generate clear or clarifying emotional states. Asked at a party what he does for a living, Earn replies, "nothing," before delivering with obscure intent a tribute to his partner: "Van does everything. She works, she raises our child, she's smarter than me, better than me. I mean, that's why I married her. She honestly doesn't get the credit she deserves. I mean, ever. But that doesn't deter her from being what she is, which is a mother, a provider, and a partner. Gun to my head, I don't think I could even look at another woman" (1.9). Van thinks the lines blatantly "mean," and they might be. He might think the gun to his head is hers, since she demands rent when he considers living with her and Lottie. A generically recognizable conflict now presents itself and (misleadingly) promises to resolve the affective ambiguity: she seems to want him to get a job as a security guard and give up "the whole 'follow your dreams' thing" (1.3).

Their first interaction suggests why that won't happen. They have just awoken, and he recounts a dream: "I was swimming in this pool, but it was like the ocean and I was swimming with the seaweed, but it wasn't seaweed, it was, like, hands. And I was swimming with this girl. And she was saying if the hands grab you, they pull you down and drown you, so swim above them" (1.1). Van intuits the hands are hers, even as we watch Earn rewrite the dream to avoid angering her. As presented, the dream anticipates a subsequent conflict between managing Alfred and being subject to Van's management. "I don't want a handout," he later says to Alfred, "I want to manage you." But "the two worlds of earn," as Alamin Yohannes calls them, Alfred's and Van's, are not so different.[39] Managing Alfred means grasping at him the way the gendered hands grasp at Earn in his dream and the way that, from his vantage, Van grasps at him. Darius asks him, "You know where the word *manage* come from? *Manus*, Latin for 'hand' " (*Atlanta* here recalls Walter White's explanation in *Breaking Bad* that the word *chiral* comes from the Greek for "hand"). Alfred disagrees with Darius's etymology but does think Earn too feminine for the job: "*Manage* come from the word *man*, and, uh, that ain't really your lane" (1.3). Alfred relents and learns to trust Earn, who learns to act aggressively on Alfred's behalf. We might be tempted to read Earn's dream as testimony to a psychological conflict akin to Walter White's, who after the onset of his cancer fears he does not earn enough to support his family. But Earn is not white and has no steady job, and so the next temptation might be to specify his putative conflict in relation to a racist tract like the "Moynihan Report," which described "the African American family" as awash in pathology because of deadbeat dads. And to be sure, Earn must risk that stereotype when doing the "the

CHAPTER 5

whole 'follow your dream' thing," which takes him from his daughter. But Earn never himself expresses his aspiration; it's attributed to him by Van, who thinks he wants to be a rapper (1.3). When asked directly by Van what he wants, he says he does not know. Here and throughout, the comedy resists the pull of melodrama: it will not make legible familiar emotions, stories, or generic conventions.

Atlanta typically refuses to explore Earn's interior states. One register of that refusal is the program's canny relation to the secret interiors that litter quality TV (and black-market melodramas). *Atlanta*'s most obvious gesture to serial quality TV is the outdoor couch it features in its advertising; just a shade lighter than the outdoor orange couch in *The Wire*, the furniture piece transforms an overgrown green field into a living room for Darius, Alfred, and Earn. In part, it's an emblem of the homelessness that finds Earn crashing on whatever couch will have him. Middle-class homelessness is one of the black-market melodrama's implicit subjects, we have seen; the genre's gothic confusions of home and work suggest that it is no longer possible to be truly at home. But homelessness is a literal prospect in *Atlanta*, even as it redounds on the program's account of interiority. The male leads of *Mad Men*, *Breaking Bad*, and *Homeland* retreat at key moments to metal containers that guard a secret they keep from their families. These containers vouchsafe their interiors, by concretizing secrets only they know, as the last remaining separate spheres, one is tempted to say. In *Atlanta*, Earn lives in a storage unit; and if this unit houses a secret, it does so as an "urn," by symbolically storing his ashes (fig. 5.6).

An urn figures prominently in Donald Glover's unproduced screenplay *Because the Internet*, released just prior to the filming of *Atlanta*, and the Childish Gambino album released in conjunction with that screenplay features the track "Urn," a homophone of our protagonist's first name that suggests the social death attendant on his inability to earn. That inability is foundational. In *Mad Men*, Don Draper fears what *he* might think of as social death. He is born Dick Whitman to poor white trash, but switches identities with a dead soldier in the Korean War. In the melodrama's present, he hides Whitman's dog tags in a small tin that is akin to an urn, insofar as it houses effects that once belonged to his

WAITING FOR THE END

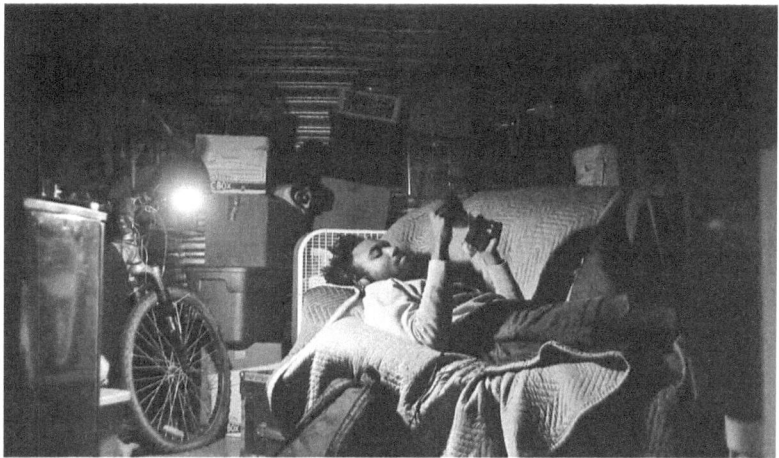

5.6. *Atlanta*: Earn's urn.

now dead former self. That dead self is dangerously Black; as Ta-Nehisi Coates put it, in an article titled "The Negro Donald Draper," Draper is, "in the parlance of old black folks, passing."[40] But Draper passes effectively and, like White, fears rather than experiences social death; his is a preeningly existential, privileged white anxiety. This is not the case for Earn, who scrapes by, unable to afford even a windowed room of his own, neither really living nor dead in a city that is as much "black purgatory" as "black heaven," to quote Maurice Garland.[41]

As in *Queen Sugar*, purgatory derives, ultimately, from the threat of prison that hangs over the program's male leads (which threat extends slavery's social death under a new guise). The pilot episode lands Earn, Alfred, and Darius in jail. And during the late-night altercation that leads to their arrest, Darius claims to experience déjà vu, and even anticipates the presence of a dog at the edge of the frame, as if to confirm that, in fact, he has been there before. Jail and recursive time work in tandem, each an expression of "the essential stasis of Black life," to recall Wilderson. The storage unit in which Earn lives expresses something similar. Superficially, it is less like Draper's tin than the cargo containers in *The Wire*'s season 2 (which house dead sex workers trafficked into the US) and *Dexter* (in which Dexter's mother, also a sex worker, is murdered). The latter drama is telling, insofar as it concretizes the psychic "crypt," as Jacques Derrida might have it, that houses Dexter's melancholic loss (as Draper's tin does his). Dexter spends the first season trying to remember the life-altering moment when as a child he discovered his mother's butchered body in the container. But on *Atlanta*, there is nothing in Earn's psychic crypt to rehabilitate with allegorical interpretation, psychoanalytic or otherwise. Except perhaps one story.

The Sopranos, *Dexter*, *Mad Men*, *Breaking Bad*, and *The Americans* use flashbacks to provide their leads with psychological etiologies. Sharing his therapy sessions, we return with Soprano, for instance, to his younger self and watch his father cut off the finger of a debtor in a butcher shop. There are limits to what that memory explains, but the drama devotes much time to unearthing Soprano's formative experiences (and representing his dreams). Relevant here is James Baldwin's account, cited by Wilderson, of white peoples' penchant for looking backward longingly. "Most of the white people I have ever known," Baldwin writes, "impressed me as being in the grip of a weird nostalgia, dreaming of a vanished state of security and order, against which dream, unfailingly and unconsciously, they tested and very often lost their lives."[42] A specified version of that nostalgia, I have argued throughout, defines the black-market melodrama, as its white families long for the return of separate spheres that have never figured prominently in the fantasy life of Black America, if only because Black America was never consistently afforded even the illusion of those spheres. Certainly no such nostalgia exists in *Atlanta*, for either historical or personal origins. And when in season 2 the comedy flashes back to Earn's childhood, we revisit a trauma that throws doubt on any notion of therapeutic personal recovery. In the flashback, the young Earn wears to school a fake FUBU jersey that his mother bought on steep discount; terrified he will be exposed, he spends the day dodging bullies who, having noticed differences between his jersey and a presumably real one worn by a classmate, but being finally convinced that Earn's shirt is the real one, descend on the classmate, who kills himself later that day.

The flashback describes something other than the trauma of being revealed as poor. "FUBU" is an acronym: "For Us, by Us." The brand dangles the prospect of nonalienated labor, even as it promises to redress the racial alienation variously described by W. E. B. Du Bois and Franz Fanon, in which the Black subject cannot but see him- or herself through the eyes of an imagined white other. Wearing a brand that is for us and by us promises an unalienated second skin impervious to racial abjection. But few at Earn's school can afford a FUBU; and the brand is not really for or by those who can. Rather, the furor surrounding the fake jersey concretizes a problem of social visibility that is both endemic to being Black in white America and specific to the labor to which the kids will be relegated. As an adult, Earn refuses to become a security guard because doing so will remake him: "I'm gonna become somebody I hate at a job like that" (1.1). As a kid, wearing a fake jersey threatens to expose not simply his poverty, but the extent to which he will be remade by future crap jobs—if he is lucky enough to get any job at all.

On *The Americans*, Philip and Elizabeth experience a pervasive unreality that stems from acting so deep as to no longer be feigned. Their work allegorizes corporate emotional labor, I argued in chapter 4, geared to the production not of a commodity but of themselves. Employment in *Atlanta* requires deeper acting. "Man, how should I talk to these white folks?" (2.2), one of Alfred's crew asks Earn before a job interview. It doesn't matter; he's dismissed the moment the interview begins. The experience is bruising, as is Van's in the episode "Juneteenth," as she pretends to be someone she is not at a party hosted by a wealthy Black socialite she hopes will land her a job. *Atlanta* is obsessed with stunting and fronting, which is what Earn does at this party when he plays the happy partner and testifies that Van "does everything." The two grin and offer an image they hope will please a likely white employer (fig. 5.7). The escapade is demeaning and at one point Earn tells Van, "This isn't real life, OK?" (1.9). But the claim is not straightforward: experiences like these make it hard to speak with confidence about "real life."

What makes *Atlanta* "the masterpiece of the decade," argues Andy Greenwald, is that "it doesn't feel like it came in any way from anything before." He adds, "It is so completely removed from any strand of television DNA that it feels separate from everything else." The comedy is "wholly unique," agrees *Mr. Robot* creator Sam Esmail, because it is "not influenced by anything but real life."[43] That is of course nonsense, and

CHAPTER 5

5.7. *Atlanta*: "This isn't real life, OK?"

of a piece with claims that *The Wire* was about "real life" in ways that other TV never had been. When white critics feel powerfully moved by but cannot adequately explain works of art about Black life, they invoke the real. But as I've been suggesting, *Atlanta* is canny and smart, often self-consciously so, about the TV that came before it. That alone makes it something more than sui generis. More fundamentally, it insists at every turn on the difficulty of identifying what is and isn't real.

People have "the wrong idea of me," Alfred tells a TV host. "Maybe you can interview me sometime? Get to know the real me." She advises him, "Play your part. People . . . want you to be the asshole. You're a rapper. That's your job" (1.5). He doesn't want to play that part. But he is far less confident than he seems about the nature of the real him and cannot forgo self-curation in any event. The episode "Woods" (2.8) casts that self-curation as feminizing housework. It begins with Alfred emerging from sleep and either dreaming or seeing a ghost of his dead mother wandering through his house. She's chastising him for his poor housekeeping: "This place is a mess. You ever hear of a trash can? I know you know how to fold." Humming gospel hymns, she cleans. Now fully awake, we think, Alfred finds Darius in his kitchen, cooking pasta from a recipe he learned in his sleep. These activities, cooking and cleaning, emerge in a crepuscular zone between sleeping and waking and set the stage for Alfred's interactions later in the episode with a fellow local celebrity, Sierra, who proposes what is in effect a work marriage. She suggests that the two "attach [their] brands." She also echoes Alfred's mother, whose insistence on housekeeping becomes Sierra's insistence on personal hygiene: Black men "be acting like grooming theirself is gay," she says, but "ain't nothing wrong with caring about your hair, your nails, your skin." They are getting a pedicure, and she is selling him the virtues of grooming and social media. "I ain't into all that fake shit," he rebuffs her. "I'm just trying to stay real." The two argue and she tells him to "wake the fuck up"—suggesting perhaps he is still asleep at home— and he leaves on foot. He's then robbed by assailants who mock him for "keeping it real" by walking instead of driving. He fights back and flees into a dark forest, which allegorical space offers an outdoor equivalent of the castrating danger already implicit in "Sierra" (both "mountain range" and "saw"). He gets lost in this purgatory and when he reemerges, he embraces the fan service and feminization that his job demands.

Relevant here is Fred Moten's analysis of "the commodity who speaks." Moten revisits a passage in *Capital* in which Marx speculates about what the commodity would say were it able to reveal its "secret." The passage is for Moten one of many in which Marx fails to register the foundational importance of slavery to the development of capitalism. The slave is for Moten the commodity who speaks—but who is given inadequate voice in Marx's system. Moten would correct that omission by turning to Black musical traditions that unsettle, as Blackness does generally, the "equivalence of personhood and subjectivity." Because "while subjectivity is defined by the subject's possession of itself and its objects . . . it is troubled by a dispossessive force [that] objects exert such that the subject seems to be possessed—infused, deformed—by the object it possesses."[44] Moten identifies a Black radical aesthetics grounded in this dispossessive force, which he finds, for example, in musical and literary evocations of the slave's scream, as that scream undoes the distinction between persons and commodities.

Moten builds on Susan Willis, who claims that "blackface is a metaphor for the commodity. It is the sign of what people paid to see. It is the image consumed, and it is the site of the actor's estrangement from self

CHAPTER 5

into role."[45] He relies more heavily on Marxist feminists who account for the genesis of labor power in women's reproductive work. For instance, he invokes Leopoldina Fortunati and her analysis of the "commodity contained within the individual: that labor power which as capacity for production has exchange value." As Moten puts it, Fortunati

> sees, along with and ahead of Marx, that . . . the commodity is contained within the individual. This presence of the commodity within the individual is an effect of reproduction, a trace of maternity. Of equal importance is the containment of a certain personhood within the commodity that can be seen as the commodity's animation by the material trace of the maternal—a palpable hit or touch, a bodily and visible phonographic inscription.[46]

All workers are commodities who speak, Moten suggests, insofar as they contain the commodity that is labor power, and all commodities, he adds, contain material traces of the maternal person who indirectly produced them. There are problems with this account. Moten renders Fortunati far more mystical than she is: as we saw in chapter 2, she argues that reproductive labor regenerates labor power not because women perform it, inside or outside of homes, and certainly not because of a woman's innate biological ability to bear children, but because of reproductive labor's structural location in the twin circuits that Marx took to be inherent in the wage relation: M-C-M' and C-M-C. And Fortunati is not really interested in the commodity's lifelike animation—the table's capacity to dance, for instance—any more than she attributes it to a lingering maternal trace.

But whether or not they are faithful to Marx and Fortunati, Moten's terms beautifully explain "Woods." Alfred's mother is a ghost that figures the origins of the commodity within and as Alfred; she is a material and musical trace who animates a confusion between Alfred the person and Paper Boi the commodity, especially as the latter will seem subsequently to require Sierra's incipiently maternal reproductive labor. Alfred's self-curation as Paper Boi, in other words, is made inextricable from his mother's reproduction of her boy Alfred, which reproduction Sierra offers to assume. Moreover, *Atlanta* casts Alfred/Paper Boi not simply as a self-alienated commodity (who speaks), but as one whose rapped speech is haunted both by his mother's hummed gospel and, ultimately, by the dispossessive force of the slave's scream.

"Woods" ends with Alfred volunteering a photo with a fan. He mugs, acting "gangster," as he puts it. He has no choice but to play the asshole, to recall the TV anchor. That's partially because, if he's in it *for* the money, he's also in it *as* the money—or as a contradictory feature of money. His stage-name "Paper Boi" invokes the cheap labor that delivers newspapers to suburban homes. *Breaking Bad* and *The Americans*, we have seen, quote iconic moments in *The Sopranos* when Tony fetches his newspaper; in each drama, a protagonist nervously scans the horizon when venturing forth from the protective confines of the home. In *Atlanta*, Paper Boi evokes the delivery of those papers but is more basically a version of the threat for which they scan, a racial threat to the white household. And his name evokes the circulation of paper money as well as newspapers. Alfred attributes his rap career to his tendency to frighten white folks at cash machines. "I scare people at ATMs," he says, "so I have to rap" (1.4). Alfred's is a cash economy, a paper economy; he's consigned to selling drugs in and rapping about black markets. But he also personifies a contradiction in the money commodity. He doesn't just frighten as someone who might steal money, in other words; he figures something frightening about money. He is the money commodity who speaks this in particular: the cash in your white hands depends on violence against Black men, which violence you project back onto Black boogeymen lurking in the shadows, waiting to rob you.[47]

Money, Marx notes, "obliterates" and renders "invisible" the "specific attributes" and "real elements" of the production process. The "real" elements in question here are money's origins not simply in the exploitations of the wage economy, or in the exchange of quanta of abstract labor, but in the racial expropriations that make the wage relation possible at all—both historically (slavery was integral not simply to US cotton production but to global industrial expansion generally) and contemporaneously (policed racial populations are for capitalists a reserve army of cheap labor). Wilderson disentangles these strands and argues that the divide between Black and non-Black (or Human), stands above and even against the divide between worker and capitalist: "The antagonism between Black and Human," he writes, "supersedes the 'antagonism' between worker and capitalist in political economy, as well as the gendered 'antagonism' in libidinal economy." His argument proceeds from the observation that, at its inception, European slavery plundered African rather than closer-to-home sources of labor, to ensure the most economically disenfranchised whites could still, even if only in theory, purchase Black slaves. "If workers can buy a loaf of bread," he writes, "they can also buy a slave. It seems to me that the psychic dimension of a proletariat who 'stands in precisely the same relationship' to other members of civil society due to their intramural exchange in mutual, possessive possibilities, the ability to own either a piece of Black flesh or a loaf of white bread or both, is where we must begin to understand the founding antagonism" between Black and Human.[48] This is a powerful claim, even if it's not finally obvious that that ostensibly founding antagonism is static and timeless. Certainly, as both *Queen Sugar* and *Atlanta* make clear, the US economy now depends fundamentally on creating heavily policed Black surplus populations. Being Black in either Louisiana or Atlanta means being permanently at risk of becoming unfree prison labor. That prospect works in tandem with what Michael Denning calls "wageless life." "Under capitalism," he writes, "the only thing worse than being exploited is not being exploited."[49] *Atlanta* confirms as much; ultimately, it is about less the fronting and stunting required by being a rapper, or by any particular job, than the posture of permanent deep acting required of those without reliable access to the wage, who must evade state violence while always hunting for their next crap job.

Coda: History Is What Hurts

"You're a simulation," or a "real fake," Darius tells Van's friend as they lounge outside Drake's mansion, having discovered the musician is not physically present for the selfies that Van hoped to take with him. "Like a sim. There is someone controlling your every movement" (2.7). Who or what might that someone be? We find one answer in the episode

"Juneteenth," at the party Earn thinks "not real." A rich white man raps spoken word poetry: "Jim Crow! Has the name of a man, but is a ghost. I am a man. But Jim Crow is haunting me, like in that movie *Poltergeist*. And I am stuck in a television, like that little girl. Just get me out of here I don't want to be in an electrical appliance." The conceit is as ridiculous for the white man as it is relevant for Alfred, say, who is trapped in social media and at every moment subject to policing. On the episode "B.A.N.," a talk-show host demands Alfred justify his music. The host looks directly at the camera, but Alfred is the one who seems trapped inside an appliance and looking out.

Atlanta's "Teddy Perkins" (2.6) extends this conceit and explains why we might consider the ghost of Jim Crow the program's most relevant "someone." Set in an Atlanta mansion, this episode is by far the most gothic of the first two seasons. Darius arrives at what is presumably an old plantation home to collect a piano with multicolored keys advertised anonymously on "a biohacking message board." But slavery's past has hardly given way before a rainbow multiculturalism; rather, the Black body here has been hacked in the name of a familiar enslavement. Darius is greeted by the "ghoulish" Teddy Perkins, played by Donald Glover in a frozen leering whiteface. Darius will later meet Teddy's brother Benny Hope, a musician who has shrouded his face in cloth to disguise what Teddy calls a debilitating skin condition. The episode's gothic spatial confusions make it hard to confidently distinguish between interior and exterior psychic states, and ostensibly separate persons. Teddy presides over the manse as a grotesque Michael Jackson, while Benny lurks in the shadows in a wheelchair, his face wrapped in blue cloth that evokes both Ralph Ellison's famous protagonist and Claude Rains in *The Invisible Man*. The brothers haunt the house as two ghosts of Jim Crow, two separate but equal halves of a single person, each having differently concealed his Black skin. Darius thinks the two are the same person. They are not, at least not exactly, but they are doppelgängers who literalize a profound self-estrangement.

"Teddy Perkins" shares many affinities with Boots Riley's *Sorry to Bother You* (2018) and Jordan Peele's *Get Out* (2017) and *Us* (2019). The latter is instructive in a general way: like Bong Joon-Ho's *Parasite*, *Us* can

CHAPTER 5

5.8. *Atlanta*: "The ghost of Jim Crow."

be read as a radical antithesis of the black-market melodrama, insofar as it depicts a doppelgänger family hunting its more affluent counterpart, as the proletariat might the petit bourgeoisie.[50] (*Us* ends by reenacting the Hands across America stunt, which updated a 1971 Coca-Cola commercial; *Mad Men* ends with that commercial and suggests Draper invented it.) More specifically, like *Get Out* and *Sorry to Bother You*, "Teddy Perkins" is about how and at what cost white voices come to issue from Black bodies (Lakeith Stanfield headlines both the second film and the *Atlanta* episode). But where *Get Out*'s Chris Washington is captured to become a host for an aging white man, Perkins has at the start already transformed into a white version of himself. Presiding over that transformation, the episode suggests, is the ghost of Jim Crow, which takes partial shape in a statue of Teddy's father.

Teddy has been turning the house into a museum that will enshrine his father's influence on him and Benny. And at one juncture he leads Darius into a dark and windowless room and there reveals a statue of the father. Like some of the painted images behind the dying artist in "Harvest" on *The Americans* (another FX program), the statue's head has no features; it is missing its face (fig. 5.8). "Harvest" aired just one month after "Teddy Perkins," in fact, and in addition to serving up similarly

254

depersonalized images, the episodes produce startlingly similar accounts of pain and artistic creation. Teddy celebrates pain while standing beneath the figure. Their father's severe parenting, he tells Darius, led to his brother's talents. He imposed an oppressive regimen on Benny because he believed "great things come from great pain." It seemed to work. Jazz pianist Amad Jamal once told Teddy, "Your brother plays pain better than anyone."

Noting the echo between the two FX programs, we might see Murdoch in Teddy's faceless father figure. Perhaps he is the "someone" controlling the characters' every move. That would be painful indeed. "History is . . . the experience of necessity," Jameson declares in *The Political Unconscious*. "History is what hurts, it is what refuses desire and sets inexorable limits to individual and collective praxis."[51] From the sublime to the ridiculous: Murdoch's "parent company" set limits on and constrained collective praxis in the making of *Atlanta* and it no doubt hurt Glover, even if only a little, to accept such limits from so noxious a company. And in fact, Glover has been as preoccupied by his corporate employers as TV creators typically are. He claimed he tricked FX into producing the show, by presenting his story in familiar terms. Two years later, the network felt less hostile. "FX, to me, feels like a safe creative place right now," he conceded, before adding that he was "hesitant to say that, because it's owned by a big conglomerate."[52] Hesitant presumably because working for News Corp meant becoming its mouthpiece (and thus assuming a white voice): in *Because the Internet*, the protagonist compares himself to Bill O'Reilly, News Corp's famous TV news host.

More backstage registers now present themselves: "Teddy Perkins" is about two brothers, one who hides in the shadows and one who curates the family's public image. *Atlanta* is made by two brothers, Donald and Stephen Glover; Donald is the family's public face while Stephen, whose trap rap is more like Alfred's than is Donald's R&B, stays invisible, writing many of the episodes and supplying the voice to which Brian Tyree Henry lip-syncs when singing as Paper Boi. And so why not see in Teddy's faceless father figure not simply the ghost of Jim Crow, but that ghost's latter-day incarnation, Murdoch, the plantation master having become the execrable CEO? Seen this way, the narrative stasis that defines the comedy springs from the unsettling ease with which one master replaces another and makes unavailable any sense of significant rather than superficial historical change.

That is useful, but insufficient. Jameson would encourage us to treat the mogul as a transitory mask, a brief stop on our way to something more impersonal. He advocates replacing "everything static about traditional personification" with "the process of identifying agencies to come." This is to use "the allegorical impulse" not to establish one-to-one correspondences between symbols and their hidden meanings, but "as a struggle against personification . . . a desperate attempt to de-reify what differentiation has brought about in the way of 'fixed ideas' and named concepts." Used this way, "allegory invents connections between dimensions of reality [that are] otherwise imperceptible," and produces "a sudden opening onto the perception of the totality as well as of the radical differences whose identities make it into a conjuncture."[53] Thus conceived, as a process rather than one fixed schema, allegory drives us beyond any one set of correspondences, toward what is otherwise unrepresentable. For Jameson, faces, names, and other marks of individuality obscure a more universal commonality. To read the faceless figure only as Murdoch would thus be to forget not simply that Murdoch was not himself News Corp, but also that the corporate person thus fronted, News Corp, is itself but a local mask worn by more systemic capitalist agencies.

The tendency in this kind of symptomatic reading is to move "up" from the local instance to still more impersonal agencies. Along the way, more encompassing accounts of capitalist relations make possible more encompassing accounts of class interest until, ultimately, we glimpse a properly utopian communist horizon in which there is but one class. In this spirit, we might say that the only partially particularized father figurine gestures toward utopian horizons, its unformed face registering what Jameson calls "agencies to come." When standing before the statue, Darius and Teddy argue about whether love or pain is more important in the raising of children. Teddy thinks the featureless head a testament to the genesis of children from pain; Darius thinks love a better origin. "Not all great things come from pain. Sometimes it's love. Not everything's a sacrifice," he says. "What if . . . you would have seen the love?" Darius is the comedy's foremost conspiracy theorist; he sees designs where others see contingency. He's also the program's funniest character, and his utopian "what if" helps explain why, over and beyond that humor, we might consider *Atlanta* a comedy at all: Darius asks Teddy to imagine a "great thing" in the generic spirit of comedy, insofar as that thing is a whole greater than the sum of its parts.

And yet, *Atlanta* offers few sudden openings; it does not transport. It places us in situations from which there are not even temporary exits—in halls of mirrors beyond which it's impossible to see. The statue's head doesn't really augur collective agencies to come. Far more concretely, it echoes a giant egg featured earlier in the episode. When Darius first arrives, Teddy offers him part of an ostrich egg. Darius demurs while Teddy plunges his fingers into the oozing innards of the soft-boiled shell, which he informs Darius is an "owl's casket." The gruesome scene suggests that however much Teddy wants to make his father Zeus, an egg from which Athena's wisdom is said to have sprung, the wisdom is dead upon arrival, entombed in a "casket," which casket seems like a skull whose insides are scooped out by probing fingers. Thus does Glover give up his intellectual labor and property to his ravenous employer. The product is not wisdom, or utopian hope, but madness. Before arriving, Darius buys a trucker's cap with a confederate flag printed next to "SOUTHERN MADE"; he colors over some of the letters such that it reads "U MAD." Teddy is made insane by white supremacy; his faceless father is first and always a slave master. Indeed, the episode suggests how southern interests were at that moment extending slavery's legacy. In Teddy's manse, a picture of Bill Clinton hangs on the wall, perhaps, to register the political conflict then underway. The episode aired just months before the 2018 election, in which Republican Brian Kemp, then Georgia's secretary of state and gubernatorial candidate, ramped up a years-long effort to suppress the African American vote. "The state has become the battleground for something deeper than the ideas of the candidates themselves," wrote Vann Newkirk in 2018; "it's now emblematic of a larger struggle over voting rights that has changed party politics markedly over the past five years."[54] We need no archival footage to know where Fox News came down. The looming election would have elucidated a fundamental continuity between "Rupert Murdoch" and "slave master," each a personification of a system of racial capitalism.

We might see Fox News or its parent company News Corp in the figurine in still another way—by recalling the longstanding legal intimacy between African American and corporate personhood. W. E. B. Du Bois claimed the Fourteenth Amendment was "the chief refuge and bulwark of corporations." And up through *Citizens United*, corporations have enshrined their status as legal persons by drawing on case law that stems from that amendment. Lisa Siraganian adds that, in the decades that followed the amendment's passage, "the era's jurisprudence and case law rendered corporations a class of abstract persons constitutively impervious to experience's marks, in pointed distinction to African Americans, whom law continued to encumber with permanent marks of race. This precisely crafted division of conceptual labor satisfied the rigid formalism of late nineteenth-century jurisprudence, while simultaneously enabling 'intangible' businesses to fortify themselves on the back of the enfeebled personhood of embodied African Americans." In sum, "African-American legal personhood and corporate personhood were bound together formally since the nineteenth century as a largely unspoken but nonetheless codified arrangement in which the attenuation of the former secured the legitimacy of the latter."[55] These terms allow us to see an affinity between Moten's account of the slave as "the commodity who speaks" and allegorical readings of Hollywood films as corporate speech. As Michael Rogin notes, all "transformative moments in the history of American film . . . organized themselves around the surplus symbolic value of blacks, the power to make African Americans stand for something besides themselves."[56] For Rogin, *The Jazz Singer* represents one such appropriative transformation: it allegorizes the industry's transition to sound, and Warner Bros. itself, when painting Al Jolson in blackface. Made Black, Jolson becomes a commodity who speaks—for and as Warner Bros., as it trailblazes new frontiers in film production.

"Teddy Perkins," of course, features not blackface but whiteface, which it uses to highlight the forcible sacrifice of Black bodies to the occult corporate agencies that speak through them. Gambino's "This Is America" gives us those agencies as they violently contort him, as if a marionette on strings. The father figurine in "Teddy Perkins" offers those agencies in still different form, I have been suggesting, as they point back to Glover's corporate employer. Jameson might say, not without reason, that those agencies limn a larger system that is not exactly or simply white. By the logic of his semiotic squares, the "negation of the negation" of "Black" is not white but the more ostensibly utopian because encompassing "not white," or "not-anti-Black." Visiting Drake's mansion, Van stumbles on his father, who speaks Spanish; she's struck with an insight: "Drake's Mexican" (2.7), by which she means, ambiguously, both not Black *and* Black and Mexican. If Darius experiences a similar insight in Teddy's mansion, it is that the statue figures the "sacrifice" of Black skin to an ideal of personhood that is the antithesis of Black embodiment, yet not exactly white either. But what cold comfort that must be. "Teddy Perkins" features no exact equivalent of the dispossessing scream that for Moten signals the slave's fateful confusion of person and commodity. Rather, the episode itself is that scream, as it reacts in horror to the fact that neither its voice nor its body is or can ever be its own.

CONCLUSION

Streaming and You

"The Streaming Revolution Has Finally Arrived. Everything Is About to Change," announced Brooks Barnes's 2019 *New York Times* article. The article went on to proclaim, "The long-promised streaming revolution—the next great leap in how the world gets its entertainment—is finally here."[1] There would be little point in asking who made the promise, so commonplace has it been for almost a decade. One version appeared in a 2014 *New Yorker* piece about Netflix, the essence of which was that new media was about to destroy TV as a distribution system, a business model, and a particular kind of content. "Television is undergoing a digital revolution," wrote Ken Auletta. He quoted the venture capitalist Marc Andreessen, who coinvented the browser that became Netscape: "TV in ten years is going to be one hundred percent streamed. On demand. Internet Protocol. Based on computers and based on software." Andreessen added, "Software is going to eat television in the exact same way, ultimately, that software ate music and as it ate books."[2]

It's safe to say that TV will not be 100 percent streamed by 2024, if by streamed we mean delivered over the internet. Streaming has gained significant ground on cable and satellite but has not yet achieved a decisive dominance: according to a Pew Research report, the percentage of Americans who watched on cable or satellite in 2021 had fallen from 76 percent in 2015 to 56 percent.[3] But enthusiasm over streaming has never been about numbers alone. From academic titles like *The Television*

CONCLUSION

Will Be Revolutionized and *Distribution Revolution* to the always enthusiastic pages of *Wired*, a legion of scholars, critics, and fans have proclaimed that internet distribution has fundamentally changed—no, revolutionized!—television, such that it has become something unprecedented, and a new medium entirely. Writing the same year as Auletta, Amanda Lotz waxed similarly breathless while describing the shift from TV's mass-market "network era" to its micro-cast "post-network era" (which shift would "revolutionize" TV). She wrote, "The changes in television that have taken place over the past two decades—whether the gross abundance of channel and program options we now select among or our increasing ability to control when and where we watch— are extraordinary and on the scale of the transition from one medium to another, as in the case of the shift from radio to television."[4]

New technologies have of course changed the industry. As this book went to press, Netflix's market capitalization was around $200 billion, roughly twice Disney's. And legacy media companies eager to compete have rushed to replicate everything from Netflix's video-on-demand interface and compression algorithms to its global coproduction arrangements and cost-plus financing (which pays production companies more up front than deficit financing but deprives them of ownership in what they produce). That rush has resulted in an unprecedented bounty of offerings, which providers tailor to consumers as never before— again, with new tech. Netflix caused a stir in 2013 when it claimed to use taste algorithms to determine viewer preferences among "76,897 micro genres." Writing in the *New York Times*, David Carr thought those algorithms would allow the company to make "the mysterious alchemy of finding a hit . . . a product of logic and algorithms."[5] Doubtful; but finding a monster hit might not be the only goal. The more advanced the algorithms, and the more diversified the field of production, the less necessity there is for single hits to tentpole mass audiences—runaway phenomena like *Squid Game* notwithstanding. Certainly, Netflix seems eager to make us each feel like an audience of one, the recipient of bespoke TV. Our customized user icons whisper to us, *this* TV is for *you*.

And yet if we look away from the dizzying array of choices on our customized home pages, we might ask not simply if Netflix really knows us all that well, but if the TV genres that we watch now are really so very different from those we watched ten or fifteen years ago. And if not, does it make sense to say that television has evolved into something unprecedented? Relative newcomers like Netflix have produced an abundance of offerings, to be sure, and in that way contributed to a new age of quantity TV. But this book argues that over the last twenty years, the US TV industry has been organized by a relatively stable conception of quality TV, and a still largely invisible meta-genre that has governed its production. That meta-genre's function has been to coordinate more longstanding and familiar genres and new ones as they emerge, and to selectively endow them with the patina of quality. In thus producing distinctions within and thereby governing TV's larger genre system, it has been the programming, the old-media software as it were, that has mattered most to the industry.[6]

That meta-genre, the black-market melodrama, has been systematically copied over the last twenty years and serials with its general features might well appear on your Netflix home page as part of this or that microgenre. Even *Squid Game*, I would argue, heavily borrows these features, in its underground allegory of capitalist precarity. But the genre proper, as described in this book, is not simply an averaging of this or that plot, style, or mood. It is also an argument about what it means to watch TV now, some fifty years into the US economy's deindustrialization. As such, it is an argument about the nature of TV's medium. Streaming—and technological innovation generally—plays only a small role in that argument.

Raymond Williams's Family Project

The precise nature of TV's medium has long occasioned versions of William Goldman's joke about the film industry: "Nobody knows anything." In 1974, Horace Newcomb said of TV, "No one seems to know just what the medium is." In 1983, Jane Feuer added, "No one is entirely sure what the entity 'television' is."[7] The *OED* offers little help. Its first definition of *television* is: "A system used for transmitting and viewing images and (typically) sound. . . . such a system used for the organized broadcast of professionally produced shows and programmes."⁸ That definition certainly lends support to those who would see in streaming a distinct evolution of TV's medium. But however tethered to transmitting and viewing, the system in question might be conceived more capaciously, such that it includes cathode tubes or coaxial cables, a TV set or smartphone, the Minimum Basic Agreement codified between the Writers Guild of America and Hollywood studios, or agreements between management and stockholders of media transnationals.

In fact, television's system should be cast in still more encompassing terms. "Every specific art," Raymond Williams writes in *Marxism and Literature*, when considering the usefulness of the term "medium," "has dissolved into it, at every level of its operations," both "specific social relationships" and "specific material means of production, on the mastery of which its production depends." Those specific relationships and materials, he adds, express local contradictions "between an increasingly collaborative production and the learned skills and values of individual production."⁹ And those local contradictions express in turn the more generalized contradictions that animate particular stages of capitalist development.

At first blush, Williams's *Television: Technology and Cultural Form* seems not to consider TV a "specific art." It understands broadcast TV not as an aesthetic medium, that is, but as a purely technological one. That's the case in part because television's distribution systems seem to dictate its content. "Unlike all previous communications technologies," Williams writes,

> radio and television were *systems primarily devised for transmission and reception as abstract processes, with little or no definition of preceding content.* When the question of content was raised, it was resolved, in the main, parasitically. There were state occasions, public sporting events, theaters and so on, which would be communicatively distributed by these new technical means. *It is not only that the supply of broadcasting facilities preceded the demand; it is that the means of communication preceded their content.*¹⁰

That said, Williams is withering when dismissing technological determinism. Andreessen lends a carnivorous agency to abstractions like

STREAMING AND YOU

software and the digital, which swallow TV as if driven by their own hunger. Williams derides a version of that thinking in Marshall McLuhan, for instance, who treats "medium" and "technology" as interchangeable and hermetically sealed, quarantined from class conflict. It is facile, Williams argues, to consider abstractions like these determinants of anything. It is much harder, on the other hand, to consider technology "at once an intention and an effect of a particular social order."[11] Media mediate the social order, which order determines their form and function. Technology is not itself the primary driver of anything.

Broadcast systems were an intention and effect of early twentieth-century industrialization, Williams contends. Their primary role was to facilitate the "transformation of industrial production, and its new social forms, which had grown out of a long history of capital accumulation." The handmaidens of "*mobile privatization*," those systems were a response to "new separations of families" and "internal and external migrations" that made it necessary to maintain "over distance and through time, certain personal connections." For Williams, "The new and larger settlements and industrial organizations required major internal mobility, at a primary level, and this was joined by secondary consequences in the dispersal of extended families and in the needs of new kinds of social organizations." TV facilitated the illusion that the newly isolated nuclear family was independent, while still connecting it to a larger world. "New homes might appear private and 'self-sufficient,'" he writes, "but could be maintained only by regular funding and supply from external sources, and these, over a range from employment and prices to depressions and wars, had a decisive and often disrupting influence on what was nevertheless seen as a separable 'family' project."[12]

Postwar TV shaped and sustained that project by drawing on antecedent literary forms. Williams unearths the long history of the TV play in particular, whose roots he traces to nineteenth-century naturalist drama—a "drama of the small enclosed room, in which a few characters lived out their private experience of an unseen public world." The TV play was "a drama of the box in the same fundamental sense as the naturalist drama had been the drama of the framed stage": "the enclosed internal atmosphere; the local interpersonal conflict; the close-up on private feeling." The TV play also updated naturalist drama's fascination with the enclosed room's exposure "to the public pressures that were seen as determining it: not just as messages from the street or the stock exchanges or the battlefields, but as the dramatic inclusion of just these elements, in an indivisible dramatic action." The TV play would extend that action serially, in soap opera, which tended to stress private experience, and in literary adaptations like *Masterpiece Theater*, which tended to stress public pressures.[13]

Williams's schema allows me to clarify the stakes of this book. For him, broadcast TV is "at once an intention and an effect" of industrialization. For me, cable, satellite, and streaming distribution systems are intentions and effects of deindustrialization. In each case, an ascendant distribution technology mediates a more general tendency: for broadcast, an expanding manufacturing base and the consolidation of the family wage; for cable, satellite, and streaming, a shrinking manufacturing base relative to the economy as a whole and work's corresponding casualization and informalization. In each case, a particular kind of TV content performs an analogous mediation: for Williams, the TV play is an "intrinsic outcome" of the "transformation of industrial production, and its new social forms," the white nuclear family above all.[14] The TV play consolidates that family's imagined autonomy, while rendering palatable its new dependencies. For me, the black-market melodrama is an intrinsic outcome of deindustrialization; it fights a rearguard battle against the breakdown of the white nuclear family's autonomy, while registering that breakdown's inevitability.

Williams also allows me, when considering TV's medium below, to stress the importance of treating genre both more broadly and more narrowly than TV studies typically does. Taking its cue from Williams, the discipline has long studied how and for what ends TV is produced. But it has been narrowly rather than broadly interested in infrastructure, and its frequently sociological terms rarely encompass Williams's "long history of capital accumulation." The discipline's "political economy" tradition, for instance, studies media industry monopolization more than the larger tendencies that drive it; analogously, significant exceptions aside, while the discipline offers rich and invaluable meso-level industry analyses, it rarely situates those analyses within broader accounts of capitalist development and crisis.[15] Conversely, if the discipline offers few comprehensive analyses of how TV functions within a capitalist system, it offers relatively little close narrative analysis (studies of individual programs and work on global TV formats are important exceptions). As pivotal as Williams has been to the evolution of TV studies, for instance, the discipline can be too eager to forget he was a gifted close reader of literature. Jeffrey Sconce for one thinks the discipline's eschewal of close reading (frequently typed as literary critical vanity) prevents it from considering TV's medium as it otherwise might: "Despite the isolated efforts of scholars . . . to initiate debate over the aesthetic properties of the medium, television remains for the most part a technological and cultural problem to be solved rather than a textual body to be engaged."[16] Jason Mittell's *Complex TV* is an outlier to this general pattern; even so, it doesn't closely read TV complexity so much as insist that it is there.

The discipline's understanding of genre can be similarly limited. It tends either to identify extremely broad rubrics (Lotz's "cable guys") or to study genres as they are supplied by the industry itself. There's good reason to focus on the industry's own understanding of genre. Hollywood writers likely did not pitch postwar TV plays as timely updates of naturalist drama, which category would not have been important to marketing departments. But identifying emergent genres as they ring a change on more longstanding and (even) literary ones pays dividends—in the case of the black-market melodrama, by allowing us to track changes in a "family project" whose history is far longer than television's. Reading that genre closely also allows us in turn to conceive of TV's medium in a new way. Because the black-market melodrama doesn't simply reproduce TV's ideological relation to deindustrialization. It comments critically upon it, and in the process makes an argument about the nature of the TV medium.

Genre-as-Medium

Quality cable melodramas have prompted frequent comparisons between distinct media (visual and print, say) and genres broadly conceived (the serial TV drama and the novel, say). As Michael Chabon put it in a representative statement, "There can't be a novelist in America who watched *The Wire* and didn't think, 'Oh my God, I want to do something like that. . . . The tapestry is so broad, it's like a 19th-century novel.' "[17] But famed futurist William Gibson offered a more confounding assessment. "Television," he said, "particularly at the HBO level in the United States—[has] become a completely new genre. Something like *Deadwood* or *The Wire* is a whole new thing—there was no equivalent to that medium before. It's like a new way of telling stories."[18] Here was the novelist who popularized "cyberspace" and first fictionalized a version of the internet announcing new serials as if they were revolutionary tech. But how can a "new way of telling stories" be both a new genre and a new medium?

Though there is no evidence he read it, Gibson's interchangeable use of *genre* and *medium* recalls Stanley Cavell's "The Fact of Television" (published in 1984, the year Gibson published *Neuromancer*). The essay appeared when the VCR was only just achieving mass-market penetration. Though HBO was at the time a decade old, MTV and cable were still in their infancy. And yet it is precisely in its attention to what now seems an antediluvian phase of broadcast that the essay is useful. Cavell is interested in the "double range of the concept of medium . . . in order to keep open to investigation the relation between work and medium that I call the revelation, or acknowledgement, of the one in the other." A medium is not simply "a familiar material," like a screen and projector, he argues (or, he might have added, like fiber optic cables and data packets). Rather, "only the art can define its media, only painting and composing and movie-making can reveal what is required, or possible (what means, what exploits of material), for something to be a painting, a piece of music, a movie."[19] A film genre does this—and thereby becomes what he calls a "genre-as-medium"—when its individual members "study" and "acknowledge" the "conditions, procedures and subjects and goals of composition" that define the film medium generally.[20]

Cavell does not think TV genres attain the status of "genre-as-medium," because he thinks TV "monitoring" fundamentally different from film "viewing," and not conducive to self-criticism. Films that make up a given "genre-as-medium" tend to study how the screen separates viewers from the diegesis, which does not acknowledge them, and which as a consequence captures "a world complete without me which is present to me."[21] But where viewing promises immortality, in its access to a world that survives our absence, monitoring is anxious and driven by the fear that the world unfolding just beyond our homes might engulf us (he defines all TV, live or not, as "*a current of simultaneous event reception*"). TV creates pseudo-events to allay that fear; Cavell writes, "as in monitoring the heart, or the rapid eye movements during periods of dreaming—say, monitoring signs of life—most of what appears [on TV] is a graph of the normal, or the establishment of some reference or base line, a line, so to speak, of the uneventful, from which events stand out with perfectly anticipatable significance."[22]

Even now, in a moment defined by streaming and the much-heralded convergence of film and television, I think it right to say that a good deal of serial quality TV remains tacitly if subtly oriented to audiences in ways that feature films are not. But it's worth noting how potentially overstated Cavell's terms are, and not simply because there now seem to be fewer differences than ever between, say, the two-hour feature film, the limited series, and the multiyear serial drama. Indeed, Cavell's terms would likely strike Linda Williams as fundamentally misguided— because they accept at face value the "classicism" of Classical Hollywood Cinema (CHC) conventions, as defined by the likes of David Bordwell and Kristin Thompson, while downplaying Hollywood cinema's more properly theatrical because melodramatic orientation to viewers.

Seen from one perspective, film and serial quality TV are just different kinds of melodrama, and as such not fundamentally opposed in their relation to audiences. Seen from another, film and serial quality TV are alike not because they are melodrama but because they are, to evoke half of HBO's most famous tagline, "Not TV"—because they defined themselves against the core genres of broadcast TV in particular. News, talk programming, reality TV, and even multicamera sitcoms filmed before live studio audiences speak to viewers as films generally do not, albeit with different degrees of explicitness. And this was exactly the hoi polloi hodgepodge from which a new generation of quality TV wanted to

CONCLUSION

distinguish itself at the start of a new millennium. In part, that ambition registered as style. For example, sloughing off TV and embracing the cinematic often meant rejecting the flamboyant camera work, over-the-top design and torqued-up reflexivity that John Caldwell considers features of "televisuality," a style palette that in the 1980s and 1990s sought to keep broadcast TV competitive in the face of new threats from the VHS and later DVD and, to a lesser extent, networks like HBO.[23] From the start, black-market melodramas eschewed televisuality, in the case of *The Sopranos*, for example, while embracing New Hollywood cinematography. Certainly David Chase, we saw in the first chapter, was vehement that he was making film and not TV.

That rejection didn't itself secure the genre's place in some imagined pantheon of cinema. Not all TV genres were or are equally televisual, Caldwell notes. He thinks some "simply do not care about style," or are stylistically conservative, because calling attention to the camera undermines their ideological function. The family sitcom typically adopted an unobtrusive style, he notes, because it aimed to "reconfigure and update the nuclear family."[24] Caldwell does not elaborate, but it's reasonable to hypothesize that sitcoms rejected televisuality in the name of stabilizing separate sphere distinctions between home and everything beyond it. Even when filmed before a live studio audience, they preserved the integrity of their households, even if only negatively, by eschewing cleverly reflexive gestures that might further collapse the difference between watched and watching families.

"Further collapse" because the watched and watching families of scripted dramas and sitcoms have long mirrored each other, as TV's dominant topic and chief addressee (or as Horace Newcomb puts it, TV's principal "'content' and object").[25] As Cavell notes, the fundamental and perhaps essential difference between TV monitoring and film viewing is that the former takes place in shared intimate spaces, whereas the later transpires in impersonal public spaces. At least until the advent of device-driven watching, TV had been what David Morely calls "a domestic medium" because it transpired in spaces where, "'if the camera pulls us in, the family pulls us out,' and where the people you live with are likely to disrupt, if not shatter, your communication with 'the box in the corner.' "[26] Cinema also transpires in shared spaces, to be sure, but after an early "cinema of attractions" gave way to CHC, the tacit subject of address has tended to be an individual in the dark, not a collective visible to itself.[27] And I'd hazard that even if much TV watching is now done on personal devices, TV remains tacitly addressed to social domestic contexts. Its capacity to produce mutual visibility is a latent core affordance, we might say, to be activated or not, repressed or not, by individual TV genres and formats, regardless of how empirical individuals watch, alone or collectively, at home or not, etc.

Following Caldwell, I'm suggesting only that, on the whole, fin-de-siècle sitcoms and family dramas repressed that core affordance: they avoided directly acknowledging their watching families, the better to advance a conservative ideological project. Black-market melodramas aim for similarly hygienic separations between their watching and watched families, on behalf of a similarly conservative project: rejecting televisuality—and stabilizing distinctions between watching and watched families—the genre consolidates the heteronormative white family's domestic autonomy. But that is only half the story. Because as we have seen throughout this book, the genre's most essential discovery is that distinctions between home and work cannot in fact be maintained.

That discovery is inextricable from the genre's filmic ambitions, which are self-consciously quixotic. Black-market melodramas want to escape TV, and those watching at home, for a more filmic condition, in conjunction with their enfeebled male leads, who want to escape the family's reproductive labor for a separate sphere of waged work. The genre's self-critical gambit, I would suggest, is that in leaving the home and the work that defines it, these men might also leave behind, on behalf of the serials themselves, the conditions of spectatorship (or "monitoring") to which TV historically has been consigned. But as they track men's failed efforts to escape reproductive labor, these serials confess they cannot escape from TV into film. To wit, the genre understands its inability to sustain separate spheres as indissociable from its inability to sustain the separateness of diegetic and nondiegetic space, as film presumably does. Taking liberties with Cavell, I would say that the black-market melodrama becomes a "genre-as-medium" as it registers its inability to transcend the "material conditions" that define TV's reception, where those conditions encompass not just the physical logistics of monitoring (as it does for Cavell), but also to the gendered reproductive labor that sustains family life.[28]

Along these lines, I argued in earlier chapters that the genre's thematic interest in men who flee their families is in part a reflexive effort to escape soap opera into something more ostensibly serious and cinematic. The genre's relation to reality TV is equally revealing. Quality TV began to take new shape in the late 1990s, even as reality TV was taking broadcast by storm. For Jane Feuer, reality TV was quality TV's object lesson; it was "the great other to quality drama," the unscripted, popular standard against which fancier fare defined its literary and cinematic ambitions.[29] This is important, but the issue is not simply the spontaneously demotic versus the planned and elite. It is also how each kind of TV situates its viewers with respect to the home's endless work. If reality TV was quality TV's other, it was so in part because of the identity it established between viewers and "the work of being watched," as Mark Andrejevic has it.[30] Frequently breaking its fourth walls, reality TV acknowledged viewers the better to insist they were working alongside those they watched. Watching and being watched were instances of "digital revolution" labor: there is no difference between producing and consuming, reality TV suggested; all of our waking hours are work, and the family home in particular is the site of new kinds of production. According to Andrejevic, reality TV embraced this account even when seeming to denounce it and even while pioneering newly exploitive production practices.[31]

Black-market melodramas also acknowledge that home is where the work is, and no longer a haven from economic life. Likewise, they grant that watching is if not work than certainly not simply leisure. But the genre makes these acknowledgments while warding them off. It goes looking for cinematic immortality (viewing), we might say, but discovers only televisual purgatory (monitoring). In a world defined by informal reproductive labor and a newly capacious category of housework, there can be nothing but soap opera, the genre dolefully concludes. And if film and TV seem more similar than ever, they are similar as TV.

Serial TV becomes serial quality TV, and something like a distinct medium, black-market melodramas insist, in the self-consciousness with which it fails to become anything other than TV.³² That self-consciousness inheres in and is calibrated by the genre's secret lives. Typically, secret lives offer some animating generic fantasy that distinguishes subject from object families. You, at home, likely do not belong to the mob, make meth, or spy for a foreign state: that fantasy makes it possible to think of watching as a vivifying escape into a diegesis that is cleanly separate from the scene of its reception. Put in Alexander Galloway's terms, secret lives are an "intraface" that represses recognition of the interface that is the boundary between the media object and the world beyond it.³³ As such, they are narrative sublimations of what might otherwise be more direct gestures to the audience of the kind common to genres like reality TV. But if secret lives are sublimations of the viewer's escape from his or her home into the melodrama at hand, they are also always potentially de-sublimations of the same, especially insofar as those melodramas also stage the impossibility of true escape.

The genre does not impose an invariant format, and a secret life alone is rarely the only way a given serial registers this double bind. *The Sopranos* uses Jennifer Melfi in the way that *Homeland*, *The Americans*, *The Leftovers*, and *Killing Eve* use their "handlers": as audience surrogates. These are oblique narrative rather than direct audience acknowledgments, and subtle ones at that. They feel more obscured, for instance, than those in *Highlander* and *Buffy the Vampire Slayer*, programs that incorporate "watchers" who surveil their superhuman subjects. But the semantic difference alone is not decisive; it falls to each serial to clarify how meaningfully or for what particular ends it narratively sublimates or de-sublimates its recognition of the audience. That clarification, I'd stress, is narrative rather than simply formal: story and plot play crucial roles in a serial's uneven and quixotic repudiation of its audience.

Analogously, a character's direct address to the camera doesn't itself determine the meaning of that address. In Michaela Coel's *Chewing Gum* and Phoebe Waller-Bridge's *Fleabag*, that address means something different than it does, say, in David Fincher's *House of Cards*. In both comedies, the protagonist speaks to the camera as if speaking to God

CONCLUSION

6.1. *Chewing Gum*: Tracey prays.

6.2. *Fleabag*: Fleabag looks back.

(figs. 6.1 and 6.2). For Fleabag, speaking to the camera is an effect of stalled mourning for a dead friend (as it is in *Weeds* for Shane Botwin, whose direct camera addresses represent a desire to speak to his dead father). Associated with therapy and confession, breaking the fourth wall signals both Fleabag's ability to straddle two worlds and a concomitant inability to be fully present to her life and those around her. Fleabag is Fleebag:

"Where did you just go?" (2.3), asks The Priest, who also speaks to God and is the only character to register her asides. "It's like you disappear" (2.4). Emotional recovery thus requires rebuilding the fourth wall and saying farewell to the audience (which is what happens in *Weeds*: Shane stops speaking to the camera when he accepts that his father is truly gone).

Similar kinds of distinctions might be made with respect to the black-market melodrama's different generic substrates. Precisely because of the extremity of their departures from everyday life, black-market melodramas with supernatural or science-fictional premises, for example, often render secret lives more explicitly escapist, and therefore more implicitly linked with those watching at home. In *Twin Peaks*, secret lives barely suppress their audience surrogacy. The malevolent and easily bored Bob, capable of inhabiting his victims, stands in for a home audience hungry for entertainment.[34] He is the prurient male spectator especially, run rampant and exposed as an ugly sadist. Subsequent science-fictional family dramas can seem to admonish not simply characters but also TV watchers to cease traveling between worlds.

That admonishment is all but explicit in *The Leftovers*, which chastises Kevin Garvey for so frequently moving back and forth between an everyday world in which he is starting a new family, having been divorced recently from his first wife, and one in which he is alternately a messiah and the president of a dystopian US. That second world is pointedly an escape from the domestic. While there, Garvey embraces policies hostile to families. "For millennia," he says, "we have believed in marriage as a cornerstone of our civilization. Our party, however, does not share this opinion. We believe that marriage is the single most destructive idea ever conceived of by humankind." But ultimately, he feels as trapped in this life as in his first. "I want to go home," he tells his handler. "Do you?" she asks. "It's just that you've been known to say that before, and yet you keep leaving home and coming here" (3.7). A version of that line appears in *Counterpart*, which offers a related doubling. "Always fleeing this life for the promise of another" (1.6), Howard Silk tells his doppelgänger, who lives in another dimension, but shows up in Silk's. Better to stay put (and not watch TV), suggests the resigned Silk, since in the end you will be reconfirmed in the life you mean to flee.

CONCLUSION

These narrative structures endow otherwise purely technical gestures with meaning. Garvey moves between realities by looking into reflective screenlike surfaces; we shuttle between worlds with him by seeing his reflection in point-of-view shots that evoke our spectatorship. Garvey also moves between worlds by drowning, and this is what Nora Durst prepares to do in the drama's final episode. She wants to find her children, lost to her along with 140 million other souls in the Sudden Departure. But as the water closes in on her, she seems to change her mind, just before the screen goes black in a hard cut. For Matt Zoller Seitz, the sequence recalls the conclusion of *The Sopranos*—which aired ten years earlier, almost to the day—and "the timing of the cut, not just mid-sentence but mid-word, is so brutal and seemingly random that at first I thought it was a glitch in HBO's signal."[35] It is to that conclusion—and the meaning with which it was endowed—that we now turn.

Cut to Black

Tony, Carmela, and AJ sit in a diner. Outside, Meadow parks her car. Strangers walk past the seated family. Some of them may or may not have been sent to kill Tony, who scans the room nervously and selects Journey's "Don't Stop Believing" on the jukebox. The song plays and the tension mounts until, in what is easily the most controversial ending in TV history, Journey's refrain suddenly stops, frozen at "don't stop," and the screen goes black.

This is David Chase, discussing the editing at work in that ending and the sequence leading to it:

> whenever Tony arrives someplace, he would see himself. He would get to the place and he would look and see where he was going.... I had him walk into his own POV every time. So the order of the shots would be Tony close-up, Tony POV, hold on the POV, and then Tony walks into the POV. And I shortened the POV every time. So that by the time he got to Holsten's [Diner], he wasn't even walking toward it anymore. He came in, he saw himself sitting at the table, and the next thing you knew he was at the table.[36]

The technique produces an uncanny effect in misleadingly implying a shot-reverse-shot structure. As we look from Tony's POV, we cut temporally, but seem to cut spatially. As a result Soprano seems to look back at himself, doubled. This culminates in the episode's final sequence, in which he looks up at the diner door one last time, awaiting the entrance of Meadow. As he does so, he looks into the camera, seeming now to look not at himself, but at us (fig. 6.3). The last shot of the drama's diegesis, in other words, is of Soprano seeming to look out of it, at the viewer. And having thus acknowledged the viewer, the screen goes black (fig. 6.4).

Had our monitors malfunctioned? Had something interrupted the transmission? In prompting these questions, the drama might be said to have called attention to the technologies on which its medium depended. But there is another way to read the conclusion as a gesture to TV's medium, one that has nothing to do with gadgets or the mechanics of cable or satellite transmission. It's certainly possible that viewers suddenly saw their screens, no longer windows and now simply black, as screens. But they might have seen something else besides in these now reflective surfaces: they might have seen themselves, in a way that spoke to the historically determined nature of TV spectatorship.

The Sopranos' final cut was the last and most implicating of its many blackouts, which overtook Soprano, and our monitors, whenever he found himself in situations he could not assimilate. The blackouts were gestures to the inadmissible, to what neither Soprano nor the drama could process. In those earlier scenes, the audience was part of what could not be processed, of the inadmissible. As I argued in the first chapter, the drama is troubled by the possibility that audiences might do more than simply watch—that they might, in effect, participate collectively in the creation of the drama's meaning. *The Sopranos* and subsequent quality TV wanting to claim properly literary forms of authorship rejected that looming heteronomy. In this respect, cutting to black and turning screens into mirrors was a devastating return of the repressed: it suggested an audience had been there all along, at the other end of the cable, determining content. Autonomy is enjoyed for a time and then, inevitably, lost.

CONCLUSION

6.3. *The Sopranos*: Tony's last look.

6.4. *The Sopranos*: The screen goes blank.

In part, that autonomy was Chase's: this drama is made, it everywhere insists, not by a corporation and certainly not by a home audience, or any crowd, but by one or at most a small handful of dedicated artisans. That's what quality means, in the crudest and most simple sense, and it's on that basis that the drama, and quality TV generally, aspires to the status of film. It's of course not the case that that autonomy is real, or definitive of film rather than TV—it is an ideological pretense, not an accurate depiction of facts on the ground. And in any event, in *The Sopranos*, autonomy is itself an ugly prospect however much desired: it inevitably references the violence with which Soprano maintains his independence from "New York" (and, analogously, Carmela's labors). And so if on the one hand Soprano stands for the drama's craft aspirations, he also exposes the violence implicit in those aspirations, as they suppress recognition of the ancillary labor upon which even the most rarefied crafts invariably depend.

"Every specific art," writes Williams, "has dissolved into it, at every level of its operations," and in its very medium, not just "specific material means of production, on the mastery of which its production depends," but a contradiction "between an increasingly collaborative production and the learned skills and values of individual production." Like film, quality TV is a collaborative production branded as if it issued from a singular vision. And as I argue in chapter 1, *The Sopranos* inaugurated a genre of serial quality TV that was particularly reflexive about that contradiction, most obviously when it depicts Soprano killing off one by one the underlings (read: staff writers) on whom his business depends. The black-market melodrama flexibly allegorizes that contradiction at multiple scales, such that dramas understand their creators or even their writers' rooms as individual units fighting for autonomy from more collectivized studios at the same moment that they understand their studios as individual units fighting for autonomy from the transnationals in which they are housed.

But ultimately, I have insisted, the genre's touchstone for that scaling is the industrious family itself, as it is riven by contradictions between the gendered, collaborative reproductive labor that sustains it and the individual waged, nominally productive labor of its typically male breadwinner, who can no longer deceive himself that his wage alone, and his "skills and values" alone, support that family. Indeed, families might be considered industrious at all to the degree that their collective informal labors make impossible any continuation of the ideological fiction that families depend primarily on a male "producer" and his income.

That contradiction came to the fore when it did, for the class that is the subject of this book, for the many reasons that I have elaborated,

CONCLUSION

primary among which is deindustrialization's erosion of the family wage. But I conclude now with a specific version of that contradiction that pressed upon the media industry when *The Sopranos* ended.

As a grumpy David Chase considered how to end *The Sopranos* from one corner of the Time Warner Empire, from another corner, a more chipper Lev Grossman considered the media landscape before him. What he saw wasn't a story "about conflict or great men"; "It's a story about community and collaboration on a scale never seen before." He wasn't writing about *The Sopranos*, but rather "You," a collective entity that *Time Magazine* had just named its Person of the Year. "For seizing the reins of the global media, for founding and framing the new digital democracy, for working for nothing and beating the pros at their own game, *Time*'s Person of the Year for 2006 is you," Grossman wrote. The cover of the issue was a computer monitor with a reflective, mirror-like surface, on which was printed "You," and in which individual readers were invited to see themselves as parts of a larger collective (fig. 6.5).

This epic story, Grossman continued, is "about the cosmic compendium of knowledge Wikipedia and the million-channel people's network YouTube and the online metropolis MySpace. It's about the many wresting power from the few and helping one another for nothing and how that will not only change the world, but also change the way the world changes."[37] Grossman was transcribing enthusiasm that had for over a decade defined the rise of the internet. New kinds of "crowds" (the term "crowdsourcing" first appeared in 2005) would baffle hoary distinctions between capital and labor while working toward brave new ends. Only this "working for nothing" wouldn't really be work. The "produsage" (productive usage) in question amounted to the self-realization of a new historical agent defined by its shared passions rather than the wage relation.

Grossman's was a pop condensation of the New Economy ideology of which reality TV was one expression. And there are interesting connections to be drawn between his account and the Italian economic theory that has appeared throughout this book. For Sarah Brouillette, autonomists like Antonio Negri and Paolo Virno offered spruced up, academically complexified versions of New Economy management

6.5. *Time Magazine*: Yes, you.

theory. These thinkers were close in spirit to Grossman and the tech enthusiasts of *Wired*, their "multitude" a version of the "crowd" that promised companies free, outsourced labor. Conversely, where male autonomists announced the postindustrial (or post-Fordist) transcendence of the wage relation, Italian Marxist feminists of the same moment, like Mariarosa Dalla Costa and Leopoldina Fortunati, exposed the gendered

CONCLUSION

expropriation on which the wage relation still depended. This book has drawn heavily from the likes of Dalla Costa and Fortunati.

Grossman worked for Time Warner, and CEO Jerry Levin had used language strikingly similar to his when selling the company's disastrous merger with AOL six years before.[38] Grossman himself would exemplify the corporate synergy promised by the merger, and not simply because he adumbrated how new media would allow consumers to add value to what they collectively consumed. More prosaically, from his lookout at *Time*, he celebrated George R. R. Martin, as "an American Tolkien" (*The Lord of the Rings* was a Time Warner film franchise) whose *Song of Fire and Ice* became *Game of Thrones* (another Time Warner franchise) and who would in turn blub Grossman's novels, themselves faithful retellings of *Harry Potter* (still another Time Warner franchise). Here were friendly corporate siblings, working together at the wonderful game of cross-promotion. These in-house appreciations, let's call them, were examples of why scale made sense.

Chase would not have called them appreciations. They would have represented to him the corrupting heteronomy that his crime drama so darkly spoofed. But more fundamentally, the capacity for produsage with which *Time* endowed "You" epitomized the reception conditions against which *The Sopranos* defined itself, and in relation to which it defined the TV medium, for itself and the genre it created. *The Sopranos* held audience produsage at bay, I have been arguing, as if it were an instance of the reproductive labor with which it had all along been preoccupied. And its finale staged a return of the repressed of that labor *as* the return of the unwaged crowd against whose looming presence it had long defined itself. Doing so afforded Chase the semblance of higher ground: *you* lionized this bloodthirsty man for years; but rather than offer a retributive ending in which his comeuppance absolves you, I offer instead a mirror for your dark desires.

At the serial's start, that looming crowd might have been an audience of web-surfing, online videogame-playing reality TV watchers, or simply fans of the lowbrow commercial TV for which Chase had long written. But the melodrama was ending, and that crowd was assuming a new name (You) in a rapidly changing context. *The Sopranos* turned blank TV screens into mirrors at the dawn of the streaming revolution. In 2007, Netflix introduced its streaming services and Apple introduced the iPhone, that portable computer that would make it all but impossible ever to cease working. The long tail of these developments would make it hard to believe that the many had wrested power from the few, or that You had "seized the reins of global media." The crowd would be gobbled up by globe-spanning predators, foremost among whom, the appropriately named FAANG group: Facebook, Amazon, Apple, Netflix, and Google. "Disintermediation" would run up against its structural limits—the primal crime of private property—and "You" would come to mean, more simply, "you." After 2007, the flimsy veneer of an ersatz collectivity became unnecessary to the NASDAQ's inexorable ascent. Seen this way, the suddenly dark screens that *The Sopranos* finale gave us evoked, but were also crucially different from, the glossy mirror on *Time*'s Person of the Year cover. What audiences saw reflected in their black screens was not the collective to which Grossman referred, but only themselves, alone and cut off.

If over the course of the 1990s the internet promised the emergence of a brave new collective beyond the wage relation, by the end of 2007 that promise had begun to lose its luster. It had never been anything but egregious bullshit to imagine an army of happy citizens "working for nothing and beating the pros at their own game." But how much more egregious would that claim quickly come to seem: when *The Sopranos* ended, or failed to end, on June 10, 2007, signs of an upcoming crash were mounting. Ten days before the finale, Standard & Poor's and Moody's downgraded over one hundred bonds backed by second-lien subprime mortgages; three days before the finale, Bear Stearns informed investors that it was suspending redemptions from its High-Grade Structured Credit Strategies Enhanced Leverage Fund. Over the next months and years, economic carnage unfolded. How many really believed, after the Great Recession, that editing Wikipedia pages amounts to wresting power from the few?

If the bursting of the dot-com bubble had not made the following sufficiently clear, then surely the Great Recession did: the New Economy was a shell game, in which it seemed for a while that the internet and related technologies would generate labor efficiencies capable of reversing deindustrialization's ravages. But all that was new were the corporate names: the internet was and is simply the latest technological fix with which capital has endeavored to decrease its living labor costs while increasing its profits. Eventually, capital within a given world-leading economic power enters into terminal decline. New technologies might for a while restore profit rates. Yet, as Giovanni Arrighi shows, economic hegemons never really escape the accumulation crises that mark their twilights. As these crises have unfolded—there have been four over the last five hundred plus years, he argues, including ours—the seat of world power has moved elsewhere, to an ascendant economy in the throes of expansion.

What a bummer of a note on which to end! But it's worth remembering that technological change tends to preserve rather than transform dominant class power. And we remain mesmerized by the New Economy shell game when we gush about the streaming revolution. Tech will save us! (if only by giving us more TV). The black-market melodrama seems beholden to a related illusion. At first blush, it seems to preserve the privilege and prestige of the besieged white family, no less than the power and position of the flagging empire that supports it. In so frequently taking up that family, the crucible of the nation's self-regard, the genre appears intent to keep the party going, if only for a little longer. But there can be no escaping the failure that suffuses these desperate melodramas. And if we watch closely, we might learn something about the real revolution through which we've all been living.

Acknowledgments

I've been lucky beyond words to have brilliant and generous friends and colleagues. None of this would have been possible, or remotely fun, without their support. Special thanks to Salman Ahmed, Paul Anderson, Adam Arvidsson, Mario Biogiolli, Evan Buswell, David Buxton, John T. Caldwell, Jed Esty, Catherine Fisk, Lauren Goodlad, Melissa Gregg, Mitchum Huehls, Eleanor Kaufman, Arin Keeble, Jonathan Lethem, Colleen Lye, Atesede Makonnen, Michael Mann, Doug Mao, John Marx, Sean McCann, Mark McGurl, Marilyn Reizbaum, Will Scheffer, Tawny Schlieski, Milette Shamir, Stephen Shapiro, Anna Shechtman, Lisa Siraganian, Rachel Greenwald Smith, and Sam Thomas. Heartfelt thanks also to friends and colleagues at UCI who have offered invaluable help: Jonathan Alexander, Elizabeth Allen, Luis Aviles, Dan Burke, Ellen Burt, Becky Helfer, Oren Izenberg, Victoria Johnson, Jayne Lewis, DeeDee Nunez, Nancy Palmer, Allison Perlman, Tony Reese, Vicki Silver, Irene Tucker, and Wylie Visconti.

Students past and present have made key contributions to this project. Thanks especially to Sarah Abolail, Nathan Allison, Devan Bailey, Maria Bose, Michelle Chihara, Jeff Clapp, Hannah Deitch, Charles Gunn, Dennis Lopez, Alexandra Lossada, Louise McCune, Philemon Roh, Alejandra Santana, and Alden Wood. At the University of Chicago Press, hearty thanks to my amazing team: James Whitman, Kyle Wagner, Kristin Rawlings, Michael Koplow, Lindsy Rice, and Nathan Petrie.

ACKNOWLEDGMENTS

I owe a special debt to Sarah Brouillette, Melinda Cooper, and Joshua Clover, each of whom has influenced this project significantly, and likely more than they realize. Thank you. The same goes for my UCI writing-group comrades Chris Fan, Richard Godden, Joseph Jeon, Ted Martin, and Annie McClanahan, who together read a great deal of this project. A special shoutout to Richard and Joe, who read still more. And endless thanks to J. D. Connor, who read every page and offered invaluable input during the project's final stages.

My deepest debt, in this and in all things, is to Andrea Henderson, without whom this book would never have been possible. 사랑해, 패블르스.

A portion from chapter 5 originally appeared as "Melodrama and Narrative Stagnation in Quality TV" in *Theory & Event*, volume 22, number 2 (April 2019). A portion of the conclusion was first published as "Streaming Enthusiasm and the Industrious Family Drama" in the *Los Angeles Review of Books*.

Notes

Introduction

1. For example: *Dead Like Me, Pushing Daisies, Lost, The Good Place, Russian Doll, The Walking Dead, The Leftovers, Westworld*, and *Upload*.
2. O'Brien, quoted in Dana Polan, *The Sopranos* (Durham: Duke University Press, 2009), 66.
3. Not every black-market melodrama has a black market; but so essential are those markets to the genre that a given serial without one can be said to belong only when it produces the "new points of compensation" that, for Stanley Cavell, allow a given genre to evolve by substituting one key feature for another. Cavell, "The Fact of Television," *Daedalus* 11, no. 4 (1982): 81.
4. "Quality TV" is a term that has evolved with the TV industry for at least five decades and was reinvented again about fifteen years ago. See Janet McCabe and Kim Akass, ed., *Quality TV: Contemporary American Television and Beyond* (New York: I. B. Tauris, 2007).
5. Stephen Holden, "Sympathetic Brutes," *New York Times*, June 6, 1999: https://www.nytimes.com/1999/06/06/movies/television-radio-sympathetic-brutes-in-a-pop-masterpiece.html.
6. Brett Martin, *Difficult Men: Behind the Scenes of a Creative Revolution: From "The Sopranos" and "The Wire" to "Mad Men" and "Breaking Bad"* (New York: Penguin, 2014), 11.
7. Egan quoted in "Channeling of the Novel," *New York Times*, December 16, 2011: https://www.nytimes.com/2011/12/18/books/review/the-channeling-of-the-novel.html.
8. Wolff, *Television Is the New Television: The Unexpected Triumph of Old Media in the Digital Age* (New York: Portfolio, 2015), 199.
9. Thatcher, Interview for *Women's Own*, September 23, 1987: https://www.margaretthatcher.org/document/106689.
10. Becker, *A Treatise on the Family* (Cambridge: Harvard University Press, 1981), back matter. Melinda Cooper explains that, for Becker, family altruism "represents an internal exception to the free market, an immanent order of non-contractual

obligations and inalienable services without which the world of contract would cease to function." See Cooper, *Family Values: Between Neoliberalism and the New Social Conservatism* (New York: Zone Books, 2017), 58.

11. Schatz, "Workplace Programs," in *Museum of Broadcast Communications Encyclopedia of Television*, vol. 1, ed. Horace Newcomb (Chicago: Fitzroy Dearborn, 1997), 1873.
12. Feuer, *Seeing through the Eighties* (Durham: Duke University Press, 1995), 115.
13. Cooper, "Family Capitalism and the 'Small Business' Insurrection," *Dissent*, Winter 2022: https://www.dissentmagazine.org/article/family-capitalism-and-the-small-business-insurrection.
14. Arvidsson, *Changemakers: The Industrious Future of the Digital Economy* (New York: Polity, 2019), 45, 5.
15. Maura Judkis, "Hard Times, Soft Pants," *Washington Post*, March 13, 2020: https://www.washingtonpost.com/lifestyle/style/hard-times-soft-pants-life-with-the-housebound-white-collar-workforce/2020/03/13/4a7243f0-62f2-11ea-b3fc-7841686c5c57_story.html.
16. See for example Melissa Gregg, *Work's Intimacy* (New York: Polity, 2018), 2, 126.
17. See Ivan Illich, *Shadow Work* (London: Marion Boyars, 1981).
18. Mies, *Patriarchy and Accumulation on a World Scale: Women in the International Division of Labor* (New York: Zed Books, 1998), ix.
19. Berlant, *Cruel Optimism* (Durham: Duke University Press, 2011), 173.
20. See Elsaesser, "Tales of Sound and Fury: Observations on the Family Melodrama," in *Imitations of Life: A Reader on Film and Television Melodrama*, ed. Marcia Landy (Detroit: Wayne State University Press, 1991): 68–91.
21. Brooks, *The Melodramatic Imagination* (New Haven: Yale University Press, 1995), 4, 40, 54.
22. Jameson, "Realism and Utopia in *The Wire*," *Criticism* 52, no. 3–4 (Summer/Fall 2010): 367.
23. Lotz, *Cable Guys: Television and Masculinities in the 21st Century* (New York: New York University Press, 2014), 43.
24. Fraser, "After the Family Wage: Gender Equity and the Welfare State," *Political Theory* 22, no. 4 (November 1994): 591.
25. For accounts of working- and middle-class families in nineteenth-century Britain and the US, see Wally Seccombe, *Weathering the Storm: Working-Class Families from the Industrial Revolution to the Fertility Decline* (New York: Verso, 1993); Deborah Valenz, *The First Industrial Woman* (New York: Oxford University Press, 1995); and Jeanne Boydston, *Home and Work: Housework, Wages, and the Ideology of Labor in the Early Republic* (New York: Oxford University Press, 1990).
26. Critics on the left and the right attributed the breakdown, variously, to feminism's undermining of the marriage contract, the extension of the family wage to African American men, and the welfare state's tendency to undermine the value of work. See Cooper, *Family Values*, introduction.
27. Karl Marx and Friedrich Engels, *The Manifesto of the Communist Party* (1848), Marxist Internet Archive, chapter one: https://www.marxists.org/archive/marx/works/1848/communist-manifesto/ch01.htm#007.
28. Fraser, "Crisis of Care? On the Social Reproductive Contradictions of Contemporary Capitalism," in *Social Reproduction Theory: Remapping Class, Recentering Oppression*, ed. Tithi Bhattacharya (New York: Pluto, 2017), 27.

29. Zaretsky, *Capitalism, The Family and Personal Life* (New York: Harper Collins, 1986).
30. Tocqueville quoted in Kerber, "Separate Spheres, Female Worlds, Woman's Place: The Rhetoric of Women's History," *Journal of American History* 75, no. 1 (June 1988): 9, 17.
31. Davidson, "No More Separate Spheres," *American Literature* 70, no. 3 (September 1998): 444.
32. See Anna McCarthy, who reveals the "distinct, if overlapping, sectors of the governing classes" that together organized TV's ideological construction of the public interest and explains how the postwar networks exerted soft power on behalf of the state as a "citizen machine," at the heart of which was a defense of the white, middle-class family. McCarthy, *The Citizen Machine: Governing by Television in 1950s America* (New York: New Press, 2010), 3.
33. Nick Browne, "The Political Economy of the Television (Super) Text," in *American Television: New Directions in History and Theory*, ed. Nick Browne (New York: Harwood, 2013), 71.
34. Pew Research Center, "The Rise of Dual Income Households," June 18, 2015: http://www.pewresearch.org/ft_dual-income-households-1960-2012-2/.
35. See for example Lillian Rubin, *Worlds of Pain: Life in the Working-Class Family* (New York: Basic Books, 1992).
36. See Gilles Saint-Paul, *Dual Labor Markets: A Macroeconomic Perspective* (Cambridge: MIT Press, 1997).
37. Cooper, *Family Values*, 24, 102.
38. Benanav, "The Origins of Informality: The ILO at the Limit of the Concept of Unemployment," *Journal of Global History* 14, no. 1 (2019): 125, 108.
39. Alejandro Portes and William Haller think neither black markets nor households should be included in the informal sector, which, for them, produces licit goods illicitly, rather than illicit goods. Alejandro Portes and William Haller, "The Informal Economy," in *The Handbook of Economic Sociology* (Princeton: Princeton University Press, 2010), ed. Neil Smelser, chap. 18.
40. Benanav, "Origins of Informality," 123.
41. Benanav, "Origins of Informality," 123, 124, 108.
42. See Castells and Portes, *World Underneath: The Origins, Dynamics, and Effects of the Informal Economy* (Baltimore: Johns Hopkins University Press, 1989). For an important account of the uncanny and the home's exposure to economic life, see Annie McClanahan, *Dead Pledges* (Palo Alto: Stanford University Press, 2016).
43. The size of any given informal economy is "to some extent indeterminate," notes Benanav, because it is by definition resistant to state measure. Still, the numbers are significant globally; a recent UN report estimates that "there are more than one billion informal workers in the world today, accounting for half of the global non-farm labor force." Benanav, "The Origins of Informality," 123, 124. Some estimates suggest that 20 percent of all US workers over the age of twenty-one generate informal income, and that about 16 percent of full-time employees do. See St. Louis Federal Reserve, "What Is the Informal Labor Market," March 18, 2001: https://www.stlouisfed.org/on-the-economy/2017/april/informal-labor-market.
Economists sometimes consider the gig economy a part of the informal economy, whether or not it generates taxed income. See for example Gary Painter, "The Scale of Informal Labor and Its Impact on the Economy," February 13, 2019: https://www

.kcet.org/shows/city-rising/the-scale-of-informal-labor-and-its-impact-on-the-economy. See also Demetra Smith Nightingale and Stephen A. Wandner, "Informal and Nonstandard Employment in the United States: Implications for Low-Income Working Families," The Urban Institute, Brief 20, 2011: http://webarchive.urban.org/publications/412372.html.

44. Mies, *Patriarchy and Accumulation*, 74.
45. Cowan, *More Work for Mother* (New York: Basic, 1983), 5.
46. Jan de Vries, "The Industrial Revolution and the Industrious Revolution," *Journal of Economic History* 54, no. 2 (June 1994): 249–70. When de Vries declared the end of the industrial family, he spoke of the demise of "the Lucy and Desi family" and then debated whether *I Love Lucy* or *Ozzie and Harriet* better captured the family that the industrious family was replacing (263). When Congress began debate about the supposed family crisis in the early 1990s, they invoked *Ozzie and Harriet* and *Leave It to Beaver*, to capture the white family ideals in whose name the act was passed. See Stephanie Coontz, *The Way We Never Were: American Families and the Nostalgia Trap* (New York: Basic Books, 1992), 23.
47. Kaoru Sugihara, "The East Asian Path of Economic Development: A Long-Term Perspective," in *The Resurgence of East Asia*, ed. Giovanni Arrighi, Takeshi Hamashita, and Mark Selden (New York: Routledge, 2003), 87–88.
48. Benanav, "Origins of Informality," 116.
49. de Vries, "The Industrious Revolution," 261, 264–65.
50. Pomeranz, "Women's Work, Family, and Economic Development in Europe and East Asia: Long-Term Trajectories and Contemporary Comparisons," in *The Resurgence of East Asia*, ed. Arrighi et al., 133.
51. Arrighi, *Adam Smith in Beijing: Lineages of the Twenty-First Century* (New York: Verso, 2007), 37; and Arrighi, *The Long Twentieth Century* (New York: Verso, 2010), 82.
52. Matt Seitz, "The Best Actress on TV is *Killing Eve*'s Sandra Oh," *Vulture*, June 27, 2018: https://www.vulture.com/2018/06/best-actress-sandra-oh-vulture-tv-awards.html.
53. Fineman, "The Structure of Allegorical Desire," in Stephen Greenblatt, ed. *Allegory and Representation* (Cambridge: English Institute, 1981), 26.
54. Polan, *The Sopranos*, 41, 5.
55. Fineman, "The Structure of Allegorical Desire," 44, 45.
56. See Benjamin, *The Origin of German Tragic Drama*, trans. John Osborne (New York: Verso, 2009).
57. Benjamin, *Selected Writings*, vol. 4, *1938–1940*, trans. Edmund Jeffcot, ed. Howard Eiland and Michael Jennings (Cambridge: Harvard University Press, 2003), 169.
58. See J. D. Connor, *The Studio after the Studio* (Palo Alto: Stanford, 2015), and Jerry Christensen, *America's Corporate Art* (Palo Alto: Stanford, 2012).
59. Jameson, *Jameson on Jameson: Conversations in Cultural Marxism* (Durham: Duke University Press, 2007), 169, 195.
60. See Jennifer Holt, *Empires of Entertainment: Media Industries and the Politics of Deregulation, 1980–1996* (New Brunswick: Rutgers University Press, 2011).
61. For Jeff Menne, Hollywood film's allegorical preoccupation with auteurism was a response to the industry's turn to post-Fordism in the sixties and seventies: "The auteur theory functioned as something like an organizational chart, always pressing authority downward to the artists in the ranks." As the studio system broke up and

as Hollywood moved to the flexible, leaned-down, and outsourced small batch-production that would define "New Hollywood," allegories of auteurism clarified what kind of unit and what kind of leadership most mattered to a given film's production. Menne, *Post-Fordist Cinema: Hollywood Auteurs and the Corporate Counterculture* (New York: Columbia University Press, 2019), 23.

62. See "The Land of the Giants" podcast, season 2, episode 1, *Vox*.
63. Martin, *The Financialization of Daily Life* (Philadelphia: Temple University Press, 2002), 55.
64. David Harvey, *The Condition of Postmodernity: An Inquiry into the Origins of Cultural Change* (New York: Blackwell, 1989), 152–53.
65. Quoted in Vincent Pecora, *Households of the Soul* (Baltimore: Johns Hopkins University Press, 1997), 11.
66. Boltanski and Chiapello, *The New Spirit of Capitalism*, trans. Gregory Elliott (New York: Verso, 2005), 155, 85; on their use of mafia, see 145 and 402.

Chapter 1

1. Fineman, "The Structure of Allegorical Desire," in *Allegory and Representation (Selected Papers from the English Institute)*, ed. Stephen Greenblatt (Baltimore: Johns Hopkins University Press, 1981), 50, 29, 44, 45, 49.
2. See Paul Grainge, *Brand Hollywood* (New York: Routledge, 20008): "According to David Bordwell, the advent of sound cinema canonized the narrativization of the credit sequence, encouraging a higher degree of graphic and aural play in the initiation of film narrative" (74).
3. Denning, *Cover Stories: Narrative and Ideology in the British Spy Thriller* (New York: Routledge, 1987), 134.
4. Devon Ivie, "Tony Soprano Is Alive and Well," *Vulture*, May 5, 2020: https://www.vulture.com/2020/05/the-sopranos-david-chase-coronavirus-scene.html.
5. Walter Benjamin, *The Origin of German Tragic Drama*, trans. John Osborne (New York: Verso, 2009), 166, 178.
6. Quoted in David Remnick, "Is This the End of Rico?," *New Yorker*, March 25, 2001: https://www.newyorker.com/magazine/2001/04/02/is-this-the-end-of-rico.
7. Warshow, "The Gangster as Tragic Hero," *Partisan Review* (February 1948), 583; Richard Pells, *Radical Visions and American Dreams: Culture and Social Thought in the Depression Years* (Middleton: Wesleyan University Press, 1973), 271–72; Mason, cited in Ron Wilson, *The Gangster Film: Fatal Success in American Cinema* (New York: Columbia University Press, 2014), 30, 11, 12.
8. C. L. R. James, *American Civilization* (New York: Blackwell, 1993), 159. Also see Andrew Berman, *We're in the Money: Depression America and Its Films* (Chicago: Ivan R. Dee, 1992).
9. Len Boselovic, "Steel Standing," *postgazette.com*, February 25, 2001: https://old.post-gazette.com/businessnews/20010225ussteel2.asp.
10. James, *American Civilization*, 127.
11. Elsaesser, *The Persistence of Hollywood* (New York: Routledge, 2011), 138.
12. Christopher Kocela, "Unmade Men: *The Sopranos* after Whiteness," *Postmodern Culture* 15, no. 2 (January 2005): http://pmc.iath.virginia.edu/issue.105/15.2kocela.html.

13. Fletcher, *Allegory: The Theory of a Symbolic Mode* (Princeton: Princeton University Press, 2012), 2.
14. Wilson, *Gangster Film*, 89.
15. Remnick, "End of Rico."
16. Matt Seitz, Alan Sepinwall, and David Chase, *The Soprano Sessions* (New York: Henry Abrams, 2021), 17.
17. Jeanne Boydston, *Home and Work: Housework, Wages, and the Ideology of Labor in the Early Republic* (New York: Oxford University Press, 1990).
18. See John Love, *Antiquity and Capitalism* (New York: Routledge, 1991), 59–109.
19. Jameson, "Reification and Utopia in Mass Culture," *Social Text*, no. 1 (Winter 1979): 146.
20. Jameson, "Reification," 146–47.
21. By *Godfather II* (1974), he argues, this dynamic has changed: now, the mafia is not a double for big business but simply big business. That film "unmasks" itself with "self-criticism": "It is as though the unconscious ideological and Utopian impulses at work in *Godfather I* could in the sequel be observed to work themselves towards the light and towards thematic or reflexive foregrounding in their own right. . . . Thus the Mafia material, which in the first film served as a substitute for business, now slowly transforms itself into the overt thematics of business itself, just as 'in reality' the need for the cover of legitimate investments ends up turning the mafiosi into real businessmen." Jameson, "Reification," 147.
22. Pecora, *Households of the Soul* (Baltimore: Johns Hopkins University Press, 1997), 48.
23. Elsaesser, *Persistence*, 141.
24. Lauren Berlant, *The Female Complaint* (Durham: Duke University Press, 2008), 1.
25. Berlant, *Complaint*, 1.
26. Polan, *The Sopranos* (Durham: Duke University Press, 2009), 23.
27. Polan, *Sopranos*, 61–64.
28. Nicholas Brown adds that Soprano and Swearengen are "the *reductio* of Hamlet" as "characters whose actions are determined by inner conflict rather than characters who embody in themselves the conflict between substantial powers." Brown, *Autonomy: The Social Value of Art under Capitalism* (Durham: Duke University Press, 2019), 175.
29. Dominik Finkelde, "The Presence of the Baroque," in *A Companion to the Works of Walter Benjamin*, ed. Rolph Goebel (New York: Camden House, 2016), 54.
30. Benjamin, *Tragic Drama*, 132. The "creaturely" is a still debated concept in Benjamin studies. See, for example, Eric Santner, *Rilke, Benjamin, Sebald* (Chicago: University of Chicago Press, 2016).
31. Benjamin, *Tragic Drama*, 139, 183–85.
32. Benjamin, *Tragic Drama*, 223, 157, 230.
33. Polan thinks the drama "represent[s] the ill-fated encounter between interpreter and text by staging scenes where interpreters fail at making meaning." Polan, *Sopranos*, 124.
34. Kantorowicz, *The King's Two Bodies* (Princeton: Princeton University Press, 1997), 337.
35. See Otto Rank, *The Double: A Psychoanalytic Study*, trans. Harry Tucker Jr. (Chapel Hill: University of North Carolina Press, 2009).
36. Benjamin, *Tragic Drama*, 56, 123, 125, 156, 70, 226.

37. Puzo, *The Godfather* (New York: New American Library, 2005), 138.
38. Quote from Stephanie Hilger, *Gender and Genre: German Women Write the French Revolution* (Newark: University of Delaware Press, 2015), 3.
39. Gledhill, "Speculations on the Relationship between Soap Opera and Melodrama," *Quarterly Review of Film & Video* 14, nos. 1–2 (June 2009), 108.
40. Samuel Weber, "Taking Exception to Decision: Walter Benjamin and Carl Schmitt," *diacritics* 22, nos. 3–5 (autumn/winter 1992): 16, 17.
41. Weber, "Taking Exception," 17.
42. Lawson interview of David Chase, in *Quality TV: Contemporary American Television and Beyond*, ed. Janet McCabe and Kim Akass (New York: I. B. Tauris, 2007), 211.
43. Polan, *The Sopranos*, 182.
44. Gottfried Kitchner notes that "for the decline of empires and the destruction of their major cities, the position on Rome is exemplary in the seventeenth century; of its earlier grandeur, there remains only an empty concept." Cited in Susan Buck-Morse, *The Dialectics of Seeing: Walter Benjamin and the Arcades Project* (Cambridge: MIT Press, 1989), 423.
45. Samuel Weber, *Mass Mediauras* (Palo Alto: Stanford University Press, 1996), 125–26. See also Anthony Curtis Adler's account of how *Buffy the Vampire Slayer* resurrects the mourning play: *The Afterlives of Genre: Remnants of the Trauerspiel in "Buffy the Vampire Slayer"* (Santa Barbara: Punctum, 2014).
46. Benjamin, *Tragic Drama*, 140.
47. Schmitt, *Hamlet and Hecuba*, trans. David Pan (New York: Telos, 2009), 45, 42.
48. On Michael Corleone's relation to JFK, see Christopher Messenger, *The Godfather and American Culture: How the Corleones Became Our Gang* (New York: SUNY Press, 2012), 304.
49. For Sean McCann, Jeb Barlett is an idealized Clinton who speaks "almost directly in the voice of god." McCann, *A Pinnacle of Feeling* (Princeton: Princeton University Press, 2008), 180. The relation of that presidential voice on *The West Wing* (made by Warner Bros. TV) and the one tacit on *The Sopranos* (made by HBO Original Programming) is instructive. Soprano was the creaturely prince-as-tyrant who shadowed the ethereal prince-as-martyr on Time Warner's proprietary stage. The programs ran alongside each other for seven years and seemed to sponsor antithetical politics. Chase abhorred *The West Wing*'s earnestness and insisted his drama had no "authority figures . . . looking out for us," no "Doctors. Judges. Lawyers. Cops." HBO exec Chris Albrecht saw matters differently: "At least when the *West Wing* creams us," he said, "it will be all in the family." Lawson interview of David Chase in McCabe and Akass, *Quality TV*, 214.
50. Schmitt, *Hamlet and Hecuba*, 65, 45, 65.
51. Charles Geisst, *Loan Sharks: The Birth of Predatory Lending* (Washington, DC: Brookings, 2017), 228.
52. James Jacobs, *Mobsters, Unions, and Feds: The Mafia and the American Labor Movement* (New York: New York University Press, 2007), 7.
53. Fitch, *The Assassination of New York* (New York: Verso, 1996), 40, 4.
54. "Mobbed Up on Wall Street," May 12, 2003: *Bloomberg Business Week*: https://www.bloomberg.com/news/articles/2003-05-18/mobbed-up-on-wall-street. See also Gary Weiss, *Born to Steal: When the Mafia Hit Wall Street* (Warner Books, 2003).
55. Quoted in Jean-Pierre Hombach, *Lady Gaga Superstar* (epubli, 2010), 384.

56. Jerry Knight, "*The Sopranos*: Scripts That Hit Home at the SEC," *Washington Post*, February 13, 2000: https://www.washingtonpost.com/wp-srv/WPcap/2000-02/13/049r-021300-idx.html.
57. The NASDAQ Composite reached a peak of 6580 in February 2000, and had fallen to 2484 in March 2001, when the episode aired.
58. For Richard Godden, the "impulse to allegory exists as a formal imperative immanent in the structure of finance capital," which "empties the world, preparing not merely 'a paper graveyard,' apt to allegorical purpose, but proposing price itself as the ur-allegorical sign." While "labor abides" as the source of all value, in moments dominated by finance, it "abides at great distance." Godden, "Labor without Value, Language at a Price: Toward a Narrative Poetics for the Financial Turn," in *The Routledge Companion to Literature and Economics*, ed. Michelle Chihara and Matt Seybold (New York: Routledge, 2019), 58, 60.
59. Alec Klein, *Stealing Time: Steve Case, Jerry Levin, and the Collapse of AOL Time Warner* (New York: Simon and Schuster, 2004), 101.
60. Nina Munk, *Fools Rush In: Steve Case, Jerry Levin, and the Unmaking of AOL Time Warner* (Harper Collins, 2009), 180.
61. Tim Arango, "How the AOL–Time Warner Merger Went So Wrong," *New York Times*, January 10, 2010: https://www.nytimes.com/2010/01/11/business/media/11merger.html.
62. Case quoted in Szalay, "'The Real Home of Capitalism': The AOL–Time Warner Merger and Capital Flight," in *The Routledge Companion to Literature and Economics*, ed. Michelle Chihara and Matt Seybold (New York: Routledge, 2019), 227.
63. Kantorowicz, *King's Two Bodies*, 5. See also Victoria Kahn, "Political Theology and Fiction in *The King's Two Bodies*," *Representations*. 106, no. 1 (Spring 2009): 77–101.
64. "AOL Learns the Price of Synergy," *Forbes*, Dec. 19, 2000: https://www.forbes.com/2000/12/19/1219aol.html#310cf6091c72; Klein, *Stealing Time*, 224.
65. See Szalay, "Real Home," 220; Phills, *Integrating Mission and Strategy for Nonprofit Organizations* (New York: Oxford University Press, 2005), 122.
66. Kevin Kelly, *New Rules for the New Economy* (New York: Penguin, 1999), 1, 72, 5. Eric Santner is indebted to this account of the economy when he traces the "metamorphosis of the king's royal flesh into the spectral materiality of the product of human labor, into the substance of value qua congelation of abstract, homogeneous human labor." He means to explain "a shift from the 'sovereign form' to the 'commodity form' of social mediation, of those processes, that is, through which people come to be bound to one another, to 'subjectivize' their social ties within a historical form of life that thereby comes to matter for them." Describing a further shift, Santner discovers his spectral materiality in "the liturgical labor that we are all, at some level, called to perform"—by being "wired" and "online." He adds, "the phrase, being 'online,' suggests participation in a virtual assembly or production line." Santner, *The Weight of All Flesh: On the Subject-Matter of Political Economy*, trans. Kevis Goodman (New York: Oxford University Press, 2016), 46, 47.
67. Greenspan quoted in Radhika Desai, *Geopolitical Economy: After US Hegemony, Globalization, and Empire* (Chicago: Pluto, 2013), 210.
68. See Munk, *Fools*, 84, 85, 272, 324.

69. See M. G. Siegler, "How Much Did it Cost AOL to Send Us those CDs in the 90s?," *TechCrunch*, December 27, 2010: https://techcrunch.com/2010/12/27/aol-discs-90s/.
70. Klein, *Stealing Time*, 2.

Chapter 2

1. Diane Shipley, "When Good TV Turns Bad," *The Guardian*, April 30, 2018: https://www.theguardian.com/tv-and-radio/2018/apr/30/when-good-tv-turns-bad-weeds.
2. Ginia Bellafante, "Is Motherhood Noble Work?" *New York Times*, August 13, 2007: https://www.nytimes.com/2007/08/13/arts/television/13weed.html.
3. Allesandra Stanley, "Life in the Suburbs," *New York Times*, September 1, 2006: https://www.nytimes.com/2006/09/01/arts/television/01weed.html.
4. Suzanne Walters and Laura Harrison, "Not Ready to Make Nice: Aberrant Mothers in Contemporary Culture," *Feminist Media Studies* 14, no. 1 (2012): 39, 51, 50.
5. Suzanne Leonard, *Wife Inc.: The Business of Marriage in the 21st Century* (New York: New York University Press, 2018), 115. *Housewives* and *Weeds*, Rebecca Feasey argues, are indebted to "heroine television" (in which women juggle family and work while raising kids) and "post-family" television (in which women struggle with "the day-to-day minutia of alternative home and family commitments"). See Feasey, *Happy Homemakers to Desperate Housewives: Motherhood and Popular Television* (New York: Anthem, 2012), 72.
6. Walters and Harrison, "Not Ready," 38.
7. Bellafante, "Pot Dealers Washed Up," *New York Times*, June 16, 2008: https://www.nytimes.com/2008/06/16/arts/television/16weed.html.
8. Emily Nussbaum, "Jenji Kohan's Hot Provocations," *New Yorker*, September 4, 2017: https://www.newyorker.com/magazine/2017/09/04/jenji-kohans-hot-provocations.
9. Kristeva, *The Powers of Horror* (New York: Columbia University Press, 1982), 2, 4, 32.
10. See for example Maya Andrea Gonzalez and Cassandra Troyan, "Heart of a Heartless World," *Blind Field*, May 26, 2016; Heather Berg, "Working for Love, Loving for Work: Discourses of Labor in Feminist Sex Work Activism," *Feminist Studies* 40, no. 3 (2014): 693–721; Annie McClanahan and Jon-David Settell, "Service Work, Sex Work, and the Prostitute Imaginary," *South Atlantic Quarterly* 120, no. 3 (2021); and Endnote Collective, "The Logic of Gender: On the Separation of Spheres and the Process of Abjection," *Endnotes 3* (September, 2013): https://endnotes.org.uk/issues/3/en/endnotes-the-logic-of-gender.
11. Fraser, "Crisis of Care? On the Social Reproductive Contradictions of Contemporary Capitalism," in *Social Reproduction Theory: Remapping Class, Recentering Oppression*, ed. Tithi Bhattacharya (New York: Pluto, 2017), 25.
12. Fraser, "Contradictions of Capital and Care," *New Left Review* 100 (July–August 2016): 103.
13. Polan, *The Sopranos* (Durham: Duke University Press, 2009), 65.
14. Cowan, *More Work for Mother* (New York: Basic Books, 1983), 14.
15. Spigel, *Make Room for TV* (Chicago: University of Chicago Press, 1992), 75, 86, 88. See also Alice Leppert, *TV Family Values* (New Brunswick: Rutgers University Press, 2019).

16. Women still do more housework than men. See Claire Miller, "Young Men Embrace Gender Equality, But They Still Don't Vacuum," *New York Times*, February 11, 2020: https://www.nytimes.com/2020/02/11/upshot/gender-roles-housework.html.
17. Kohan cited in Garin Pirnia, "Ten Facts about *Weeds*," *Mental Floss*, November 8, 2017: https://www.mentalfloss.com/article/503233/facts-about-weeds.
18. See Lakshmi Padmanabhan on *Sex and the City*: the comedy gives "women narratives of belonging that could account for the anxiety of freedom from the heterosexual couple form and family ties while still reproducing these modes as desirable, if perpetually deflected or deferred, structures for their lives." *Post45*, October 13, 2018: https://post45.org/2018/10/sex-and-the-city-lakshmi-october-13/.
19. Kristeva, *Powers of Horror*, 2.
20. Yeager, *Desire and Dirt* (Chicago: University of Chicago Press, 2000). Weeds are "a suburban scourge if ever there was one," notes Kera Bolonik, "a hearty little uninvited plant that pops up on a beautifully manicured lawn like a squatter and symbolizes the people and the problems that unexpectedly turn up, that isn't easily removed and reemerges often stronger and worse than before." See Bolonik, *In the Weeds* (New York: Simon and Schuster, 2007), xi.
21. See Donnalyn Pompper, *Rhetoric of Femininity: Female Image, Media, and Gender Role Stress/Conflict* (Minneapolis: Lexington Books, 2016), 114.
22. See Lexico, s.v. "husband": https://www.lexico.com/definition/husband.
23. Evelyn Nakano Glenn, "From Servitude to Service Work: Historical Continuities in the Racial Division of Paid Reproductive Labor," *Signs* 18, no. 1 (Autumn 1992): 1–43.
24. Federici, *Revolution at Point Zero: Housework, Reproduction, and Feminist Struggle* (San Francisco: PM Press, 2012), 19.
25. Federici, *Revolution at Point Zero*, 20.
26. Dalla Costa and James, *The Power of Women and the Subversion of Community* (Bristol: Falling Wall, 1975), 29.
27. Kathi Weeks, *The Problem with Work: Feminism, Marxism, Antiwork Politics, and Postwork Imaginaries* (Durham: Duke University Press, 2011), 121.
28. Dalla Costa and James, *The Power of Women*, 33–34.
29. Maya Gonzalez, "The Gendered Circuit: Reading *The Arcane of Reproduction*," *Viewpoint Magazine*, September 23, 2013: https://viewpointmag.com/2013/09/28/the-gendered-circuit-reading-the-arcane-of-reproduction/.
30. Federici, *Revolution at Point Zero*, 7–8.
31. This obscured use value creation, Nancy Fraser adds in different context, is "hidden" for another reason as well: its "dirty secret" is that it is compelled with a version of the abstract, impersonal violence that compels wage workers. Nancy Fraser, "Behind Marx's Hidden Abode," *New Left Review* 86 (March–April 2014).
32. Fortunati, *The Arcane of Reproduction*, trans. Hilary Creek (Brooklyn: Autonomedia, 1995), 17, 23.
33. Gonzalez, "Notes on the New Housing Question: Home Ownership, Credit, and Reproduction in the Post-war U.S. Economy," *Endnotes* 2 (April 2010): https://endnotes.org.uk/issues/2/en/endnotes-notes-on-the-new-housing-question.
34. Endnote Collective, "The Logic of Gender."
35. Mies, *Patriarchy and Accumulation on a World Scale: Women in the International Division of Labor* (New York: Zed Books, 1998), xi, 4.
36. Mies, *Patriarchy*, 33.

37. Mies, *Patriarchy*, 116, 127.
38. Mies, *Patriarchy*, 96, 105, 110.
39. Mies, *Patriarchy*, 110, 127.
40. See "Labor-Force Participation Rate," The World Bank: https://data.worldbank.org/indicator/SL.TLF.CACT.FE.ZS?end=2019&start=1990; for data that distinguishes between formal and informal labor force participation, see: "Women's Employment," *Our World in Data*, March 2018: https://ourworldindata.org/female-labor-supply.
41. Quoted in Kyle Ryan, "Mary Louise Parker," *AV Club*, June 17, 2009: https://www.avclub.com/mary-louise-parker-1798216811.
42. Limon, *Stand-up Comedy in Theory; or, Abjection in America* (Durham: Duke University Press, 2000), 4, 5, 105.
43. For an important account of comedy and gig work, see Annie McClanahan, "TV and Tipworkification," *Post45*, January 10, 2019: https://post45.org/2019/01/tv-and-tipworkification/.
44. Wanzo, "Precarious Girl Comedy: Issa Rae, Lenah Dunham, and Abjection Aesthetics," *Camera Obscura* 31, no. 2.92 (2016): 32, 33, 38.
45. Benson-Allott, "No Such Thing Not Yet: Questioning Television's Female Gaze," *Film Quarterly* 71 no. 2 (2017): 65, 68, 69.
46. Emphasis added. Kohan, quoted in Nussbaum, "Jenji Kohan's Hot Provocations."
47. Though notoriously hard to estimate, the US-Mexico weed trade was valued between $6 and $29 billion during the comedy's run. See Salvador Rizzo, "Do Mexican Drug Cartels Make $500 Billion a Year?," *Washington Post*, June 24, 2019: https://www.washingtonpost.com/politics/2019/06/24/do-mexican-drug-cartels-make-billion-year/.
48. See Stephen Shapiro, *The Culture and Commerce of the Early American Novel: Reading the Atlantic World System* (University Park: Penn State Press, 2008), 39.
49. Alvarado, *Abject Performances: Aesthetic Strategies in Latino Cultural Production* (Durham: Duke University Press, 2018), 8–9.
50. Lonnie Firestone, "David Simon Doesn't Want His Pornography Show to be Sexy," *Vanity Fair*, September 7, 2017: https://www.vanityfair.com/hollywood/2017/09/the-deuce-hbo-david-simon-james-franco-maggie-gyllenhaal-porn, and Andy Serwer, "David Simon's New Show *The Deuce* Is Really About . . . Business," *Yahoo Finance*, September 11, 2017: https://finance.yahoo.com/news/hbos-hot-new-show-deuce-really-business-140300111.html.
51. Jameson, "Reification and Utopia in Mass Culture," *Social Text*, no. 1 (Winter 1979): 147.
52. Shuster, *The New Television: The Aesthetics and Politics of a Genre* (Chicago: University of Chicago Press, 2017), 169.
53. Limon, *Stand-up Comedy in Theory*, 117.
54. Evan Narcisse, "The Biggest Problem with *The Handmaid's Tale* Is How It Ignores Race," *io9*, June 20, 2017: https://io9.gizmodo.com/the-biggest-problem-with-the-handmaids-tale-is-how-it-i-1796235427.
55. Lewis, *Full Surrogacy Now: Feminism Against Family* (New York: Verso, 2019), 10, 12–13.
56. Mies, *Patriarchy*, 123.
57. Yvonne Griggs, *Adaptable TV: Rewiring the Text* (New York: Palgrave, 2018), 122, 123.
58. "World Prison Populations," BBC News: http://news.bbc.co.uk/2/shared/spl/hi/uk/06/prisons/html/nn2page1.stm.

59. "Criminal Justice Fact Sheet," NAACP: https://www.naacp.org/criminal-justice-fact-sheet/.
60. Jessica Pishko, "A History of Women's Prisons," *JSTOR Daily*, March 4, 2015: https://daily.jstor.org/history-of-womens-prisons/.
61. Genevieve LeBarron, "Rethinking Prison Labor: Social Discipline and the State in Historical Perspective," *WorkingUSA: The Journal of Labor and Society* 15 (September 2012): 328.
62. LeBarron, "Rethinking," 333, 348; Petchesky cited in LeBarron, 335.
63. LeBarron, "Rethinking," 338.
64. LeBarron, "Rethinking," 327–28, 343, 348, 345.
65. Thompson, "Rethinking Working-Class Struggle through the Lens of the Carceral State," *Labor: Studies in Working-Class History of the Americas* 8, no. 3 (2011): 39–40.
66. Kara Gotsch and Vinay Basti, "Capitalizing on Mass Incarceration," *Sentencing Project*, August 2, 2018: https://www.sentencingproject.org/publications/capitalizing-on-mass-incarceration-u-s-growth-in-private-prisons/.
67. Jack O'Keeffe, "How '*OITNB*' Gets Real about Trump's Immigration Policies," *Bustle*, July 27, 2018: https://www.bustle.com/p/is-polycon-a-real-private-prison-company-orange-is-the-new-black-season-6-is-a-little-too-real-9896049; Gotsch and Basti, "Capitalizing."
68. Shane Bauer, "The True History of America's Private Prison Industry," *Time Magazine*, September 25, 2018: https://time.com/5405158/the-true-history-of-americas-private-prison-industry/.
69. Griggs, *Adaptable TV*, 114–15.
70. As Fortunati puts it, "reproduction work—housework and prostitution—has a dual character. The former presents itself to capital as a natural force of social labor, hence as non-work, and posits itself to the worker as a personal service, thus not directly waged work. The latter is for capital an unnatural force of social labor, and for the worker is a personal service paid for by money, but not directly with a wage." Fortunati, *Arcane*, 21–22.
71. Fortunati, *Arcane*, 23.

Chapter 3

1. Martin, "How Tony Soprano Paved the Way for Donald Trump," *Vanity Fair*, June 29, 2016: https://www.vanityfair.com/hollywood/2016/06/donald-trump-tony-soprano; Weiss, "What TV Can Tell Us about How the Trump Show Ends," *Politico*, January 16, 2021: https://www.politico.com/news/magazine/2021/01/16/donald-trump-post-presidency-television-459771.
2. Segal, "The Dark Art of *Breaking Bad*," *New York Times*, July 6, 2011: https://www.nytimes.com/2011/07/10/magazine/the-dark-art-of-breaking-bad.html; Goldberg, "*Breaking Bad* Breaks Through," *National Review*, September 23, 2013: https://www.nationalreview.com/2013/09/breaking-bad-breaks-through-jonah-goldberg/.
3. Harris, "Walter White Supremacy," *New Inquiry*, September 27, 2013: https://thenewinquiry.com/walter-white-supremacy/.
4. Linnemann, *Meth Wars: Police, Media, Power* (New York: New York University Press, 2016), 42; Bill Bradley, "Vince Gilligan Finally Reveals Why Walter White

Left Gray Matter," *HuffPost*, March 17, 2015: https://www.huffpost.com/entry/vince-gilligan-walter-white-gray-matter_n_56e85f27e4b0b25c91838d57.

5. As Chris Prioleau notes, "The body count on *BB* is extremely high and almost exclusively Latino." Prioleau, "Walter White and Bleeding Brown," *Apogee*, October 3, 2013: https://apogeejournal.org/2013/10/03/walter-white-bleeding-brown-on-breaking-bads-race-problem/.
6. Marez, "From Mister Chips to Scarface; or, Racial Capitalism in *Breaking Bad*," *In the Moment/Critical Inquiry*: https://critinq.wordpress.com/2013/09/25/breaking-bad/.
7. Cooper, "Family Capitalism and the 'Small Business' Insurrection," *Dissent* (Winter 2022): https://www.dissentmagazine.org/article/family-capitalism-and-the-small-business-insurrection.
8. See Barbara Ehrenreich and John Ehrenreich, "The Professional-Managerial Class," in *Between Labor and Capital*, ed. Pat Walker (Boston: South End Press, 1999).
9. Duménil and Lévy, *The Crisis of Neoliberalism* (Cambridge, MA: Harvard University Press, 2011), 329.
10. Kat Eschner, "How Detroit Went from Motor City to the Arsenal of Democracy," *Smithsonian Magazine*, April 28, 2017: https://www.smithsonianmag.com/smart-news/when-detroit-was-arsenal-democracy-180962620/.
11. Dennis Riches, "*Breaking Bad* and the New Mexican Nuclear Uncanny," *Nuclear Free by 2045?*, August 17, 2014: https://nf2045.blogspot.com/2014/08/breaking-bad-and-new-mexican-nuclear.html.
12. Lotz, *Cable Guys: Television and Masculinities in the 21st Century* (New York: New York University Press, 2014), 60.
13. Melinda Cooper, *Family Values: Between Neoliberalism and the New Social Conservatism* (Zone Books, 2017), 10–12.
14. Martin, "Historicizing White Nostalgia: Race and American Fordism," *Blind Field*, August 3, 2017: https://blindfieldjournal.com/2017/08/03/historicizing-white-nostalgia-race-and-american-fordism/.
15. See Kristin Hunt, "A Brief History of Evil Twins in Soap Operas," *Mental Floss*, July 12, 2016: http://mentalfloss.com/article/82952/brief-history-evil-twins-soap-operas.
16. Gutkin, "*Twin Peaks: The Return*—Allegory and Dislocation," *post45*, September 16, 2017: https://post45.org/2017/09/twin-peaks-the-return-allegory-and-dislocation/.
17. Alex Diedrick, "*Breaking Bad* Fan Theory," *Uproxx*, September 15, 2016: https://uproxx.com/tv/what-if-breaking-bad-finale-was-a-dream/.
18. See Otto Rank, *The Double: A Psychoanalytic Study*, trans. Harry Tucker Jr. (Chapel Hill: University of North Carolina Press, 2009).
19. Harris, "Supremacy."
20. Linnemann, *Meth Wars*, 177.
21. Pine, "The Economy of Speed," *Public Culture* 19, no. 2 (2007): 359.
22. Matthews, "Here's What *Breaking Bad* Gets Right, and Wrong, about the Meth Business," *Washington Post*, August 15, 2013: https://www.washingtonpost.com/news/wonk/wp/2013/08/15/heres-what-breaking-bad-gets-right-and-wrong-about-the-meth-business/.
23. National Drug Intelligence Center, *New Mexico Drug Threat Assessment*, April 2002: https://www.justice.gov/archive/ndic/pubs07/803/meth.htm.
24. Brenner, *The Economics of Global Turbulence: The Advanced Capitalist Economies from Long Boom to Long Downturn, 1945–2005* (New York: Verso, 2006), 99.

25. Harvey, *The Condition of Postmodernity: An Inquiry into the Origins of Cultural Change* (New York: Blackwell, 1989), 141–201.
26. See Michael J. Piore and Charles Sabel, *The Second Industrial Divide: Possibilities for Prosperity* (New York: Basic, 1984), and James P. Womack et al., *The Machine That Changed the World* (New York: Rawson Associates, 1990). See also Jasper Bernes, "Logistics, Counterlogistics, and the Communist Prospect," *Endnotes* 3, and Deborah Cowen, *The Deadly Life of Logistics: Mapping Violence in Global Trade* (Minneapolis: University of Minnesota Press, 2014), 1.
27. Brenner, *Global Turbulence*, 129.
28. Brenner, "The Boom and the Bubble," *New Left Review* 6, November/December 2000: https://newleftreview.org/issues/ii6/articles/robert-brenner-the-boom-and-the-bubble.
29. Brenner, "Boom," 131.
30. Brenner, "What Is Good for Goldman Sachs Is Good for America: The Origins of the Current Crisis," *Verso Blog*, November 13, 2018: https://www.versobooks.com/blogs/4122-what-is-good-for-goldman-sachs-is-good-for-america-the-origins-of-the-current-crisis. Peter Gowan adds that the end of the 1990s saw "unprecedentedly high levels of public and household debt, a deep structural imbalance of payments deficit and a business cycle dependent on asset price bubbles" sustained by "inward flows of finance from all over the world." Gowan, *The Global Gamble: Washington's Faustian Bid to Maintain World Dominance* (New York: Verso, 1999), 123. Giovanni Arrighi adds that by the early 2000s, deficits in the account of the US balance of payments had grown steadily to nearly $3 trillion and were being added to at a rate of $1.5 billion a day at the time of the invasion of Iraq. Arrighi, *Adam Smith in Beijing: Lineages of the Twenty-First Century* (New York: Verso, 2007), 191–93. David Graeber adds that federal debt, held by foreign and international investors, rose from below $200 trillion in 1985 to just under $2,000 trillion in 2005. Graeber, *Debt: The First 5,000 Years* (New York: Melville House, 2011), 369. David Harvey noted the foreign ownership of nearly one third of stock assets on Wall Street, and one half of US Treasury bonds in 2005. Harvey, *A Brief History of Neoliberalism* (Oxford: Oxford University Press, 2005), 193.
31. Brenner, "Good for Goldman," 38, 24.
32. Brenner, *Global Turbulence*, 293.
33. Deepankar Basu and Ramaa Vasudevan summarize: "In Brenner's account, the crisis was precipitated by intensification of competition, which squeezed profit margins and led to persistent overcapacity in manufacturing (Brenner, 2006). For Shaikh (1987) the crisis tendency stems from a falling rate of profit due to a process of increasing capital intensity and labor-saving technical change that is reflected in a rising 'materialised composition of capital'; for Duménil and Lévy (1993), the crisis stems from exhaustion of the technological progressivity of the post-war period; Moseley (1992), on the other hand, highlights the growth of the ratio of unproductive to productive labor as the main reason for declining profitability and stagnation." See Deepankar Basu and Ramaa Vasudevan, "Technology, Distribution, and the Rate of Profit in the U.S. Economy: Understanding the Current Crisis," *Cambridge Journal of Economics* 37, no. 1 (January 2013): 57–89.
34. Harvey, *Condition*, 180.

35. See Arrighi, "The Social and Political Economy of Global Turbulence," *New Left Review* 20 (March/April 2003): https://newleftreview.org/issues/ii20/articles/giovanni-arrighi-the-social-and-political-economy-of-global-turbulence.
36. Randy Martin, *Financialization of Daily Life* (Philadelphia: Temple University Press, 2002), 23.
37. Robert Gordon, *The Rise and Fall of American Growth* (Princeton: Princeton University Press, 2017), 2, 17.
38. Basu and Vasudevan, "Technology," 57–88.
39. See Federal Reserve, "Industrial Production, Capacity, and Utilization": https://www.federalreserve.gov/releases/g17/current/ipg1.svg.
40. The company name suggests Marx's "fictitious capital," which, according to David Harvey, is "money that is thrown into circulation as capital without any material basis in commodities or productive activity." Harvey, *Limits to Capital* (New York: Verso, 2006), 95.
41. "Manufacturing: NAICS 31–33," *US Bureau of Labor and Statistics*: https://www.bls.gov/iag/tgs/iag31-33.htm.
42. Quoted in Michael Lanigan, "Ten Things You Never Knew about *Breaking Bad*," *Joe*: https://www.joe.ie/movies-tv/10-things-never-knew-breaking-bad-613362.
43. Quoted in Andrew Romano, "*Breaking Bad*: The Finest Hour on Television," *Newsweek*, June 26, 2011: https://www.newsweek.com/breaking-bad-finest-hour-television-67999.
44. Williams, *Playing the Race Card: Melodramas of Black and White* (Princeton: Princeton University Press, 2002), 30.
45. See also Jesse's conversation with Jane about doors, after visiting a Georgia O'Keefe exhibit (3.11).
46. On the TV's historical association of women and home audiences, see Lynn Joyrich, *Re-viewing Reception: Television, Gender, and Postmodern Culture* (Bloomington: Indiana University Press, 1996), 46.
47. Inspired by *The Sopranos*, *Mad Men* was, Weiner would recall, "obviously written for HBO." Weiner twice offered his show to the network, shot it in the studios used by *The Sopranos* and employed the same production crews. See Gary R. Edgerton, "The Selling of *Mad Men*: A Production History," in *Mad Men, Dream Come True TV*, ed. Gary Edgerton (New York: I. B. Tauris, 2010), 6.
48. Quoted in Edgerton, "The Selling," 4, 8, 13.
49. Andrew Sarris, "Towards a Theory of Film History," in *Theories of Authorship*, ed. John Caughie (London: Routledge and Kegan Paul, 1981), 49.
50. Mann, "It's Not TV, It's Brand Management TV," in *Production Studies*, ed. Vicki Mayer, Miranda Banks, and John Caldwell (New York: Routledge, 2009), 99.
51. Mittell, *Complex TV: The Poetics of Contemporary Television Story Telling* (New York: New York University Press, 2015), 88.
52. See Miranda Banks, *The Writers: A History of American Screenwriters and Their Guild* (New Brunswick: Rutgers University Press, 2015).
53. Rod Lurie, quoted in Catherine Fisk and Michael Szalay, "Story Work: Nonproprietary Autonomy and Contemporary Television Writing," *Television and New Media* 18, no. 7 (2017): 613.
54. Hamilton, quoted in Fisk and Szalay, "Story Work," 611.

55. Max Horkheimer and Theodor Adorno, *The Dialectic of Enlightenment* (Palo Alto: Stanford University Press, 2007), 96.
56. See John Caldwell, *Production Culture: Industrial Reflexivity and Critical Practice in Film and Television* (Durham: Duke University Press, 2008); Vicki Mayer, *Below the Line: Producers and Production Studies in the New Television Economy* (Durham: Duke University Press, 2011); Banks, *The Writers*.
57. See Alisa Perren and Thomas Schatz, "Theorizing Television's Writer-Producer: Reviewing *The Producer's Medium*," *Television & New Media* 16, no. 1 (2015): 86–93; and Matt Stahl, "Nonproprietary Authorship and Uses of Autonomy: Artistic Labor in American Film Animation, 1900–2004," *Labor: Studies in Working-Class History of the Americas* 2, no. 4 (2015): 87–105.
58. When writers are not subject to the direction and control of the employer in the creation of the work, employers can acquire the copyright only if the writer assigns it. *Community for Creative Non-violence v. Reid*, 490 U.S. 730 (1990).
59. Barnouw, *The Television Writer* (New York: Hill and Wang, 1962), 19.
60. See Fisk and Szalay, "Story Work," 618.
61. Duménil and Lévy, *Crisis*, 14, 9.
62. Miller, quoted in Marc Leverette, Brian L. Ott, and Cara Louise Buckley, ed., *It's Not TV, It's HBO* (New York: Routledge, 2008), x.
63. See Brian Stelter, "Season 5 of 'Mad Men' Is Delayed Until 2012," *New York Times*, March 29, 2011: https://www.nytimes.com/2011/03/30/arts/television/mad-men-delayed-as-matthew-weiner-and-amc-dispute-contract.html.
64. Subsequent amendments to the suit made clear that the issue for which Darabont was seeking redress was less his firing than AMC's failure to pay him a percentage of the profits generated by the serial and "derivative productions" like *Fear the Walking Dead*. See Dominic Patten, "Walking Dead Lawsuit," *Deadline Hollywood*, August 4, 2015: https://deadline.com/2015/08/walking-dead-lawsuit-frank-darabont-caa-amc-amended-complaint-1201491755/.
65. See Nellie Andreeva, "AMC Studios Becomes a Standalone Unit," *Deadline*, June 25, 2014: https://deadline.com/2015/06/amc-studios-standalone-rick-olshansky-stefan-reinhardt-leadership-1201456458/.
66. Andy Greenwald, "The Zombie Network," *Grantland*, October 16, 2013: https://grantland.com/features/the-state-amc/.
67. Quoted in "With *Halt and Catch Fire*, AMC Hopes for Another *Mad Men*," *LA Weekly*, May 29, 2014: https://www.laweekly.com/with-halt-and-catch-fire-amc-hopes-for-another-mad-men/.
68. See Michael C. Mims, "Don't Bake—Litigate!: A Practitioners Guide on How Walter White Should Have Protected His Interests," *New Mexico Law Review* 45, no. 2 (2015).
69. See Fan Yang, "Science and Intellectual Property in *Breaking Bad*," *Flow*, December 12, 2013: http://flowtv.org/2013/12/science-and-intellectual-property-in-breaking-bad/.
70. Russell Moy, "A Case against Software Patents," *Santa Clara High Technology Journal* 17, no. 1 (2000): 71, 73.
71. In *Gottshalk v. Benson* (1972) and *Parker v. Flook* (1978), the Supreme Court held that software, algorithms, and mathematical formulae not connected to a patentable physical process could not be patented. But *Gottshalk* and *Parker* were limited a few

years later in *Diamond v. Diehr* (1981), which made possible the radical expansion of the software and tech industry, by allowing the patenting of software and algorithms. And in *Alice v. CLS* (2014), the Supreme Court issued its fourth ruling in four years on the section 101 issue raised in *Gottshalk* and *Parker*.

72. Galloway, *The Interface Effect* (New York: Polity, 2012), 22. Moy argues that IBM might have patented their BIOS, and thus protected it. Moy, "A Case," 95. On the analogy between software and TV programming, see Szalay, "Pimps and Pied Pipers," *Journal of American Studies* 49, no. 5 (2015).

Chapter 4

1. Kaplan, "Manifest Domesticity," *American Literature* 70, no. 3 (September 1998): 581.
2. Edgerton, cited in Glen Creeber, ed., *The TV Genre Book* (London: BFI, 2015), 36; Alyssa Rosenberg, "In Praise of Carrie Mathison's Feminine Instincts," *Slate*, December 22, 2012: https://slate.com/human-interest/2012/10/homeland-episode-4-carrie-mathison-female-super-spy.html; Sophie Gilbert, "The Case against Carrie," *Atlantic*, October 12, 2014: https://www.theatlantic.com/entertainment/archive/2014/10/homeland-the-case-against-carrie/381369/.
3. Elizabeth Anker, *Orgies of Feeling: Melodrama and the Politics of Freedom* (Durham: Duke University Press, 2014), 2.
4. See Szalay, *Hip Figures: A Literary History of the Democratic Party* (Palo Alto: Stanford University Press, 2012), ch. 3.
5. Hofstadter, *The Paranoid Style in American Politics* (New York: Knopf, 2012), 25.
6. Quote in June Thomas, "A Conversation with *The Americans* Showrunners," *Slate*, January 31, 2013: https://slate.com/culture/2013/01/the-americans-fx-spy-series-creators-joe-weisberg-and-joel-fields.html.
7. Rothman, "The Cruel Irony of *The Americans*," *New Yorker*, March 16, 2016: https://www.newyorker.com/culture/culture-desk/the-cruel-irony-of-the-americans; Nussbaum, "Change Agents," *New Yorker*, March 24, 2014: https://www.newyorker.com/magazine/2014/03/31/change-agents.
8. See Walzer, *The Revolution of the Saints: A Study of the Origins of Radical Politics* (Cambridge: Harvard University Press, 1982).
9. See Michael Rogin, *Ronald Reagan the Movie* (Berkeley: University of California Press, 1987), 242.
10. Stephanie Coontz, *The Way We Never Were: American Families and the Nostalgia Trap* (New York: Basic Books, 1992), 29.
11. The postwar automation of household chores and the suburban home's decreased reliance on waged labor led to significant increases in the time spent on housework by middle-class women. See Glenna Mathews, *"Just a Housewife": The Rise and Fall of Domesticity in America* (New York: Oxford University Press, 1987).
12. Betty Friedan, *The Feminine Mystique* (New York: W. W. Norton, 1963), 204.
13. Marx, "Notebook Seven—The Chapter on Capital," *Grundrisse*: https://www.marxists.org/archive/marx/works/1857/grundrisse/ch14.htm.
14. Hochschild, *The Managed Heart* (Berkeley: University of California Press, 2012), 153, 156.
15. Hochschild, *Managed*, 109, 33.

16. Boltanski and Chiapello, *The New Spirit of Capitalism*, trans. Gregory Elliott (New York: Verso, 2005), 80.
17. Hochschild, *Managed*, 35.
18. Hochschild, *Managed*, 133.
19. Hochschild, *Managed*, 51.
20. Hochschild, *Managed*, 161, 167.
21. Julie Beck, "The Concept Creep of Emotional Labor," *Atlantic*, November 26, 2018: https://www.theatlantic.com/family/archive/2018/11/arlie-hochschild-housework-isnt-emotional-labor/576637/.
22. Hochschild, *Managed*, 171.
23. *The Americans* has an "added layer," Nussbaum claims, because "we're watching actors give brilliant performances as actors who give brilliant performances." Nussbaum, "Change Agents."
24. Jeremy Egner, "The Spy Who Married Me," *New York Times*, January 24, 2013: https://artsbeat.blogs.nytimes.com/2013/01/24/the-spy-who-married-me-keri-russell-and-matthew-rhys-on-the-americans/.
25. Hochschild, *Managed*, 192.
26. Jameson, *Representing Capital* (New York: Verso, 2014), 109.
27. Seccombe, *Weathering the Storm: Working-Class Families from the Industrial Revolution to the Fertility Decline* (New York: Verso, 1993), 8.
28. Marx, "Private Property and Communism," *Economic and Philosophical Manuscripts of 1844*: https://www.marxists.org/archive/marx/works/1844/manuscripts/comm.htm.
29. Marx, "Estranged Labor," *Economic and Philosophical Manuscripts of 1844*: https://www.marxists.org/archive/marx/works/1844/manuscripts/labour.htm.
30. E. Urbánek, "Roles, Masks, and Characters: A Contribution to Karl Marx's Idea of the Social Role," *Social Research* 34, no. 3 (1967): 531.
31. Brennan, "The Free Impersonality of Bourgeois Spirit," *Biography* 37, no. 1 (Winter 2014): 5.
32. Beverungen, Murtola, and Schwartz, "The Communism of Capital?," *ephemera: theory & politics in organization* 13, no. 3 (2013): 484.
33. Marx, *Capital*, vol. 3, part 3, chap. 15.4: https://www.marxists.org/archive/marx/works/1894-c3/ch15.htm.
34. Virno, *A Grammar of the Multitude* (Los Angeles: Semiotext(e), 2004), 110.
35. Virno, *A Grammar*, 56, 61; Max Horkheimer and Theodor Adorno, *The Dialectic of Enlightenment* (Palo Alto: Stanford University Press, 2007), 96.
36. For a withering critique of Virno, Hardt, and Negri, see Timothy Brennan, "The Empire's New Clothes," *Critical Inquiry* 29, no. 2 (2003): 337–67.
37. Virno, *A Grammar*, 108, 110.
38. Berardi, *The Soul at Work* (Los Angeles: Semiotext(e), 2009), 108–9.
39. Eliot, "Tradition and the Individual Talent," *Poetry Foundation*: https://www.poetryfoundation.org/articles/69400/tradition-and-the-individual-talent.
40. Wolff, *The Man Who Owns the News: Inside the Secret World of Rupert Murdoch* (New York: Broadway Press), 249, 251.
41. Hochschild, *Managed*, 133, 34.
42. Scott W. Fitzgerald, *Corporations and Culture Industries* (Minneapolis: Lexington Books, 2012), 351.

43. Harvey, *A Brief History of Neoliberalism* (New York: Oxford University Press, 2005), 35.
44. Wolff, *The Man*, 188.
45. Fitzgerald, *Corporations*, 351, 352.
46. See for example Meg James, "Fox's Newman and Walden one of Hollywood's Most Lucrative Partnerships," *LA Times*, November 16, 2014: https://www.latimes.com/entertainment/envelope/cotown/la-et-ct-fox-duo-20141116-story.html.
47. Fox News became part of 21st Century Fox and would later remain with Murdoch (as part of the newly minted Fox Corporation) in the wake of Disney's purchase of 21st Century Fox in 2019.
48. Galloway, *The Interface Effect* (Malden, MA: Polity, 2012), ch. 4.
49. See, for example, Robert Merry, "The Deep State Is Very Real," *National Interest*, February 12, 2018: https://nationalinterest.org/feature/the-deep-state-very-real-24474.
50. Harvey, *Brief History*, 31.
51. Kang, "How Fox News, Terrorists, and Truthiness Ruined *The X-Files* for Me," *Vulture*, September 10, 2013: https://www.vulture.com/2013/09/x-files-ruined-by-fox-news-terrorists-truthiness.html.

Chapter 5

1. Newcomb, cited in Trisha Dunleavy, *Complex Serial Drama and Multiplatform Television* (New York: Routledge, 2017), 100; Jason Mittell, *Complex TV: The Poetics of Contemporary Television Storytelling* (New York: New York University Press, 2015), 10.
2. Martin, *Difficult Men: Behind the Scenes of a Creative Revolution: From "The Sopranos" and "The Wire" to "Mad Men" and "Breaking Bad"* (New York: Penguin, 2014), 11.
3. Dunleavy, *Complex Serial Drama*, 102.
4. Polan, *The Sopranos* (Durham: Duke University Press, 2009), 59.
5. See Lev Grossman in "Contemporary Seriality: A Roundtable," *Columbia Commons*, January 24, 2019, 111.
6. Elsaesser, "Tales of Sound and Fury: Observations on the Family Melodrama," in *Imitations of Life, A Reader on Film and Television Melodrama*, ed. Marcia Landy (Detroit: Wayne State University Press, 1991), 76.
7. Williams, *Playing the Race Card: Melodramas of Black and White* (Princeton: Princeton University Press, 2002), 30–35.
8. Benjamin, *The Arcades Project*, trans. Howard Eiland and Kevin McLaughlin (Cambridge, MA: Harvard University Press, 1999) [J50,5], 319. See also Robert S. Lehman, "Allegories of Reading: Killing Time with Walter Benjamin," *New Literary History* 39, no. 2 (2008): 240–41.
9. Porter, quoted in Jane Feuer, *Seeing through the Eighties* (Durham: Duke University Press, 1995), 121–22.
10. Linda Williams: "Part of the reason for the masculine dominance of so many contemporary serials from *The Sopranos*, through *The Wire*, *Breaking Bad*, and *Mad Men* is the desire to dissociate such work from the taint of the feminine family

melodrama and their earlier soap opera origins." Williams, On "The Wire" (Durham: Duke University Press, 2014), 46.
11. Brunsdon, "Crossroads: Notes on Soap Opera," in Regarding Television, ed. E. Ann Kaplan (New York: American Film Institute, 1983), 78.
12. Modleski, "The Rhythms of Reception: Daytime Television and Women's Work," in Regarding Television, 71.
13. Michèle Mattelart, "Everyday Life (Excerpt)," in Feminist Television Criticism, ed. Charlotte Brunsdon, Julie D'Acci, and Lynn Spigel (Oxford: Clarendon Press, 1987), 30, 32, 34.
14. Feuer, Seeing through the Eighties, 116.
15. See Trotsky, History of the Russian Revolution (Chicago: Haymarket Books, 2008), and Bloch, Heritage of Our Times (Cambridge: Heritage, 1991).
16. Harootunian, Marx after Marx (New York: Columbia University Press, 2017), 55, 64, 10, 62, 24.
17. Marx, Capital, vol. 1, ch. 25, sec. 3.
18. See also Hamilton Carroll, "Policing the Borders of White Masculinity: Labor, Whiteness, and the Neoliberal City in The Wire," in The Wire: Race, Class, and Genre, ed. Liam Kennedy and Stephen Shapiro (Ann Arbor: University of Michigan Press, 2012), 262–63.
19. See Brenner, The Boom and the Bubble: The U.S. in the World Economy (New York: Verso, 2003), 8.
20. Toscano and Kinkle, Cartographies of the Absolute (New York: Zero Books, 2015), 154.
21. Toscano and Kinkle, Cartographies of the Absolute, 151, 156.
22. Cited in Hua Hsu, "Walking in Somebody Else's City: The Wire and the Limits of Empathy," Criticism 52, nos. 3–4 (2010): 511.
23. See Laura Mulvey, "Melodrama In and Out of the Home," in High Theory/Low Culture, ed. Colin MacCabe (New York: St. Martin, 1986), 81; Peter Brooks quoted in Williams, On "The Wire," 215.
24. Williams, On "The Wire," 220.
25. Hsu, "Walking," 510; Williams, On "The Wire," 133–34.
26. For an account of these terms, see Ted Martin, "Temporality and Literary Theory," Oxford Research Encyclopedia of Literature (December 2016): http://oxfordre.com/literature/view/10.1093/acrefore/9780190201098.001.0001/acrefore-9780190201098-e-122?rskey=WMprac&result=1.
27. Quoted in "A Look Back at As the World Turns: The Beginning," Soaps.com; https://soaps.sheknows.com/as-the-world-turns/news/11637/a-look-back-at-as-the-world-turns-the-beginning/.
28. Patterson, Slavery and Social Death: A Comparative Study (Cambridge: Harvard University Press, 2018). See also Vincent Brown, "Social Death and Political Life in the Study of Slavery," American Historical Review 14, no. 5 (December 2009): 1248, 1233.
29. Wilderson, Afro-Pessimism: An Introduction (Minneapolis: Racked and Dispatched, 2017), 18.
30. Wilderson, Red, White, and Black: Cinema and the Structure of U.S. Antagonisms (Durham: Duke University Press), 340, 27; and Wilderson, Afro-Pessimism, 18.

31. See Dan Berger, "Mass Incarceration and Its Mystification: A Review of *The 13th*," *Black Perspectives*, October 22, 2016; https://www.aaihs.org/mass-incarceration-and-its-mystification-a-review-of-the-13th/.
32. On social death, race, and prison, see Joan Dayan, "Legal Slaves and Civil Bodies," in *Materializing Democracy: Toward a Revitalized Cultural Politics*, ed. Russ Castronovo and Dana D. Nelson (Durham: Duke University Press, 2002), 53–94; and Colin Dayan, "Legal Terrors," *Representations* 92, no. 1 (Fall 2005): 42–80.
33. Harootunian, *Marx after Marx*, 118.
34. Natalie Baszile, *Queen Sugar: A Novel* (New York: Penguin, 2015), 80.
35. Fredric Jameson, "Realism and Utopia in *The Wire*," *Criticism* 52, nos. 3–4 (2010): 360.
36. Jameson, "Realism and Utopia," 367.
37. Jameson, *Allegory and Ideology* (New York: Verso, 2019), 50.
38. Jameson, *Allegory*, 325.
39. Yohannes, "Donald Glover's Two Worlds of Earn," *NBC News*, September 7, 2016: https://www.nbcnews.com/news/nbcblk/two-worlds-earn-fx-comedy-atlanta-n642181.
40. Coates, "The Negro Donald Draper," *Atlantic*, October 27, 2008: https://www.theatlantic.com/entertainment/archive/2008/10/the-negro-donald-draper/6129/.
41. Garland, "Donald Glover's *Atlanta* Reveals How the Black Heaven Is Also a Black Purgatory," *HipHopWired*, September 6, 2016: https://hiphopwired.com/513285/donald-glovers-atlanta-brings-normalcy-citys-multi-layered-image/.
42. Baldwin, cited in Wilderson, *Red, White, and Black*, 11.
43. Chris Ryan and Andy Greenwald, "The Ten Best TV Shows of the Decade," *The Watch* podcast, December 19, 2019.
44. Moten, *In the Break* (Minneapolis: University of Minnesota Press, 2003), 1.
45. Susan Willis, "I Shop Therefore I Am: Is There a Place for Afro-American Culture in Commodity Culture?" in *Changing Our Own Words*, ed. Cheryl Wall (New Brunswick: Rutgers University Press, 1989), 189.
46. Moten, *Break*, 17–18.
47. *Atlanta* is preoccupied with money as "an idea" (2.3), and with fake money. Earn's cash is twice refused, at a movie theater and strip club, because vendors declare it fake. George Floyd's murder was precipitated by a convenience store refusing his money as fake. See Nicholas Bogul-Burroughs and Will Wright, "Little Has Been Said about the $20 Bill That Brought Officers to the Scene," *New York Times*, April 19, 2021: https://www.nytimes.com/2021/04/19/us/george-floyd-bill-counterfeit.html.
48. Wilderson, *Red, White, and Black*, 26, 13.
49. Denning, "Wageless Life," *New Left Review* 66 (November/December 2010).
50. See Sheri Marie-Harrison, "Us and Them," *Commune Magazine* June 6, 2019: https://communemag.com/us-and-them/.
51. Jameson, *The Political Unconscious* (Ithaca: Cornell University Press, 1981), 102.
52. Glover, quoted in Matthew Shaer, "Most Creative People," *Fast Company*, May 17, 2017: https://www.fastcompany.com/40412346/why-atlanta-creator-donald-glover-is-one-the-most-creative-people-in-business-2017.
53. Jameson, *Allegory*, 346–47.

54. Vann Newkirk, "The Georgia Governor's Race," *Atlantic*, November 6, 2018: https://www.theatlantic.com/politics/archive/2018/11/how-voter-suppression-actually-works/575035/.
55. Lisa Siraganian, *Modernism and the Meaning of Corporate Person* (New York: Oxford University Press, 2021), 179, 180, 181.
56. Rogin, *Blackface White Noise: Jewish Immigrants in the Hollywood Melting Pot* (Berkeley: University of California Press, 1998), 14.

Conclusion

1. Barnes, "The Streaming Revolution Has Finally Arrived. Everything Is About to Change," *New York Times*, November 18, 2019: https://www.nytimes.com/2019/11/18/business/media/streaming-hollywood-revolution.html.
2. Auletta, "Outside the Box. Netflix And the Future of Television," *New Yorker*, January 26, 2014: https://www.newyorker.com/magazine/2014/02/03/outside-the-box-2.
3. Lee Rainie, "Cable and Satellite TV Use," *Pew Research Center*, March 17, 2021: https://www.pewresearch.org/fact-tank/2021/03/17/cable-and-satellite-tv-use-has-dropped-dramatically-in-the-u-s-since-2015/.
4. Lotz, *The Television Will Be Revolutionized* (New York: New York University Press, 2014), 6.
5. David Carr, "Giving Viewers What They Want," *New York Times* February 24, 2013: https://www.nytimes.com/2013/02/25/business/media/for-house-of-cards-using-big-data-to-guarantee-its-popularity.html.
6. For a version of this argument, see Michael Wolff, *Television Is the New Television: The Unexpected Triumph of Old Media in the Digital Age* (New York: Portfolio, 2015).
7. Newcombe, *TV: The Most Popular Art* (New York: Anchor Press, 1974), 1; Feuer, "The Concept of Live Television," in *Regarding Television*, ed. E. Ann Kaplan (Frederick, MD: University Publications of America, 1983), 12.
8. *Oxford English Dictionary*, s.v. "television."
9. Williams, *Marxism and Literature* (Oxford: Oxford University Press, 1984), 163–64.
10. Williams, *Television: Technology and Cultural Form* (London: Routledge, 2003), 18–19.
11. Williams, *Television*, 132.
12. Williams, *Television*, 10, 19, 20.
13. Williams, *Television*, 52–53, 58.
14. Williams, *Television*, 12.
15. For important exceptions, see Scott W. Fitzgerald, *Corporations and Culture Industries* (New York: Lexington, 2011), and the works of Michael Curtin.
16. Sconce, "What If: Charting Television's New Textual Boundaries," in *Television after TV*, ed. Jan Olsson and Lynn Spigel (Durham: Duke University Press, 2004), 94.
17. Quoted in Alexandra Alter, "TV's Novel Challenge," *Wall Street Journal*, February 22, 2013: https://www.wsj.com/articles/SB10001424127887323478004578306400682079518.
18. Zack Handlen, "Williams Gibson," *The AV Club*, September 7, 2010: https://www.avclub.com/william-gibson-1798221636.
19. Cavell, "The Fact of Television," *Daedalus* 11, no. 4 (1982): 80.
20. Cavell, "Fact," 82.

21. Cavell, "Fact," 95.
22. Cavell, "Fact," 85, 89.
23. See Caldwell, *Televisuality: Style, Crisis, and Authority in American Television* (New Brunswick: Rutgers University Press, 1995).
24. Caldwell, *Televisuality*, 23, 18.
25. Newcomb, "'This Is Not Al Dente': *The Sopranos* and the New Meaning of Television," in *Television: The Critical View*, ed. Horace Newcomb (New York: Oxford University Press, 2007), 566.
26. Morely, *Family Television: Cultural Power and Domestic Leisure* (New York: Routledge, 1988), 1–2, 8.
27. Tom Gunning, "Cinema of Attraction[s]: Early Film, Its Spectators, and the Avant-Garde," *Wide Angle* 8, nos. 3–4 (1986): 63–70.
28. Cavell, *Pursuits of Happiness* (Cambridge, MA: Harvard University Press, 1981), asks why the films that interest him "emerge and disappear" during the 1930s. It can't be that they are "fairy tales for the Depression," he says, and he is not "drawn to an economic interpretation" (2–3).
29. Feuer, "HBO and the Concept of Quality TV," in *Quality TV: Contemporary American Television and Beyond,* ed. Janet McCabe and Kim Akass (New York: I. B. Tauris, 2007), 156.
30. Reality TV harks back to "the lateral surveillance and mutual monitoring associated with life in traditional, pre-modern communities," which mutuality is betrayed by the factory floor and Fordist production. "A certain nostalgia for the lost 'golden era' of participatory media production thus comes to characterize the rhetoric of the digital revolution." Andrejevic, *Reality TV: The Work of Being Watched* (New York: Rowman and Littlefield, 2003), 25, 40, 26.
31. Reality TV has led the industry in replacing unionized with nonunionized, informal, and frequently unwaged labor. It has led the industry, in Michael Curtin and Kevin Sanson's words, in chasing "lower labor rates and less regulated environs." Curtin and Sanson, "Precarious Creativity: Global Media, Local Labor," in *Precarious Creativity: Global Media, Local Labor, ed. Michael Curtin and Kevin Sanson* (Oakland: University of California Press, 2016), 1–3. Reality TV also relies on free digital infrastructures "to collectively generate marketing or productions proper for film and video companies," in John Caldwell's words. Its reliance on crowdsourcing "helped U.S. film and television companies . . . by laying off 'inside' employees and sending production work outside of the studios and networks where it would be produced more cheaply"—or freely. "Crowd-sourcing" is "the new out-sourcing," he concludes, and continues "a half-century trend—from the breakup of the studio system, the development of the package system, to contract outsourcing, to visual effects boutiques, digital sweatshops, and vast cadres of nonunion reality-TV workers who have absolutely no upward career mobility in Hollywood." Caldwell, "Worker Blowback: User-Generated, Worker Generated, and Producer-Generated Content: Within Collapsing Production Workflows," in *Television as Digital Media*, ed. James Bennett and Niki Strange (Durham: Duke University Press, 2011), 285–86; and Caldwell, "Hive Sourcing Is the New Out-Sourcing: Studying Old (Industrial) Labor Habits in New (Consumer) Labor Clothes," *Cinema Journal* 49, no. 1 (Fall 2009): 162.
32. This is a conclusion opposed to Martin Shuster's in *The New Television*, which uses Cavell's work on film and all but ignores his essay on TV, while arguing, ultimately,

that "New TV" is new because it understands itself as film. See Shuster, *The New Television: The Aesthetics and Politics of a Genre* (Chicago: University of Chicago Press, 2017).

33. Galloway, *The Interface Effect* (New York: Polity, 2012), 40.
34. See Helen Deutsch, "Is It Easier to Believe?: Narrative Innocence from *Clarissa* to *Twin Peaks*," *Arizona Quarterly* 49, no. 2 (1993): 137–58.
35. Seitz, "*The Leftovers* Final Review," *New York Magazine*, June 6, 2017: http://www.vulture.com/2017/06/the-leftovers-finale-review.html.
36. Chase, quoted in James Greenberg, "This Magic Moment," *DGA Quarterly*, Spring 2015: http://www.dga.org/craft/dgaq/all-articles/1502-spring-2015/shot-to-remember-the-sopranos.aspx.
37. Grossman, "You, Yes You, Are *Time*'s Person of the Year," *Time Magazine*, December 25, 2006: http://content.time.com/time/magazine/article/0,9171,1570810,00.html.
38. See Szalay, "'The Real Home of Capitalism': The AOL–Time Warner Merger and Capital Flight," in *The Routledge Companion to Literature and Economics*, ed. Michelle Chihara and Mathew Seybold (New York: Routledge, 2018), 361–73.

Index

Page numbers in italics refer to figures.

ABC, 24
abjection, 84–86, 93–95, 102–11, 163, 247
abstractions, 224–25
accumulation crises, 31, 152, 206, 223–25. *See also* capitalism; neoliberalism
Adlon, Pamela, 104–5
Adorno, Theodor, 62, 162, 225
affect, 43, 66–67, 105, 242–43
affluence. *See* wealth
agricultural household, 23, 29–30, 57
Akira, Hayami, 29
Alabama 3, 46–48
Albrecht, Chris, 293n49
Alice in Wonderland, 3
Alice v. CLS, 302n71
alienation, 179–80, 183, 195, 197–99, 201, 247
allegorical melodrama, 16–17, 20, 66
allegory: of allegorical desire, 34–36; and *The Americans*, 247; and *Atlanta*, 246, 249; and black-market melodramas, 6, 16, 28, 93, 112, 115–16, 141, 149, 168, 177, 204, 206; of the Cave, 34; and class, 183–84; and the Cold War, 175; and corporate agencies, 38, 40, 71–75, 177–78, 208–11, 216, 218, 247, 258–59; of deindustrialization, 34–35, 39, 49, 224; discussions of, 35–36, 38–39, 49–50, 55, 63, 69–70, 80–81, 256, 294n58; and family, 41, 57, 93–94, 178–82; and the formal economy, 224; and gangster

films, 9, 57, 70; and housework, 32; literary, 46; and masculinity, 11; and origins, 46–48; and prison, 116, 121; synchronic, 36–38
Alley, Robert, 160
All in the Family, 18–19, 89. *See also* Bunker, Archie (character)
All My Children, 140
alternate realities, 3–4, 36–38, 165–66, 174–76, 179, 190–91, 196, 202, 214, 247, 256
Alvarado, Letitia, 110
AMC Networks (AMC Studios), 157–58, 166–72
Americans, The, 4, 6, 21, 32, 43, 120, 173, 177–93, 196–97, 201–10. *See also* "Harvest" (*The Americans*); Jennings, Elizabeth (character); Jennings, Philip (character)
Andreessen, Marc, 261, 264–65
Andrejevic, Mark, 272
Andy Griffith Show, The, 18
Anker, Elizabeth, 174
antiheroes, 17, 84, 129
AOL–Time Warner merger, 75–80, 282
Apple v. Franklin, 171
Arcane of Reproduction, The (Fortunati), 99
archaic households, 58, 221
Arrighi, Giovanni, 30–31, 152–53, 284, 300n30
Arvidsson, Adam, 10
As the World Turns, 231–32, 240

311

INDEX

Atlanta, 15, 215–16, 242–57, 307n47. *See also* Glover, Donald; Glover, Stephen; "Teddy Perkins" (*Atlanta*)
Auletta, Ken, 261
auteur theory, 160–61, 290n61
authenticity, 197, 248–49
authority (state), 26, 64, 66, 184
awakenings, 5–6. *See also* purgatory

Baldwin, James, 246
Banks, Miranda, 162
Barnes, Brooks, 261
Barnouw, Erik, 163
Basu, Deepankar, 152, 300n33
Because the Internet (Glover), 244, 255
Becker, Gary, 7, 287n10
Beeman, Stan (character), 186, 188. *See also Americans, The*
Bellafante, Ginia, 83–84
Benanav, Aaron, 27–28, 289n43
Benjamin, Walter, 35–36, 49, 61–65, 67, 69–70, 80–81, 215
Benson-Allott, Caetlin, 107–8
Berardi, Franco, 199–201
Berlant, Lauren, 7, 13, 23, 60–61
Bernanke, Ben, 148
Better Things, 104–6. *See also* Adlon, Pamela
Beverungen, Armin, 199
Bewkes, Jeffrey, 80
Big Love, 6, 15–16, 38, 43, 89, 149. *See also* Henrickson, Bill (character)
blackface, 114, 249–50, 258
black-market melodramas. *See* allegorical melodrama; allegory; family life; melodrama; meta-genre; repetition (looping); second lives; stasis; temporality; title sequence; *and specific television shows*
Bloch, Ernst, 220–21
Boltanski, Luc, 41–42, 138, 194
Bonanza, 140
Bordwell, David, 269
Botwin, Andy (character), 2, 86, 92, 94, 111. *See also Weeds*
Botwin, Nancy (character), 83–86, 91–96, 107–12. *See also Weeds*
Boydston, Jeanne, 56
Bracco, Lorraine, 53. *See also* Hill, Karen (character); Melfi, Jennifer (character)
Braudel, Fernand, 10
Breaking Bad, 12; and allegory, 86, 120, 130–31, 135–36, 140–41, 147–49, 159, 164; and change, 155; and chiral doubles, 141–43; and class, 129–31, 133–36, 149; and cleanliness, 143–44; and defamiliarization, 156–57; and deindustrialization, 2, 16, 131, 136–37, 148–55, 216; and family life, 6–7, 156; and the Feds, 184, *185*; and gender anxiety, 137–39, 144–46; and housework, 97, 120; and IP, 170; and Madrigal, 143, 153–54; and purgatory, 2; and race, 13–14, 138; and rot, 147–48, 154; and secret lives, 3, 5–6; as a serial, 105, 215; and white privilege, 11; the writers of, 156–60, 166. *See also* crystal meth; Fring, Gus (character); Gilligan, Vince; Pinkman, Jesse (character); White, Skyler (character); White, Walter (character)
Brecht, Bertolt, 57
Brennan, Timothy, 199
Brenner, Robert, 78, 149–54, 300n33
broadcast TV, 10, 24–25, 35, 264–65, 270
Brodhead, Richard, 23
Brody, Nicholas (character), 32, 174, 184. *See also Homeland*
Brooks, Peter, 16–18, 65–66, 226, 230–31
Brouillette, Sarah, 280–81
Brown, Gillian, 23
Brown, Nicholas, 292n28
Browne, Nick, 24
Brunsdon, Charlotte, 219
Buffy the Vampire Slayer, 17, 209, 215
Bunker, Archie (character), 18, 20. *See also All in the Family*
Burnham, James, 209
Burns, Alex, 78
Byrde, Martin (character), 7–8, *12*. *See also Ozark*

Caldwell, John, 162, 270–71, 309n31
Cantwell, Chris, 168–69
Capital (Marx), 199, 249
capital gains, 223
capitalism, 41–42, 85, 98–104, 122–23, 201, 252. *See also* accumulation crises; deindustrialization; economic crises; family wage; Fordism; industrial capital; neoliberalism; racial capitalism; two-income household
Carr, David, 262
cartels, 14, 92, 110, 146. *See also* Mexico
Carter, Chris, 210
Case, Steve, 76

Castells, Manuel, 28
Cavell, Stanley, 268–69, 271, 287n3, 309n32
CBS, 24
Chabon, Michael, 268
Chapman, Piper (character), 94, 113–14, 119, 125–28. See also *Orange Is the New Black*
Chase, David, 49–50, 68–69, 73–75, 79–80, 160, 270, 276–78, 280, 282, 293n49. See also *Sopranos, The*
Chase-Dunn, Christopher, 109
Cheever, John, 6
Chewing Gum, 273–74
Chiapello, Eve, 41–42, 138, 194
Childish Gambino, 244, 259
China, 29–30, 32, 150
Christensen, Jerry, 38
Chun, Wendy, 172
cinematography, 45–47, 81, 113–14, 156–57, 216, 276–77
circle of domestic life, 23
Citizens United, 258
Classical Hollywood Cinema (CHC), 269, 271
closeted identities, 4
Coates, Ta-Nehisi, 245
Cobb, Jonathan, 196
Coca-Cola, 159
Coel, Michaela, 273–74
Cohle, Rustin (character), 20. See also *True Detective*
Cold War, 32, 174–75, 177, 192
colonialism, 27, 103
comedy (genre), 85, 87, 104–6, 242, 244, 257
commodity fetish, 199
communication (media and tech), 77–78
communism (philosophy or ideology), 198, 200–201
Communism (specific political party), 174, 188–89, 201, 204, 207, 209–10
Complex TV (Mittell), 267
Condon, Richard, 174
Connor, J. D., 38
Cooper, Gary, 60
Cooper, Melinda, 9, 26, 133, 138, 287n10
Coppola, Frances Ford, 51, 57, 68–69
CoreCivic, 124, 126
Corleone, Michael (character), 57–58. See also *Godfather II, The*
Corleone, Vito (character), 57, 65. See also *Godfather, The*
corporations, 199, 201, 203–8, 258. See also synergy; *and specific companies*
Corrections Corporation of America, 124

Counterpart, 4, 28, 173, 175–77, 189, 275
COVID-19 pandemic, 10, 49
Cowan, Ruth Schwartz, 29, 86, 93
Crain, Juliana (character), 175, 177. See also *Man in the High Castle, The*
creativity, 168–70
cruel optimism, 7
crystal meth, 146, 149, 159
culture industry, 162, 200
Curtin, Michael, 309n31
Cynical Reason, 18, 241

Dalla Costa, Mariarosa, 97–99, 281–82
Dallas, 8–9, 20, 215, 219, 241
Darabont, Frank, 166, 302n64
Dark Angel, 209
Davidson, Cathy, 23
Deadwood, 62, 268
debt, 26, 151–52, 300n30
deep acting, 194–96, 247, 252
deep state, 209–11
deindustrialization: and *Breaking Bad*, 2, 16, 131, 136–37, 148–55, 216; the complex processes of, 39, 41; and the developing world, 27; and family life, 20, 22, 41–42, 58, 75, 89, 280; and the global dynamics of, 149–53; and the internet, 284; and New York, 72–73; and *The Sopranos*, 16, 20–21, 48–50, 58, 71, 75, 216, 280; and the Telecommunications Act, 39; and television, 24–26, 36, 49, 136, 219; and the United States, 149–54; and the white middle class, 2, 9–10, 28; and *The Wire*, 215, 223–25, 228. See also capitalism; manufacturing
Delta Airlines, 194–95
Denning, Michael, 49, 252
Departed, The, 54–55
deregulation, 39
Derrida, Jacques, 246
Desperate Housewives, 83–84
Detroit, 21
Deuce, The, 112
developing world, 27, 31–32. See also third world
de Vries, Jean, 29–30, 290n46
Dexter, 4, 90, 140, 245–46
Diamond v. Diehr, 302n71
Dickens, Charles, 41
directly market mediated sphere (DMM), 101–2
disintermediation, 283

distribution (miracle of), 30–31
Distribution Revolution (Curtin, Holt, and Sanson), 262
domestic (in black-market melodramas): airlines and the, 195; border crises, 31; consequences of Reagan's revolution, 32; dilating space in the, 216, 223; a double meaning of, 173–74; entrapment, 10–11, 60, 222; escape, 275; family, 47–48, 55, 58, 60; homelessness and the, 228–29; ideology, 22–24, 58, 139; idyll, 16, 18; innocence, 94, 228; labor, 7, 22, 28, 86–87, 98–99, 102–3, 116, 119, 177, 189, 219, 234; life, 8, 116–17, 176–77, 223, 226–27; listlessness, 6, 176, 240; medium (TV), 270–71; neoliberal models of the, 40–41; pastoral, 56, 58; race and the, 184, 186–87, 217, 271; servitude, 26. *See also* family life; housework; separate spheres; white middle-class families
dot-com bubble, 74–75, 79, 283
doubling (symbolic), 53–54, 140–41, 176, 184, 222, 250–51, 253–54
Douglas, Ann, 23
Douglas, Susan, 83, 106
Dow, Bonnie, 106
downward mobility, 9, 32, 95, 114, 156, 164, 184
drama (genre), 105
Draper, Don (character), 2, 19, 159–60, 167, 170, 184, 244–46. *See also Mad Men*
Dr. Jekyll and Mr. Hyde (Stevenson), 141
dual labor markets, 25–26. *See also* labor
Du Bois, W. E. B., 247, 258
Duménil, Gérard, 135, 163, 300n33
Dunleavy, Trisha, 215
DuVernay, Ava, 235. *See also Queen Sugar*; *13th* (documentary)
Dynasty, 8–9, 20, 215, 219, 241

East Asia, 29–31
economic crises, 51–52, 74–75, 152, 224–25. *See also* dot-com bubble; Great Depression; Great Recession
Edgerton, Gary, 174
Egan, Jennifer, 4
Ehrenreich, Barbara, 135
El Camino, 135
elective affinity, 189
Eliot, T. S., 202
Ellison, Ralph, 253
Elsaesser, Thomas, 16, 53–54, 60, 215, 220
Emmy Awards, 85, 105

Empire, 9
Endnotes, 100–104, 125
Enron, 79
escape (from purgatory), 1–3, 6, 10–12, 28, 32, 106, 232, 234, 245, 249, 272
Esmail, Sam, 247. *See also Mr. Robot*
espionage, 3–4, 32, 177–79, 189, 196
Europe, 29
exploitation, 13–14, 28, 31, 59, 88–89, 103–4, 110, 134, 184. *See also* labor; race; slavery
expropriation, 28, 53, 103, 221–22, 235, 251, 281–82. *See also* labor; race; slavery

fabula, 230–31
"Fact of Television, The" (Cavell), 268
family altruism, 8, 287n10
family business, 7–9, 20, 28, 30, 40–42, 47–48, 57, 71, 133, 138, 146. *See also Americans, The*; *Queen Sugar*; *Weeds*
family life: and *The Americans*, 180–82, 186–87; and *Breaking Bad*, 6–7, 156; and broadcast TV, 265, 270–71; and corporate business, 40–43; and the individual, 6–7; and industrial capitalism, 22; and love, 181–82; and Nazism, 175; and nostalgia, 36, 58; and *Orange Is the New Black*, 43, 116–20; and prison, 116–19, 125; and purgatory, 2, 10; and *Queen Sugar*, 240; and Raymond Williams, 263–67; the reinvention of, 26; and *The Sopranos*, 6, 43, 47, 49, 55–60, 66–67, 97, 222; and *Twin Peaks*, 216–19, 222–23, 228; and *Weeds*, 6, 112–13; and *The Wire*, 226–28; and women, 15. *See also* housework; separate spheres; *Sopranos, The*; white middle-class families
family values, 8, 41
family wage: and black-market melodramas, 16, 89, 136, 138, 215, 222; and broadcast TV, 24–25; and crisis, 85; the decline of the, 9–10, 22, 25, 206, 288n26; and gangster movies, 21–22; and nostalgia, 138, 216; and race, 12–13; and state Fordism, 19, 42
Fanon, Franz, 247
Fargo, 13
Feasey, Rebecca, 295n5
Federal Writers' Projects, 162
Federici, Silvia, 97, 99
feminism, 25, 85–87, 97, 107, 137–38, 221. *See also* gender; masculinity

feminization, 97–99, 134, 143, 190, 243, 248–49
Feuer, Jane, 9, 219–20, 263, 272
Fincher, David, 273–74
Fineman, Joel, 34–35, 46–47
Fitch, Robert, 72
Fitzgerald, Scott W., 205, 207
flashbacks, 45, 71, 117–18, 159, 246
Fleabag, 273–75
Fletcher, Angus, 55
flexible accumulation, 150
Fordism, 19, 25–26, 40–42, 85, 156, 164, 200–201, 290n61. *See also* capitalism
foreign (in black-market melodramas), 173
Forever, 1–2
Fortunati, Leopoldina, 99–100, 125–26, 250, 281–82, 298n70
Fourteenth Amendment, 258
fourth wall. *See* speaking to the camera
Fox News, 209–11, 258, 305n47
Fraser, Nancy, 22–23, 85, 138, 296n31
fraud, 72–73, 79, 148
Freamon, Lester (character), 225–27. *See also Wire, The*
Freud, Sigmund, 111
Friedan, Betty, 193
Fring, Gus (character), 13–14, 96, 130, 132, 135, 144–46, 157–58, 164, 166. *See also Breaking Bad*
FUBU, 246–47
FX, 254–55

Galloway, Alexander, 172, 209, 273
Game of Thrones, 2, 14, 43
gangster movies, 3–4, 9, 21–22, 43, 49–50, 52–57, 65. *See also* mourning plays; *and specific movies*
Garland, Maurice, 245
Garvey, Kevin (character), 275–76
gender, 19–23, 28, 53, 84, 136, 186, 191, 198. *See also* feminism; labor; masculinity
General Intellect, 200
Genette, Gérard, 230–31
genre, 3–16, 19–43, 50–55, 69, 89–90, 105–25, 136, 160, 182–91, 216–19, 244, 262–84, 287n3. *See also* medium (as a term); meta-genre
geopolitical gothic, 174, 213
Get Out, 253–54
Gibson, Mel, 77
Gibson, William, 268
Gilbert, Sophie, 174

Gilligan, Vince, 130–31, 141–42, 154–67. *See also Breaking Bad*
Gilligan's Island, 140
Gimme a Break!, 89
Girls, 107
Gledhill, Christine, 16, 66
Glover, Donald, 244, 255, 257. *See also Atlanta*; Childish Gambino
Glover, Stephen, 255
GLOW, 107
Godden, Richard, 294n58
Godfather, The, 20–21, 49, 51, 56–58, 65, 70, 112
Godfather, The (Puzo), 65
Godfather II, The, 51–52, 57, 71, 112, 292n21
Goldberg, Jonah, 130
Goldman, William, 263
Gonzalez, Maya, 98–100
good and evil, 17–18, 36, 140–42, 241
Goodfellas, 52, 53, 56, 65
Good Place, The, 35
Gorbachev, Mikhail, 187–88, 209
Gordon, Robert, 152–53
Gottshalk v. Benson, 302n71
Gowan, Peter, 300n30
Grace under Fire, 20
Grammar of the Multitude, A (Virno), 200
Gramsci, Antonio, 221, 235–36
gray markets, 27
Great Depression, 18, 21, 51. *See also* economic crises
Great Expectations (Dickens), 41
Great Recession, 146–51, 153, 283. *See also* economic crises
Greenspan, Alan, 78–79, 151–52
Greenwald, Andy, 247
Greggs, Kima (character), 226–27, 229. *See also Wire, The*
Griggs, Yvonne, 118, 124–25, 127
Grimes, Rick (character), 116–17, 167, 232–33. *See also Walking Dead, The*
Grossman, Lev, 280–83
Grundrisse, The (Marx), 200
Gutkin, Len, 140–41

Haller, William, 289n39
Halt and Catch Fire, 34, 136–37, 167–72
Hamilton, Ian, 162
Hamlet (Shakespeare), 62–63, 67, 69–71, 292n28
Hamlet or Hecuba (Schmitt), 70
Handmaid's Tale, The, 15, 117–18. *See also* Osborne, June (character)

Hardt, Michael, 199–200
Harootunian, Harry, 221, 235–36
Harris, Malcolm, 130, 133
Harrison, Laura, 83–84
"Harvest" (*The Americans*), 254–55
Harvey, David, 41, 150, 152, 206, 210, 225, 300n30, 301n40
Hastings, Reed, 40
Hawthorne, Nathaniel, 55
HBO, 24–25, 37–38, 40, 77, 80, 128, 164, 269–70
Hegel, Georg Wilhelm Friedrich, 41
Henrickson, Barbara (character), 89–90. See also *Big Love*
Henrickson, Bill (character), 38, 89–90, 184. See also *Big Love*
Hidden Injuries of Class, The (Sennett and Cobb), 196
Hilger, Stephanie, 65–66
Hill, Henry (character), 52–54. See also *Goodfellas*
Hill, Karen (character), 53–54. See also *Goodfellas*
Hill Street Blues, 8, 160–61, 215
histoire, 230–31
Hobbes, Thomas, 200
Hochschild, Arlie Russell, 88, 177, 180, 193–97, 205
Hofstadter, Richard, 174–75
Homeland, 32, 90, 173–74, 184, 186, 209. See also Brody, Nicholas (character); Mathison, Carrie (character)
homelessness, 228–29, 242, 244–45. See also unemployment
Honeymooners, The, 88
Horkheimer, Max, 162
Hortis, C. Alexander, 72
Horvath, Hannah (character), 107
housekeeping, 189
House of Cards, 273–74
housewifization, 11, 28, 87, 102–4
housework, 11, 28–29, 86–104, 111–12, 119–20, 125–26, 177, 189–93, 196, 248–49. See also family life; gender; labor; laundry; masculinity
Hsu, Hua, 227
Humans, 167
Hung, 3, 21

IBM, 170–72
I Dream of Jeannie, 140
Illich, Ivan, 196

I Love Dick, 107
I Love Lucy, 88, 290n46
immigration, 110
indirectly market mediated sphere (IMM), 101–2, 125–26
industrial capital, 220–24, 227. See also capitalism
industrious family, 9–11, 15, 29–31, 43, 89, 92–93, 177, 236, 279, 290n46
industrious revolution, 29–30
informal economies: and agriculture, 235; and black markets, 3, 12, 14, 27, 87, 124, 287n3; definition of, 27–28, 289n43; and drugs, 224, 289n39; and family businesses, 9–10; and prison, 126–27; and race, 13; and survival, 11; and the white middle class, 26–27; and women, 102–4
International Labor Organization (ILO), 27
International Wages for Housework Campaign, 97, 99, 102–3, 221
internet, 6, 78–80, 261–62, 280, 283–84
Invisible Man, The (Ellison), 253
Invitation to Love, 223
IP (intellectual property), 170–72

James, C. L. R., 51–52
James, Selma, 97–98
Jameson, Fredric, 18, 38–39, 43, 57, 71, 112, 197, 227, 240–42, 255–56, 259, 292n21
Japan, 29–30, 150–51, 154
Jazz Singer, The, 258
Jeffersons, The, 88
Jennings, Elizabeth (character), 177–84, 186–93, 196, 201–2, 204, 207–11, 247. See also *Americans, The*
Jennings, Paige (character), 182, 187–90, 193
Jennings, Philip (character), 10, 177–83, 186–91, 196–97, 201, 203–4, 207–10, 247. See also *Americans, The*
Jim Crow, 253–56
Joon-Ho, Bong, 253–54
justice, 226–27, 229
Justified, 21

Kang, Inkoo, 211
Kantorowicz, Ernst, 64, 76–77
Kaplan, Amy, 173
Kelly, Kevin, 77–78
Kemp, Brian, 257
Kerber, Linda, 23
Kerman, Piper, 125

INDEX

Khrushchev, Nikita, 192
Killing Eve, 4–6, 10, 32, 33, 34. *See also* Polastri, Eve (character)
Kinkle, Jeff, 225
Kitchner, Gottfried, 293n44
Klein, Alec, 77
Kocela, Christopher, 54, 58
Kohan, Jenji, 87, 91, 107–8, 113–14, 160. *See also Orange Is the New Black*; *Weeds*
Kristeva, Julia, 84–85, 106

labor: affective, 193–94; agricultural, 221, 236–37; and allegory, 177; blue-collar, 133–34; casualized, 25–27, 31, 150; digital revolution, 272; division of, 9, 20, 23, 28, 90, 103–4, 121, 138–39, 177, 186–87, 189, 198; domestic, 86–87; emotional, 177, 180, 192–97, 247; and family life, 2, 6, 10–11, 21–22, 47–48, 55, 89–90, 188, 193, 195, 198, 213, 219, 226–29, 240, 272; immaterial, 194; informal, 27–30, 87, 289n43, 309n31; managerial, 200, 224; markets, 25; and masculinity, 11, 18; nonwhite, 22, 25, 28, 95, 97, 108–9, 132, 138, 146, 192; organized, 135, 224; prison, 87, 122–27, 235–36, 252; and race, 15, 25–26, 235–36, 247, 251–52; and redundancy, 223–24; reproductive, 85–87, 97–102, 109, 119–21, 126, 131, 143–44, 146, 189, 206, 236, 238, 250, 271–72, 279, 282, 298n70; shadow, 195–96; and TV writers, 162–64; wage, 9–11, 22–31, 52–53, 59–60, 85–87, 90, 93, 97–104, 121–26, 132–33, 138–39, 145–46, 150, 162–63, 177, 189, 198–201, 219–22, 235–36, 250–52, 271, 279–82, 296n31, 298n70, 303n11, 309n31; and women, 25–26, 30, 59, 88–89, 91, 96, 103–4, 219–21. *See also* exploitation; housework; manufacturing; office work; race; unemployment
Lasch, Christopher, 7
late style, 62
laundry, 13–14, 96, 119–20, 144, 190, 192–93. *See also* housework
Laverne & Shirley, 20
Lazzareto, Maurizio, 199–200
Leave It to Beaver, 88–89, 290n46
LeBarron, Genevieve, 122
Leftovers, The, 275–76
legalization (weed), 112–13
Legion, 34
Leibovitz, Annie, 65

Leonard, Suzanne, 84
Levin, Jerry, 75–76, 282
Lévy, Dominique, 135, 163, 300n33
Lewis, Sophie, 117–18
Limon, John, 106, 108, 113
Linnemann, Travis, 131
Lisco, Jonathan, 168
literature, 16, 58, 141, 161, 265
Little Caesar, 21–22, 51
Lodge 49, 34–35
"Logic of Gender, The" (*Endnotes*), 100–101
Long Twentieth Century, The (Arrighi), 31
Los Alamos National Laboratory, 136
Lost, 3, 35, 215
Lotz, Amanda, 21, 137, 262

Mad Men: and allegory, 136, 159; and IP, 170; precursors to, 4, 6; and purgatory, 2; and secret lives, 244–45; as a serial, 215; and women, 89. *See also* Draper, Don (character)
mafia, 57, 71–73, 112, 222, 292n21. *See also* gangster movies; *Sopranos, The*
magical realism, 217, 242–43
Malcolm in the Middle, 140–41
Man, Paul de, 35
Managed Heart, The (Hochschild), 194, 205
Managerial Revolution, The (Burnham), 209
Manchurian Candidate, The, 174, 177–78, 184, 186
Maniac, 1
Manicheanism, 17, 20, 54, 59, 140, 174, 178
Man in the High Castle, The, 4, 19, 173, 175–76, 183, 190
Mann, Denise, 161
manufacturing, 19–24, 36, 49, 71–72, 130–31, 135–36, 149–54, 206. *See also* deindustrialization; labor
Marez, Curtis, 132
Marks, Earn (character), 15, 242–47, 253, 307n47. *See also Atlanta*
marriage contract, 58–59, 288n26
Martin, Brett, 4, 21, 129–30, 215
Martin, Laura Renata, 138
Martin, Randy, 40–41, 152
Marx, Karl, 22–23, 59, 85–87, 97–99, 103, 181, 197–200, 223–24, 236, 249–51. *See also* communism (philosophy or ideology)
Marxism and Literature (Williams), 264
masculinity, 11, 21, 42, 91–92, 105, 144–45, 234, 243, 249, 305n10. *See also* feminism; gender

INDEX

Mason, Fran, 51
mass industriousness, 10
Masterpiece Theater, 266
Mathews, Dylan, 149
Mathison, Carrie (character), 174, 186. See also *Homeland*
Matrix, The, 3, 213
Mattelart, Michèle, 219–22, 236–38
Mayer, Vicki, 162
Mazzara, Glen, 166
McCann, Sean, 293n49
McCarthy, Anna, 289n32
McLuhan, Marshall, 265
McNulty, Jimmy (character), 223–29. See also *Wire, The*
Mean Streets (Scorsese), 51
medium (as a term), 264–73, 277. See also genre
Melfi, Jennifer (character), 17, 45, 50, 53, 61–62, 81, 273. See also *Sopranos, The*
melodrama, 16–18, 36, 65–66, 226. See also soap operas
Menne, Jeff, 290n61
Merish, Lori, 23
meta-genre, 5, 263. See also genre
metaphor, 47, 93–94, 162, 228
Mexico, 32, 86, 108–10, 130. See also cartels
Michaels, Meredith, 83
Mies, Maria, 11, 28, 87, 102–4, 110, 118, 122
Miles, Alfred (character), 242–43, 245, 248–51, 253. See also *Atlanta*
Miller, Toby, 164
Minimum Basic Agreement (MBA), 163
mise-en-scène, 16–17, 220
misogyny, 13, 52, 105
Mittell, Jason, 161, 214, 267
Modleski, Tania, 219
Moltisanti, Christopher (character), 68–69, 73, 79. See also *Sopranos, The*
Mommy Myth, The (Douglas and Michaels), 83
moral legibility, 17–18, 66
moral occult, 17
Morely, David, 270–71
Moten, Fred, 242, 249–50, 258–59
mourning plays, 62–71. See also gangster movies
Moy, Russell, 171–72
Moynihan Report, 243
Mr. Inbetween, 28
Mr. Robot, 32, 213–15
Mulvey, Laura, 226

murder, 3–4
Murdoch, Rupert, 163, 177, 204–8, 210–11, 255–58, 305n47
Murtola, Anna-Maria, 199
music, 16, 46–48, 237, 249

narrative, 47–48, 214–16, 273. See also serial narratives
Nazism, 19
NBC, 24
Negri, Antonio, 199–200, 280–81
neoliberalism, 6, 26, 40–41, 123, 163–64, 205–7, 210. See also accumulation crises; capitalism
Netflix, 4–5, 40, 78, 128, 231, 261–63, 283
Netscape, 78, 261
Newcomb, Horace, 160, 214, 263, 270
New Deal, 123, 135
New Economy, 75–78, 123, 136, 280–81, 283–84
New Jersey, 48–49
Newkirk, Vann, 257
Newman, Gary, 208
New Mexico, 149
new momism, 83–84, 93, 95, 192
New Rules for the New Economy (Kelly), 77–78
News Corp, 204–11, 255–56, 258
News of the World, 208
Nietzsche, Friedrich, 220
Nixon, Richard, 192
nostalgia, 18–20, 35–36, 43–46, 50–52, 57–60, 136, 138, 215–16, 227, 246. See also white middle-class families
Nurse Jackie, 15, 90–91, 149
Nussbaum, Emily, 84, 108, 179

O'Brien, Geoffrey, 2
office work, 213–14. See also labor
Oh, Sandra, 32
oikos, 23, 57
Orange Is the New Black, 1, 15, 34, 43, 87, 94, 100, 113–21, 124–28, 160. See also Chapman, Piper (character); Kohan, Jenji; prison; Warren, Suzanne "Crazy Eyes" (character)
Origin of German Tragic Drama, The (Benjamin), 49, 62, 69
origins, 21, 46–50, 183–84
Osborne, June (character), 117–18. See also *Handmaid's Tale, The*
Oz, 116–17, 128

INDEX

Ozark, 3, 6–8, 13–14. *See also* Byrde, Martin (character)
Ozzie and Harriet Show, The, 87, 88, 290n46

Padmanabhan, Lakshmi, 296n18
Palmer, Laura (character), 218–19, 222–23. *See also Twin Peaks*
paranoia, 174–75, 184
Parasite, 253–54
Parker, Mary-Louise, 104–5. *See also Weeds*
Parker v. Flook, 302n71
pastoralism, 56
patents, 171–72, 302n71
patriarchy, 28, 107, 222
Patriarchy and Accumulation on a World Scale (Mies), 104
Patterson, Orlando, 233
Peaky Blinders, 1, 3, 6, 19, 149
Pecora, Vincent, 58
Peele, Jordan, 253–54
Pells, Richard, 51
Percy Amendment, 123
Personal Responsibility and Work Opportunity Reconciliation Act (PRWORA), 26, 39
Petchesky, R., 122
petrified unrest, 215–16, 223, 238, 242
Phillips, Irna, 232
Phills, James, 77
picaresque, 62
Pine, Jason, 149
Pinkman, Jesse (character), 134–36, 142–43, 145–46, 157–58, 164–66. *See also Breaking Bad*; White, Walter (character)
Plaza Accord, 150–51
Polan, Dana, 34, 62, 86, 215
Polastri, Eve (character), 32, 34. *See also Killing Eve*
Political Unconscious, The (Jameson), 255
Pomeranz, Ken, 29–30
populism, 9, 210
pornography, 112, 124–25
Porter, Dennis, 219
Portes, Alejandro, 28, 289n39
postfeminist television, 106–7
poverty, 26, 31, 246–47
power, 31, 65, 174
Power of Women and the Subversion of the Community, The (Dalla Costa and James), 97–99
Powers, Tom (character), 52–54, 60. *See also Public Enemy, The*

Prioleau, Chris, 299n5
prison, 117–25, 235, 238, 245. *See also Orange Is the New Black*
Prison Industry Enhancement Act, 123
produsage, 78, 280, 282
Prohibition, 71–72
La Promesse, 13
prosumer, 78
Protestantism, 188
psychotherapy, 17, 45–47, 53, 60–64, 81, 197, 222
Public Enemy, The, 21–22, 51, 54, 60
purgatory, 1–2, 11, 14–15, 28, 48–49, 106, 245. *See also* awakenings
Puzo, Mario, 65

quality TV: and allegory, 34 (*see also* serial narratives); and auteurs, 159–60; comparisons, 267–68; and corporate control, 167, 172; and doubles, 140; the evolution of, 272–73, 287n4; and film, 269–70, 278–79; introduction to, 4–5; and meta-genre, 263; and nostalgia, 20; the secret interiors of, 244; and soap operas, 167, 191, 215, 219, 237; and temporality, 230–32; title sequences of, 238
Queen Sugar, 1, 15, 117, 215–16, 229–40, 252. *See also* DuVernay, Ava

race, 12–14, 32, 34, 95, 107–8, 113–17, 146, 186, 232. *See also* exploitation; labor; slavery; *and specific races*
racial alienation, 247, 251
racial capitalism, 242, 258
racism, 13, 15, 56, 116–18, 121–23, 184, 238, 241–42. *See also* blackface; Jim Crow; slavery; white supremacy
Rains, Claude, 253
Rank, Otto, 64, 141
Reagan, Ronald, 32, 150, 187, 204, 207
reality TV, 272, 309nn30–31
récit, 230–31
Rectify, 117
reflexivity, 40–41, 67–68, 112, 121, 124, 127, 154, 157, 159, 164, 168, 177, 208, 210, 214, 279
Reformation, 64
reindustrialization, 216
relative surplus value, 236
Remnick, David, 56, 58
repetition (looping), 214, 216, 225–26, 228, 238, 240–41

INDEX

revenge fantasies, 13–15, 69, 131–32
Reverse Plaza Accords, 78, 150–52
Riley, Boots, 253
Rogers, Christopher, 168
Rogin, Michael, 258
romance, 7–8, 88–89
Rome, 69, 293n44
Roseanne, 20, 88
Rosenberg, Alyssa, 174
Rosetta, 13
Ross, Steve, 163
Rothman, Joshua, 178–79
Roy, Logan (character), 20. See also *Succession*
Roy Donovan, 90
Russian Doll, 1

Sack, Johnny (character), 49. See also *Sopranos, The*
safe houses, 49, 67
Said, Edward, 62
Sanson, Kevin, 309n31
Santner, Eric, 294n66
Sarris, Andrew, 160
Scarface, 21–22, 51
Schatz, Thomas, 8
Schmitt, Carl, 70–71
scholarship, 39–40, 62, 262
Schwartz, Gregory, 199
Sconce, Jeffrey, 267
Scorsese, Martin, 51, 54, 68–69
Seccombe, Wally, 197–98
second industrious revolution, 30
second lives: and black-market melodramas, 3–6, 11, 89–93, 139–40, 173, 244; and gangster movies, 54; and geopolitics, 173–74, 177; and men, 11, 89; and the viewer, 273, 275; and women, 17, 90–93, 117
second shift, the, 88
Segal, David, 130
Seitz, Matt Zoller, 56, 276
Sennett, Richard, 196
sentimentality, 60–61, 66
separate spheres: the absence of, 6, 25, 34–35, 42, 58, 85, 90, 168, 188, 191; and black-market melodramas, 7, 11, 19, 24, 36–38, 89, 244, 271; and domestic space, 98, 228; and the first world, 103; and the mafia, 35, 56–57; and Marx, 22–23, 198; and nostalgia, 140, 216, 222, 227, 246; as a political imperative, 23–24; and race,

15, 222, 246; and secret lives, 89, 92, 117; and sitcoms, 270; and the workplace, 42. See also family wage; white middle-class families
Sepinwall, Alan, 56
serial narratives, 214–16, 219–20, 222, 230–31, 268–69, 273, 305n10. See also narrative; quality TV
Sex and the City, 92, 296n18
sex work, 85–86, 100, 110–11, 119, 125–27, 187, 189
shadow work, 11
Shaikh, Anwar, 300n33
Shakespeare, William, 62, 67–71
Shameless, 90
Shipley, Diane, 83
showrunners, 160–67, 172. See also specific showrunners
Showtime, 90
Shuster, Martin, 112–13, 309n32
Simon, David, 62, 112
simultaneity of the non-simultaneous, 220–21
Siraganian, Lisa, 258
Sirk, Douglas, 16–17
sitcoms, 270
Six Feet Under, 1–2, 38
sjužet, 230–31
slavery, 216, 229, 233–35, 237–38, 249, 251–53, 255–59. See also exploitation; race
soap operas, 7, 11, 94, 105, 140, 191–95, 215, 219–23, 237–38, 240, 266, 272. See also melodrama; *and specific shows*
social conservatives, 26, 130, 133
social death, 233–34, 240, 244–45
social engineering, 194, 205
Sons of Anarchy, 3, 8, 13–14, 43
Sony Corporation, 154, 158–59
Soprano, AJ (character), 67, 129, 182
Soprano, Carmela (character), 49, 53, 56, 58–61
Soprano, Livia (character), 47, 60–61, 63
Soprano, Meadow (character), 56–57, 79, 182, 276–77
Soprano, Tony (character), 45–50, 55–70, 73–74, 81, 86, 89, 129, 276–79, 293n49
Sopranos, The: and abjection, 85–86; and allegory, 34–38, 45–50, 55–57, 70–71, 80–81, 86, 279; the conclusion to, 276–78, 282–83; and deindustrialization, 16, 20–21, 48–50, 58, 71, 75, 216, 280; and the dot-com bubble, 79–80; family life

320

of, 6, 43, 47, 49, 55–60, 66–67, 97, 222; and the Feds, 184, *185*; and gangster films, 4; as genre, 105; and nostalgia, 20–21, 222; praise for, 4; and purgatory, 2, 48–49; and race, 13–14; scholarship on, 34, 62; and second lives, 3; and serial narratives, 215, 279; and Shakespeare, 67–69, 292n28; and the viewer, 277–78, 282; and the welfare state, 8. *See also* Chase, David; mafia
Sorry to Bother You, 253–54
Spangler, Lynn, 106
speaking to the camera, 273–75, 277
Spigel, Lynn, 87
Squid Game, 262–63
Stanislavski, Constantin, 195
Stanley, Allesandra, 83
Star Trek, 140
stasis, 215–20, 223–24, 227–28, 230, 232, 234, 241–42, 245, 255–56
St. Elsewhere, 8
Stranger Things, 28
streaming (online), 261–64, 269, 283–84
Streeck, Wolfgang, 138
strike (Writers Guild), 161–64
Succession, 9, 20
Sugihara, Kaoru, 29–30
Superman, 214
synergy, 77–78, 80, 282. *See also* corporations

Tea Party movement, 211
technological determinism, 264–65
"Teddy Perkins" (*Atlanta*), 253–56, 258–59
Telecommunications Act, 39–40
television (definition of), 263–64
Television (Williams), 264
Television Will Be Revolutionized, The (Lotz), 261–62
televisuality, 270–72
temporality, 155–56, 215, 222–23, 229–31. *See also* stasis; time accountancy
terrorism, 32, 184
Thatcher, Margaret, 6, 150, 204
third world, 27, 31–32, 102–4, 108–10, 118. *See also* developing world
13th (documentary), 235
thirtysomething, 215
"This Is America" (Glover), 259
Thompson, Heather Ann, 123–24
Thompson, Kristin, 269
Time (magazine), 280, *281*, 282–83

time accountancy, 235–38. *See also* temporality
Time Bind, The (Hochschild), 193
Time Warner, 3, 38, 40, 50, 70, 75–80, 280–82, 293n49
title sequence: *Breaking Bad*, 159, 235; *Homeland*, 184–86; *Humans*, 167; *Oz*, 128; *Queen Sugar*, 235, 238, 240; *The Sopranos*, 21, 45–49, 80–81, 85; *Twin Peaks*, 217
Tocqueville, Alexis de, 23
Toffler, Alvin, 78
Toscano, Alberto, 225
Tracy and Hepburn, 59–60
transition, 47
transnational corporations, 40
Trotsky, Leon, 220–21
True Detective, 14–15, 20
Truman, Harry, 174
Trump, Donald, 129–30, 133–34, 138, 210
TV play, 265–66
20th Century Fox, 207–9
21st Century Fox, 208
24 (TV show), 209
Twilight Zone, The, 67–68
Twin Peaks, 17, 20, 36, 140–41, 215–19, 222–23, 228, 275. *See also* Palmer, Laura (character)
Twin Peaks: The Return, 90
two-income household, 25, 30, 85, 104, 186

Undone, 2–3, 5–6
unemployment, 27–28, 75, 98, 223. *See also* homelessness; labor
unions, 72
United States, 2, 23, 31, 39, 130, 192
United States of Tara, The, 90
Updike, John, 6
upward mobility, 52, 96, 183
Urbánek, E., 199
Us, 253–54
USSR, 32, 43, 183, 192
U.S. Steel, 51–52, 71
utopianism, 43, 57, 178, 201, 241, 256–57

Vasudevan, Ramaa, 152, 300n33
Victoria's Secret, 77
Virno, Paolo, 199–201, 280–81
Visit from the Goon Squad, A, 4
voting, 257

Walden, Dana, 208
Walker, Richard, 73

Walking Dead, The, 14, 43, 116–17, 166–67, 232–33. *See also* Grimes, Rick (character)
Waller-Bridge, Phoebe, 273–75
Walters, Suzanne, 83–84
"Walter White Supremacy" (Harris), 130
Waltons, The, 18
Walzer, Michael, 188
want satisfaction, 57
Wanzo, Rebecca, 106–7
Warren, Suzanne "Crazy Eyes" (character), 113–14, 116. *See also Orange Is the New Black*
Warshow, Robert, 50–51
wealth, 26, 31, 83, 110, 183
Weber, Max, 57, 189
Weber, Samuel, 67, 69–70
Weeds: and abjection, 86, 106–8, 110; and affective illegibility, 105–6; and allegory, 17, 86–87, 111–13; background on, 83–84; and family life, 6, 112–13; and housework, 91–97, 100, 112, 120; and men, 94–95; and motherhood, 83–86, 92–93, 97, 111–13, 295n5; and purgatory, 2, 15, 86, 92; and race, 13–14, 107–8; and second lives, 3, 92–93. *See also* Botwin, Nancy (character); Kohan, Jenji; Parker, Mary-Louise
Weeks, Kathi, 98
Weiner, Matthew, 68, 157–58, 160, 166–67
Weisberg, Joel, 178
Weiss, Joanna, 129
welfare state, 8, 19, 22, 26, 31, 85
West Germany, 150
Weston, Kath, 118
West Wing, The, 8, 293n49
Wexler, Lara, 23
White, Skyler (character), 7, 137, 139, 142, 144, 148, 155–58, 183
White, Walter (character), *12, 121*; and cancer, 148–49, 155; and entitlement, 132–34, 138; and labor, 86, 120, 143–44, 164–66; and masculinity, 137–38, 144–45; motivations of, 7, 164; and paternalism, 134–35, 142; in purgatory, 2; and second lives, 11, 89, 139–41; and the third world, 31. *See also Breaking Bad*; Pinkman, Jesse (character)
whiteface, 258–59
white invisibility, 13
white middle-class families, 117; and allegory, 6; ambitions of, 146–47; and deindustrialization, 2, 9, 50, 138; and hired help, 88–89; and labor, 6, 9, 25, 27–29, 189; and meaning, 43; and race, 11–15, 116; and survival, 26–27, 31; and television history, 18; and the welfare state, 8. *See also* downward mobility; family life; nostalgia; separate spheres
white privilege, 11, 13, 19, 26, 107, 138
white supremacy, 127–28, 130–33, 135, 186, 230, 257. *See also* racism
Wilderson, Frank, 233–34, 245–46, 251–52
Williams, Linda, 16, 155, 216, 226–28, 241, 269, 279, 305n10
Williams, Raymond, 24, 264–67
Willis, Susan, 249–50
Wilson, Ron, 51, 55
Wire, The, 18, 62, 215–16, 223–29, 233, 240–41, 245, 268. *See also* Simon, David
Wizard of Oz, The, 3
Wolff, Michael, 4, 204–5
workplace dramas, 8, 48
Writers Guild of America (WGA), 161–63
Wylie, Philip, 192

X-Files, The, 140, 209–11, 215

Yates, Richard, 6
Yeager, Patricia, 94
Yohannes, Alamin, 243

Zaretsky, Eli, 23

www.ingramcontent.com/pod-product-compliance
Lightning Source LLC
Chambersburg PA
CBHW022032290426
44109CB00014B/836